Rocky Mountain

Gardener's Guide

Published by Cool Springs Press, a Division of Thomas Nelson, Inc., P. O. Box 141000, Nashville, Tennessee, 37214.

Cretti, John L.
    Rocky Mountain gardener's guide / John Cretti.
      p. cm.
    Includes bibliographical references and index.
    ISBN: 1-59186-038-5 (pbk.)
    1. Landscape plants--Rocky Mountain Region. 2. Landscape gardening--
    Rocky Mountain Region. I. Title.
SB407 .C75 2003
635.9'0978--dc21

                              2003014660

First printing 2003
Printed in the United States of America
10 9 8 7 6 5 4 3 2

Managing Editor: Billie Brownell
Designer: Sheri Ferguson Kimbrough
Horticulture Editor: Karen L. Panter, Ph.D.
Production Design: S.E. Anderson
Illustrator: Bill Kersey, Kersey Graphics

On the cover: 'General Sikorski' Clematis in 'Montgomery' Spruce Tree,
    photographed by J. Paul Moore

Many thanks to the following, who graciously reviewed the plant list for the
    Rocky Mountain Gardener's Guide for regional appropriateness:
        Teresa A. Cerny, Ornamental Horticulture Specialist, Utah State University
        Dr. Robert Gough, Professor of Horticulture and Extension Specialist, Montana
            State University
        Wayne S. Johnson, Ph.D., Extension Specialist, PAT, IPM, and Horticulture,
            University of Nevada
        Karen L. Panter, Ph.D., Extension Horticulture Specialist, Department of
            Plant Sciences, University of Wyoming
        Robert R. Tripepi, Professor, Plant Science Division, University of Idaho

Visit the Thomas Nelson website at www.ThomasNelson.com

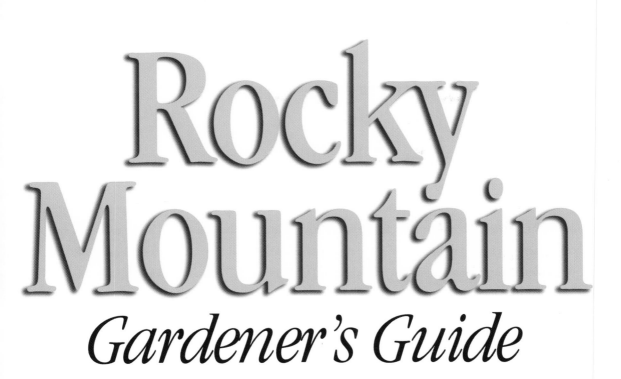

Rocky Mountain
Gardener's Guide

John Cretti

COOL SPRINGS PRESS

Nashville, Tennessee
A Division of Thomas Nelson, Inc.
www.ThomasNelson.com

Dedication

To the Zang Family; for their simplicity of life and inspiring me to garden by following the wisdom of Nature.

Acknowledgments

One of my greatest fortunes in life is sharing "down to earth" gardening information with gardeners throughout the Rocky Mountain region. It is not just my knowledge alone, but the shared experiences of many amateur and professional gardeners that have made this book possible. Thanks to friends and colleagues who helped me along this journey. They include Liz Ball, horticultural communicator; Bob Polomski at Clemson University; Michael A. Dirr, author of *Manual of Woody Landscape Plants*; Eleanor Welshon for her insight on growing perennials; Jo Kendzerski for sharing her secrets on growing roses; Patt Dorsey, Colorado Division of Wildlife; Don Schlup of Scienturfic Turf; Dave Woodman, landscaper; and the late horticulturist George Kelly, author of *Rocky Mountain Horticulture*, who emphasized the uniqueness of our region.

For her friendship and generosity with her time, I am grateful to Nancy Perry who encouraged me to stay the course and complete this project.

I also wish to thank the staff of Cool Springs Press, my publisher, particularly Hank McBride for his confidence and understanding and Billie Brownell for supporting and helping me through all the technicalities of writing this book.

Thanks to my family—Jeri, Jason, Justin, Jinny, and Jonathan—who put up with me during all the time I spent putting together this publication.

Above all, thanks to the Master Gardener of all time, our Lord and Savior, who invites us to grow in His earthly garden, rest as He stills the waters of our lives, and trust Him as he leads us through life's tribulations.

Table of Contents

Featured Plants for the Rockies 6

Welcome to Gardening in the Rockies 9

How to Use the *Rocky Mountain Gardener's Guide* 18

USDA Cold Hardiness Zones 19

Annuals 20

Bulbs, Corms, Rhizomes & Tubers 40

Conifers 60

Deciduous Trees 76

Ground Covers 106

Lawns 124

Ornamental Grasses 134

Perennials 146

Roses 186

Shrubs 200

Vines 240

Butterfly Gardening 252

Coping with Browsing Deer 255

Old-Time Remedies for Pest and Disease Problems 256

Glossary 262

Bibliography 265

Photography Credits 265

Plant Index 266

Meet John Cretti 272

Featured Plants *for the Rockies*

Annuals
Calendula, 22
Cleome, 23
Cosmos, 24
Dusty Miller, 25
Flowering Kale, 26
Four o'Clock, 27
Geranium, 28
Impatiens, 29
Larkspur, 30
Love-in-a-Mist, 31
Marigold, 32
Morning Glory, 33
Moss Rose, 34
Pansy, 35
Petunia, 36
Snapdragon, 37
Sunflower, 38
Zinnia, 39

Bulbs, Corms, Rhizomes, & Tubers
Bearded Iris, 44
Canna, 45
Crocus, 46
Daffodil, 47
Dahlia, 48
Dwarf Iris, 49
Gladiolus, 50
Glory-of-the-Snow, 51
Grape Hyacinth, 52
Lily, 53
Meadow Saffron, 54
Ornamental Onion, 55
Siberian Squill, 56
Snowdrop, 57
Tulip, 58
Windflower, 59

Conifers
Arborvitae, 64
Austrian Pine, 65
Bristlecone Pine, 66
Colorado Spruce, 67
Concolor Fir, 68
Creeping Juniper, 69
Douglas Fir, 70
European Larch, 71
Limber Pine, 72
Pinyon Pine, 73
Rocky Mountain Juniper, 74
Yew, 75

Deciduous Trees
Amur Maple, 84
Cottonwood, 85
Flowering Crabapple, 86
Goldenrain Tree, 87
Green Ash, 88
Hawthorn, 89
Hedge Maple, 90
Kentucky Coffee Tree, 91
Linden, 92
Mayday Tree, 93
Norway Maple, 94
Oak, 95
Ohio Buckeye, 96
Ornamental Pear, 97
Quaking Aspen, 98
River Birch, 99
Serviceberry, 100
Thornless Honeylocust, 101
Weeping Willow, 102
Western Catalpa, 103
Western Hackberry, 104
White Ash, 105

Ground Covers
Carpet Bugleweed, 108
Creeping Oregon Grape
    Holly, 109
Creeping Phlox, 110
Creeping Veronica, 111
False Rockcress, 112
Hardy Iceplant, 113
Heart-leafed Bergenia, 114
Kinnikinick, 115
Lily-of-the-Valley, 116
Periwinkle, 117
Pussytoes, 118
Snow-in-Summer, 119
Spotted Dead Nettle, 120
Stonecrop, 121
Sweet Woodruff, 122
Woolly Thyme, 123

Ornamental Grasses
Blue Fescue, 136
Blue Oat Grass, 137
Feather Reed Grass, 138
Fountain Grass, 139
Hardy Pampas Grass, 140
Little Bluestem, 141
Maiden Grass, 142
Northern Sea Oats, 143
Prairie Dropseed, 144
Switchgrass, 145

Perennials

Artemisia, 148
Aster, 149
Blanket Flower, 150
Blazing Star, 151
Bleeding Heart, 152
Blue False Indigo, 153
Butterfly Weed, 154
Chiming Bells, 155
Coneflower, 156
Coral Bells, 157
Coreopsis, 158
Daylily, 159
Evening Primrose, 160
Gentian, 161
Goldenrod, 162
Hardy Chrysanthemum, 163
Hardy Geranium, 164
Hosta, 165
Hyssop, 166
Japanese Anemone, 167
Joe-pye Weed, 168
Lamb's Ears, 169
Lenten Rose, 170
Lupine, 171
Oriental Poppy, 172
Penstemon, 173
Peony, 174
Perennial Flax, 175
Perennial Salvia, 176
Purple Coneflower, 177
Rocky Mountain
    Columbine, 178
Russian Sage, 179

Sedum 'Autumn Joy', 180
Shasta Daisy, 181
Siberian Iris, 182
Sneezeweed, 183
Sweet William, 184
Veronica, 185

Roses

Climbing Rose, 192
Floribunda Rose, 193
Grandiflora Rose, 194
Hybrid Tea Rose, 195
Miniature Rose, 196
Modern Shrub Rose, 197
Old Garden Rose, 198
Species Rose, 199

Shrubs

American Plum, 204
Apache Plume, 205
Barberry, 206
Beauty Bush, 207
Blue Mist Spirea, 208
Burning Bush, 209
Butterfly Bush, 210
Common Ninebark, 211
Cotoneaster, 212
Currant, 213
Daphne, 214
Dwarf Artic Willow, 215
Firethorn, 216
Forsythia, 217
Glossy Buckthorn, 218
Honeysuckle, 219

Hydrangea, 220
Leadplant, 221
Lilac, 222
Mockorange, 223
Mountain Mahogany, 224
Oregon Grape, 225
Potentilla, 226
Redtwig Dogwood, 227
Rock Spirea, 228
Rose-of-Sharon, 229
Saucer Magnolia, 230
Scotch Broom, 231
Sea Buckthorn, 232
Siberian Pea Shrub, 233
Silver Buffaloberry, 234
Snowberry, 235
Spirea, 236
Sumac, 237
Viburnum, 238
Witchhazel, 239

Vines

American Bittersweet, 242
Clematis, 243
Climbing Honeysuckle, 244
Climbining Hydrangea, 245
Common Hop, 246
English Ivy, 247
Porcelain Vine, 248
Silver Lace Vine, 249
Trumpet Vine, 250
Virginia Creeper, 251

Welcome to
Gardening
in the Rockies

Welcome to the Rocky Mountain region, where gardening is an adventure. It is truly a pleasure to awaken to a day when the early fog melts before a warm sun that beholds snow-capped peaks in a majestic morning blush.

Few regions on earth possess such diversity of climates and plant communities—from the higher elevations to the large expanses of the High Plains. Rugged, rocky slopes and snow-capped mountain peaks rise above vast basins, lakes, and alpine meadows. We have some of the most breathtaking scenery in the world. But our region is separated from large bodies of water by expanses of soaring mountains, foothills, plains, and even deserts. You are likely to find moist conditions at higher elevations and along the river drainages. It is not uncommon for drought to occur anywhere in our region at almost any time of year. To many of us who settle here, it is often a challenge to grow the plants with which we were familiar in other parts of the country.

Gardening in the Rockies is different, but with proper planning and maintenance, cultivating a "green thumb" reaps rewarding and enjoyable results.

Designing Your Rocky Mountain Landscape

When it comes to the different aspects of gardening, few are as intimidating as garden design. This may stem from the belief that landscape design is a practice best left to the trained garden experts who have "artistic" skills. But when you really think about it, we all design things every day, from arranging the furniture in our homes to setting the dinner table, hanging pictures on a wall, placing books on a bookshelf, and getting dressed.

There's nothing really mysterious about the process of designing your landscape. It can be as simple as dragging out the garden hose and outlining a proposed flower bed by shaping the hose in a pattern to please the eye, grouping shrubs together, and choosing a location for shade trees. These practices are all part of landscape design. Like an artist, you control what goes on the landscape canvas; it's up to you to choose a variety of adaptable plants for the palette and create a garden of distinction and diversity. A well-planned landscape reflects your lifestyle and gardening personality. It should be a place where you can relax and be comfortable. Beginning gardeners are generally already nervous about what they don't know; don't confuse this "beginner's nervousness" with an inability to design.

Observe nature to discover the inexhaustible source of designs reflected all around you. Nature is also the most reliable source for horticultural information. Notice what grows where, the type of soil, the exposure of sun or shade, the type of climatic conditions, rocky slopes versus low-lying wet areas, and potential drought tolerance. Carefully selecting your plants helps you create a landscape that can bring pleasure from the moment it is installed, and as the plants mature, the landscape continues to have interest year after year.

Landscaping Goals

There are many added benefits to a well-conceived landscape design. Diversity in plant species supports an abundance of wildlife, including birds and butterflies. Such natural habitats are less vulnerable to insect pests and diseases that can devastate a single plant species. Landscaping for wildlife also has an economic dimension. It presents the opportunity to save on heating and cooling costs for your home. Evergreens planted on the north and west sides of your home reduce the cooling effect of harsh winter winds and concurrently provide shelter for overwintering wild birds. Deciduous trees planted on the side of your home shade it in summer and reduce cooling costs. Additionally, they provide nesting sites and food sources for birds. When the leaves are shed in autumn, your home then receives the sun's rays during the winter.

Start small and continue to grow with confidence. Attempting too much too soon can quickly lead to frustration. Don't feel as if you have to tackle everything at once. Let your landscape evolve along with your knowledge, skills, and of course, your interests. Landscaping in phases is a lot easier on your bank account, too!

Tulips and Birch Tree

Rocky Mountain Soils

When you get a group together to talk gardening, the conversation inevitably turns to the topic of "dirt." But to be technically correct, we should call it *soil.*

The physical properties of Rocky Mountain soils are as diverse as the climate. A description of a soil type generally includes the percentage of organic matter, the kind and percentage of soil particles (sand, silt, clay), information on mineral content, soil consistency (the amount of resistance to cultivating), and soil structure (the kind and amount of soil particle aggregates). Most soils in our region are alkaline with a pH range of 7.2 to 8.3. In the High Country, we often find soils that are slightly acidic from the continuing decomposition of deciduous foliage and evergreen needles over many years.

The key to successful gardening lies in the soil, and throughout our region, soils can pose problems for the many plants introduced here. Plants from the east or west coast perform best in organically rich soils with a pH of 6.8. Except for soils in many mountain communities, the organic content of Rocky Mountain soils is generally low, ranging from 0.8 to 1.4 percent. Native soils have sufficient potassium for normal plant growth, and micronutrients such as iron, manganese, copper, and zinc should be sufficient, but the high alkalinity in some areas makes these nutrients unavailable to the plants. The yellowing of foliage in some plants is often caused by an iron deficiency, a condition known as "iron chlorosis." It usually occurs because high-calcium (calcareous) soils hold the iron in a form that the plants cannot access. Adding iron such as ferrous sulfate to the soil is, at best, a temporary solution—the soil soon makes this source inaccessible, too. An alternative solution is to select plants that tolerate alkaline soil conditions.

Beware the advice of miracle soil improvement! Many quick fixes come from sources unfamiliar with our region. They may advocate adding lime, gypsum, vitamins, kelp, liquid soil conditioners, or other miracle concoctions to the soil. Disregard such advice; using these additives is an effort in futility, not a solution to our soil problems. When something sounds too good to be true, it usually is!

But soil modification can be useful; it often helps improve soil conditions so that the soil can sustain many of the traditional plants introduced from other parts of the United States. Since little can be done to modify our dry air and wind, successful gardening is partly due to good soil conditions. In most situations, the best soils for growing a diversity of plants should have a balance of minerals, air, and moisture. Whether your soil is too sandy, rocky, or high in clay, the solution is essentially the same: add some good quality organic amendment.

Remember, though, that too much soil modification can also pose problems in Rocky Mountain soils. Our semiarid, highly alkaline soils can accumulate natural soluble salts when too much organic matter is added all at once. When these accumulated salts stay in the amended layer around the root zone of plants, roots are soon injured. It is important to loosen the soil as thoroughly and as deeply as possible; this makes it more porous so that the salts can be leached away with proper watering practices.

Patio Garden

Plants have trouble making their roots explore compacted clay, and roots cannot obtain enough moisture in fast-draining sand or crushed-granite-based soils. Gardeners often compound the problem by overcompensating with water; too much water ultimately displaces oxygen in the soil and leaves the plant waterlogged. It is a strange paradox that in semiarid climates, trees, shrubs, perennials, and rock garden plants are doomed by too much water just as they are doomed by severe drought.

Watering

Water is a precious resource throughout the Rockies, so be sure to plan your landscape so that it is water thrifty and in harmony with your surroundings. But you don't have to deprive yourself of a carpet of lawn for you, your children, and your pets to play and relax on, and you don't have to deny yourself the pleasure of growing a favorite flowering shrub or flower garden. There are many creative ways to design your

Woolly Veronica and Aspens

home landscape so that it includes many of the native plants, as well as adaptable plants from other regions of the world that have climates similar to our own.

It seems simple enough to water outdoor plants, but most of us tend to either overwater or underwater. There is no magic rule to watering plants; watering properly depends on several factors, including the type of soil you inherit or create, sun exposure, shade, and wind. Sandy soils drain so quickly that water for such soils must be applied more frequently—but in lower quantities. Clay soils hold water longer; they should be watered less often, or plants can become waterlogged. As you "learn

Well-Designed Lawn

by doing," get a feel for your soil and local weather conditions; your observations help you best determine when and how much to water specific plants and garden areas.

Mulching

If you take a walk through the High Country forests, you will notice that the soil beneath our native vegetation is covered with aspen leaves, evergreen needles, and other woodland debris. Take a lesson from nature and imitate these forest conditions in your own landscape by using organic mulches.

Mulch acts like a blanket. It keeps moisture in the soil, prevents roots from becoming too hot or cold, and helps reduce annual weed growth. In turn, the plants respond with healthier growth. As organic mulches break down, they enrich the soil with humus and provide valuable slow-release nutrients. The ideal mulch permits water and air to penetrate the underlying soil. One of my favorite mulches is pine needles—I often refer to it as "Rocky Mountain mulch." Even though evergreen needles are acidic, there's no need to worry about making the soil "too acidic." Naturally alkaline soils resist quick transformation; it takes decades of needle accumulations to significantly change the pH of calcareous soils.

Shredded leaves, dried grass clippings, pole peelings, wood chips, clean straw, and shredded wood products are some other organic mulch materials.

Remember that soil is alive and must have oxygen. Don't smother the soil around plants with black plastic. Instead, if needed, use a top-quality fabric weed barrier. Cover the fabric with mulch to prevent rapid degradation from sunlight.

Pests and Diseases

The same conditions that allow our gardens to thrive also create an ideal environment for insects and diseases.

Insects are an integral part of gardening; there are the good, the bad, and the ugly. Most are benign; many are beneficial and feed on undesirable pests, while some, such as the tomato hornworm, are endowed with fearsome size and an evil-looking horn at the rear end of the body. Compared to other areas of United States, our problems with insect pests and diseases are moderate. Freezing winter temperatures, unpredictable temperature fluctuations, strong winds, and low humidity discourage pests and diseases from taking a stronghold in our landscapes.

As I often say on my radio and television shows, "A healthy, vigorous plant is the best defense against pests." Plants that grow vigorously can quickly overcome some insect damage, and plants not stressed by environmental conditions can resist most diseases. A stressed plant, on the other hand, is more susceptible to insect and disease invasions. Most of the plants chosen for this book have a strong resistance to insects and diseases. If you follow suggestions about proper placement and care of the plants, you should rarely have to use pesticides. Remember, successful gardens are by nature "user friendly" when it comes to the gardener, wildlife, pets, and the environment.

Plant Hardiness and Light Requirements

The U.S. Department of Agriculture (USDA) Plant Hardiness Zone map on page 19 was created by using weather data to divide our country into minimum-temperature zones. Other than annuals, each plant listed here includes a zone designation. The zone tells you where the plant can survive winter conditions. That is, if a plant is listed as hardy to zone 5, but you live in zone 4 (where colder winter

Winter Landscape

temperatures occur), that particular plant may not survive a severe winter in your area without additional protection.

The USDA Plant Hardiness Zone map in this book reflects a new view of changing climatic conditions. Zones designated as "A" are 5 degrees Fahrenheit cooler than those designated "B." These additional designations reflect differences in the climates and microclimates of specific areas. A and B plant hardiness is not specified in the text of this guide, however, because current, reliable USDA information on the hardiness ratings of all plants listed is not yet available. Ongoing research is leading to the development of new data, including extremes of cold and heat in which landscape plants will thrive. The zone ratings given in this book serve as guidelines to help you select plants suited to your geographic region's climatic conditions.

Keep in mind, however, that conditions *other* than zone hardiness can determine whether a plant thrives in your landscape in the winter. The lay of the land, wind, sunlight intensity, rainfall, exposure, humidity, soil, pH, drainage, and microclimates can all affect plant hardiness. Valleys or low areas frequently have late-spring frosts. City dwellers generally find their average temperatures warmer than

Hardy Geranium

those in surrounding rural areas. The plants listed in this book comprise some of my favorites and are proven performers in many parts of the region, but do remember there is a wide diversity of climates across the Rocky Mountain region. Under certain circumstances—for example areas of high wind, low humidity, high temperatures, prolonged drought, higher elevations, or soil alkalinity—some of my favorite plant recommendations may not perform to optimum growth potential. Carefully consider the plants' site preferences and any special soil conditions of your area. With a little ingenuity, you might be able to create a spot in your landscape that replicates conditions suited for certain plants that are native to other areas. Plants don't know geography; they know only whether they are happy in the site you've chosen.

Take time to analyze a planting site—the amount of sun it gets and its soil, wind exposure, and drainage. Try to match the plant to the site; this gives the plant the best chance of staying healthy and vigorous, which is the best way for it to resist pests and diseases.

Bristlecone Pine

Exposure

The symbols in this book represent the range of sun exposure for each plant. The symbol representing "Full Sun" means the plant does best with six or more hours of direct sunlight daily. "Partial Sun" tells you the plant can thrive in four to six hours of sun daily. "Partial Shade" designates locations with fewer than four hours of sunlight daily, including dappled shade or indirect light all day. "Full Shade" represents protection from direct sunlight and includes locations such as the north side of buildings or large boulders and beneath the spread of evergreens. Some plants can be grown successfully in more than one exposure, so you sometimes see more than one exposure symbol with a plant entry.

Now, on your mark, get set, start growing!

How to Use the *Rocky Mountain Gardener's Guide*

Each entry in this guide provides you with information about a plant's particular characteristics, its habits and its basic requirements for vigorous growth, as well as my personal experience and knowledge of it. I have tried to include the information you need to help you realize each plant's potential. Only when a plant performs at its best can one appreciate it fully. You will find such pertinent information as mature height and spread, bloom period and seasonal colors (if any), sun and soil preferences, planting tips, water requirements, fertilizing needs, pruning and care, and pest information. Each section is clearly marked for easy reference.

Sun Preferences

For quick reference, I have included symbols representing the range of sunlight suitable for each plant. "Full Sun" means a site receiving at least 6 to 8 hours of direct sun daily. "Part Sun" means a site that receives at least 4 to 6 hours of direct sun daily. "Part Shade" means a site that receives about 4 or fewer hours of direct sun daily. "Shade" means a site that is protected from direct sun. Some plants grow successfully in more than one range of sun, which will be indicated by more than one sun symbol. (Also see page 17 "Exposure" paragraph.)

Full Sun   **Part Sun**   **Part Shade**   **Shade**

Additional Benefits

Many plants offer benefits that further enhance their appeal. The following symbols indicate some of the more notable additional benefits:

Attracts Butterflies

Attracts Hummingbirds

Produces Edible Fruit

Has Fragrance

Produces Food for Birds and Wildlife

Drought Resistant

Suitable for Cut Flowers or Arrangements

Long Bloom Period

Native Plant

Supports Bees

Provides Shelter for Birds

Evergreen or Colorful Fall Foliage

Companion Planting and Design

In this section, I provide suggestions for companion plantings and different ways to showcase your plants. This is where many people find the most enjoyment from gardening.

My Personal Favorite

This section describes those specific cultivars or varieties that I have found to be particularly noteworthy. Or, I sometimes suggest other species that are also good choices. Give them a try or perhaps you'll find your own personal favorite.

USDA Cold Hardiness Zones

Colorado, Idaho, Montana, Utah, and Wyoming

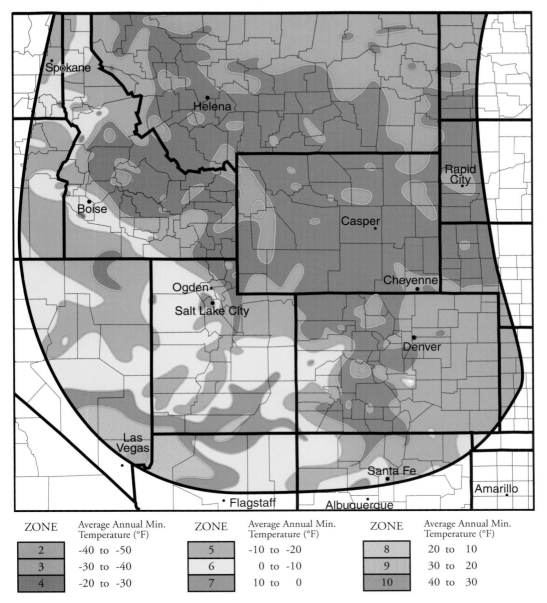

ZONE	Average Annual Min. Temperature (°F)	ZONE	Average Annual Min. Temperature (°F)	ZONE	Average Annual Min. Temperature (°F)
2	-40 to -50	5	-10 to -20	8	20 to 10
3	-30 to -40	6	0 to -10	9	30 to 20
4	-20 to -30	7	10 to 0	10	40 to 30

Cold-hardiness zone designations were developed by the United States Department of Agriculture (USDA). They are based on the minimum average temperatures all over the country. Each variation of 10 degrees Fahrenheit represents a different zone, indicated by colored bands on a zone map. Because perennial plants, whose roots survive winter, vary in their tolerance for cold, it is important to choose those plants that are suitable for the zone for your region of the Rockies. Consult this map to learn in which zone you live. Most of the plants in this book will perform well throughout the region. Though a plant may grow (and grow well) in zones other than its recommended cold-hardiness zone, it is best to select plants labeled for your zone, or warmer.

In this book, the zone notation means the plant is hardy down to the stated zone. However, these zones are only guidelines and not hard and fast rules limiting what you can or cannot grow. Each landscape includes mini-zones (called microclimates) that no zone map can indicate. Microclimates vary from the surrounding area due to topography, exposure to wind, heat, and sun, drainage, soil texture, and other factors. These differences in microclimates may affect zone ratings by as much as two hardiness zones. The important thing to remember is that no zone system is perfect and they should be only used as a guide. Experiment growing different plants and have fun in your gardening endeavors.

Annuals
for the Rockies

If you're looking for a riot of color, in a short amount of time, then annuals are your answer. Not only do annuals bloom profusely, but they do so quickly and with little effort on your part. There are many ways to use annuals in your landscape. Use them to fill barren spots or in mass plantings; plant them in a mixed border or as a touch of summer color in front of the mailbox. Annuals make a fine addition to the perennial border, too. Many annuals make wonderful cut flowers, so if you have the room, plant an annual cut-flower garden. Annuals make ideal container plants set on a deck or patio, in window boxes, or in a sunroom for the winter months.

Cosmos

Annual Definitions

An annual is a plant that completes its entire life cycle in one season; it starts from seed, grows, flowers, reproduces seeds, and dies when the frost ends its growth period. Some annuals, such as marigolds, morning glories, and zinnias, if they are grown in suitable sites and soils, reward you again the next year. At season's end, they often self-sow seeds that then overwinter in the ground and sprout the following spring, starting the cycle over again.

Annuals start to bloom soon after they are planted, bringing excitement and color in a relatively short time. They generally grow in the top 6 in. or so of soil and demand less elaborate soil preparation than the perennial plants in your landscape.

Most seed companies classify annuals based on the temperature needed for germination, healthy growth, and bloom. They divide annuals into three categories: hardy, half-hardy, and tender. Hardy annuals can withstand a reasonable degree of frost. Though they die back in the fall, their seeds survive outside and germinate in the spring. In fact, the alternate freezing and thawing of late winter does not harm them and is often necessary for germination (sweet pea, calendula, cleome). Half-hardy annuals are generally damaged, stunted, or killed by continued exposure to frost, but do stand up to an occasional light frost and cooler temperatures (snapdragon, petunia, marigold). Tender annuals, such as impatiens, coleus, and cosmos, are those that are immediately killed by frost. They need warm soils for germination and vigorous growth.

Getting Them Off to a Good Start

If you purchase annuals as "bedding plants" instead of growing your own, look for healthy plants with dark-green leaves that are neither too spindly nor too compact. I prefer plants that are not in bloom.

They have less transplant shock and come into bloom faster in your garden if they are not in bloom when planted. If you can't plant them right away, keep the plants in a lightly shaded spot and water them as needed to keep them from wilting. Carefully lift or punch the plants from their individual cell packs or containers, keeping the rootball together to prevent damage. If the roots have grown extremely compacted, loosen them gently before planting or score the rootball with a pocketknife. This allows the roots to spread out readily once they make contact with the soil. Dig the planting hole slightly larger than the root system, set the plant at the same level at which it was growing in the container, and gently firm the soil around the roots. Water thoroughly after planting, and again when the soil begins to dry out 2 in. deep, until the plants are well established. An application of a high phosphorous fertilizer (5-10-5) helps get the transplants off to a good start.

A Giant Canvas

Hybridizers are constantly developing new varieties of annuals, many with disease resistance and other desirable characteristics that were not available years ago. While perennials make up the framework for the flower garden, let the annuals act like weavers and binders, helping to tie plants together and bridging the gap between seasons. Though the majority are sun lovers, many annuals will grow in shade. Many can also withstand dry summer winds, heat, and drought conditions. Annuals are available in an unlimited variety of colors, flower shapes, and forms. Think of your landscape as a giant canvas and the flowers as the paint. A combination of annuals and perennials will keep the garden in color all season long.

Petunia 'Purple Wave'

21

Calendula
Calendula officinalis

Calendula is an easy-to-grow annual that was thought to possess wondrous medical virtues and grown in every medieval garden. The almost luminous colors of the flowers are sure to draw attention. Seeds of this annual can be sown in early spring, even as the snow melts, and they will germinate and grow. Within six weeks, calendulas put on their display of silky-petaled flowers, blooming from late spring to late fall. They thrive with cool nights and are outstanding for gardens in high altitudes. In the heat of summer, calendula may take a rest from blooming because it lacks heat resistance. Plant it in light afternoon shade to prolong the bloom period in summer. The flowers have been used for culinary, cosmetic, and medicinal purposes.

Other Common Name
Pot marigold

Bloom Period and Seasonal Color
Early summer to frost blooms in bright orange, apricot, yellow, and cream

Mature Height × Spread
12 to 24 in. × 15 to 18 in.

When, Where, and How to Plant
Calendula seed can be sown directly into the garden in early spring. Sow it outdoors as soon as the ground can be worked. This annual tolerates cooler temperatures and can be sown a few weeks before the frost-free date. Calendula thrives in full sun, but tolerates a bit of shade, particularly during the heat of summer. Sow seeds in moderately moist and well-drained soil. Improve heavy clay and sandy soils with some compost before planting. Keep the flower bed moistened daily to ensure good germination within ten to fourteen days. Thin plants 6 to 10 in. apart, depending on variety.

Growing Tips
Water regularly during hot, dry summer weather. A 1- to 2-in. layer of mulch maintains soil moisture and keeps the soil cool. Fertilize in spring and early fall with a slow-release 5-10-5, and water well.

Care
These generally pest-free and carefree annuals may begin to languish in summer, but don't fret. Trim the plants back by half to stimulate new growth and repeat blooming when cool weather returns. Deadhead spent flowers to stimulate more blooms. Calendulas are quite cold tolerant and continue to bloom profusely into late autumn until a hard frost while other flowers are waning. They self-sow generously and produce an abundance of volunteers. Thin plants to encourage vigorous growth and better flowering.

Companion Planting and Design
Use calendulas in an annual flower bed, cutting garden, herb garden, and containers. Good companions are love-in-a-mist, nasturtiums, borage, and 'Dark Opal' basil. I like to combine them with purple and blue flowers. Sow blue larkspur seeds at the same time you sow calendula for a wonderful blue and orange combination.

My Personal Favorites
The 'Pacific' series grows taller (24 to 30 in.) and makes wonderful cut flowers. 'Touch of Red' (14 to 16 in.) is outstanding, with silky flower petals edged with dark red, giving an antique look.

Cleome

Cleome hassleriana

When, Where, and How to Plant

Cleome can be sown directly outdoors in late spring as the soil warms. Start seeds indoors four weeks before the last killing frost, and harden young transplants before setting them into the garden. Young transplants may be available at garden retailers. Plant cleome in a sunny location with well-drained soil. This annual tolerates light shade, but the more sun it gets, the more blooms it produces. Space plants or thin seedlings 18 to 24 in. apart. When sowing seeds outdoors, plant them at the recommended depth on the seed packet. Set transplants at the same level they were growing in their original container. Gently firm the soil around the roots, and water well.

Growing Tips

After planting, apply an all-purpose 5-10-5 granular fertilizer, lightly scratch it into the soil, and water well. Cleome tolerates dry soils, but should be watered during hot, dry spells to ensure vigor and blooms. In poor soils, apply an all-purpose fertilizer such as 5-10-5 or 10-10-10 a couple of times during the summer.

Care

This easy-to-grow annual thrives in hot weather. Deadhead spent flowers to encourage additional blooms and to reduce self-seeding. Mature flowers develop interesting seedpods later in the season. Just be prepared for an onslaught of volunteer seedlings next season. Cleome can grow quite tall and may require staking in wind-prone areas. This annual is usually free of serious pests or diseases.

Companion Planting and Design

Since it grows so tall, keep cleome in the background. It works well behind a border of perennials or shorter annuals. Use cleome as an annual screen, or grow it against a wood fence or retaining wall. The handsome lobed foliage and tall stems topped with lacy flowers add eye appeal to island gardens and cutting gardens.

My Personal Favorite

Cleomes in the 'Queen' series (4 ft.) are available in shades of pink, rose, purple, lilac, and white.

If you desire an airy, colorful tall annual, you will appreciate the colorful, long-blooming, floriferous cleome. Cleome—or spider flower—gets its name from its spider-like flowers with long, waving stamens. As the flowers mature, the seedpods are also attractive. Cleome is wonderful for informal, sunny gardens; it can be used behind other plants in a flower border or planted in a bed all its own. Whether you plant it from seed or transplants, cleome grows rather quickly to 4 ft. or more, and it spreads about 2 ft. wide. The globe-shaped flowers appear in midsummer and are quite interesting with curving stamens. Because it self-seeds so prolifically, cleome may not be for the gardener who detests pulling out volunteer plants.

Other Common Name
Spider flower

Bloom Period and Seasonal Color
Midsummer to frost blooms of pink, lavender, purple, rose, and white

Mature Height × Spread
3 to 4 ft. × 18 to 24 in.

Cosmos
Cosmos bipinnatus

The tall, wispy stems and daisylike flowers of cosmos are a favorite in an old-fashioned garden. They are among the easy-to-grow annuals that can be grown from seed sown directly in the garden in late spring. These dependable plants quickly grow to several feet tall. The blooms consist of flower petals, which are actually separate ray flowers that have notched edges as though they were trimmed with pinking shears. The bright-yellow centers of the blooms are really disk flowers. Cosmos make excellent cut flowers for floral arrangements. Children enjoy these annuals because they grow so easily from seed and quickly stretch taller than the young gardeners who plant them. Their lacy elegance, abundant blooms, and ease of growing make cosmos a must for every garden.

Bloom Period and Seasonal Color
Midsummer to frost blooms in pink, white, rose, and lavender

Mature Height × Spread
1 to 4 ft. × 16 in.

When, Where, and How to Plant
Sow cosmos seeds directly in the garden as soon as the soil is workable in the spring. Transplants set out after the last spring frost establish quickly as the soil warms. Cosmos prefers a location in full sun with well-drained, average-to-poor soils. Soils that are too rich make for lush leafy growth and sparse flowers. Space plants 10 to 15 in. apart. They branch out freely as they grow, so allow plenty of room. Pinch back young transplants to encourage bushier growth and branching. Set transplants at the same level they were growing in their original containers. Gently firm the soil around the roots, and water well.

Growing Tips
Too much fertilizer produces rank foliage and sparse flowering, so don't use fertilizer with these rugged annuals. Give them an occasional drink of water during hot spells. They can tolerate dry conditions.

Care
This annual self-sows readily, but the flower colors may not be exactly the same as those of the parent plants. You may want to yank out volunteer seedlings and plant new ones each year—or experiment and enjoy the show. Insects and diseases generally do not bother cosmos, but good air circulation is essential to reduce problems with powdery mildew in late summer. Also, avoid wetting the foliage in the evening. Deadhead spent flowers to keep the flower bed tidy and to encourage more blooms.

Companion Planting and Design
Grow cosmos in cutting gardens or in mass plantings. Use them as background for other annuals and perennials. The fernlike foliage, branching form, and height create an old-fashioned, romantic effect. Cosmos are great annuals for hot, sunny spots and are excellent for a water-thrifty garden.

My Personal Favorites
'Picotee' is one of my favorites (30 in.); its icy-white blossoms are boldly bordered, splashed, or stippled with crimson. For something different, try 'Seashells' (3 ft.) with petals that curve inward like fluted seashells around a buttonlike center.

When, Where, and How to Plant

Set out transplants in late spring. Dusty miller prefers full sun, but tolerates filtered sun. Whether your soil is sandy or clay, dusty miller does best in well-drained soils. Amend heavy, compacted clay soil or extremely sandy soil with compost before planting. Then remove transplants from their containers and set them at the same level they were growing. Gently firm the soil around the roots, and water well. Space the plants 6 to 12 in. apart. After planting, water thoroughly.

Growing Tips

After transplanting, apply an all-purpose 5-10-5 or 10-10-10 fertilizer around the plants and lightly rake it in. Water new transplants once or twice a week to ensure healthy establishment. Once established, dusty miller is drought resistant—if you mulch with a few inches of shredded cedar or pine needles.

Care

Dusty miller is virtually free of insects and diseases. In poorly drained sites, it can suffer root rot. To encourage bushier growth, pinch back flowers as soon as they appear. If plants start to grow leggy, prune them back once or twice during the summer. These plants continue to maintain their handsome foliage into late autumn, even after a frost. Dusty miller often survives a mild winter. Though the top of the plant may die back, the crown survives and sprouts new growth the following spring. If live buds are present, cut the dead foliage within 2 in. of the ground in spring and wait for regrowth.

Companion Planting and Design

An effective foil for other bedding plants, this foliage annual is excellent for edging, for formal beddings, and to create patterns. Use it in container gardens for accent. For a visually cooling effect, combine dusty miller with pink geraniums in a border planting or half whiskey barrel.

My Personal Favorites

Some varieties have deeply cut leaves, including 'Silver Dust' (8 in.), covered with dense, woolly white hairs. *Senecio cineraria* 'Cirrhus' has spoon-shaped leaves that are woolly and silvery white. It can grow to 15 in. tall.

If you're looking for handsome foliage in the garden, plant dusty miller. One of the few foliage plants that prefers a sunny location, it helps cool down the bold colors in the flower garden. Dusty miller easily tolerates heat and performs well as a water-thrifty annual. The word senecio *comes from the Latin for "old man"; the name refers to the thick mat of white whiskers covering the leaves. If the colors in your garden seem overwhelming, plant dusty miller. The silvery-gray foliage cools the bold reds, oranges, and yellows of many annuals and perennials. Dusty miller is wonderful for edging flower beds and for borders, as well as to create patterns in your garden. Dusty miller can be grown successfully in full sun or partial shade.*

Bloom Period and Seasonal Color
Grown for its silvery-gray foliage

Mature Height × Spread
6 to 15 in. × 12 in.

Flowering Kale

Brassica oleracea

If you live at the higher elevations where temperatures are cooler, flowering kale and ornamental cabbage are prized for their highly ornamental leafy rosettes in deep, rich colors. They are actually two different types; flowering kale develops a looser head and has fringed leaves, whereas flowering cabbage develops a tighter head with smooth-edged leaves. In the High Plains or lower elevations, flowering kale begins to show its true colors in late summer through autumn. The waxy, tough foliage and rosettes range in colors from white, cream, and pink to red and maroon, and some have variegated foliage. Flowering kale retains its crispy foliage well into the fall, despite the cool weather and brushes with frost. Use this annual in mass plantings to create a bold display.

Other Common Name
Ornamental kale

Bloom Period and Seasonal Color
Late summer through early winter foliage in white, cream, purple, maroon, and variegated

Mature Height × Spread
10 to 18 in. × 18 to 24 in.

When, Where, and How to Plant
The best time to obtain transplants of flowering kale or cabbage is early spring; transplants can be set out in early fall, if they are available. To achieve the best foliage color, plant in full sun, though this annual grows fine with partial shade in afternoon. Flowering kale performs best in well-drained, compost-enriched soil. Loosen the soil to a depth of 6 in. or more, and work 2 to 3 in. of compost uniformly into the soil. Rake the planting area level, and dig planting holes wide enough to accommodate the root system. Position the transplants at the same level they were growing. Gently firm the soil around the roots, and water thoroughly. If planting in containers, use a quality, compost-based potting soil.

Growing Tips
Provide ample water during the summer heat and throughout the growth cycle. Avoid overwatering—waterlogged plants die. Mulch to maintain moisture and to keep the soil cool. After transplanting young plants, scatter an all-purpose fertilizer like 5-10-5 throughout the planted bed and lightly rake the fertilizer into the soil. Then apply a 2-in. layer of organic mulch over the entire annual bed.

Care
These easy-to-grow plants require little attention—usually just the removal of an occasional unsightly or old leaf throughout the growing season. Unlike edible cabbage, ornamental cabbage is usually not bothered by cabbage loopers or aphids. If caterpillars become a problem, engage in bacterial warfare by using Bt (*Bacillus thuringiensis*). Read and follow label directions.

Companion Planting and Design
Plant in flower beds near the driveway or curb; flowering kale is especially effective when planted as a single color in groups of six or more. Plant single colors to outline beds of other cool-tolerant plants such as pansies, calendulas, snapdragons, or dianthus. Use in containers for accent and late-season color.

My Personal Favorite
Flowering kale with fringed foliage is my favorite for accents in the fall and early winter garden.

Four o'Clock

Mirabilis jalapa

When, Where, and How to Plant

Four o'clocks in my garden sow themselves from seeds dropped the previous summer and autumn. I let them grow where they are or transplant young seedlings elsewhere in the spring. Spring is also when seeds can be sown directly into the garden. Four o'clocks do best in full sun, but tolerate light shade. Grow them in well-drained soil amended with aged manure or compost. To sustain the plants all season, scatter some organic 5-10-5 or slow-release fertilizer into the soil at planting time. Plant seedlings 1 ft. apart to allow for uniform growth and to accommodate their spreading habit.

Growing Tips

Four o'clocks grow with minimal care. Water them deeply once a week, and they'll do the rest. Plants grown in soils that are too rich tend to grow leggy and flop over. Avoid fertilizing with high nitrogen, and don't overwater. Four o'clocks don't require additional fertilizer; this may induce weaker stems and fewer flowers. During periods of drought, mulch to help conserve water and to reduce weed invasions.

Care

You may cut four o'clocks back a bit or stake the plants if they become too large or bushy. Pests and diseases rarely bother them. Grasshoppers pose the greatest threat, but they can be controlled by chickens, guineas, or hand picking. **Caution:** All parts of this plant can be toxic, so choose another annual if you have young children or curious pets.

Companion Planting and Design

Four o'clocks work well as background plants, as edging along stone walls, in flower beds, and in mixed-flower borders. Their fragrant blooms attract sphinx moths and hummingbirds during the evening hours, and both are delightful to watch. Since they self-sow so prolifically, four o'clocks make excellent pass-along plants.

I Also Recommend

'Jingles' is a shorter variety with sturdy, dense foliage and handsome striped flowers. The perennial four o'clock *Mirabilis multiflora* is a favorite for a xeriscape or water-thrifty garden.

Four o'clocks are among my favorite flowers for the old-fashioned garden. They have followed me through the years, standing the test of time and proving their toughness in all kinds of climates. As their name suggests, four o'clocks put on their flower display late in the day. Newly opening trumpetlike flowers brighten the afternoon and evening garden. Hummingbirds love to sip nectar from the fragrant blooms. Attuned to the sun, the flowers don't open on cloudy or rainy days. With tough roots and sturdy stems, these durable plants survive drought and heat. Annual four o'clocks self-seed freely for future years. A native perennial four o'clock, Mirabilis multiflora, produces magenta trumpets from July to September and is my favorite for dryland settings.

Other Common Name
Beauty-of-the-night

Bloom Period and Seasonal Color
July to frost blooms in rose, red, yellow, white, or striped

Mature Height × Spread
2 to 3 ft. × 2 ft.

Geranium

Pelargonium × hortorum

Geraniums continue to be among the most popular annuals for containers and borders. The bright globes of clustered flowers are a welcome sight in midwinter. From the time they are set outdoors in late spring, geraniums display their colors continuously until a hard frost. By summer's end, the plants may be woody, so they will benefit from a good pruning if you plan to bring them indoors. Pruning makes for a tidy plant and helps it develop fresh, new foliage. To keep geraniums blooming vigorously, deadhead the spent flowers regularly. Those plants with darker markings around the leaves are called zonal geraniums; they are vegetatively propagated. Seed-grown geraniums have gained popularity with their single flowers and use in mass plantings. Scented geraniums are prized for their fragrant foliage.

Bloom Period and Seasonal Color
Early summer to hard frost in colors of red, salmon, pink, orange, and white

Mature Height × Spread
12 to 24 in. × 12 to 16 in.

When, Where, and How to Plant
Geraniums thrive in the Rocky Mountains' bright sunshine and cool evenings. Plant in late spring after the danger of frost has passed, and locate them in a sunny exposure with well-drained soil. Before planting, enrich the soil with compost to retain moisture and to improve drainage. Loosen the soil in a prepared bed to a depth of 6 in. or more. Scatter an all-purpose 5-10-5 or 10-10-10 fertilizer over the bed, and lightly rake it into the soil. Dig the planting hole wide enough to accommodate the root system, and position the plants at the same depth they were growing. Gently firm the soil around the roots, and water well. Space plants 12 to 15 in. apart. To conserve moisture and reduce weed growth, apply shredded cedar or aspen mulch around the plants.

Growing Tips
Provide geraniums with water throughout the growing season, and use a general flower fertilizer such as 5-10-5 according to the manufacturer's recommendations. Avoid watering in late evening; the flower clusters tend to stay wet and become more susceptible to fungus problems.

Care
Remove faded flowers to encourage more blooms. With these proper growing conditions, geraniums are usually troublefree and will bloom until a hard frost. Geraniums are frequently attacked by a notorious pest known as tobacco/geranium budworm. The tiny caterpillars tunnel into the developing buds and reduce flowering. If this becomes a problem, you may need to treat the plants early in the season with a systemic insecticide. Read and follow label directions.

Companion Planting and Design
Geraniums look best in a mass display. Use them effectively in containers, in flower beds, as accent plants, and in windowboxes. Geraniums grown from cuttings are best for container gardens. When it comes to your garden, let your imagination decide!

I Also Recommend
Ivy geranium (*Pelargonium peltatum*) is my favorite for hanging baskets beneath the patio or covered deck. Trailing stems spill over the containers with brilliant colored blooms.

When, Where, and How to Plant

Set transplants outdoors after the danger of frost has passed, usually late May to mid-June. These tender annuals grow best after the soil has warmed. Plants set out in cool soil will sulk. They flower more profusely where they receive some morning sun although the newer varieties can tolerate more sunlight. Use soil that is rich in humus and well drained. In heavy clay or sandy soils, add compost before planting. Space 10 to 12 in. apart. Position transplants at the same level they were growing. Gently firm the soil around the roots, and water well. After planting, fertilize with an all-purpose 5-10-5 plant food. Do not use high nitrogen—this results in more foliage and few flowers.

Growing Tips

Water impatiens sparingly if they are planted in the shade to avoid waterlogged soil. Impatiens growing in more sun require more water. Wilting foliage signifies that the plants need a good drink. Mulch helps conserve and maintain uniform moisture. Fertilize monthly with a 5-10-5 granular plant food.

Care

Impatiens can be plagued by slugs. If you begin to see leaf damage, take appropriate control measures. My favorite way is to place homemade slug traps throughout the shade garden. Mix 1 teaspoon sugar and 1/4 teaspoon yeast dissolved in 1 cup water. Place this bait in shallow containers (empty tuna or cat food cans), and bury them with the rims level to the ground. Lightly pinch off faded flowers to encourage more blooms and to keep the plants tidy.

Companion Planting and Design

Impatiens are ideal as mass plantings and in containers on shaded patios or decks. Use paler impatiens in shade and brighter ones in the sun. These annuals make excellent companions with other shade plants such as ferns, hostas, pulmonaria, or lungwort.

I Also Recommend

Impatiens balsamina is an old-fashioned favorite with double flowers in yellow, pink, or salmon. Its common name, touch-me-not, comes from the way the ripe seedpods erupt when touched with pressure.

So you have a shady garden and you can't grow flowers. Have you tried impatiens? These brightly colored annuals dress up a shady garden. Use impatiens in containers or windowboxes, and watch the bright blossoms spill over the sides. Older varieties are well adapted to shade, while some of the newer varieties tolerate some sun. Single plants can grow into a flower-covered mound up to 16 in. tall and wide. Impatiens blooms all summer until touched by frost. Look for double impatiens, with flowers that resemble fluffy miniature roses. In late summer and early fall, collect the seedpods and watch them disperse their seeds. Place one in a child's palm; the youngster will be fascinated how the light-green seedpods split open and launch tiny seeds.

Other Common Names
Busy lizzie, touch-me-not

Bloom Period and Seasonal Color
Summer to frost blooms in shades of pink, coral, red, scarlet, orange, white, bicolors, and striped

Mature Height × Spread
6 to 16 in. × 6 to 24 in.

Larkspur

Consolida ambigua

Larkspur is a wonderful annual that resembles our perennial delphinium. It blooms prolifically in the cool weather of late spring, early summer, and on and off through summer and fall. Unlike delphinium, which struggles in warmer conditions and windy areas, lark-spur grows easily, its erect blooms supported on handsome, deeply cut, almost fernlike foliage. The showy flower spikes are thick single or double blooms in beauti-ful shades of blue, lilac, violet, purple, pink, or white. Larkspur florets are about 1 in. long and spurred. The flowers are often tightly clustered along the stems, but some varieties produce more widely spaced blooms. A compact variety, 'Dwarf Butterfly Blue', is perfect for con-tainer gardening. **Caution:** All parts of the larkspur, especially the seeds, are poisonous if eaten.

Other Common Name
Annual delphinium

Bloom Period and Seasonal Color
June through autumn blooms in blue, lavender, purple, pink, and white

Mature Height × Spread
1 to 4 ft. × 2 to 3 ft.

When, Where, and How to Plant
Sow larkspur seeds directly in the garden in late April to early May or in autumn as a dormant seeding. Be patient—seeds take fourteen to twenty days to germinate. Locate in full sun and, for best performance, in well-drained garden soils. Enrich heavy clay and extremely sandy gar-den soils with compost to encourage healthy and vigorous growth. Prepare the soil by loosening it to a depth of 6 to 8 in. Mix in a handful of 5-10-5 or slow-release granular fertilizer. Sow seeds as directed on the package or transplant seedlings in holes slightly larger than their root-balls. Space the plants 10 to 12 in. apart. To avoid crowding, thin young seedlings once they grow to a few inches tall.

Growing Tips
Water young plants regularly until they become well established. During drought, water weekly with 1 to 2 in. of water. Mulch to conserve water and to reduce weed invasions, if needed. Organic or slow-release 5-10-5 fertilizer is all that's neces-sary to maintain these easy-to-grow annuals.

Care
Once established, this annual often becomes self-sowing. Taller varieties benefit from staking to keep the blossom-heavy plants from blowing over. Crowding and poor air circulation can promote powdery mildew on the foliage, so thin plants as needed. Occasionally slugs or aphids become a problem. Cut off faded blooms to groom the plants and to stimulate more flowers. For self-sowing, allow the flowers to mature and form seeds.

Companion Planting and Design
Larkspur's deeply cut, fernlike foliage and colorful flowers create a wonderful effect with the coarser textured foliage of neighboring perennials. Plant taller varieties as background plants and shorter types at the front of flower beds and borders. Larkspur is a must for the cut flower garden and can be used fresh or dried.

My Personal Favorite
'Earl Grey' is one of my favorites, with its beautiful silvery-mauve double blooms.

Love-in-a-Mist
Nigella damascena

When, Where, and How to Plant
Love-in-a-mist is easy to grow from seeds sown in the garden as soon as the soil can be worked in the spring. Love-in-a-mist tolerates cooler temperatures. The seeds germinate in about two weeks. Plant in average garden soil with good drainage and full to partial sun. Nigella has a taproot and resents being transplanted. Sowing seed directly in the garden produces the best results. If you are transplanting from cell-packs, be careful not to disturb the roots. Set at the same level they were growing in their containers. Thin the seedlings to 6 to 8 in. apart.

Growing Tips
Water during dry spells to maintain healthy plants. Love-in-a-mist thrives with the normal watering provided to neighboring plants. If you plant in average garden soil conditioned with compost, extra fertilizer is not needed. This annual is a true easy grower.

Care
When planted early, love-in-a-mist provides the greatest show before the summer heat. Plants mature in about six weeks, when blooming slows down. Successive sowings made from spring through early summer can prolong bloom. Ripening seedpods inflate like balloons crowned with jester's caps, only without the bells. Pick the seedpods right as the maroon begins to develop. If you wait too long, they're not as striking. Pests and diseases generally don't bother this plant.

Companion Planting and Design
Use love-in-a-mist in the perennial garden to fill open spots, or let it self-sow in the vegetable and herb garden for special accents. It's best used as a filler in perennial beds, cottage gardens, and herb gardens, but works effectively in the cut flower garden. Used in the rose garden, this annual's fernlike foliage and flowers accent the roses.

I Also Recommend
'Oxford Blue' (to 30 in.) is a tall double-flowered form with a unique deep-blue color and delicate grace. 'Mulberry Rose' (15 in.) is a beautiful single pink. The species *Nigella hispanica* (16 in.) has black centers and scarlet stamens.

Love-in-a-mist, or fennel flower, is an old-fashioned favorite. Its romantic name refers to the pastel blossoms that hover above soft, green, fernlike foliage. The most beautiful forms of this annual are those with clear sky-blue or delphinium-blue blossoms, an uncommon color for flowers. The horned seedpods give this plant another common name, devil-in-a-bush. Love-in-a-mist's inflated seedpods, with their maroon stripes, are quite attractive and can be used, either fresh or dried, in floral arrangements and herbal wreaths. Each seedpod contains many black seeds, which can be shared with friends or allowed to self-sow. These aromatic seeds are used by cooks and physicians in eastern countries, and both the leaves and the seeds are used in India to prevent moths from chewing clothing.

Other Common Names
Fennel flower, nigella, devil-in-a-bush

Bloom Period and Seasonal Color
Early summer to frost blooms in blue, rose, and white

Mature Height × Spread
12 to 18 in. × 6 to 8 in.

Marigold

Tagetes spp.

Marigolds appeal to both beginning and experienced gardeners who like a riot of color in orange, yellow, and mahogany; cultivars are even available with red and yellow stripes. The full round flowers resemble small carnations or chrysanthemums. They are the sunshine of the annual flower bed and end the season with a burst of vigor. Plants grow from just a few inches tall to 3 ft. The French marigold (Tagetes patula), with fernlike foliage, grows 6 to 14 in. tall. Flowers may be single, double, or crested. African marigolds (Tagetes erecta) grow as tall as 3 ft. and are best planted in masses. 'Crackerjack Mixed' produces bold flowers of orange, gold, and lemon. 'Galore' hybrids (16 to 18 in.) are self-cleaning—spent flowers disappear under new blooms.

Bloom Period and Seasonal Color
Early summer to frost blooms in orange, reddish orange, yellow, mahogany, and bicolors

Mature Height × Spread
6 to 36 in. × 6 to 18 in.

When, Where, and How to Plant
Marigold seeds can be started indoors four to six weeks before the last frost date. Wait to sow seeds outdoors until the soil begins to warm up in mid- to late May. Seeds sown directly in the garden germinate in seven to ten days, depending on soil temperature. Transplants should be set out in the garden after the danger of frost has passed. Marigolds prefer warm weather and full sun, but tolerate some light shade. In heavy clay or sandy soils, add some compost to the soil before planting. This improves drainage and aids in moisture retention. Depending on the type, space marigolds 6 to 15 in. apart.

Growing Tips
After planting, apply an all-purpose 5-10-5 fertilizer. If the soil is too rich or if you use high-nitrogen fertilizer, marigolds grow lush foliage, but few flowers. Keep plants watered once or twice a week or as the soil dries out. Apply mulch around the plants to maintain soil moisture and to prevent weeds.

Care
Don't get water on the flowers, or you will shorten their lives. Deadhead or remove faded flowers often to stimulate more blooms and to keep the plants tidy. During hot weather, watch for spider mites, which cause the foliage to turn silvery gray. Hose down foliage to discourage these pests. Many gardeners interplant their vegetable garden with marigolds, believing that these annuals repel certain pests. The pungent, distinctive aroma of the old-fashioned species seems to be the most effective.

Companion Planting and Design
Marigolds create an explosion of color in mass plantings or can be mixed with ageratum, zinnias, cosmos, and other annuals. Dwarf varieties are superb for containers.

My Personal Favorites
Look at any seed catalog; the many interesting cultivars will mesmerize you. The single French marigolds are among my favorites. Signet marigolds (*Tagetes tenuifolia*), which grow 6 to 10 in. tall, bear single flowers on handsome fernlike foliage and are particularly useful for edging.

Morning Glory

Ipomoea purpurea

When, Where, and How to Plant

Sow morning glories in spring after the danger of frost has passed and the soil is warm. Start transplants indoors a month before the last frost-free date. Morning glories prosper in sunny locations and well-drained soils. To bloom profusely, they need at least six hours of sun daily. Avoid heavily shaded areas or poorly drained soils. If you live in an area with heavy clay soil, amend the soil with compost before planting. Seeds planted directly outdoors germinate in ten to twenty days. To hasten germination, nick the ends of the seeds with a file, pocket knife, grinder, or hacksaw. You can also soak the seeds in warm water for twenty-four hours before planting. Morning glories can be successfully grown in large pots in which you have erected an upright structure or trellis. Fill the container with a compost-based potting soil, and make sure there is proper drainage at the bottom or sides of the container.

Growing Tips

Morning glories take care of themselves once they become established. Water thoroughly once a week. Regular watering is necessary to prevent stress and severe wilting, which can delay flowering, but don't overwater. During periods of drought, mulch to conserve water and to keep the soil cool. Use an all-purpose 5-10-5 or 10-10-10 fertilizer in the spring to get them started; that's all that is needed. Those growing in containers can be fertilized once a month since they are watered more frequently.

Care

Morning glories are not bothered by many insect pests or diseases. No pruning is needed, but you can train the vines to grow in specific directions.

Companion Planting and Design

Morning glories twine with abandon on chain-link fences and trellises, around gazebos, and on fence posts. They make excellent summertime flowering screens.

I Also Recommend

The cardinal climber (*Ipomoea* × *multifida*) is my favorite to attract hummingbirds. It has delicate, deeply fringed foliage and glowing scarlet 2-in. tubular blooms.

Morning glories are among the favorite annual flowering vines that Rocky Mountain gardeners have grown in their landscapes for generations. The vigorous, quick climbers twine around upright supports such as chain-link fences, trellises, pergolas, and branches of dead trees to provide a temporary summer screen. Trumpetlike flowers are large and showy, up to 5 in. across, contrasted by the handsome heart-shaped foliage. Morning glories bloom prolifically in bright, sunny spots. Each flower lasts for a day, but flowers are borne continually. They are among the few plants that bloom in mid- to late summer when other plants are winding down. If you want to get plants to grow and bloom earlier, try starting seeds indoors four weeks before the last frost-free date in your area.

Bloom Period and Seasonal Color

Summer to frost blooms in blue, white, purple, lavender, pink, and red

Mature Height × Spread

8 to 10 ft. × 6 to 12 ft.

Moss Rose
Portulaca grandiflora

Moss rose is able to survive and bloom in the most inhospitable places. Even dry, parched, and poor soils, and the heat of the sun do not faze the vigorous growth of this attractive annual ground cover. The bright, glowing flowers with satiny petals in red, yellow, scarlet, magenta, orange, and white bloom profusely on succulent reddish stems. When other plants are wilting in summer's heat, moss rose grows on, creeping and spreading to cover a spot where nothing else dares to grow. Flowers are 1 to 2 in. of single or double forms. Moss rose is noted for its ability to self-sow and return the following season. Due to cross-pollination, the second year's flowers may not be quite as vigorous or colorful as the originals.

Other Common Name
Portulaca

Bloom Period and Seasonal Color
Early summer to frost blooms in red, rose, pink, orange, yellow, and white

Mature Height × Spread
4 to 6 in. × 6 to 10 in.

When, Where, and How to Plant
You may set young transplants of moss rose out in the garden after the danger of frost has passed and the soil has warmed. Seeds can be started indoors six weeks before the last frost date in your area. To thrive and bloom profusely, moss rose prefers full sun. It tolerates poor soils, but the site should be well drained. Avoid planting in areas that remain wet. Set young plants 6 to 8 in. apart. If you start seeds indoors, mix the fine seed with sand for easier sowing—and do not cover; portulaca seeds need light for germination.

Growing Tips
After setting the plants outdoors, apply an all-purpose 5-10-5 or 10-10-10 fertilizer. Avoid fertilizing with any high-nitrogen fertilizer or flowering will be diminished. You need fertilize only this once. Moss rose doesn't require supplemental food. Water the soil as it becomes dry. This plant can withstand drought conditions, but should be watered regularly to maintain vigorous growth.

Care
Moss rose is quick to establish, sprawling and trailing its way along the ground. It has no serious pest or disease problems. Once you put in all this initial effort, moss rose blooms profusely with minimal care and needs only light deadheading of its spent flowers.

Companion Planting and Design
The creeping stems hug the ground, making moss rose an excellent ground cover when grouped in front of a perennial bed or along the sidewalk or driveway. An excellent complement to dusty miller, moss rose provides a nice contrast to that plant's fuzzy silvery-gray foliage. Another good companion is the petunia. Moss rose makes a wonderful container garden plant, too; the fleshy leaves help the plant retain moisture even in dry, windy spots.

My Personal Favorites
'Sundial' hybrid mix produces double flowers in cream, fuchsia, pink, orange, scarlet, yellow, and white. 'Afternoon Delight' has flowers that stay open all day, even on the hottest days.

Pansy

Viola × wittrockiana

When, Where, and How to Plant

Set out transplants two to three weeks before the last frost. Plants are readily available in late summer for flowers in autumn and the following spring. Pansies thrive in full sun to light shade. Exposure to the afternoon sun dries the plant out faster. Partial shade in summer helps prolong bloom. Pansies do best in cool weather and are well suited to high-altitude gardens. Plant in well-drained soils that have been amended with compost. Avoid heavy clay soils that stay wet all winter. Set transplants 6 to 8 in. apart; try a checkerboard pattern for dramatic effect. Position the plants at the same level they were growing in their containers. Gently firm the soil around the rootball, and water well. Apply a mulch of evergreen boughs over fall-planted pansies after the ground freezes.

Growing Tips

Apply an all-purpose 5-10-5 fertilizer throughout the prepared bed, and lightly rake it in. Provide water on a regular basis; pansies resent dry, hot periods. They perform best in soils kept uniformly moist. Mulch to keep the soil cool and moist.

Care

Pinching off spent flowers encourages more blooms and keeps the flower bed tidy. Cut pansies back after the big flush of bloom to stimulate the plants to repeat bloom as the weather begins to cool. Slugs can become a problem; they cherish the tender leaves. To repel these pests, surround the plants with wood ashes.

Companion Planting and Design

Use pansies in flower beds, plant them in masses, or grow them in containers. In autumn, plant them over newly planted bulb beds. They bloom into early winter and return in spring with colorful flowers skirting the bases of daffodils, tulips, and other bulbs. Pansies perform beautifully in spring and autumn container gardens.

I Also Recommend

Johnny-jump-up (*Viola tricolor*), 10 to 12 in., is always a welcome sight in the garden. Its tricolored flowers—purple, yellow, and white—are about 3/4-in. long.

These old-fashioned flowers perform with gusto in the spring and fall. Pansies make wonderful filler plants to disguise the old or ripening foliage of spring-flowering bulbs. There have been numerous improvements in pansies over the years. A multitude of colors—blue, purple, violet, rose, gold, yellow, orange, lavender, white, and bicolors—are available, and many types have markings that create a tiny cheerful face. Although they grow like a perennial, pansies are best treated as annuals since they begin to lose their vitality by the second year. Fall-planted pansies continue to flower through November and even poke their faces out of melting snow in the winter. Mulched over the winter, they revive and begin to bloom at the first hint of spring.

Other Common Name
Viola

Bloom Period and Seasonal Color
Spring and autumn blooms in blue, violet, purple, white, splotched, orange, mahogany, and multicolors

Mature Height × Spread
6 to 10 in. × 8 to 12 in.

Petunia

Petunia × hybrida

Among the bedding plants that provide a long season of bloom and color in the garden, petunias are the most common. Even if they are shredded or beaten down by a summer hailstorm, these resilient plants grow back to continue flowering until a hard frost. Petunias are remarkable in the High Country—they thrive in cool conditions and display bright colors at higher elevations. And they take the heat in stride. Many new introductions offer additional advantages compared to the older petunias. 'Purple Wave', an All-America Selections winner, was the first ground cover petunia to produce a dense carpet of burgundy-purple blooms on compact plants. Petunias come in all kinds of colors. Some are veined or striped, and others ruffled; flowers come single or double.

Bloom Period and Seasonal Color
Early summer to frost blooms in white, yellow, red, purple, lavender, light blue, and bicolors

Mature Height × Spread
6 to 12 in. × 12 to 24 in.

When, Where, and How to Plant
Set out young transplants in the spring after the danger of frost has passed. Petunias prefer sunny locations with at least six hours of sun daily. Partial shade is acceptable, but flowering may be sparse. Plant in humus-enriched and well-drained soil. Amend heavy clay and sandy soil with compost before planting. Space petunia plants 6 to 12 in. apart, depending on the cultivar; then apply an all-purpose 5-10-5 or 10-10-10 fertilizer. Set the plants at the same depth they were growing. Gently firm the soil around the roots, and water well. Pinch off the flowers to promote a bushier plant.

Growing Tips
These easy-to-grow annuals thrive in the summer heat. Keep the soil watered regularly during hot, dry spells. Avoid watering late in the evening— plants that stay wet overnight are more prone to diseases. Fertilize about once a month to keep the foliage vigorous and the flowers developing.

Care
Remove faded blooms to encourage new growth and more flowers. This can be accomplished by pinching off spent flowers, making sure to remove the seedpod. Petunias that become tall and scraggly can be sheared in early July to rejuvenate the plants and promote another flush of bloom. Cut such plants back by half, and then fertilize. Petunias can be bothered by the tobacco/geranium budworm. This pest tunnels through the flower buds and reduces flowering. Use an appropriate systemic control to keep these pests at bay.

Companion Planting and Design
With their velvety textures, funnel-shaped flowers and distinctive fragrance, petunias work well in annual flower beds, as well as hanging baskets and containers. Petunias are well suited to sunny garden beds and make good companions for sweet alyssum and plants with silver foliage, such as artemisia, dusty miller, and lamb's ears.

My Personal Favorites
So many cultivars are available that it would take another chapter to do them justice. Choose colors and growth habits that fit your garden or containers.

Snapdragon
Antirrhinum majus

When, Where, and How to Plant
Sow seeds in mid- to late spring. Set out young transplants in early May. Snapdragons tolerate cooler conditions, so you can plant them a few weeks before the last frost date. Plant in full sun, but flowers last longer with afternoon shade. They do best in well-drained soil enriched with compost. Space plants 8 to 10 in. apart, depending on the plant's ultimate size. Transplants should rest at the same depth as they were growing. If you sow seeds outdoors, make a shallow trench in the prepared soil and lightly cover (1/8 in.) with fine compost or peat moss. Water lightly, and keep the seed bed moist so the seeds germinate quickly.

Growing Tips
Once established, snapdragons produce bright, long-lasting blooms with little effort. Snaps dislike conditions that are too wet or too dry. With trial and error, you will find the right balance. To conserve water, apply mulch around the plants when they are young. Fertilize with a balanced plant food such as 5-10-5 early in the season, but don't fertilize again until after the first flush of blooms. At that time, cut back the spent flower spikes and fertilize.

Care
In windy areas, taller types may need to be staked. Deadhead regularly to keep plants tidy and to redirect energy to new plant growth. Snaps self-seed if flowers are left to mature. Rust disease can infect older types of snapdragons. It appears as tiny, brownish, powder-filled dots on the undersides of leaves. Select varieties that resist rust. Improve air circulation by adequate spacing and pinching.

Companion Planting and Design
Snapdragons are especially suited to old-fashioned and cutting gardens, or as a background for perennial beds. Dwarf-sized snaps work well in containers. Combine snapdragons with candytuft, pinks, coneflowers, cosmos, marigolds, and zinnias.

My Personal Favorites
The 'Liberty' series produces extra-long, sturdy spikes (18 to 24 in.), making them superb cut flowers. The floriferous 'Royal Carpet Mix' (8 to 12 in.) resists rust disease.

Few flowers provide the opportunity for interaction as do colorful snapdragons. Children are fascinated as they play with the blossoms, pushing the "dragon jaws" open and then allowing them to snap shut. These old-fashioned favorites are easy to grow, either from seed or from young transplants. Groups of these stately flower spikes in exuberant colors make a vertical statement in an old-fashioned garden. Snapdragons are excellent cut flowers, so plant them in your cut flower garden. These tough annuals tolerate cool temperatures, and they often dispense seeds that germinate the following spring. Dwarf and intermediate types do not require staking. Some cultivars, such as the 'Butterfly Series', produce double flowers. Some of the dwarf kinds, such as 'Floral Carpet' and 'Tahiti', are excellent for containers.

Other Common Name
Snaps

Bloom Period and Seasonal Colors
June through frost blossoms in white, red, rose, pink, yellow, orange, and lavender

Mature Height × Spread
6 to 30 in. × 8 to 18 in.

Sunflower

Helianthus annuus

This North American native, with its distinctive big, dark disk surrounded by a single row of yellow petals, is recognized throughout our region. Wild sunflowers adorn the roadsides and prairies during the summer. In the High Plains, sunflowers are grown for their edible seeds and for the oil they produce. Many cultivars suit the home landscape, from the short 'Teddy Bear' (1 ft. tall) to the 'Russian Giant' (10 ft. or taller). As you thumb through seed catalogs, you find sunflowers in a wide range of colors, flower types, and sizes. Some are hybridized to be pollenless, making them desirable for cut flowers. Sunflowers grow on sturdy, fuzzy stems, and they sport sandpaper-textured, bristly green leaves that withstand the wind and heat.

Other Common Name
Annual sunflower

Bloom Period and Seasonal Color
July through September blooms in yellow, gold, mahogany, red, or bicolors

Mature Height × Spread
2 to 12 ft. × 2 to 4 ft.

When, Where, and How to Plant
Sunflowers are remarkably easy to grow just by sowing the seeds directly in the garden in May. To extend the blooming period, you may plant every few weeks into early July. Sunflowers do best in full sun. Plant in well-drained soil that has been amended with aged manure or compost. Sustain them for the entire growing season by adding an all-purpose 5-10-5 or slow-release granular fertilizer when you plant. Thin seedlings according to suggestions on the seed packet. They don't respond well to transplanting, so plant sunflowers where they can grow and thrive undisturbed.

Growing Tips
Keep the seedbed moist until the seeds have germinated. Once sunflowers are established, water them weekly to encourage vigor and strong growth. During periods of drought, mulch to conserve water and to reduce weed invasions. Don't fertilize after the one application when planting; too much nitrogen tends to weaken plants and to delay bloom.

Care
Sunflowers are generally not bothered by pests and diseases. Deer may occasionally visit the garden and strip off the flower heads. Try the homemade repellent on page 257. Squirrels can be a major pest. When the back of the sunflower head turns pale-yellow and then brown, cover the sunflower head with a paper bag tied tightly at the stem to thwart squirrels from collecting the ripening seeds. To harvest the seed heads, cut the flowers off and hang them in a cool garage or shed to dry.

Companion Planting and Design
Since most are large and coarsely textured, use sunflowers as background plantings or as specimens in the flower bed. Smaller varieties are suitable for beds, borders, or even large containers. They also make a nice screen for the vegetable garden. Sunflower seeds are prized by many birds, especially the finch family, and by squirrels and chipmunks, too.

My Personal Favorite
'Indian Blanket' (3- to 4-ft. tall) produces red to mahogany blooms tipped with yellow.

Zinnia

Zinnia spp.

When, Where, and How to Plant

Not frost tolerant, these seeds won't germinate in cold soils, so plant in mid- to late spring after frost danger has passed. They germinate in seven to ten days. Set young transplants in the garden after the soil has warmed in mid- to late May. Zinnias do best in full sun and well-drained soils. Work compost into the soil before planting. Classic zinnias tolerate poor, dry soils better than common zinnia. Set transplants at the same level they were growing. Gently firm the soil around the roots, and water well. Thin common zinnia 10 to 15 in. apart and classic zinnia 6 to 10 in. apart, depending on the mature height and the effect you desire.

Growing Tips

Zinnias thrive in hot, dry summers, but require weekly watering for profuse flowering. Classic zinnia is more drought resistant than common zinnia. Fertilize with a slow-release 5-10-5 plant food monthly. Apply mulch to maintain soil moisture, conserve water, and prevent weeds.

Care

Zinnias produce more flowers if you deadhead regularly. Some taller types may require staking in wind-prone areas. Zinnias are prone to foliar diseases, including powdery mildew, so provide good air circulation. Water at ground level to avoid wetting the leaves. To prevent powdery mildew, apply this homemade remedy to foliage: Dissolve 2 tablespoons of baking soda in 1 gallon of water, and add one tablespoon Murphy's oil soap. Use a tank sprayer or spray bottle to apply to the upper and lower surface of the foliage, starting in midsummer. Apply every seven to ten days or as needed.

Companion Planting and Design

Plant in annual flower beds, as borders, and in cutting gardens. Avoid shady areas and locations where air movement is restricted. Dwarf varieties grow well in containers.

My Personal Favorite

Narrowleaf zinnia (*Zinnia angustifolia*), 12 to 18 in., is my favorite water-thrifty zinnia; its trailing stems work well for beds and borders, and as an annual ground cover.

True to their Mexican origin, these rugged and durable annuals are perfect for a water-thrifty flower garden. Zinnias make wonderful cut flowers. Butterflies, bees, and hummingbirds love them. The bright showy blossoms come in various colors and forms. Dahlia-flowered types sport wide petals that form a rounded bloom up to 6 in. across. Cactus-flowered types, with blooms up to 6 in., have quilled, ruffled petals. Dwarfs such as 'Thumbelina' grow no more 8 in. and bloom when only a few inches tall. Don't hesitate to pick lots of these flowers, since more will soon follow. Classic zinnia (Zinnia angustifolia) differs from traditional zinnia (Zinnia elegans)—narrow, dark-green foliage supports a multitude of small daisylike blooms with orange centers. Classic zinnia creates an excellent annual ground cover.

Other Common Names

Common garden zinnia, classic zinnia

Bloom Period and Seasonal Color

Late spring to frost bright, showy blooms in red, orange, yellow, pink, lavender, white, and striped

Mature Height × Spread

6 in. to 3 ft. × 1 to 2 ft.

Bulbs, Corms, Rhizomes & Tubers *for the Rockies*

Whether you're a novice or well-seasoned gardener, growing flowers from bulbs is a simple and rewarding experience. Just the mention of bulbs brings to mind colorful spring flowers—bouquets of tulips, bunches of bright yellow daffodils, and carpets of crocus—but various bulbs also bloom in summer, autumn, and winter. For example, pink and lavender colchicum bloom atop naked stems in the autumn garden. Many bulbs can be coaxed (some say "forced") to bloom ahead of their normal flowering season to give us weeks of color, fragrance, and pleasure during the cold winter months.

Grace summer gardens with gorgeous blooms of spiking gladiolus, dahlia blooms as big as dinner plates, and the beautiful arching stems of lilies. The bright blossoms of begonias create pools of brilliant color to awaken shady gardens.

The Bulb Family

Most gardeners have come to use the word *bulb* as a catch-all term for a variety of plants including corms, rhizomes, and tubers. Usually round, a bulb is a living bud—a subterranean bud that grows roots below and produces a stem to the surface. From the stem emerge foliage and blooms. Some examples of true bulbs are tulips, hyacinths, and daffodils. They are truly miracles of nature. Hidden within bulbs are embryos that contain all the ingredients of next year's flowers, surrounded by fleshy layers of stored food energy.

The other various plants referred to as bulbs are generally solid masses of storage tissue. For example, gladiolus and crocus are corms, dahlias are tubers, and cannas grow from rhizomes. Whatever term you choose to use, these plant structures have living buds with a reserve of stored food. Succeeding with bulbs is

Fringed Tulip

Dahlias

easy. Each contains within itself the nutrients necessary for one full season of growth and miraculous bloom. All you need to do is provide the proper growing conditions of light, water, and soil.

Some bulbs, including paper-whites and hyacinths, don't even need soil, and colchicum can be forced to bloom without soil or water.

Hardy and Not So Hardy Bulbs

Hardy bulbs are those classified by their ability to survive the minimum temperatures that occur during winter. They can be left in the ground year-round and are treated as perennials. These hardy bulbs need a period of cold during their dormancy or they do not flower reliably. Planting in the autumn ensures the proper chilling and rewards you with colorful blossoms each spring.

Nonhardy or "tender" bulbs, corms, and tubers are unable to withstand cold temperatures so generally they are dug from the garden and stored inside during the winter. They are treated as annuals and planted anew each spring. This group includes dahlias, gladiolus, and cannas.

Hardy bulbs are able to endure more neglect than suspected, and they are easy to grow. Tulips are among the most drought tolerant when planted in soil with good drainage. If you're a beginner, select easy-to-grow bulbs first. They are economical in large quantities and conveniently available from local and mail-order sources. Daffodils, crocuses, grape hyacinths, snowdrops, and scilla fit this category. You will find a good range of colors and flower shapes. Once you've succeeded with these basic bulbs, you can add others in following years. Caution: Bulb gardening can become addictive.

Guarding Against Critters

Plant tulips, crocuses, lilies, and other tasty morsels in wire baskets to keep rodents from devouring them. Wire baskets are easy to make from ¹/₂-inch mesh hardware cloth; this size allows stems and roots to grow

through, but keeps critters out. Cut a 6- to 8-in. strip of any length, and make a circle. Then cut a bottom piece to fit, and wire it to the circle. Dig the planting hole at the proper depth for the specific bulbs, place your homemade basket in the hole, set the bulbs in, and cover with soil. Finish by laying a piece of wire mesh directly onto the basket, then add more backfill soil.

It's Better to Be Generous

My *Rule of Green Thumb* for landscaping with bulbs is to plant the same types together and don't be stingy. Naturalize an area by throwing a handful, and plant them where they fall. Plant bulbs in clumps of a dozen or more to create uniformity of color and foliage texture. Massing bulbs provides enough flowers to cut for indoor bouquets.

Place tall-flowering bulbs such as late tulips, lilies, and crown imperials in the background of a border or among similarly sized shrubs or perennial flowers. Crocus, snowdrops, glory-of-the-snow, scilla, and colchicum can be used as carpets in shrub borders or perennial beds, or naturalized in lawns and meadow gardens.

Bearded Iris

When you purchase bulbs, make sure they are firm and large for their type. Bigger bulbs generally bloom the first season and have larger blooms. To encourage the best growth and root development, plant your spring flowering bulbs when the ground temperatures are below 60 degrees Fahrenheit. If you don't get the bulbs planted right away, store them in a cool, dry place, but don't forget about them. Even if you plant them in December, they generally bloom the following spring; if they don't, they should be back on schedule the following year.

Buried Treasures

Bulbs are nature's miracles, tiny bundles of stems, leaves, and flowers compressed into well-tuned organs that resume growth when conditions are appropriate. They are so naturally dramatic that wherever you plant them, a spotlight shines. The simplest and most dramatic idea for adding bulbs in the landscape is to plant them in masses; a lot of one variety closely spaced in groups provides the biggest show.

Gladiolus

Bearded Iris

Iris germanica and hybrids

The bearded irises, a favorite from my grandmother's garden, are also called German irises or flags. These durable and long-lived perennials withstand the test of time. Among my favorites is 'Eversweet', a smaller tall bearded iris with graceful, well-branched, sturdy stems. Irises adapt to the wide range of soils and environmental conditions found throughout the region. With their many colors, these plants play a spectacular role in the spring garden. The leaves of tall bearded irises are sword shaped and up to 1 ft. long; their waxy coating rubs off easily. The root system consists of fleshy, modified plant stems, called rhizomes, which store nutrients. Shortest and earliest to bloom are the miniature dwarf bearded irises. Create a rainbow of colors in your garden with bearded irises!

Other Common Names
Flag, German iris

Bloom Period and Seasonal Color
May and June blooms in white, reds, pink, yellow, orange, blue, purple, lilac, lavender, and almost black, as well as bicolors

Mature Height × Spread
6 in. to 2 ft. × as permitted by clumping

Zones
To zone 3

When, Where, and How to Plant
Plant iris rhizomes in late July through August (six to eight weeks before the ground is likely to freeze). Transplant potted plants from spring through summer. Irises perform best in a sunny location with well-drained soils. Enrich the soil with aged manure or compost, and mix in an all-purpose 5-10-5 granular fertilizer before planting. Make a narrow, shallow furrow; set the rhizomes horizontally so that the roots nestle into the soil indentation. Space the plants about 12 in. apart, pointing the ends with the foliage fan in the direction the clump is to spread. Cover the rhizomes with soil to blanket the roots, but leave the shoulder slightly exposed. Water well.

Growing Tips
Water regularly if the soil is dry. Once bearded irises are established, avoid overwatering—which can rot the rhizomes. A good soaking once every seven to ten days should be adequate during the growing season. Fertilize in the fall with a slow-release or organic fertilizer. A light organic mulch protects irises during snowless winters.

Care
General care includes thinning or dividing irises every three to five years, depending on how crowded the plants are. Trim off any injured, damaged, or diseased foliage, but leave the healthy foliage undisturbed—it manufactures food for the rhizomes. Keep the iris bed free of weeds and debris so the shoulders of the rhizomes can bask in the sun. Cut or snap the faded bloom stems off close to the ground. Aphids may attack the buds in the spring; use appropriate control measures.

Companion Planting and Design
The swordlike foliage combines handsomely with peonies and works well as a background in the perennial garden. Irises are cold hardy and can be grown in containers that are at least 12 in. deep.

My Personal Favorite
Reblooming irises, known as *remontants*, bloom in the spring, then bloom again in late summer and autumn. 'Clarence', with white standards and violet falls washed with white, is my favorite.

Canna

Canna × generalis

When, Where, and How to Plant

Plant canna rhizomes in the spring after the soil has warmed to 68 degrees Fahrenheit—use a soil thermometer to verify soil temperature. To get a head start, start the rhizomes in pots indoors about four weeks before the last expected spring frost for your area. Locate in full to partial sun. Cannas do best in moist soils enriched with compost. Amend the soil to a depth of 8 to 10 in., and add an organic all-purpose 5-10-5 granular fertilizer when preparing the planting site. Plant the rhizomes 3 to 4 in. deep; space them 18 to 24 in. apart. Cover with soil, and water well. Plant container-grown plants at the same depth they were growing in their pots.

Growing Tips

Cannas require supplemental watering in order to maintain moist soil conditions, especially during drought. Use a good organic mulch to retain moisture and to reduce weeds. Slow-release fertilizer added to the soil at planting is sufficient to sustain the plants throughout the growing season.

Care

Groom the plants and stimulate more flowers by removing the faded blooms. Cut *just below* each faded flower cluster—cutting too far down may remove potential secondary flower stalks. Stake taller varieties, if needed. After frost kills back foliage in late fall, cut off the stalks and dig up the rhizomes. Let the rhizomes dry for a few days; then place them in a wooden box, cover them with sphagnum peat, and store in a frost-free location over winter. Check the rhizomes monthly; lightly mist them with water if they are shrinking or drying. It suffers from no serious problems.

Companion Planting and Design

Cannas' tropical look should be relegated to the back of the garden as an accent against fences, walls, or flower borders. Smaller varieties can be planted with annuals or in large containers around a patio, deck, or pool.

My Personal Favorite

A taller growing variety (to 6 ft.), 'Bengal Tiger' sports dramatic green and yellow striped leaves and bright orange blooms. (If you don't find it listed as 'Bengal Tiger', try looking for 'Pretoria' or 'Striata'.)

If you want a bold, tropical accent in your garden, plant cannas. These summer bloomers boast big, showy, irregularly shaped flowers atop equally showy foliage that ranges from red, green, and blue-green to bronze. Some foliage, such as 'Bengal Tiger', is striped. Canna leaves are typically 1 to 2 ft. long, with blunt edges and prominent veins. Cannas come as dwarfs, which grow only a few feet high, and giants, which reach 6 ft. or taller. Numerous varieties are available, including 'Pretoria', with green and yellow-striped foliage; 'Wyoming', with bronzy purple foliage and orange blooms; and 'Pfitzer Crimson Beauty' and 'Pfitzer Chinese Coral', which grow 2 to 3 ft. tall. Canna glauca is an aquatic variety; use it in the water garden.

Other Common Name
Hybrid canna

Bloom Period and Seasonal Color
Mid- to late summer and early fall blooms in red, pink, salmon, yellow, or orange

Mature Height × Spread
2 to 6 ft. × as permitted

Zones
Not hardy; annual rhizome; needs to be harvested in fall

Crocus
Crocus spp. and hybrids

Though the first day of spring doesn't arrive until late March, you know spring is just around the corner when the bright yellow and lavender chalices of crocus blooms unfurl in Rocky Mountain sunshine. With the right selections, the crocus season can span several weeks. Crocuses are known to multiply and spread if they like their location. The petite snow crocus (Crocus chrysanthus) blooms two weeks earlier than the larger flowered Dutch hybrids. Even though smaller, the blooms are most welcome in the landscape with the first stirrings of spring and the arrival of honeybees. Plant crocuses where you can enjoy them often—along the driveway, along garden pathways, and near the doorway. Tomasini's crocus, Crocus tommasinianus, is ideal for naturalizing in lawns and multiplies over the years.

Other Common Name
Common crocus

Bloom Period and Seasonal Color
Late winter through spring blooms in purple, white, yellow lavender, and stripes

Mature Height × Spread
3 to 6 in. × as desired

Zones
To zone 3

When, Where, and How to Plant
Plant crocus corms in autumn. Crocuses prefer full sun, but grow fine in partial sun to partial shade. Plant them in well-drained soil. Amend clay, sandy, and crushed granite soils with compost before planting. This helps retain moisture and improve drainage. Plant the species crocus generously and densely, about 3 in. deep and 2 in. apart. Within a few years, the plants will have multiplied from seed and new cormlets. Plant the large-flowered Dutch crocuses 4 in. deep and 4 in. apart. You can also follow the general rule by planting the corms three times as deep as the bulbs measure in diameter.

Growing Tips
Water thoroughly after planting and during extended dry periods in the fall and winter when temperatures are above freezing. You may apply bulb fertilizer (5-10-5) into the soil at planting time. In autumn, apply 5-10-5 fertilizer to garden beds where crocuses are planted. This gives them an extra boost for the next spring flowering cycle.

Care
These long-lived plants require little attention. But field mice, squirrels, and voles find crocus irresistible. Prevent rodent damage by covering newly planted areas with rabbit or chicken wire, or enlist an active, hungry cat or dog to stand on patrol.

Companion Planting and Design
Crocuses can be naturalized in lawns as long as you're willing to wait to mow the grass until the narrow leaves die back. Plant them generously along garden paths, sidewalks, and driveways; in flower beds; and near the doorway. Don't forget autumn-flowering crocuses for a colorful display for both gardener and the last of those foraging honeybees. The thin leaves ripen relatively quickly and are not bothersome when planted among other perennials.

My Personal Favorites
Though spring-blooming crocuses are delightful, my favorites include the autumn-flowering crocuses *Crocus speciosus*, with violet flowers, and *C. kotschyanus* in lavender-blue. A highly prized plant is saffron crocus (*C. sativus*); its bright orange-red stigmas impart flavor and a golden glow to fine cuisine.

Daffodil
Narcissus spp. and hybrids

When, Where, and How to Plant

Plant bulbs in the fall—before the ground freezes—in moisture-retentive, yet well-drained soil. Daffodils prefer sunny locations, but tolerate light shade from deciduous trees as the trees leaf out in the spring. They do best in soils that remain moist from planting until their leaves have died down in early summer, but they will tolerate drier conditions in the summer. Amend clay soils by adding compost. Loosen soil to a depth of 12 in., and mix in a granular bulb fertilizer. Plant large trumpet daffodils 6 to 8 in. deep and 4 to 6 in. apart. Smaller varieties can be planted 4 to 6 in. deep and 3 to 4 in. apart. For the best effect, plant clusters of seven or more, making sure the bulbs' pointed tips face up. To naturalize in open areas, cast handfuls of bulbs randomly across the area and plant them where they fall. After planting, water well.

Growing Tips

Water periodically during fall, winter, and spring drought conditions. A 2-in. cover of organic mulch insulates soil in the winter and maintains moisture. Fertilize established plantings in the fall to encourage healthy blooms next spring. Scatter a complete 5-10-5 granular fertilizer over naturalized areas, and water well.

Care

Leave daffodils undisturbed for years. Remove each spent flower head, but leave the foliage intact until it naturally ripens. Don't waste your time braiding or tying up the leaves. Every five to seven years, dig and divide daffodil bulbs to increase stock and to reduce crowding. They are disliked by insects and four-legged critters—including squirrels, rabbits, deer, and elk—because all parts are toxic.

Companion Planting and Design

Plant drifts in shrub borders, under deciduous trees, and among ground covers. Mass plantings near the doorway and mailbox are always welcome. Daffodils make excellent cut flowers.

My Personal Favorite

Pheasant's eye daffodil (*Narcissus poeticus*) is my favorite for naturalizing; it blooms later than most varieties. It's a very fragrant old-fashioned favorite that has broad white petals and a small "eye" on the cup.

Whether you call them jonquils, narcissus, or daffodils, no landscape can have too many of these heralds of spring. Tulips may announce spring in a bold fanfare of upright stems, but daffodils, with their graceful nodding heads in yellow, peach, pink, and white, are the quintessential spring flowers. These plants differ from other bulbs in that they prefer the cooler, moister areas of the garden and endure drought during the summer. Thousands of cultivars are available—some with ruffled flowers, double flowers, split cups and coronas, and peachy-pink blossoms. The smaller types of daffodils, close to the species and wild forms, bloom reliably without a lot of maintenance. In our landscape, their virtue is that deer and rabbits don't disturb them!

Other Common Names

Narcissus, jonquil

Bloom Period and Seasonal Color

Mid-March into May blooms in yellow, orange, peach, pink, white, and bicolors

Mature Height × Spread

6 to 18 in. × 6 to 8 in.

Zones

To zone 3, depending upon the species

Dahlia

Dahlia spp. and hybrids

Dahlias are strong, handsome plants that adorn the summer garden. Native to Mexico, these colorful plants adapt well to summer growing in the Rockies. Few summer garden plants offer such variety of flower shapes, sizes, and colors, plus a long season of bloom. More than two thousand kinds are available, including miniatures, pompom, ball, cactus, formal, informal, stellar, waterlily, peony, anemone, and giant—and these are just a few of the classifications. Dahlias come in a riot of colors. They reach their flowering peak in mid- to late summer. Since they have a long season of prolific flowering, they provide cut flowers for much of the summer. Dahlias work well in outdoor containers, too. Glossy green leaves densely cover the thick, almost succulent stems.

Bloom Period and Seasonal Color
Mid- to late summer blooms in many colors

Mature Height × Spread
1 to 7 ft. × as permitted

Zones
Not hardy; treat as an annual; harvest tubers after frost

When, Where, and How to Plant
Plant the tuberous roots outdoors in mid- to late spring. They bloom best in full sun, but can tolerate light shade in the afternoon. The soil should be well drained. Condition heavy clay and sandy soils with compost to a depth of 12 in. or more. Mix in slow-release or organic, all-purpose fertilizer during soil preparation. Dig planting holes 6 in. deep. Set the tubers on their sides with the eyes, or buds, pointing up. Space plants 2 to 3 ft. apart to ensure good air circulation.

Growing Tips
Dahlias require a deep soaking at least weekly to promote healthy and vigorous plants. Apply liquid fertilizer weekly until the plants develop flower buds. Mulch to conserve moisture; provide additional water if necessary during dry spells.

Care
To avoid poking the tuber, insert stakes into the soil near the tuber at planting. Taller growing varieties do best when staked and protected from wind damage. Deadhead spent flowers to encourage more blooms. If you desire bushier plants with more flowers, pinch out the central stem after four to six leaves develop. Once the plants die back after a hard frost, cut back the tops to within an inch of the tubers and dig them up. Store the tubers in a frost-free location; cover them with a layer of sawdust or sphagnum peat moss inside a wooden box. In early spring, divide the tubers, being careful not to damage the eyes. Get a jump on the season by starting the tubers in pots indoors in March. Earwigs can become a nuisance in the flowers. Place rolled-up moistened newspaper at the base of the plants to trap these critters. Spider mites can be a problem in the heat of summer, but they can easily be controlled by hosing down foliage.

Companion Planting and Design
Dahlias are effective as mass plantings in their own flower bed. You can also use them in mixed flower beds or as a background or screening. Plant dwarfs as edging.

My Personal Favorite
'Weston Pirate' is an eye-catching cactus form with a nice, dark-red color.

Dwarf Iris
Iris reticulata

When, Where, and How to Plant

Plant the bulbs of dwarf iris in the fall. *Iris reticulata* performs best in full to partial sun. Dwarf irises prefer any well-drained, good garden soils. Avoid heavy clay soils that do not drain. Loosen the soil thoroughly and augment it with compost to improve drainage in clay soils and to retain moisture in sandy or gravelly free-draining soils. Plant the bulbs 4 in. deep, and place them 3 to 6 in. apart. These plants can be grown in containers in ordinary potting soil. For the best effect, plant dwarf irises in groups of twelve or more.

Growing Tips

After planting dwarf irises, water the bed thoroughly—but keep in mind that overwatering is sure doom for this diminutive flowering bulb. During extended dry spells in late fall and winter, water when temperatures are above freezing. Lightly mulch with pine needles or compost in late fall. In autumn, scatter a granular 5-10-5 fertilizer over the area where irises are planted.

Care

These plants don't require a lot of attention. Dwarf irises are generally reliable plants throughout the Rockies if we grow them hot and dry. Poor drainage dooms these tiny bulbs, so it is best to avoid wet, clay soils. They require little care and will multiply if conditions are ideal. Dwarf irises have no significant pest or disease problems.

Companion Planting and Design

Dwarf irises work well in rock gardens, near sidewalks and driveways, or wherever drainage is good. Combine them with other spring-blooming bulbs to add interest in early spring. They are ideal for rocky slopes, underplanted with woolly thyme or creeping ground cover junipers. One of my favorite uses is to naturalize them in native grass lawns.

I Also Recommend

Iris reticulata danfordiae grows to 4 in. tall. It features bright-yellow and brown speckles and it is very fragrant. Its flowers form early in the spring, competing with snowdrops and crocuses for first place in the early spring bloom contest. (It may be sold as *Iris reticulata danfordiae* or *Iris reticulata* 'Danfordiae'.)

The fragrant and petite flowers of *Iris reticulata, also known as dwarf or snow iris, awaken the spring garden. They are among the earliest to bloom, along with crocuses and snowdrops. Given a proper, well-drained home, snow irises thrive year after year. These diminutive beauties (6 to 8 in. tall) prefer to grow hot and dry, so avoid frequent watering from the sprinkler system. The characteristic flowers have upright standards and downward falls in shades of purple, blue, and violet. The falls have a golden-orange beard bordered in white. Because they bloom so early, plant dwarf irises where they will be appreciated. Come spring, the early flowers brighten the landscape. Later the leaves die back discreetly before it's time to mow the grass.*

Other Common Names
Reticulated iris, snow iris, dwarf bulbous iris

Bloom Period and Seasonal Color
Early spring blooms in blue, purple, or violet

Mature Height × Spread
6 to 8 in. × 6 in.

Zones
To zone 3

Gladiolus

Gladiolus × hortulanus

Gladiolus is named for its distinctive swordlike leaves. The Latin word gladius *means "little sword," and glads were an integral part of Roman culture. They are reputed to be the floral emblem of the Roman gladiators. Paintings of gladioli are found in the ruins at Pompeii. For a great effect in your garden, stagger plantings to add vertical accent, colorful spiked blooms, and summer-long bloom to your garden. Gladiolus blooms open successively from bottom to top over several days. The stiff, upright foliage completes the attractive display. Although glads are technically "tender corms" in our region, they are usually grown as an annual but they can sometimes survive on a south or southwest exposure if mulched over the winter.* Gladiolus byzantinus *are winter hardy. They grow into delicate clumps and bloom in summer.*

Other Common Name
Glad

Bloom Period and Seasonal Color
June to frost blooms in white, cream, yellow, orange, salmon, red, rose, violet, and bicolors

Mature Height × Spread
2 to 3 ft. × 6 to 8 in.

Zones
Not hardy; treat as an annual; harvest corms after frost

When, Where, and How to Plant
Plant around mid-April; set corms out every two weeks in succession until mid-June to assure a continuous supply of flowers over the growing season. Flowers mature every eight to ten weeks. Glads bloom best in full sun, but grow well in partial sun, too. Plant them in well-drained soil. Lighten heavy clay soils by digging 10 to 12 in. deep and adding compost. Mix in a slow-release or organic granular 5-10-5 fertilizer while preparing the bed. Planting depth varies with corm size: Corms smaller than $1/2$ in. across go 3 in. deep, 1-in. corms go down 4 in., bigger corms go 6 in. deep. Plant with the pointed side facing up and the flat base down. Instead of lining up glads like soldiers, plant them in groups of seven or more, spacing them 6 in. apart.

Growing Tips
To maintain moisture and discourage weeds, keep the soil evenly moist and mulch. Water when the soil below the mulch feels dry to the touch, but avoid overwatering; it can rot the corms. No additional fertilizer is needed beyond that supplied at planting.

Care
Taller varieties benefit from staking, particularly in windy areas. Place bamboo stakes near the corms at planting time; they are soon camouflaged as the foliage grows. When the foliage ripens or frost kills the tops, dig up the corms, trim off dying stems, and allow the corms to dry. Store them in netted produce bags or old nylon panty hose in a well-ventilated, frost-free location. Tiny pests called thrips attack the leaf sheaths and flower buds, causing foliage to become stippled and brown, buds to shrivel, and flowers not to open. Use a systemic insecticide labeled for thrips, and follow label directions carefully.

Companion Planting and Design
Plant glads in the cutting garden especially, and as background in a flower border. They attract hummingbirds and sphinx moths.

My Personal Favorite
The bright-red *Gladiolus* 'Oscar' really attracts hummingbirds.

Glory-of-the-Snow
Chionodoxa luciliae

When, Where, and How to Plant

Plant the small bulbs of glory-of-the-snow in the fall. Choose a sunny location, though glory-of-the-snow tolerates light shade from the emerging foliage of deciduous shade trees. *Chionodoxa* will grow in short grasses, through ground covers, and under shrubs and ornamental trees. They require well-drained soil. Amend heavy clay soils with compost, and loosen deeply to help improve drainage. Plant the small bulbs 3 to 4 in. deep, and space them 3 in. apart. Bold plantings of fifty to one hundred bulbs produce the best displays. You can dig out an entire bed, plant the bulbs as suggested, and then cover them with the backfill soil. If you prefer, use a strong, bulb-planting trowel marked at the proper depth and plant in lawn areas for naturalizing.

Growing Tips

Water the bulbs thoroughly after planting. When planting in large masses, incorporate a bulb fertilizer (5-10-5) into the planting area at the time of planting to give glory-in-the-snow a boost as it becomes established. During extended dry periods in the fall and winter, water areas where glory-of-the-snow bulbs are planted. Do this when temperatures are above freezing to allow the water to soak in.

Care

Chionodoxa needs little attention. These plants are generally free of pests and disease. When using glory-in-the-snow in lawns, allow the foliage to mature or ripen before mowing. This allows them to store food energy before going dormant.

Companion Planting and Design

While making a bold display on its own, glory-of-the-snow combines well with other early flowering bulbs and perennials. Use with Lenten rose (*Helleborus orientalis*), daffodils, and early-blooming tulips. Allow them to naturalize in meadow and woodland gardens or in front of shrubs or perennial beds.

My Personal Favorites

Chionodoxa comes in various colors. 'Alba' is white, 'Blue Giant' is sky blue with a white center, and 'Pink Giant' is bright pink with a white center.

The traditional sky-blue blossoms of Chionodoxa are a cheerful sight in the early spring, and as befits their name, the flowers often get caught by a spring snow. The star-shaped, 1-in.-wide flowers number ten or more per spray or stem. Flower stalks grow 2 to 3 in. high over handsome grassy foliage. Each flower has a starry white center and faces skyward, which distinguishes this plant from the Siberian squill (Scilla), which nods its head and has deeper blue flowers. This bulb naturalizes nicely. It multiplies by both seeds and offsets to form a carpet of blue. Glory-of-the-snow is effective near the front entry and along walkways or spots where it can be viewed from the windows. They are a welcome delight to the winter weary.

Bloom Period and Seasonal Color
Early spring blooms in blue, lilac, or white

Mature Height × Spread
4 to 5 in. × 4 in.

Zones
To zone 4

Grape Hyacinth
Muscari armeniacum

Reliable and easy to grow, grape hyacinths resemble bunches of little grapes and create striking combinations of sky blue, powder blue, or deep lavender to charm the daffodils, tulips and pansies in your spring garden. The true species including M. armeniacum, M. latifolium, and M. azureum, are prolific, spreading by seed to naturalize meadows, lawns, and rock gardens. Plant them in groups of fifty or more for a bold display that lasts for weeks. Muscari frequently sends up its grasslike foliage in the late summer and fall. In spring, spikes of fragrant blue flowers appear and the leaves continue to grow. Eventually the foliage dies down and bulbs enter a dormant state, but later their growth cycle begins again and they produce many more plants.

Bloom Period and Seasonal Color
Mid-spring blooms in blue, purple, pink, yellow, or white

Mature Height × Spread
6 to 8 in. × 6 in.

Zones
To zone 3

When, Where, and How to Plant
Plant grape hyacinths in the fall as soon as possible because the foliage begins to grow in the early fall. Grape hyacinths perform well in full to partial sun. They grow in a wide range of soils, but well-drained soils are best, so loosen the soil deeply and augment with compost if needed. Work the compost uniformly into the soil to a depth of 6 in. Add a bulb fertilizer to the soil before planting. Plant the bulbs 3 in. deep, and space them 3 to 4 in. apart. After planting, water well. If squirrels watch as you plant, consider covering the beds with rabbit or chicken wire to protect the plants.

Growing Tips
Grape hyacinths only need be watered weekly or just as the soil dries out. Keep newly planted grape hyacinths watered during dry periods in the fall and winter. If you like, scatter an all-purpose 5-10-5 granular fertilizer over the planting site in the fall and water well.

Care
Once established, grape hyacinths need little care; they are among the easiest bulbs to grow. Pest and disease-free, these plants spread freely by seed, so if you want to control them, deadhead spent flowers to prevent infiltration into areas where you don't want them to grow.

Companion Planting and Design
Plant grape hyacinths in drifts under shrubs and trees where they will remain and spread undisturbed. Great for rock gardens, these plants also make good companions for daffodils and set off the flaming hues of tulips. They make effective edging around beds and walkways. Plant some of the unusual species, such as *M. comosum* with its tassels of lilac blooms and golden *M. macrocarpum* for added accents. Grow *M. armeniacum* 'Christmas Pearl' in pots; you will enjoy blooms a few weeks after potting.

I Also Recommend
Muscari botryoides is regarded as the true grape hyacinth. It has sky-blue flowers and a white rim at the mouth.

When, Where, and How to Plant

Plant in the spring. Unlike tulips, these bulbs have no protective covering, so plant them immediately before they dry out. Avoid moldy bulbs or those that have dried out and have no roots. Most prefer moist, well-drained, humus-rich soil and full to partial sun. Good drainage is essential; if your soil is particularly clayey, consider growing lilies in containers or raised beds. Plant bulbs 6 to 8 in. deep, depending on the size. Madonna lily (*Lilium candidum*) is the exception: plant it so that the top of the bulb is at soil level. Work a generous supply of compost into the planting area, toss in a handful of bulb fertilizer, and incorporate it to the bottom. For dramatic displays, plant lilies of the same variety in groups of three, spaced 12 to 18 in. apart.

Growing Tips

Lilies in well-drained soils tend to be long-lived. They need fertilizer such as 5-10-5 or 10-10-10 in the spring as the shoots emerge. Be sure to provide adequate moisture during the active growth cycle. Water weekly to ensure healthy and vigorous growth early in the season.

Care

Some tall lilies may need staking when grown in partial shade—be careful not to pierce the bulb. Deadhead spent blooms to prevent seed formation, unless you are hybridizing. Leave as much foliage as possible to store food energy for next year's blooms. Divide clumps if they become overcrowded and lose vigor (usually every five years). Transplant in the fall when the leaves have died back: Lift bulbs with a spading fork, separate, and replant. Pests and diseases do not bother lilies.

Companion Planting and Design

Plant lilies in perennial gardens with ferns, in mixed borders, and as background accents. Consider their expected height, and plant them to be enjoyed and to use as cut flowers.

My Personal Favorites

My favorites include 'Star Gazer' which has crimson-red flowers spotted in darker maroon and 'White Elegance'.

True lilies are aristocrats of the garden. They come in stunning colors and various heights; some have a delightful fragrance that attracts butterflies and hummingbirds. With a little planning, you can have lilies in bloom from early summer to early fall. These exotic and eye-catching flowers can be erect, pendant trumpets, upward-facing stars or ruffled, speckled, and fragrant—who can ask for more? Well-drained and fertile soil is essential to grow both Asiatic hybrids and trumpet lilies. Oriental lilies prefer light shade in the afternoon and slightly acidic soil. Try growing these in large pots or containers filled to the brim with humus-enriched potting soil. This growing technique works well with Asiatic hybrids, as well, especially if your garden soil is heavy clay.

Other Common Name
Garden lily

Bloom Period and Seasonal Color
Summer to late-summer blooms in white, yellow, gold, orange, pink, and red

Mature Height × Spread
18 in. to 6 ft. × 2 ft.

Zones
To zone 3, depending upon the species

Meadow Saffron
Colchicum spp. and hybrids

With the right planning, your autumn garden can hold many surprises. As surely as daffodils and tulips emerge in the spring, the late summer and fall garden comes alive with Colchicum autumnale or autumn crocus. Perhaps the showiest of fall bloomers, it features luminous pink blossoms that look wonderful amid a ground cover of santolina or dusty miller. The wispy, rosy-pink, goblet-shaped flowers are borne on 6- to 8-in. stems in late summer and fall. Colchicum is not a true crocus, but a member of the lily family. A single bulb may produce up to ten flowers, in bunches that add dimension to the perennial garden or border. The double-flowered hybrid colchicum 'Waterlily' resembles a waterlily bloom and is sure to catch an eye in your garden.

Other Common Names
Autumn crocus, colchicum

Bloom Period and Seasonal Color
Late summer and autumn blooms in pink, lavender, mauve, and white

Mature Height × Spread
6 to 12 in. × 6 in.

Zones
To zone 4

When, Where, and How to Plant
Plant meadow saffron in late summer to early fall, and plant immediately. These plants have a schedule all their own and will bloom on time, whether the bulb is stashed on a shelf or planted. Plant bulbs in well-drained, yet moisture-retentive soil that is compost enriched. They grow best in full sun to partial shade. In a woodland garden, plant meadow saffron near the front edge to receive more sun. Place each bulb with 4 in. of soil over its top. Space them 6 to 9 in. apart. Water well after planting.

Growing Tips
Though colchicum tolerates heat and dry periods while its foliage is growing in the spring, it needs moisture to help the bulbs store energy for the autumn display. Keep the soil moist after planting to ensure healthy establishment, but don't overwater. A light layer of organic mulch helps maintain moisture and reduce weeds. Apply bulb fertilizer (5-10-5) in the spring when the foliage is growing, and water thoroughly.

Care
Plants slowly form colonies if you don't disturb the bulbs when working in the perennial border. They require little except adequate moisture when the foliage is growing in the spring. In late spring or early summer, the foliage turns yellow, but leave it in place until the leaves die back or ripen naturally. Removing the leaves too early robs the plant of nutrients for the flowering cycle. Pests are not a problem.

Companion Planting and Design
Plant meadow saffron close to garden pathways and walkways where the emerging flowers invite passersby to admire the fall color. Use them in rock gardens, under perennials, and among various silver-leaved ground covers such as santolina, lamb's ears, and dusty miller. Some of the prettiest displays are at the foot of a burning bush (*Euonymus alatus*).

My Personal Favorites
C. speciosum (showy colchicum) offers large flowers of luminous lavender or rosy pink. Many showy colchicums are hybrids, including 'Waterlily', 'Lilac Wonder', and 'The Giant'.

Ornamental Onion
Allium spp.

When, Where, and How to Plant
Plant these plump, white-skinned bulbs in late September through mid-November. Ornamental onions prefer full sun, but tolerate some light shade. They prosper in average to rich, well-drained soils. Loosen the soil deeply to a depth of 6 in. or more. Add moisture-retentive compost if the soil is extremely sandy, gravelly, or primarily clay. Dig deeply enough so that the base of the bulb is 5 in. below the soil surface. A bulb fertilizer can be added to the bottom of the planting holes before placing the bulbs. Use at least three bulbs to a grouping; space taller types 12 in. apart and dwarf species 4 to 6 in. apart. Water well after planting.

Growing Tips
Once established, ornamental onions are perfectly happy on their own. Provide moisture during the growing season. Fertilize each fall with a 5-10-5 granular plant food, and water thoroughly. During dry winter periods, water when temperatures are above freezing.

Care
The globular heads of ornamental onions self-seed readily. If you don't want this, deadhead the spent flower heads before they scatter seed. The foliage is attractive when young, but by flowering time can become ragged, so grow alliums among other plants to hide the leaves. My children find these plants fascinating when they bloom because they grow so tall. Alliums are free of pests and diseases.

Companion Planting and Design
Plant in perennial beds, as a background or accent, and in mixed plantings. Plant groups of *Allium aflatunense* at regular intervals to create an interesting accent and unifying rhythm to the perennial garden. Many species of *Allium* can be grown successfully, including dwarf selections such as *A. cernuum* (12 in. tall) and the tallest species, *Allium giganteum* (4 to 5 ft.). The dried flower heads provide a nice accent in floral arrangements.

My Personal Favorite
Drumstick allium (*A. sphaerocephalum*) is easy to grow and produces purple-crimson flowers atop stems that reach up to 3 ft. Bees love it!

Many species of ornamental onions are prized for their handsome foliage and spherical flowers. Allium is Latin for garlic, but onions, leeks, chives, and shallots, which are confined to the kitchen, also belong in the genus Allium. Allium aflatunense is one ornamental onion that shows off dense, rounded 3- to 4-in. flower heads held high on strong straight stems (2 to 3 ft.). 'Purple Sensation', which may be listed as A. hollandicum, is a popular selection. Its lilac-purple to rose-purple blossoms appear in May and June and are a strong accent to the perennial garden. Each flower bursts from the bud to form a near perfect globe that lasts for several weeks. Even after bloom, the spent flower heads are attractive for months until they break apart in the wind. Deer leave them alone.

Other Common Names
Flowering onion, allium

Bloom Period and Seasonal Color
May to June blooms in lilac, purple, reddish purple, and white

Mature Height × Spread
20 in. to 3 ft. × 1 ft.

Zones
To zone 4

Siberian Squill
Scilla siberica

The beautiful blue blossoms of Siberian squills enhance the garden in early spring. You can't miss this little gem. The six-petaled, downward nodding flowers, usually arranged five to six to a clump, are particularly effective along pathways, in rock gardens, or scattered in lawns. Like many of the other minor bulbs, squills seed themselves throughout the garden, quickly forming a carpet of electric blue to complement other spring flowers. Their pendant, star-shaped flowers are among the earliest to open, following snowdrops. The deep-green foliage and bright color, sometimes Prussian blue, are bold contrasts for yellow and white daffodils. Squills make pretty companions for the smaller narcissus such as 'Jetfire', 'Peeping Tom', 'February Gold', and 'Jenny'. For a big splash of color in the spring, plant squills by the hundreds.

Bloom Period and Seasonal Color
Early spring dark-blue blooms

Mature Height × Spread
4 to 6 in. × 4 in.

Zones
To zone 3

When, Where, and How to Plant
Plant squill bulbs, like other minor bulbs, in the fall. All are easy to grow and thrive in well-drained soils and full sun to partial shade. If the soil is compacted, be sure to loosen it thoroughly and augment with compost for moisture retention and to improve drainage. Avoid planting in heat traps, such as southern exposures near buildings; those flowers won't last as long. Squills prefer some shade, especially during the warmest part of the day. Plant the small squill bulbs 3 in. deep, and space them 4 to 6 in. apart. You can mix a granular 5-10-5 fertilizer into the soil before planting. After planting, lightly firm the soil over the bulbs and water the area well.

Growing Tips
Be sure to provide adequate moisture while squills are growing, but when they are in their rest period, keep them on the dry side. The area where you plant squills may be fertilized in the fall by scattering a granular 5-10-5 throughout the bed. Water thoroughly. Spread a thin layer of compost in the fall to retain moisture.

Care
Squills thrive in any well-drained soil. Once established, they endure for years if undisturbed. Those planted in lawns should be allowed to grow and the foliage ripen and turn brown before mowing. There are few, if any, pests.

Companion Planting and Design
Use squills generously at the edges of shrubs and ornamental trees, in rock gardens, in lawns, and along pathways. These little blue gems are wonderful when crowded together and should be planted in bold clumps with other bulbs and perennials. Squills immediately brighten the spring garden before other bulbs or other perennials begin to open.

My Personal Favorite
One of my favorites is 'Spring Beauty' which has vivid blue flowers. The flowers appear before the foliage, and the blooms tend to last well. There is a white form listed as 'Alba', but it is not nearly as bold as the blue types.

Snowdrop
Galanthus nivalis

When, Where, and How to Plant

Plant snowdrops with other minor bulbs in autumn. Snowdrops prefer some sunlight for part of the day and appreciate partial shade from the hot afternoon sun. While tolerant of most garden soils, *Galanthus* does best in well-drained soils with lots of humus. Snowdrops prefer conditions that are similar to those of the forests—semishade, moist, fertile soils, rich in humus and nutrients found in the continuous decay of organic materials. You may need to add compost before planting. Plant snowdrops 3 to 4 in. deep, and space them 4 in. apart. If you like, mix 5-10-5 fertilizer in the soil of a prepared bed before planting. Once planted, gently firm the soil and water well.

Growing Tips

Once established, snowdrops are easy to maintain. In the High Country, they need no additional moisture beyond melting snow and spring rains. In drier areas, some fall and winter watering may be needed and a light organic mulch is beneficial. Moisture is necessary during the active growth cycle until the leaves mature and die down. Each autumn, you can top-dress the bulb area with a layer (1/2 to 1 in.) of pulverized compost or leaf mold. If you like, sprinkle a granular 5-10-5 fertilizer over the bed and water thoroughly.

Care

Snowdrops thrive and increase freely to form colonies. They may be left in place for many years without being divided. If grown in lawns, don't mow until the snowdrop foliage has ripened or turned brown. They are not bothered by pests or diseases.

Companion Planting and Design

Plant snowdrops in bold groupings beneath shrubs and trees, in rock gardens, in a woodland setting, in the front of a shady border, and in lawns.

My Personal Favorite

You can't beat this aptly named species as it has the attributes to withstand late snowstorms and thrive through freezing temperatures. Snowdrops generally open in mid- to late February and continue into April.

Snowdrop is among the earliest heralds of spring. These petite gems have popped up in my garden as early as mid-February, often while snow still covers the ground. Snowdrops' distinctive translucent flowers are composed of three petals tipped with green, surrounded by three longer outer petals of pure white. The smooth leaves of snowdrops measure about 6 in. long. Along with squills and grape hyacinths, these plants are most effective when arranged in drifts or bold clumps in the landscape. They are similar to snowflakes (Leucojum vernum), but the segments of snowdrops are not of equal length as are those of snowflakes. In Galanthus species, the inner segments are shorter and notched at the tips, with green tips around each notch.

Bloom Period and Seasonal Color
Early spring in pure-white blooms

Mature Height × Spread
6 in. × 3 to 4 in.

Zones
To zone 3

Tulip
Tulipa spp.

Harbingers of spring, these classic, cup-shaped flowers awaken the landscape. The sounds of bees working the flowers means the garden season is about to begin. Tulips come in a rainbow of colors and various forms and heights. Darwin hybrids have excellent cold tolerance and endure drought during their dormant summer period. With so many choices, I like to grow various types to extend the flowering season and to add interest throughout the landscape. Look for varieties that naturally perennialize or multiply in your garden. Tulips are also favored green treats by rabbits and deer. Should these visitors appear in your garden, you need to develop a control strategy. Tulips are most effective in mass plantings and can be used in informal clumps near the doorway or mailbox.

Other Common Name
Garden tulip

Bloom Period and Seasonal Color
Early March, April, and May blooms in all colors except true black and blue

Mature Height × **Spread**
12 to 24 in. × 10 to 12 in.

Zones
To zone 3, depending upon the species

When, Where, and How to Plant
Plant tulip bulbs in autumn, anytime before the ground freezes solid. If planting is delayed, keep the bulbs in a cool spot like the refrigerator or garage. Bulbs exposed to hot temperatures produce smaller flowers. Locate tulips in full sun in well-drained soils that have been enriched with compost. Mix in a slow-release, granular bulb fertilizer at planting time. I prefer to dig out an entire bed for mass planting and uniform tulip height. Plant bulbs 6 to 8 in. deep with the pointed tips up. In colder areas, plant 10 in. deep; this delays early flowering, but yields bigger flowers and reduces rodent damage. Cover the bulbs with prepared soil, and water thoroughly.

Growing Tips
Water tulips regularly during the growing season, but leave them on the dry side when the foliage ripens and during the summer. To help ensure survival and good repeat flowering in subsequent years, scatter bulb fertilizer over the bed in early spring and again in autumn; water thoroughly.

Care
Remove faded flowers by cutting the stems at ground level. Leave foliage to ripen and collapse on its own as it stores food energy for future blooms. During the winter, cover tulip beds with mulch to retain moisture and to delay early emergence. Deer, rabbits and gophers love tulips, so protect them as needed. You can grow them in mesh baskets and apply repellents to the foliage as soon as it emerges.

Companion Planting and Design
Plant tulips in shrub borders, island beds, mixed perennial beds, and among evergreen ground covers. Plant among violas and pansies for dramatic spring color.

I Also Recommend
One of my favorites is a Darwin hybrid called 'Orange Bowl', an intense red striped with yellow flames. I like botanical tulips for rock gardens and water-thrifty perennial gardens. I particularly like *Tulipa greigii* 'Red Riding Hood' which bears bright-red, cup-shaped flowers on short stems. The distinctive maroon-striped foliage accents the blooms.

Windflower

Anemone blanda

When, Where, and How to Plant

Plant the brown fibrous tubers in the fall before the ground freezes. For the most effective mass displays, be bold: plant in groups of thirty or more. Choose a sunny to partially shady location such as under high trees and at the edges of shrubs. Windflower does best in moist, but well-drained soils rich in organic matter. Good drainage is essential for these fussy plants. Compost, scoria (crushed volcanic rock), perlite, and pea gravel improve soil structure and improve drainage in heavy clay soils. Plant tubers 2 to 3 in. below the soil surface and 4 to 6 in. apart. Check for the buds or "eyes" and plant them facing up. If you can't determine which way is up, don't worry. Set the tubers sideways and gently push them down into the soil at the proper depth. (I prefer to prepare a designated area for windflowers and plant them all at once.) Then gently firm the soil over them, and water well.

Growing Tips

Mix all-purpose 5-10-5 granular fertilizer with the soil before planting, and water the bulbs thoroughly after planting. Watering is beneficial during extended dry periods in the fall and winter. Scatter a light layer of organic mulch over the planting area in late fall to maintain moisture.

Care

These shallow-rooted plants can be a bit temperamental in colder zones, but will survive if an organic mulch is applied over the growing area. A winter mulch of evergreen boughs, pine needles, or shredded cedar prevents heaving and maintains soil moisture. There are no serious pest problems.

Companion Planting and Design

Windflowers appreciate dappled shade from the foliage of other spring-flowering bulbs. They make good companions to snowdrops, winter aconite, hyacinths, and squills. Plant in drifts to create a woodland setting.

My Personal Favorites

One of the most reliable, 'Charmer' has deep-pink flowers; 'Radar' offers reddish flowers and white centers, and 'White Splendor' features pure-white flowers. Mixes of blue, white, and pink are also commonly available.

The daisylike flowers of windflower are a welcome sight in early spring, though they are more closely related to buttercups than daisies. These low-growing beauties are covered in mid-spring with masses of blooms in blue, pink, or white with cheery bright-yellow centers. The masses of flowers almost hide the starburst-shaped foliage hugging the ground. A border of these little gems in front of daffodils, tulips, and other bulbs catches the eye. 'Charmer', with its deep-pink blossoms, is a favorite in my garden, where it thrives in the sandy loam soil. The flowers are set off by the ground-hugging, deep-green, and dissected foliage. Windflowers are impressive when planted in large groupings, so don't be stingy. When spring arrives, you won't be disappointed.

Bloom Period and Seasonal Color
Early spring blooms in blue, pink, red, and white

Mature Height × Spread
3 to 6 in. × 2 to 3 in.

Zones
To zone 4

Conifers *for the Rockies*

The diversity of those hardy evergreens that endure cold and drought are apparent from the high peaks of the Rocky Mountains at treeline—that ragged line where trees stop and tundra begins—where the twisted bristlecone pines reside, to the subalpine forests, where spires of firs rise to the sky, to the montane forests, with ponderosa pines growing on the south-facing slopes and Douglas firs residing on wetter, north-facing exposures, to the pinyon woodlands in western Colorado and New Mexico, where pinyon and juniper grow in harmony. Some of the wind-sculptured bristlecone pines on Mount Evans in Colorado have survived over two thousand years.

Thinking Like a Native

When you plan to plant evergreens in your landscape, keep their native habitat in mind. A pinyon pine planted in the middle of the lawn soon develops weak branches, falls under attack by borers, and is on its way to plant heaven. Similarly, Colorado blue spruce becomes stunted and struggles to survive if planted in the corner of the yard where snow seldom remains and water never reaches. Finding an evergreen that looks good is useless if the tree does not survive.

One important consideration is the tree's winter hardiness. The U.S. Department of Agriculture (USDA) has divided the country into areas called hardiness zones based on the average minimum winter temperatures of that region. These regional zones are identified numerically. But these hardiness zone numbers are not always an exact guide. Even within a particular zone, significant variations in soil, rainfall, exposure, and humidity can affect a plant's ability to acclimate to a certain locale. If you can simulate the growing conditions for native evergreens in your landscape, experiment by growing various species.

Creeping Juniper 'Nana'

Know the ultimate height and spread of an evergreen *before* you plant it. If you value your view of the mountains, don't plant a spruce in front of the living room window. It eventually blocks the view. Look up, as well; growing evergreens can interfere with overhead power lines and utility areas. The spread of an evergreen is often referred to as the "skirt" and, without your proper planning, can have consequences in your landscape. The skirt of our native spruces can grow to 25 ft. or more. What a shame it is to have to prune a beautiful spruce by removing the lower branches to open up a view or clear a driveway. Raising a spruce's skirt is tree butchery and endangers the tree. Cutting away a large portion of the lower branches destroys the spruce's fulcrum of balance. It becomes more prone to blowing over when high winds hit your neighborhood.

Swiss Pine

Planning for Success

Evergreens are best planted in the spring, though fall planting can be successful if you get it done by mid-October. Root growth slows down as soil temperatures approach 45 degrees Fahrenheit. Trees planted in the fall need to be mulched more heavily (4 to 6 in.) in an effort to delay the freezing of the soil and allow more time for root development. Autumn and winter watering is absolutely essential before the soil freezes; even after a freeze, continue to monitor moisture in the soil, watering monthly when there is no snow cover throughout the winter.

Planting evergreens is relatively simple: Dig a wide, shallow hole; add backfill soil; water slowly to eliminate air pockets under the roots; cover the soil with an organic mulch; and water only as needed after planting. In heavy-clay soils, score the side walls of the planting hole to break up the soil compaction created from the digging process. You don't need to loosen the soil below where the rootball is to rest; doing so can cause the evergreen to settle too deeply after planting. Transplanted evergreens acclimate to their new environment if planted in concert with native soil conditions.

Making the Most of Your Soil

Few plants thrive in "contractor dirt," compacted clay, or poorly drained soils. Such soils lack the oxygen needed for root growth. My favorite planting recommendation has been to amend the entire planting area prior to digging the planting holes. However, many Western horticulture experts now recommend that *no* soil amendments be added to planting sites. Instead, loosen the native soil thoroughly to alleviate soil compaction. This preparation creates a more suitable environment for root growth. Adding *some* organic matter helps improve drainage and aeration, but don't add large amounts of organic matter into the backfill soil. If the soil is made too rich, the tree's roots may decide to remain within the planting hole and never attempt to explore the surrounding native soil. Roots grow into soil that has a balance of oxygen and water, so the best recommendation is to dig the hole wider rather than deeper and loosen the soil thoroughly.

How much organic matter is needed? Mix in high-quality organic matter equal to one-third of the volume of native soil removed from the planting hole. In high-clay, alkaline soils, organic matter provides the roots with better aeration. In sandy and rocky soils, organic matter provides the water-holding capacity that helps prevent drought stress to the root system.

ABCs of Planting

If you're planting in heavy-clay soil, dig the planting hole 1 to 2 in. shallower than the height of the tree's rootball. Shallow planting in clay soils prevents the tree from sinking too deeply. If your soil is sandy, the hole should be no deeper than the rootball. Here, the idea is to place the rootball on a solid foundation so the roots can grow in the top 15 to 18 in. of soil.

Juniper Berries

Now you're finally ready to plant. Handle the rootball with care; breaking the rootball is often fatal to young trees and shrubs, especially evergreens. Remove the tree from its container and place it in the hole. If the roots have become potbound, growing in circles and compacted, tease out the roots by hand or score (nick) the sides of the rootball with a sharp knife. This stops the roots from growing in a spiral pattern (girdling each other) and encourages them to spread out into the soil.

On larger balled-and-burlapped evergreens, remove at least the top half of the wire basket *after* the tree is situated in the planting hole. Cut off remaining nylon twine and rope, as well. Cut off as much of the burlap wrap around the top of the ball as possible, or tuck it back into the soil. Cut several slits through the remaining material to permit the roots to venture into the new soil. Shovel backfill soil into the hole about halfway up, and gently firm it to keep the tree from tipping over. Then water slowly and allow the soil to settle in, eliminating air pockets. Once the water has soaked in, add more backfill soil to complete the planting. Water again. Use the extra soil to construct a dike at the edge of the planting hole. In four to five days, fill this reservoir with water. Don't overwater—more evergreens die from overwatering than under-watering. Give the soil a good soaking when it begins to dry out at 4 to 6 in. deep. Mulch the planting area 3 to 4 in. deep with old pine needles, compost, or shredded wood chips. In later years, an appropriate ground cover can be planted as a living mulch.

Douglas Fir

You don't have to add fertilizer during the planting operation or afterwards. Research has shown that no fertilizer is needed for the first growing season. Evergreens planted in turf areas generally receive adequate nutrients from regular fertilizing of the turf grasses during the growing season. After the second or third spring, you may apply a slow-release granular 10-10-10 fertilizer around the drip line. Apply 1 cup of fertilizer per inch of trunk thickness; measure the thickness of the trunk 4 ft. from the ground. Use a crowbar or an old ski pole to punch holes 8 to 10 in. deep at 12 in. intervals, and scatter the fertilizer granules where the holes were punched. Water until the fertilizer granules dissolve or wash into the holes.

All-Season Interest

You may choose a variety of evergreen trees for the home landscape to use for privacy screening, wind abatement, and year-round accent. Evergreens make highly effective windbreaks to buffer the force of the wind, absorbing it rather than redirecting it over a fence or wall. I've planted many Austrian pines, whose branches grow all the way to the ground, to stop the force of the westerly winds in my High Plains wind-break. Combined with deciduous trees and shrubs, evergreens provide ornamental interest and wildlife habitat throughout the seasons.

Arborvitae
Thuja occidentalis

Arborvitae tend to be small to medium evergreen trees or shrubs with soft, flattened branches. Some arborvitae cultivars are not highly desirable—they may discolor and dehydrate in the winter from prolonged exposure to sun and wind. But they are adaptable to alkaline soils and poor growing conditions. This evergreen's adaptability to both moist and dry sites makes it a valuable plant for small spaces. If you do have limited space, consider some of the dwarf varieties, such as 'Globosa', which grows in a compact, rounded form and maintains its shape with minimal pruning. The cultivar 'Brandon', with its narrow, columnar growth habit, works well for vertical accent. Touchable evergreen foliage makes arborvitae a nice year-round accent in the landscape when they are sited properly.

Other Common Names
White cedar, American arborvitae

Bloom Period and Seasonal Color
Soft evergreen foliage ranging from bluish green to emerald green

Mature Height × Spread
15 to 20 ft. × 3 to 7 ft.

Zones
To zone 3

When, Where, and How to Plant
Plant arborvitae from spring to early summer. If you plant in the fall, water regularly when rain and snow are scarce. Keep plants away from rooflines; sliding snow may result in branch damage. Plant in a semiprotected location in partial sun or shade. *Semiprotected* means protection from direct exposure to winter sun and winds that tend to desiccate the foliage. Container-grown plants are easy to transplant. After removing the plant, carefully pull apart any compacted or circling roots that have built up. Thoroughly break up the soil, and add compost to sandy soils to retain moisture. If your soil is heavy clay, dig the planting hole 2 in. shallower than the rootball. In sandy soils, the hole should be no deeper than the root system. It is more important to dig the hole wide to encourage strong root development. Refer to page 62.

Growing Tips
Once established, arborvitae endure heat and tolerate short periods of drought. They adapt well in deep, well-drained soils and benefit from deep watering periodically during prolonged drought. In mid- to late spring, you may apply a fertilizer around the drip line of the tree or shrub. Consult page 63 for more information on fertilizing evergreens.

Care
Pruning is best done in the spring just as new growth begins. To provide protection from heavy snow loads, you might support the branchlets with twine or heavy plastic-coated wire wrapped in a spiral around the plant to hold the foliage and stems together. Eventually, the dense foliage hides the supports. If the foliage becomes chlorotic (pale yellow), apply chelated iron in the spring. Generally, arborvitae are not bothered by pests or diseases.

Landscape Merit
Protected from intense winter sun, arborvitae make effective foundation plantings on a north, northeast, or eastern exposure.

My Personal Favorites
Emerald-green 'Smaragd' grows into a neat pyramid and holds its color through the winter. 'Brandon' has handsome dark-green foliage with a bluish cast.

Austrian Pine

Pinus nigra

When, Where, and How to Plant

Container-grown and balled-and-burlapped specimen pines should be transplanted in the spring to early summer. Avoid late fall planting. Locate in full sun for the best growth and uniform development. Austrian pine prefers well-drained soils, but adapts to clay soils that are made to drain with good soil preparation and modifications. It will grow in clay and sandy soils and tolerates poor soil conditions better than spruces or firs. Planting on raised berms in heavy-soil sites helps ensure survival and prevents overwatering. The planting hole should be two to three times as wide as the rootball or the container-grown root system. If your soil is heavy clay, dig the planting hole 2 in. shallower than the rootball. In sandy soils, the hole should be no deeper than the root system. It is more important to dig the hole wide to encourage strong root development. Follow the general planting guidelines for evergreens on page 62.

Growing Tips

Treated with too much love and care, as often happens, this pine soon becomes stressed from overwatering and overfertilizing, particularly when planted in a lawn area. Consult page 63 for information on watering and fertilizing evergreen trees.

Care

Pines can be pruned in mid-to late spring to maintain height and spread. To keep them in bounds, remove one-half to three-quarters of the new candle growth. Keeping the tree healthy discourages the onset of diseases and pests.

Landscape Merit

Austrian pine is relatively fast growing and makes an effective windbreak, screen, or specimen tree. Allow plenty of space so it can develop properly and naturally. It helps soften the open-growing characteristics of our native ponderosa pine (*Pinus ponderosa*).

My Personal Favorite

Austrian pine is the most commonly available in the trade. My favorite for the water-thrifty garden or a bonsai effect is the dwarf cultivar 'Hornibrookiana'.

One of the most adapted pines for the landscape is the Austrian pine. Perhaps one of the most hardy, this pine withstands dry, windy conditions much better than white pine. It can grow in fairly heavy clay soils and alkaline conditions throughout the region. It is well adapted to sandy soils of the High Plains. Austrian pine's stout, pyramidal growth makes it an excellent choice for windbreaks and screening, or as a nice specimen tree. The mature tree's distinctive silhouette of graceful horizontal branches creates unique character in the landscape. Austrian pine is classified as fast growing, which makes it ideal for screening, for windbreaks, or as a specimen tree. Once it becomes established, it can endure drought conditions and maintain its beauty and character.

Bloom Period and Seasonal Color
Evergreen foliage

Mature Height × Spread
30 to 60 ft. × 20 to 40 ft.

Zones
To zone 3

Bristlecone Pine

Pinus aristata

The bristlecone pine is one of our beloved natives that grows in the subalpine forests and at tree lines, where it grows slowly. Its dark-brown cones have small prickles on the scales, giving this pine its common name. The wind twists and contorts bristlecone pines. These uniquely shaped trees are called krummholz, from the German word for "crooked wood." Some specimens are among the oldest trees in the world—over two thousand years old. The dark-green needles are densely clustered along the stems and branches, giving it another common name— foxtail pine. They are covered with tiny pitch nodules, which are often mistaken for insect pests. Another interesting feature is that bristlecone pines hold their needles for ten to fifteen years before normal needle drop occurs.

Other Common Name
Foxtail pine

Bloom Period and Seasonal Color
Dark-green evergreen needles followed by brown cones

Mature Height × Spread
10 to 30 ft. × 8 to 20 ft.

Zones
To zone 2

When, Where, and How to Plant

The preferred time to plant bristlecone pine is spring. This gives the pine a longer season to establish roots before winter. Fall planting can be successful if you follow certain guidelines. Consult general directions for proper soil preparation and planting techniques on page 62. Bristlecone pine does best in full sun and in well-drained soils. It tolerates wind very well, luckily for us. Avoid areas that don't drain well, as poor drainage means certain death for this native pine. Dig the planting hole two to three times as wide as the rootball or container. If your soil is heavy clay or poorly drained, plant the top of the root system 2 in. above the surrounding grade.

Growing Tips

Bristlecone pine can be a long-lived evergreen—if it is not overwatered or overfertilized. Provide water during long, dry spells to maintain the tree's vigor. Water deeply, but infrequently. In early spring, after the first growing season, you may apply 1 cup of a 10-10-10 fertilizer for each inch of trunk thickness. This helps make the tree grow a bit faster. Be sure to water the fertilizer into the soil thoroughly after application.

Care

Bristlecone pines have unique growing characteristics and should not be pruned. Allow them to grow and develop naturally. A truly tough species that endures in alkaline, rocky, poor, well-drained soils and in the wind, this tree is not bothered by pests or diseases.

Landscape Merit

Plant it as a specimen conifer, as a backdrop for a perennial garden, or in a rock garden. I have used it in foundation plantings because it grows slowly and for its picturesque growth habit. Irregular shrubby, spreading branches make this pine an ideal accent conifer, and it retains its growth habit with age. Plant *Juniperus horizontalis*, creeping juniper, at its feet for an extra-special effect.

My Personal Favorite

The native bristlecone pine is my favorite for its unique character, which endures with age.

Colorado Spruce
Picea pungens

When, Where, and How to Plant

Plant blue spruce in early spring through early fall. Container-grown and balled-and-burlapped nursery stock are readily available and easily transplanted. Seedling trees are available through mail-order nurseries, but beware: Not all have what we most seek in this plant—blue genes! Allow plenty of space when picking a location for your spruce. Some cultivars grow more slowly and some have a columnar habit, both can be used for special situations. Spruce does best in full sun and prefers moist, well-drained soils. Prepare the planting hole equal in depth to the rootball and two to three times as wide. Follow instructions for soil preparation and planting techniques for evergreens on page 62.

Growing Tips

The first few growing seasons are critical in establishing your blue spruce. Provide adequate moisture to keep the roots thriving and to prevent heat stress. Do not apply weed-and-feed fertilizers near spruce trees; herbicides can accumulate near the root zone and result in distorted growth and possible dieback. Follow fertilizing guidelines on page 63.

Care

In the summer heat, spider mites can become a problem, causing the needles to develop a salt-and-pepper appearance. Control them by syringing the tree with water or an appropriate miticide. Spruce adelgids cause new growth to develop purple galls that turn brown by August. These pests can be controlled in early spring as new growth begins to expand. Use an appropriate insecticide, and follow label directions. Be very cautious when using dormant sprays on spruce; oil sprays remove the bluish green coloration. Pruning alters spruce's natural growth habit and is generally not recommended.

Landscape Merit

Colorado blue spruce makes a beautiful and stately specimen evergreen. Combine it with colorfully stemmed shrubs, such as red and yellow twig dogwood, spring-blooming forsythia, and witch hazel.

My Personal Favorite

Picea pungens 'Hoopsii' has the most glaucous (blue-green color) needles and an informal growth habit. It makes a striking specimen tree in the landscape.

The majestic Colorado spruce is noted for its silvery-blue needles that form a stately pyramid with stiff horizontal branches sweeping the ground. Known also as blue spruce, this tree is a favorite for landscape use. Seedling trees vary in needle color from bright-green to gray-green to silver-blue. When selecting a spruce for your landscape, look for some of the grafted cultivars that have outstanding color variations and growth characteristics. My favorites include 'Hoopsii', 'Fat Albert', 'Iseli Fastigiate', 'Montgomery', and 'Thompsenii'. Since spruces naturally grow beside rivers and streams throughout the Rocky Mountain region, it is important to plant them where they will receive adequate moisture. Give the blue spruce adequate room to grow so you won't have to prune it later and destroy its natural growth habit.

Other Common Name
Blue spruce

Bloom Period and Seasonal Color
Beautiful blue-green evergreen needles in a conical form

Mature Height × Spread
60 to 100 ft. × 20 to 30 ft.

Zones
To zone 2

Concolor Fir

Abies concolor

The concolor fir is one of the most beautiful of the pyramidal conifers. Its soft, bluish green needles exhibit even more intensity when the new blue growth expands in spring. Soft, short, flattened needles make white fir a favorite, and this native's dense, full growth is displayed in beautiful tiered branches to create a bold look in the landscape. Reaching 60 ft. or more with a conical growth habit, this majestic evergreen sports bluish green coloration year-round. Among the firs, white fir is noted for its outstanding tolerance of hot and dry conditions. If you want a dwarf evergreen fir for the rock garden, be sure to check out Abies concolor 'Compacta' (3 ft.), which features beautiful silvery-blue needles.

Other Common Name
White fir

Bloom Period and Seasonal Color
Wonderful bluish green evergreen needles

Mature Height × Spread
30 to 60 ft. × 15 to 30 ft.

Zones
To zone 3

When, Where, and How to Plant

Plant white fir in early spring through early fall. Avoid late fall planting—there's not enough time for the tree to develop strong roots before winter. If you're planting in the heat of summer, provide ample water and mist the foliage to reduce stress. This large evergreen requires a spot with full sun or afternoon shade, with plenty of room to grow. It prefers moist, well-drained soils, but endures drought if watered properly. See page 62 for specific details on soil preparation and planting. Prepare the planting hole two to three times wider than the rootball. After positioning the tree in the hole, add backfill soil and then water slowly to eliminate air pockets. Mulch with 2 to 3 in. of pine needles or other organic matter.

Growing Tips

Able to withstand hot, dry conditions once established, concolor fir requires regular watering the first few years to encourage strong roots. Construct a dike or water basin at the edge of the planting hole. When the soil begins to dry out 4 to 6 in. deep, fill the reservoir with water to soak the soil. Avoid frequent light waterings. Consult page 61 for details on winter watering. Refer to page 63 for fertilizing tips.

Care

In windy and exposed sites, construct a burlap screen on the windward side of the tree to reduce windburn and needle desiccation. Giant conifer aphids may visit the needles and twigs in late summer, attracting ants and yellow jacket wasps. Control them with insecticidal soap.

Landscape Merit

Known for its softening evergreen effect on the landscape, white fir matures to produce interesting purplish brown cones. This prized specimen tree can be integrated into a windbreak if you provide regular moisture.

I Also Recommend

Also try our native, high-country species alpine fir (*Abies lasiocarpa*). If you don't have space for a large growth habit, 'Candicans' features outstanding bright silver-blue needles and a narrow upright growth habit.

Creeping Juniper
Juniperus horizontalis

When, Where, and How to Plant

Plant creeping junipers from early spring through early fall. They perform best in full sun, but tolerate some light shade. Don't plant in deep shade. Creeping junipers can be used in many difficult soil situations from sandy and dry to heavy clay. Just be sure the soil is well drained. For use as a ground cover, space the plants 2¹/₂ to 3 ft. apart—they will spread over time. Dig the planting holes as deep as the rootball or container and three times as wide. Follow the general directions for planting evergreens on page 62.

Growing Tips

Once established, creeping junipers are long lived. Water them deeply, but not frequently. As new growth begins in the spring, apply a quality long-lasting slow-release fertilizer such as 10-10-10. To avoid foliage burn, water thoroughly after application.

Care

Pruning is not generally required, but occasionally do trim dead or broken branches. Cut back to a side branch to allow new growth to fill in. Spider mites may visit during hot, dry periods. They can cause yellowing and browning of the scalelike needles; a fine webbing may be present throughout infested branches. Hose mites off with water regularly to prevent a severe problem, or use an appropriate control for mites.

Landscape Merit

Plant a grouping to cascade over a rock wall or in planters. Or use creeping juniper as a foundation planting, to cover a steep slope, to fill in the area between the sidewalk and street, or anywhere you want winter interest. Its salt tolerance makes it useful along sidewalks and driveways where deicing salts are used.

My Personal Favorites

'Wiltonii' or 'Blue Rug' grows very prostrate (4 to 6 in.) and can spread to 8 ft. with silvery-blue foliage that turns plum red during the winter months. 'Bar Harbor', 'Hughes', and many other cultivars are available with differing heights, foliage color, textures, and winter coloration.

Creeping juniper and many other juniper species are incredibly diverse and are among the most effective and drought-enduring ground covers. These incredible evergreens have adapted to minimize water loss by developing the small, scalelike needles packed densely along the stems and a growth habit that shades the soil over the root system. After becoming established, they spread to form an almost impenetrable weed barrier. You will find cultivars with dark-green, steel-blue, or bluish gray foliage and some that produce attractive blue berries. Others, such as 'Wiltonii', turn purplish in the winter. Creeping mountain juniper (Juniperus communis var. montana) is a prostrate species that thrives in the High Country; its female plants feature handsome blue berries. This evergreen is excellent for underplanting around taller conifers.

Bloom Period and Seasonal Color
Evergreen with year-round interest; colors vary depending on species

Mature Height × Spread
6 to 18 in. × 6 to 12 ft.

Zones
To zone 3

Douglas Fir
Pseudotsuga menziesii

Douglas fir is a native of the forests harvested primarily for lumber. But I recall childhood days taking winter trips to the mountains to cut a "Doug fir" for the family Christmas tree. It can be found growing in dense forests, and it benefits from thinning. Often seen as an ornamental conifer in the landscape, Douglas fir can also be used as a garden backdrop. The short, thin needles are shiny-green above with a whitish band beneath. One of this evergreen's best features is its downward hanging cones with decorative three-pronged bracts. Douglas fir grows into an open pyramidal form, with upper branches that grow upright while lower branches descend. With age, this fir prunes itself, creating a more open appearance.

Bloom Period and Seasonal Color
Medium- to dark-green evergreen foliage

Mature Height × Spread
30 to 60 ft. × 15 to 20 ft.

Zones
To zone 3

When, Where, and How to Plant
Plant container-grown or balled-and-burlapped trees in early spring. Locate them in full sun or partial shade. With a new planting, it is advisable to construct a burlap screen on the windward side of the tree to reduce sunburn. The screen is needed only the first few years as the tree becomes established. It does best in moist, well-drained soils and does not tolerate dry sites. Dig the planting hole two to three times wider than the rootball. Loosen the soil well beyond the planting hole, and add compost to the area. Follow the general planting guidelines for evergreens on pages 62 to 63.

Growing Tips
Douglas fir can be long lived, provided it receives adequate moisture. Soak the soil deeply on a regular basis with a soaker hose or twin-eye sprinkler placed at the drip line and beyond. Move the sprinkler every fifteen to twenty minutes until you have watered the entire root area. Trees growing in lawn areas receive some nutrients from applications of lawn fertilizers, but do not apply weed-and-feed products near evergreens; herbicide contamination in the root zone can result in dieback.

Care
If soils become compacted, aerate once or twice a year with a crowbar, metal rod, or old ski pole. Punch holes 10 to 12 in. deep all around the drip line to allow oxygen, water, and nutrients into the root zone. This tree serves as the winter host of the spruce adelgid, a pest that causes the purplish brown galls on blue spruce.

Landscape Merit
Douglas fir is an excellent specimen evergreen. If you have space, consider planting it in groups for screening or background.

I Also Recommend
I like the native Douglas fir, but also look for the blue-needled *P. menziesii* var. *glauca*, a slow-growing type whose form is somewhat more pyramidal. *P. menziesii* 'Glauca Pendula' is the weeping cultivar; it's a good choice for rock gardens, as is the dwarf cultivar *P. menziesii* 'Densa'.

When, Where, and How to Plant

Plant larch in early spring to allow plenty time for strong root development. Choose an open area with full sun and plenty of space; larch has considerable spread. It prefers well-drained soils, so it's beneficial to amend the planting area with compost or other suitable organic matter. Follow the guidelines on soil preparation and planting techniques on pages 62 to 63.

Growing Tips

European larch is easy to establish provided you supply consistent moisture during the growing season. It does not tolerate extreme drought. Use a "frog-eye" sprinkler set at the drip line. Allow the water to soak in for twenty-five to thirty minutes, and move the sprinkler to provide good overlap. Water periodically throughout winter, particularly when there is little or no snow cover, but water only when temperatures are above freezing and the soil is not frozen. Watering may be necessary every five to six weeks during extended dry spells in late fall and winter. Consult page 61 for more details on fall and winter care. A tree planted in a lawn area receives some nutrients from lawn fertilizers; otherwise, see page 63 for fertilizing guidelines. Do not apply weed-and-feed fertilizer products; the herbicides accumulate in the soil and can be absorbed by the tree.

Care

European larch is generally pest and disease free. Prune in summer to control height and spread and to allow pruning wounds to heal properly before winter.

Landscape Merit

Prized for its wonderful fall coloration, larch is also lovely when new foliage emerges in the spring. For a nice effect, underplant with spring-flowering bulbs and ground covers such as *Galium odoratum*, *Euonymus fortunei*, or *Ajuga reptans*. If you have space, use this unusual deciduous evergreen as a specimen tree or in a group planting for an elegant background accent.

My Personal Favorite

If space is limited, search out 'Fastigiata', a cultivar with a narrow, columnar growth habit and shorter ascending branches.

Belonging to a class of conifers that shed their leaves in autumn and remain barren throughout the winter, the larch is native to northern and central Europe and is extremely well adapted to our Rocky Mountain climate and soils. It catches the eye in the fall when its foliage turns a rich, golden yellow. In the spring, the branches reclothe themselves with delicate, bright-green foliage. If you want to capture solar radiation in the winter to help warm your home, European larch is a good substitute for larger spruces or pines planted on southern exposures. The broad pyramidal growth habit, typical when the tree is young, becomes irregular with age. The cold-hardy larch tolerates alkaline soils. If you have space in your landscape, plant this impressive deciduous conifer and enjoy its spectacular form.

Other Common Name
Common larch

Bloom Period and Seasonal Color
Delicate light-green foliage in spring turns golden yellow in autumn

Mature Height × Spread
70 to 80 ft. × 25 to 30 ft.

Zones
To zone 3

Limber Pine
Pinus flexilis

One of my favorites, limber pine is adapted to many growing situations throughout the region, with hardiness to zone 2. It is a medium-sized pine that fits well in a smaller landscape setting. With its informal growth habit, limber pine has outstanding characteristics that add interest as a specimen tree, accent, or background planting. It develops real character as it matures and creates a stunning silhouette with silvery-gray bark. A Rocky Mountain native, limber pine can be found growing on exposed slopes at higher elevations. It is well adapted to drought and windy conditions. Several cultivars have outstanding characteristics—'Extra Blue' has intense blue needles, 'Glauca Pendula' grows along the ground and develops an irregular shrub form, and 'Nana' is a dwarf form that works well in rock gardens.

Bloom Period and Seasonal Color
Evergreen bluish green foliage for year-round interest

Mature Height × Spread
30 to 45 ft. × 25 to 30 ft.

Zones
To zone 2

When, Where, and How to Plant
Container-grown and balled-and-burlapped limber pines can be planted from early spring through summer. Avoid late-fall planting. Locate in full sun for the best growth and uniform development. Limber pine prefers well-drained soils but can adapt to clay soils that are made to drain with good soil preparation and modifications. Follow the guidelines on pages 62 to 63. The planting hole should be two to three times as wide as the rootball or the container-grown root system. If your soil is heavy clay, dig the planting hole 2 in. shallower than the rootball. In sandy soils, the hole should be no deeper than the root system. It is more important to dig the hole wide to encourage strong root development. When the rootball is set on undisturbed soil, there is no need to loosen soil in the bottom of the planting hole. There is less chance it will settle too deep.

Growing Tips
Keep newly planted pines healthy by providing adequate moisture during establishment. After planting, add 2 to 3 in. of organic mulch. It's especially important to supply water during the fall and winter months when rain or snow cover is scarce or lacking. Consult information on fall and winter care on page 61. Limber pines generally don't need additional fertilizer the first year after transplanting. In the spring of the second season of growth, you may apply a complete fertilizer such as 10-10-10. Refer to more fertilizing guidelines on page 63.

Care
Pruning is not necessary, unless you are trying to maintain limber pine to a specific height and spread. If so, prune in the spring when new candle growth expands. Limber pine is not bothered by pests or diseases.

Landscape Merit
Limber pine, with its pyramidal growth habit, can be used in smaller spaces. It is an effective accent or specimen planting and works well in a naturalistic grouping.

My Personal Favorite
A distinctive, densely branched specimen, *Pinus flexilis* 'Vanderwolf's Pyramid' features twisting bluish green needles accented underneath with a pale-blue line.

Pinyon Pine

Pinus cembroides edulis

When, Where, and How to Plant

Container-grown and balled-and-burlapped pinyon pines transplant best in the spring. Locate them in full sun for best growth and uniform development. Well-drained soils are preferred, but pinyon tolerates poor soil conditions better than spruces and firs. Follow the planting guidelines on pages 62 to 63. Planting on raised berms in heavy soil helps ensure the tree's survival and prevents overwatering. Use some of the extra soil to make a dike or water basin at the edge of the planting hole for future watering. When the soil dries out 4 to 6 in. deep, fill the reservoir with water to soak the soil. After planting, mulch with pine needles, shredded wood chips, or other organic material.

Growing Tips

Pinyon does not tolerate "wet feet." Once it's established, water deeply once a month. Avoid frequent light waterings—which often occur if the tree is in or near lawn areas. Additional fertilizer is not necessary, but if you feel the urge to fertilize, follow the guidelines on page 63.

Care

Pinyons are often treated with too much love and care and quickly become stressed from overwatering, overfertilizing, and improper pruning. They generally do not need pruning unless you are trying to grow a bonsai or control height and spread. Allow it to grow with its natural form. Pitch mass borers attack stressed trees. These pests are very difficult to control. In late summer, giant conifer aphids may congregate on the needles, becoming a nuisance. Hose them off with water or a homemade soap spray.

Landscape Merit

Pinyon provides year-round color in the water-thrifty landscape and is an excellent drought-resistant pine for screening or windbreaks. Underplant with *Juniperus horizontalis* (creeping juniper) for a nice contrast year-round.

My Personal Favorite

The native pinyon pine is my favorite, but keep in mind that it is slow growing. When allowed to develop naturally without pruning, though, it eventually grows into a picturesque specimen.

This southern Rocky Mountain native prefers south-facing slopes and thrives on neglect. When cutting firewood, it's great fun to collect the pine cones for a bountiful harvest of delicious pinyon nuts. Pinyon pine is perhaps the most drought-tolerant pine species and can grow into picturesque forms with twisted trunk and limbs. The resin deposits and needles release an enjoyable pine fragrance during hot summer evenings. Under cultivation in the home landscape, pinyons do best planted on berms or raised island beds where drainage is good. Pinyons planted in heavily watered turf areas often fail. Landscape placement is key for this pine to grow and survive. Combine it with our native sumac, Rhus trilobata, which grows in dry conditions, for a spectacular Rocky Mountain autumn display.

Bloom Period and Seasonal Color
Fragrant, short evergreen needles; pine cones covered with pungent pitch contain delectable, edible seeds

Mature Height × Spread
12 to 20 ft. × 12 to 15 ft.

Zones
To zone 3

Rocky Mountain Juniper
Juniperus scopulorum

The natural pyramidal growth habit of our native Rocky Mountain juniper and its grayish shaggy bark are characteristic of this strong survivor of drought and alkaline soils. It is relatively untouched by insect pests, unless stressed from overwatering or bark injuries. Drought-enduring shrubs or trees as a group, junipers are an integral part of the water-thrifty landscape. They provide cover for wildlife, and the bluish to green berries are both attractive and a food source for birds. Junipers are a diverse group and easy to grow in a wide range of soils from sandy to clay and in soils of high pH. Once established, they tolerate dry conditions. Other species, such as Juniperus chinensis and many of its cultivars, are also excellent drought-resistant conifers for use as small trees, shrubs, and ground covers. Also see the creeping juniper entry on page 69.

Other Common Name
Colorado redcedar

Bloom Period and Seasonal Color
Green to bluish green evergreen scalelike foliage; colorful, fragrant berries on the female plants of some cultivars

Mature Height × Spread
15 to 40 ft. × 8 to 20 ft.

Zones
To zone 2

When, Where, and How to Plant
Plant container-grown Rocky Mountain and other junipers from spring through early fall and bare-root trees in early spring. Provide adequate moisture if planting in the heat of summer. Locate junipers in full sun; those that grow in dense shade soon become thin, open, and ratty. Junipers are quick to establish in well-drained soils with moderate moisture. Proper soil preparation in clay, sandy, or granite-based soils is key. Refer to pages 62 to 63 for information on soil preparation and planting guidelines.

Growing Tips
Junipers take strong hold if they are watered regularly during the first few years. Soak the soil deeply and infrequently for the strongest root development. Once upright junipers are established, they are drought resistant. After the first growing season, fertilize lightly in the spring with a 10-10-10. Follow fertilizing guidelines on page 63.

Care
During the frenzy of spring, many homeowners take pruners in hand and shear their juniper, but this can actually shorten its life and turn the inside of the evergreen brown. Allow junipers to grow naturally, and resist shearing outer growth. Unless you're growing a formal hedge or topiary, junipers live longer and look best left untouched. To reduce excessive limb breakage, protect the plant from heavy, wet snow loads. Poor drainage, oxygen starvation to the roots, and bark injuries are the most common causes of decline in juniper plantings. Spider mites often attack stressed trees in the heat of summer, but they can be repelled by syringing the foliage with water.

Landscape Design
Upright-growing junipers can be used for windbreaks, hedges, and group plantings, and as specimen trees. The green to bluish green foliage provides nice contrasts to the bark of many deciduous shrubs in winter.

I Also Recommend
I like *J. scopulorum* 'Moonglow' with its dense silvery-gray foliage and a broad pyramidal growth habit (18 ft. tall × 12 ft.). Eastern red cedar (*Juniperus virginiana*) grows taller, up to 35 ft., and is and excellent screen or windbreak.

When, Where, and How to Plant

Plant in the spring to allow yews to establish strong roots before fall. Choose an area that is partial shade to full shade. Though yews are perfectly hardy in our region, plant them out of extremely exposed windy locations and winter sun; otherwise, the needles brown. To avoid root rot, don't plant yews in low areas where water accumulates; be sure the soil drains well. Dig the planting hole two to three times wider than the rootball. Prepare heavily compacted soils by adding a generous supply of compost, up to 40 percent by volume to native soil. Loosen the soil to improve porosity. Follow the general planting directions on pages 62 to 63.

Growing Tips

Yew does not tolerate prolonged droughts, so be sure to water regularly during dry periods throughout the growing season—especially in late fall and winter if weather conditions are dry. Water when temperatures are above freezing and the soil is not frozen. Fertilize sparingly in early spring or when new growth emerges; use 10-10-10 or a similar analysis, and follow label directions. Consult page 63 for information on fertilizing evergreens.

Care

To maintain a natural look, prune the longest growth in the spring as new growth begins to expand. Avoid shearing, which can brown the foliage and make the plant appear ragged. Extreme exposure to winter sun and wind causes the needles to turn yellow or brown, so consider location carefully. **Caution:** If eaten, the needles are poisonous, as are the inner hard seeds of the red fruits.

Landscape Merit

Yews add handsome winter color. Use them as hedges, foundation plantings, bonsai (pruned to smaller proportions), or for screening. Be sure to space the plants appropriately and site them in areas protected from severe wind exposure.

My Personal Favorite

Taxus × media 'Hicksii' has a narrow upright growth habit with soft green needles and grows to 10 ft. high with a 6-ft. spread

Placed in shady areas of the landscape, yews are among the most attractive evergreens. They are best grown with protection from winter sun and wind on an east or north exposure. Some fine specimens can be seen in Fort Collins, Colorado, where their handsome dark-green needles create a nice contrast to the harsh university building walls. In the proper location, yews can be used in mass plantings, in shrub borders, or as foundation planting. They need well-drained soils and prefer moist conditions, thus shady locations are best. If desired, yews can be pruned into a more formal hedge, but the natural growth form is quite attractive. Planted in combination with other deciduous trees and shrubs, yews offer a striking contrast in color and textures.

Other Common Names

Anglojap yew, Hick's yew

Bloom Period and Seasonal Color

Handsome dark-green evergreen foliage

Mature Height × Spread

15 to 20 ft. × 6 ft.

Zones

To zone 4

Deciduous Trees *for the Rockies*

Planted in the proper location, a tree will live for generations, silently cleaning the air while providing shade, beauty, and shelter for wildlife. They are a living link between the past and the future.

Deciduous trees give us shade in summer, cooling our living environment by blocking out the hot sun. But bare of their leaves in winter, the same trees allow sunlight and warmth to reach us when we need it most. They remove carbon dioxide and pollutants from the air, and return oxygen to the air we breathe. They are one of Nature's gifts.

Heritage Birch

Making Good Choices

The most important consideration in growing trees successfully in the Rockies is choosing the right type of tree for your specific site and needs.

What is it that you are looking for? Maybe a tree that has an ever-changing seasonal display? A tree just for shade? Or is it a tree that will grow fast for privacy and shade? After a long chilly winter, who doesn't look forward to the beauty of a flowering plum or crabapple?

Planting Tips

Trees may be transported and sold any of these three ways. Bare-root trees are grown in a nursery field, harvested when dormant (early spring or late fall), and made available to gardeners. Once dug, these trees should be planted as soon as possible so the roots don't dry out, and preferably before the leaves emerge in the spring.

Specimen trees are often sold balled and burlapped (their rootballs wrapped and secured with a wire basket and twine). It is important to remove at least the top $1/3$ to $1/2$ of the wire basket *after* the tree is situated in the planting hole. Use a bolt cutter to cut through the stiff wire, and then carefully pull it away. This allows the upper portion of the rootball to develop healthy roots. The top of the rootball should be planted level with the surrounding grade. Also, remove any nylon twine around the trunk; this material does not decompose and can girdle roots and the trunk of the tree even years later.

Container-grown trees are also available. Look for signs of healthy new growth when selecting these trees. When planting containerized trees, check the root system. If the roots have grown into a mass encircling the rootball, they should be teased or even cut at planting to encourage lateral growth. The nice thing about container-grown trees is they can be planted just about anytime of the year, but spring is the ideal time, as soon as the ground can be worked. A note about those so-called "plantable" containers— they *aren't*. When you take the tree out of its container for planting, carefully remove the plastic or fiber pot.

The Secret to Success

As with all types of plants, the secret to growing trees successfully is to start with good soil. Few trees thrive in clay, heavy, compacted, or poorly drained soils. The lack of available oxygen to the roots results in stunted growth or eventual death. Nor do trees survive drought in sandy or rocky soils that have no ability to retain moisture. Trees produce vigorous, healthy growth if they are planted in soil that is well drained, loosened as deeply as possible, and amended with some organic matter. But there is one caveat: Don't overamend the soil with too much "stuff"! If too many amendments or too much amendment is added to the planting hole, the tree's roots may decide to remain within the hole, growing in circles, and never explore the surrounding soil. This causes a "bathtub" effect. Remember, roots *will* grow and move into soil that contains oxygen. After years of research, gardeners have learned the best rule is to dig the planting hole *much wider* than deep. And loosen the soil around the planting hole thoroughly.

So how much organic matter should be added to your native soil? A *rule of thumb* is to use up to 4 yards of organic matter for every 1,000 sq. ft. of area to be planted. This varies, of course, depending on what kinds of trees you select; some species prefer less pampering with special soil amendments.

If you are moving to a new home site that is not yet landscaped, the ideal way to prepare the soil is to incorporate organic amendments into the soil as deeply as possible and adjust the planting height. A tractor with plow or disk attachments works best for large areas; a heavy-duty rototiller is good for smaller areas. When planting trees in an existing landscape or when replacing trees, amend the soil taken from the planting hole; be careful not to make the soil too rich in organic material.

Urban Legends

You don't have to cut the branches back by one-third to balance the top of the tree with the roots. The branch tips on a small tree produce plant hormones that direct the growth of roots. If you prune to compensate for lost roots, the tree's energy goes into replacing the lost foliage. While this happens, root growth stops temporarily. This is exactly opposite what the new tree really needs to do. Except to remove broken, damaged branches or to correct shape, don't prune a new tree for a year after planting.

You don't need to feed the tree with vitamins and hormones at the time of planting. This is a myth; at worst, they impede root growth by increasing the soluble salt levels in the planting hole. A tree manufactures its own vitamins and hormones, so why waste your money?

Don't fertilize trees during transplanting; allow the roots to become established the first growing season so they are able to use supplemental nutrients in future years.

Much About Mulch

After planting, spread a 2- to 3-in. layer of organic mulch over the root zone, but not up against the trunk. Piling mulch on or over the base of the tree trunk can keep the bark soft and wet (conditions that favor diseases); it may also encourage rodents to gnaw on the bark. Appropriately applied mulch helps to reduce weed growth, keeps the soil cooler, and maintains and conserves moisture. Water deeply and thoroughly to moisten the rootball *and* the surrounding soil. This encourages new roots to grow into your native soil.

Important Watering Tips

Watering Newly Planted Trees

Watering the first year is critical—young, transplanted trees need ample moisture to become established. With backfill soil, build a dike about 3 in. high around the root zone. This forms a reservoir to hold water and allow it to soak down to the roots. Apply 1 to 2 in. of water to the root zone each week, but do not overwater. A good way to determine whether the tree needs water is to dig down around the root zone (to a depth of 4 to 6 in.) and feel the soil. If the soil is dry, it's time to water. If the soil is still moist, wait a few days.

Watering Established Trees

As trees grow and mature, watering practices vary, depending on the species and their tolerance for drought. It is important to deeply saturate the soil around the drip line (the area on the ground beneath a tree's outermost branches). For larger, maturing trees, the area *beyond* the drip line should be watered too. The most effective way to provide water is to place a "frog-eye" sprinkler at the outer edge of the drip line. Move the sprinkler around this zone every ten to fifteen minutes to allow for overlap and to completely cover the root zone.

A Row of Maples

How much water does a tree need? An easy way to determine this is to measure the tree's trunk diameter at knee height, then multiply by ten. For example, a tree with a 7-in. diameter tree trunk needs 70 gallons of water.

How long to water? When using the frog-eye sprinkler, set a medium pressure and multiply the trunk diameter by five to calculate total watering time. For example, that 7-in. tree should be watered for thirty-five minutes, moving the sprinkler as needed for overlap. Slow watering allows water to percolate deeply where roots can use it more efficiently.

Fall and Winter Watering

Lack of available subsoil moisture can take its toll on trees during the fall and winter seasons. When there is little or no rain or snow, it is critical to *winter water* trees when temperatures are above freezing and as long as the ground remains unfrozen. This may need to be done every four to five weeks, depending on weather conditions. After winter watering, don't forget to drain your hoses and return them to storage for use later as needed.

The ABCs of Fertilizing Trees

If you're uncertain about applying fertilizer to trees, a soil test can help you determine when it becomes necessary to do so. You can also look for symptoms of nutrient deficiency—including small leaves, light-green or yellow leaves, stunted or short shoot growth, dead twigs at the ends of branches, and general lack of vigor. If these symptoms are present and are not a result of other variables such as drought stress, root injuries, herbicide damage, or diseases, then tree fertilization may be necessary.

Apply tree fertilizer when environmental conditions are most favorable for root growth. This is best done in late spring or early summer when the soil is moist and temperatures are between 68 and 84 degrees Fahrenheit.

Tree fertilizer is most effective and best used by the root system when applied to the soil surface over the root system of the trees (the tree's drip line and several feet beyond). Research has shown that surface placement of a complete fertilizer (N-P-K such as 10-10-10) is as good as, or better than, subsurface applications to shade trees growing outside of lawn areas. Trees growing within lawn areas benefit from lawn fertilizer (but do *not* use weed-and-feed formulations) and generally do not need additional tree fertilizer applications. Trees can absorb nutrients applied to the soil surface because the nutrients move downward with water that percolates through the soil; tree roots near the soil surface can

absorb the migrating nutrients. A rate of 1 to 2 lb. of actual nitrogen per 1,000 sq. ft. per growing season supplies the nutrient needs of most trees. Just remember, fertilizer applications are not to be used as a rescue effort for stressed, injured, or declining trees.

Since the root zone of most trees lies just below the soil surface (6 to 12 in.), applying fertilizer to the surface of the soil is the easiest and most effective method of getting nitrogen to the root zone. Scatter the fertilizer at the drip line of the tree and several feet beyond this area, using the required amount to cover the total square feet. Water thoroughly after fertilizing to allow the nutrients to reach the root system. **Caution:** Do *not* use

Flowering Crabapple 'Eley'

too much fertilizer. If you apply more than the manufacturer's recommendations, tree roots can be burned or killed.

The Kindest Cut

Pruning—More Harm Than Good Sometimes

You'll be surprised how much outdated information about pruning trees can still be found in gardening books. Two common outdated pruning procedures are these: "Prune flush with the trunk" and "Paint the cut to prevent the wood from rotting." Both of these old recommendations have been shown by research to cause more harm than benefit to the tree.

Here's why: By pruning flush with the trunk, the larger cut that results takes longer to heal or close over. And you are eliminating the growing point. Another name for the branch growing point is the *branch collar*. When pruning branches, try to cut the branch so as to maintain the branch collar.

Pruning Wounds and Wound Closure

Quaking Aspen

Trees do not heal wounds the way people do. Trees grow callus tissue in response to pruning. This tissue grows over the wound or injured area, but the damaged tissues are not repaired. Trees chemically wall off the wounded tissue, a process called *compartmentalization*.

Japanese Maple Autumn Foliage

Make pruning wounds as small as possible so the tree can close the wounds more quickly. The longer a wound remains open, the greater the chance that decay will occur. Research has shown that flush cuts may open large wounds that are unable to close rapidly.

Wound dressings or paints inhibit the tree from healing itself and should not be applied. If a tree is pruned at the proper time and pruned correctly, the plant heals itself quickly. So do not paint cuts. Also, do not leave stubs sticking out from the trunk. They will die back into the trunk and cause the heartwood to decay.

When to Prune

Trees can be pruned anytime of year, but pruning at different seasons brings different plant responses. Late winter and early spring, after a general warming trend, is a good time to prune because callus tissue then forms rapidly. This is the period of fastest redevelopment and readjustment to pruned limbs. Even though outwardly the cut may look the same, underneath the tree has sealed off that cut to prevent decay, insects, and diseases from invading.

Prune trees that "bleed" from wounds (dripping sap), such as maples, birches, and walnuts, in late summer or early fall. Bleeding, though, does not generally harm the tree.

Removing large quantities of foliage after (not during) a flush of growth, such as late spring or early summer, tends to dwarf a tree. If that's the effect you desire, this is a good time to prune. For more rapid development, pruning before leaf emergence in the spring is better.

Pruning in late summer or early fall can cause vigorous regrowth, which in some species does not have time to harden off by winter. Late-fall or early-winter pruning subjects the tree to a greater incidence of dieback around the cut, and the wound closes more slowly.

What to Prune

Prune to remove dead, diseased, or damaged wood; to eliminate rubbing, interfering, or poorly placed branches; and to shape the tree.

Dead wood should be cut back to—but not *into*—live wood. Sometimes you may prune out diseased wood to stop the disease's spread. When pruning diseased wood, make a thinning cut well below the infected site into the healthy wood. Disinfect your pruning equipment between each cut with 70 percent alcohol or rubbing alcohol. Do not use chlorine bleach because it rusts tools. Cut back damaged branches to another branch. This damage includes previous poor pruning cuts or stubs.

Eliminate rubbing, interfering, or poorly placed branches. Cut off branches that are or will eventually rub or grow in the wrong direction.

Narrow "V" crotches (bark incursions) occur when a layer of bark gets squeezed between two branches growing very close together. Cut off one of the trunks or branches. Bark incursions may cause one of the limbs to split under strong winds or under a heavy snow or ice load.

Prune the tree to the shape you want. Such pruning is done to accentuate the tree's normal shape. When planting young or new trees, do not prune off one-fourth to one-third of the top as is sometimes recommended. Severe pruning at the time of planting reduces shoot and root growth the following year. When planting a tree, prune out the dead, diseased, and damaged branches and cut the rubbing, interfering, and badly placed branches. Select the main scaffold branches as early as possible.

Water sprouts or suckers sometimes emerge when a tree has been severely pruned and almost always grow from a stub cut. Some species of trees are notorious for producing many vigorous shoots. These shoots are generally poorly placed and interfere with growth. Prune them off when young, or physically rub them off when they are quite small.

Protecting Young Tree Bark

Protect the tree trunk bark of young trees by wrapping $1^1/2$-in.-diameter or wider white plastic swimming pool hose around the trunk. Cut the hose to a length equal to the distance between the ground and the first branch. Make a vertical cut the length of the hose, pry it open, and snap the hose around the trunk. **My Rocky Mountain Gardening Tip:** Apply reflective tree wraps around Thanksgiving, and remove the wrapping around Easter.

The Beauty of Trees

Trees are functional all year. They sharpen our awareness of the changing seasons, from the first green buds in spring through the cool, lush summer foliage. The brilliant autumn yellow and gold of native aspen trees stir visitors and residents alike to enjoy a drive to the High Country. As winter arrives, deciduous trees can be dramatic and sculptural as they bring interest to the otherwise stark landscape.

Amur Maple
Acer ginnala

One of amur maple's outstanding characteristics is its brilliant yellow-orange to red foliage in autumn. With our customary lack of red in the fall, this tree is a must for the Rocky Mountain landscape. The winged samara seeds are quite attractive in the summer and persist through the winter, but often become a nuisance in the flower bed and the cracks of sidewalks the following spring when they drop and begin to germinate. The foliage is an attractive dark, glossy green. Amur maple's small size makes it a good choice for a patio setting or for screening, grouping, or accenting an unadorned wall of the house, garage, or garden shed. Use it to grace the entry to your home. Several good cultivars are available for our region.

Other Common Name
Ginnala maple

Bloom Period and Seasonal Color
Early spring yellowish white flowers with a mild fragrance; glossy green summer leaves turning yellow and red in autumn

Mature Height × Spread
18 to 25 ft. × 15 to 30 ft.

Zones
To zone 3

When, Where, and How to Plant
The best time to plant amur maple is in the spring once the ground has thawed, but it can be planted in early fall while the soil remains warm. This allows for strong root growth before winter. Plant in full sun to partial shade. Amur maple adapts to most Rocky Mountain soils, but grows best in moist, well-drained areas. Its roots tend to grow shallow and quickly explore surrounding soil. It is important to dig the planting hole three times wider than the original rootball. Mulch after planting with 2 to 3 in. of pine needles or coarse compost. See pages 76 to 77 for more planting tips.

Growing Tips
Keep newly planted trees moist until they become well established. Regular watering in the summer is a must. Symptoms of scorched leaves usually indicate moisture stress. Refer to pages 78 to 80 for advice on watering and fertilizing techniques. Trees not growing in lawn areas should be mulched with 2 to 3 in. of pine needles or aspen humus.

Care
Amur maple grows gracefully without much pruning, but minor pruning may be done in late spring or early summer to remove crisscrossing branches and to allow for good air circulation. A common problem in midsummer is the appearance of yellow leaves and scorched leaf tips. Yellowing may be a symptom of iron chlorosis. Remedy this by applying a chelated iron. Determine whether scorched leaf tips indicate a lack of available water in the soil or soil that is too compacted, and correct the condition.

Landscape Merit
A relatively small specimen tree, amur maple works well for patio plantings, screening, and mass plantings; it makes a good corner accent. Plant it near entryways so you can enjoy its beauty daily. This extremely hardy tree displays quite dramatic fall coloration.

My Personal Favorite
Acer ginnala 'Compactum' grows vigorously and has larger leaves that are dark green. Its autumn color is brilliant red-purple.

Cottonwood
Populus spp.

When, Where, and How to Plant
Plant cottonwood from spring through fall. Bare-root trees should be planted as soon as the soil can be worked in the spring. Locate them in full sun in an open area far away from buildings and sewer systems. Dig the planting hole three times wider than the spread of roots or the rootball. Cottonwood does best in moist, deep loamy soil. Follow the general instructions for planting trees on pages 76 to 77.

Growing Tips
During drought periods, water trees regularly to maintain vigor and health and to reduce leaf scorch. Otherwise, water deeply and as infrequently as possible to discourage shallow rooting. These trees grow vigorously with proper watering. Consult pages 78 to 80 for moe information on watering trees effectively. Apply a slow-release 10-10-10 fertilizer in the spring.

Care
Prune each year and after storm damage to maintain this tree's health and for your safety. Prune in late winter or early spring. The poplar family is notorious for producing sucker growth in lawns, gardens, and flower beds; to prevent such problems, carefully consider location before planting. Female trees produce catkins followed by cottony seeds—which become a nuisance and may require frequent cleanup. Diseases and insect pests are common. Inspect trees weekly for pests, and take appropriate control measures.

Landscape Merit
Some species have a narrow growth habit and can be used for screening. *Populus alba* 'Pyramidalis', with a spread of 15 to 20 ft., is one. Cottonwood is a good replacement for the short-lived lombardy poplar. The poplar family is known for its ability to grow fast. Poplars need plenty of space to grow upwards and outwards. Older trees have magnificent trunk and branch structure that adds winter interest.

My Personal Favorites
My favorite is the pioneer native species, *Populus deltoides* spp. *monilifera*, which grows along streams, rivers, and drainage basins. Silver poplar (*Populus alba*) has chalky-white bark with leaves that are dark green on top and silvery white on the bottom.

Newcomers are always asking for the names of trees that grow fast and provide "instant" shade. Many are awed by the fall gold in the High Country and want aspen (Populus tremuloides) somewhere in their landscape. But aspens eventually become problem trees that are weak wooded, subject to storm damage, and prone to insects and diseases. Learn about the various Populus trees and make appropriate choices for your landscape so you can prevent potential problems. In the home landscape, cottonwood's brittle and weak branches can be a hazard. Female trees produce inordinate amounts of cottony seeds. Poplars are especially useful for planting in wet sites, but their fast growth rate, rapidly expanding crowns, and vigorous greedy roots make them poor candidates near buildings, septic systems, sewers, and underground drainage pipes. Balance their good qualities against their shortcomings.

Other Common Names
Plains cottonwood

Bloom Period and Seasonal Color
Bright-yellow fall foliage

Mature Height × Spread
70 to 100 ft. × 50 to 60 ft.

Zones
To zone 3

Flowering Crabapple
Malus spp.

Among the most popular ornamental landscape trees, flowering crabapple offers many wildlife-friendly species. After a long, cold winter, their colorful, cheerful blooms welcome early spring. In the fall, a variety of birds enjoy this tree's ornamental fruits—but some cultivars are fruitless. Flowering crabapple's primary growth habit is that of a deciduous tree, but over the past several years of evaluating crabapple varieties for disease resistance, some forms are more shrublike and attractive in the landscape. The bacterial disease fireblight is particularly destructive to this tree's ornamental value, but some of the new selections have shown good resistance to this common problem. Among the top-performing crabapples in our landscape are 'Donald Wyman' and 'Prairie Fire', with beautiful flowers, clean foliage, persistent fruit, and disease resistance.

Bloom Period and Seasonal Color
Spring flowers in pink, rose red, white with pink blush, or white; persistent and wildlife-edible fruit throughout summer and early winter

Mature Height × Spread
15 to 25 ft. × 10 to 25 ft.

Zones
To zone 3

When, Where, and How to Plant
Crabapples are easily transplanted from early spring through early fall. To achieve the best growth, prolific flowering, and bright fruit, plant crabapples in full sun with good air circulation. Locate the tree far enough away from other trees so that shade and root competition do not become a problem. Crabapples adapt to a wide range of soil conditions, but do best in well-drained soils. Dig the planting hole at least two to three times wider than the rootball or spread of the roots. Amend the soil with one-third by volume of good compost. For more detailed information on soil preparation, see pages 76 to 77. Mulch the root zone with shredded bark or cedar shavings to a depth of 2 in. Water the soil thoroughly, and check it every few days; water again when it dries out to a depth of 6 to 8 in.

Growing Tips
Once established, crabapple trees thrive with little care other than occasional deep watering. But avoid overwatering crabapples once they are established—these trees do not appreciate wet feet. See watering and fertilizing tips on pages 78 to 80. To avoid potential herbicide contamination to the tree, it is important not to use weed-and-feed combinations.

Care
To maintain tree health, proper air circulation, and beauty, prune crabapples every few years in late winter. Most varieties are grafted to a more vigorous rootstock that often sprouts growth off the base of the trunk. Remove these sprouts or suckers as soon as they appear. When pruning crabapple trees, have a bottle of denatured alcohol on hand to prevent the spread of bacterial fireblight. You can easily clean pruners and saw blades with the alcohol or a spray disinfectant after each pruning cut.

Landscape Merit
Whether a tree or shrubby, crabapples are all-season plants with unique structural accents and colorful bark.

My Personal Favorite
'Donald Wyman' has beautiful pink buds that open to white. Flowers are followed by long-lasting, tiny, glossy, bright-red fruit.

Goldenrain Tree
Koelreuteria paniculata

When, Where, and How to Plant

Early spring is the best time to plant to allow for good root development—or early autumn while the soil is still warm. Avoid planting in midsummer; heat stresses the tree, and the foliage requires more moisture than the roots can possibly supply. Plant in full sun for the best flower development, but in a semiprotected spot away from prevailing winds and temperature fluctuations. Goldenrain tree adapts to our alkaline soils and tolerates air pollution. Dig the planting hole three times wider than the rootball and as deep as the rootball. Follow soil preparation and planting instructions on pages 76 to 77. Mulch newly planted trees with 2 to 3 in. of compost or other suitable organic material to maintain and conserve moisture.

Growing Tips

Water regularly during dry periods to encourage healthy growth and drought endurance. Misting the foliage in the morning and evening reduces heat stress and leaf scorch while this tree becomes established. Once the tree is established, apply an all-purpose fertilizer such as 10-10-10 in late spring or early summer. Trees located in lawn areas generally do not require supplemental fertilizer since they derive some nutrients from lawn fertilization. Avoid high-nitrogen fertilizers that induce soft growth—which is more susceptible to breakage. Consult pages 79 to 80 for information on fertilizing trees.

Care

Young trees can suffer from sunscald injury—splitting or cracking of the bark. Protect young trees by wrapping 1 1/2 in.-diameter white plastic swimming pool hose around the trunk: Cut the hose to a length equal to the distance between the ground and the first branch. Make a vertical cut the length of the hose, pry it open, and snap the hose around the trunk. Prune in late winter or early spring.

Landscape Merit

Goldenrain tree is prized for its stunning yellow flowers in the summer. Clusters of lanternlike, papery seedpods add interest.

My Personal Favorite

The species is the most reliable and cold hardy.

One of the few trees that flower in midsummer, goldenrain tree features panicles of fragrant yellow flowers followed by clusters of papery, lanternlike seedpods. Goldenrain tree is a perfect size for a smaller landscape—it grows relatively quickly, but not so large that it overpowers a house or small landscape. This tree grows best at elevations below five thousand feet, including the High Plains and foothill regions. The compound leaves emerge purplish red, mature to green, and change to orange-yellow in the fall. Place this attractive ornamental tree where it can be enjoyed from a window, or put it near the flow of pedestrian or automobile traffic. With its clusters of yellow flowers, goldenrain tree offers unexpected color in the summer.

Other Common Names
Varnish tree, pride of India

Bloom Period and Seasonal Color
Showy yellow flower clusters in summer; clusters of papery seedpods like oriental lanterns appear in late summer and fall

Mature Height × Spread
25 to 40 ft. × 20 to 30 ft.

Zones
To zone 4 (with a protected site)

Green Ash

Fraxinus pennsylvanica

The green ash has become one of the most dominant trees in Rocky Mountain landscapes because of its adaptability and drought tolerance. In some cases, green ash has been overplanted and trees can be compromised should a disease outbreak occur. Green ash trees adapt to alkaline soils and grow relatively quickly. The pyramidal young tree becomes broadly oval as it matures. Dark-green compound foliage turns radiant yellow in autumn. The maturing, gray-brown bark is rather attractive with diamond furrows separated by narrow ridges. Green ash is very heat and cold tolerant, which makes it an ideal landscape tree. 'Marshalls Seedless' has glossy green leaves and is pest and disease free. 'Summit' grows with a straight central leader and has wonderful golden-yellow fall foliage.

Bloom Period and Seasonal Color
Greenish to reddish green flowers before leaves; glossy green summer foliage turning yellow to golden yellow in the fall

Mature Height × Spread
50 to 60 ft. × 25 to 30 ft.

Zones
To zone 3

When, Where, and How to Plant
Green ash tree can be planted from spring through early fall. If planting during the heat of summer, provide adequate moisture for good establishment. Locate the tree where it will receive full sun for the best growth and development. Green ash is very adaptable to the region's varied soil conditions and survives elevations to 8,500 ft. Dig the planting hole three times as wide as the rootball. If your soil is a heavy clay, dig the planting hole 2 in. shallower than the rootball. In sandy soils, the hole should be no deeper than the rootball. Trees have a hard time establishing in clay, compacted, or poorly drained soils. Follow general instructions for soil preparation and planting techniques on pages 76 to 77.

Growing Tips
Keep green ash trees healthy and encourage drought tolerance by watering on a regular basis. Water deeply once a week or as the soil begins to dry out. Consult pages 78 to 80 for methods of watering and tips on fertilizing. During extended dry periods in the fall and winter, water every four to six weeks when temperatures are above freezing. See page 79 for information on winter watering.

Care
It is important to maintain tree vigor and health. Avoid overwatering, which can waterlog the soil and displace oxygen, causing the tree's leaves to turn yellow. The tree's rapid decline follows. In early spring, green ash tree is frequently attacked by the larvae of sawfly. These wimpy pests can be easily controlled merely by hosing them off the leaves with a strong stream of water as often as they appear. Prune green ash tree in late winter or early spring.

Landscape Merit
Some outstanding selections are available for street plantings or specimen shade trees. Green ash tree is widely adapted to western and alkaline soil conditions and is durable.

My Personal Favorite
'Cimmaron' has an upright oval form with dramatic reddish fall foliage. It tolerates alkaline soils.

Hawthorn
Crataegus spp.

When, Where, and How to Plant
Plant hawthorns in spring through early fall. Container-grown nursery stock can be planted anytime they are available, but avoid late-fall planting. To promote vigorous growth and prolific flowering, plant in a location with full sun. Performance is best in moist, well-drained soils, but trees adapt to dry conditions once established. Dig the planting hole two to three times wider than the rootball. Be sure the top of the rootball or container root system is planted level with the surrounding grade. In heavy clay soils, the planting hole can be 2 in. shallower than the rootball. Mulch after planting with 2 to 3 in. of compost or other organic material.

Growing Tips
Water deeply and infrequently. In soils with a high pH, hawthorns can develop a problem with iron chlorosis. Even though iron is in most Rocky Mountain soils, it is often unable to be used by the plant. Apply a chelated iron fertilizer by punching holes (8 to 10 in. deep) around the drip line, spacing them 10 to 12 in. apart. Broadcast the fertilizer over the area, and water well. Follow guidelines for watering and fertilizing on pages 78 to 79.

Care
Once established, hawthorns are low maintenance and need only periodic pruning in late winter or early spring. Some suckering around the base of the tree may occur occasionally, but these can be pruned away as soon as they appear. Trees that become stressed may become susceptible to fireblight, rusts, leaf spots, cedar hawthorn rust, aphids, and mites. Most hawthorns are pH adaptable, but occasionally a selection may develop chlorosis.

Landscape Merit
Hawthorns produce showy white flower clusters followed by persistent fruit for wildlife. Very attractive fall colors range from red-maroon to yellow-gold. Mature trees have handsome exfoliating bark.

My Personal Favorite
My favorite is Russian hawthorn (*Crataegus ambigua*). Small dark-red fruits decorate the branches for several weeks, attracting birds. Its gnarled growth habit makes a beautiful silhouette in our landscape.

A group of small trees with a wide range of adaptability and moderate drought tolerance, hawthorns are tough, hardy, and easy to grow where few other trees survive. This makes hawthorns valuable trees in difficult sites, but don't overlook their ornamental qualities in the landscape as attractive specimen trees. They work nicely in limited space. The clusters of showy white flowers are followed by applelike fruit in late summer that persist through fall. Many wild birds favor the fruit. Fall foliage colors range from bronze to red-orange. Crataegus laevigata 'Crimson Cloud' is a delightful low-branching tree with an upright growth habit. Crimson-red blossoms with white star-shaped centers appear in late spring. There are many desirable varieties that grow well throughout the region.

Bloom Period and Seasonal Color
Spring blooms in white, followed by fall berries; colorful fall foliage

Mature Height × Spread
15 to 25 ft. × 15 to 30 ft.

Zones
To zone 3

Hedge Maple
Acer campestre

Many gardeners are not familiar with the hedge maple, but this tree has proven to be a durable small maple that is surprisingly pest and disease free. Even though it is a slow-growing tree, its unique foliage and lightly ridged bark makes the hedge maple a great choice for a smaller landscape. The attractive dark-green leaves change to a yellow-green or yellow in the autumn. One of hedge maple's merits is its ability to adapt to our alkaline soil conditions; it does not exhibit iron chlorosis as other maples often do. Once the tree becomes established, it makes a great choice for a water-wise landscape; it tolerates dry soils and soil compaction. I highly recommend that you include this maple tree in your landscape.

Other Common Name
Field maple

Bloom Period and Seasonal Color
Greenish, inconspicuous flowers in early spring; yellowish green to yellow-gold leaves in autumn

Mature Height × Spread
15 to 25 ft. × 12 to 25 ft.

Zones
To zone 4

When, Where, and How to Plant
Plant in early spring through early fall. Site in a location that receives full sun to part sun. When planting in summer, provide ample moisture to ensure healthy establishment. It is quite adaptable to a wide range of soils, but prefers a rich, well-drained location. Soils that are typically alkaline do not seem to bother this fine tree, and after a few years of establishment, it soon tolerates dry soil conditions. Dig the planting hole at least three times as wide as the rootball, though it need not be deeper than the rootball. Use a good soil conditioner such as compost or sphagnum peat moss at the rate of 25 to 30 percent by volume with your native soil. Follow the general planting guidelines on pages 76 to 77. Spread a 2-in. layer of shredded cedar mulch or pine needles over the root zone.

Growing Tips
Water hedge maple regularly during the first few years while it becomes established. Fertilizer can be applied in late May or early June. Follow the guidelines for watering and fertilizing trees on pages 78 to 80.

Care
Once your hedge maple becomes established, it is a low-maintenance tree. The hedge maple attracts no serious pests and is relatively disease free. Occasionally, a few caterpillars may chew on the foliage, but they are easy to control with biological or insecticidal soap sprays. Light pruning, if needed, can be done during the summer months; avoid pruning in late fall and winter.

Landscape Merit
Hedge maple is a wonderful tree to replace old, diseased, or dying aspens. It has attractive, lightly ridged, and furrowed bark. The hedge maple is not a large tree, so it can be planted near sidewalks, driveways, and entrances where it can be appreciated.

My Personal Favorites
'Queen Elizabeth' has strong branch development and darker green leaves. 'Fastigiatum' is an upright-growing cultivar with corky branches and five-lobed leaves.

Kentucky Coffee Tree
Gymnocladus dioica

When, Where, and How to Plant

Plant this tree in the early spring or early fall. Even though the Kentucky coffee tree grows slowly, it eventually becomes quite large and needs plenty of room to develop. Locate in full sun. This tree adapts to a wide range of soil types and tolerates drought. Dig the planting hole two to three times as wide as the rootball. If your soil is a heavy or compacted clay, dig the planting hole 2 in. shallower than the rootball. In sandy soils, dig no deeper than the rootball. Check the soil moisture weekly by digging down 4 to 6 in. near the edge of the rootball. If the soil is becoming dry, water deeply. Apply a layer of organic mulch over the root zone after planting. Also see pages 76 to 77 for more planting advice.

Growing Tips

Once this tree becomes established, it requires minimal care. Soak the root zone deeply, but infrequently. Using a frog-eye sprinkler set at the drip line, water each area for fifteen to twenty minutes. Move around the tree until the watering is completed. Refer to watering practices on pages 78 to 80. Trees planted in lawn areas rarely need additional fertilizer since they receive some nutrients from lawn fertilizer.

Care

The very hardy Kentucky coffee tree has few insect pest problems and is disease free. Prune in the dormant season to remove dead or broken limbs. You may have to remove basal suckers that emerge around the bottom of the trunk. Bear in mind that the fruits on female trees and large leaf stalks that support the many leaflets drop in mass and require periodic cleanup.

Landscape Merit

Kentucky coffee tree makes a good, permanent shade tree. Its majestic presence in the winter landscape is unique. The large, divided leaves cast a dappled shade that enables shade-tolerant grasses to grow beneath its canopy.

My Personal Favorites

There are a few fruitless male trees such as 'Stately Manor' and 'Espresso'. Check with local nurseries for their availability.

The strong and very hardy Kentucky coffee tree is one of the most stately trees in the winter landscape. Its distinctive rough bark is deeply furrowed. As the bark matures, it develops scaly, recurving ridges for year-round interest. Female trees bear greenish white panicles of flowers followed by long, beanlike pods that persist through the winter. Male flowers are smaller and less fragrant. It is one of the latest trees to leaf out in the spring and generally avoids being damaged by late-spring frosts. Foliage has a purplish tinge when emerging that gradually changes to dark bluish green in summer. Kentucky coffee tree has a narrow growth habit when young, but matures to an open, broad-spreading crown. It makes an excellent shade tree with superior drought endurance.

Bloom Period and Seasonal Color
Clean green foliage; yellow-gold in the fall; interesting winter structure

Mature Height × Spread
50 to 60 ft. × 40 to 50 ft.

Zones
To zone 4

Linden
Tilia spp.

With their heart-shaped leaves, linden trees are remarkably attractive. They are noted for their uniform pyramidal growth and make excellent shade and street trees. The fragrant flowers that droop from the branches appear in midsummer and act as a magnet for honeybees. In the fall, clusters of tiny pea-sized fruits hang delicately from papery bracts, adding another decorative quality to the fall landscape. The littleleaf linden (Tilia cordata), with its dense pyramidal form, is an excellent street, lawn, or specimen tree. The American linden (Tilia americana) generally grows larger but has the same pyramidal growth habit of littleleaf linden. These trees are very tolerant of our region's alkaline soil conditions. In autumn, the linden's handsome foliage turns yellow and gold.

Bloom Period and Seasonal Color
Attractive yellow and gold foliage in the fall

Mature Height × Spread
50 to 60 ft. × 30 to 45 ft.

Zones
To zone 3

When, Where, and How to Plant
Plant linden in the spring through early fall. If planting in midsummer, provide ample moisture to prevent stress and subsequent leaf scorch. Locate in full sun for the best growth and development. Lindens adapt to a wide range of soils, including alkaline conditions. Follow soil preparation recommendations on pages 76 to 77. Dig the planting hole two to three times wider than the rootball. For larger, balled-and-burlapped specimen trees, set the tree in the planting hole, remove all nylon twine, and use a bolt cutter to remove as much of the wire basket as possible. Add backfill soil to the hole, and water slowly to eliminate air pockets. Use some of the extra soil to make a dike or water basin for future watering.

Growing Tips
When the soil begins to dry out in the top 4- to 6-in. layer, fill the water basin to soak the soil thoroughly. Lindens do best when watered regularly. They do not tolerate prolonged drought well; be sure to water them during dry periods because stressed trees are more susceptible to spider mites and leaf scorch. See watering techniques for trees on page 78. Mulch newly planted trees with a 2-in. layer of organic mulch to maintain moisture and conserve water. Fertilize in early to mid-spring. See page 79 for details on how to fertilize trees.

Care
Lindens are usually pest and trouble free. Prune these trees in late winter to early spring as needed. Sucker growth at the base of the tree can be a nuisance with some varieties, remedy this by pruning suckers off as soon as they appear.

Landscape Merit
Among the best street trees, lindens thrive in some of the most difficult sites and make excellent choices for specimen shade trees in the home lawn.

My Personal Favorite
My favorite, *Tilia cordata* 'Greenspire'; grows in a dense, formal shape and has an abundance of spicy, fragrant flowers in June and July.

When, Where, and How to Plant

Plant Mayday tree in early spring. For the best flowering and growth form, locate in full sun with good air circulation. It does best in well-drained soils, so be sure to condition clay soils with a good soil amendment. Follow the general instructions for planting trees on pages 76 to 77. Dig the planting hole two to three times wider than the original rootball to encourage healthy, vigorous root growth. In clay soils, set the rootball so that the top is level with or an inch above the surrounding ground. Form a berm just beyond the edge of the root zone to provide a basin in which to water deeply as needed.

Growing Tips

Proper watering is essential to establish newly transplanted trees, especially the *Prunus* genus. Overwatering can cause stress and poor root growth. Most ornamental cherries are shallow rooted, so provide ample moisture and keep the root zone cool. Once the tree is established, water deeply once a week or as the soil begins to dry out. Spread a 2- to 3-in. mulch around the root zone to maintain moisture and reduce annual weed growth—but keep the mulch away from the tree's trunk. Follow the watering guidelines on page 78. The second growing season, sprinkle a complete granular fertilizer such as 10-10-10 on the mulch and water well. Consult page 79 for more details on fertilizing trees.

Care

Prune rubbing branches and dead or broken limbs in late winter or early spring. Keep trees healthy to discourage pests and diseases. If cherry or pear slugs attack the foliage, hose them off with water or sprinkle with wood ashes.

Landscape Merit

A medium-sized tree with a fairly dense, rounded crown, Mayday works well in smaller spaces; its early foliage and blooms are a welcome sight after a long winter. Excellent for shelterbelt and wildlife plantings.

My Personal Favorite

My favorite is the species Mayday tree, due to its fragrant spring blossoms.

Species in the genus Prunus *are noted for their fragrant early blossoms throughout the region, but tend to be short lived when planted in heavy clay soils. Frequent temperature fluctuations cause stress, which often results in diseases and insect problems. Despite this, a few cultivated varieties have performed admirably in our landscape and are highly recommended. Canada red chokecherry (Prunus virginiana) grows well in my windbreak and attracts wildlife. Prunus padus or Mayday tree is one of my favorites; it is prized for its spring-fresh, fragrant, drooping flower clusters in late April to early May. Small black fruit ripen in July to early August and are a favorite of visiting birds. Mayday tree has nice fall color with foliage turning yellow-gold to bronze-red.*

Other Common Name
Birdcherry

Bloom Period and Seasonal Color
Fragrant white flower clusters in early spring; yellow-gold to bronze-red fall foliage

Mature Height × Spread
18 to 25 ft. × 20 to 30 ft.

Zones
To zone 3

Norway Maple
Acer platanoides

Norway maples mark the beginning of spring with their greenish yellow flowers which emerge in April before the leaves appear. Once established, Norway maple and many of its cultivars provide a canopy of dense shade during the hottest part of the summer day. Summer's green foliage canopy transforms in the fall to shades of yellow, orange, and sometimes reddish orange. One of the oldest cultivars, 'Crimson King' features maroon leaves all season. Flowers are maroon-yellow in early spring. The attractive rounded outline of Norway maple is common to both young and older trees. It adapts to clay or sandy soils and withstands hot, dry conditions better than sugar maple. The winged seeds are fun to watch as they "helicopter" down from the branches in the fall.

Bloom Period and Seasonal Color
Early spring greenish yellow blooms appear before foliage; bright-yellow fall foliage

Mature Height × Spread
30 to 50 ft. × 25 to 50 ft.

Zones
To zone 3

When, Where, and How to Plant
Plant Norway maple spring through early fall. Fall planting should be done as early as possible to allow for strong root growth before winter. Locate in full sun for the best growth. Norway maple does best with lots of space, so plan accordingly. Its shallow root system may limit its use in lawn areas as the tree matures. It prefers a well-drained, moderately moist, and fertile soil. Dig the planting hole two to three times wider than the rootball. If your soil is heavy clay, the planting hole can be dug 2 in. shallower than the depth of the soil ball. In sandy soils, dig no deeper than the rootball. Follow the general planting instructions on pages 76 to 77.

Growing Tips
To ensure good establishment the first growing season, water deeply each week or as the soil dries out. Encourage drought endurance by watering deeply and applying mulch. Trees growing in lawn areas generally don't need additional fertilizer, but those in other areas benefit from supplemental fertilizer. See the section on tree fertilizing on page 79. During dry, windy conditions in the fall and open, dry winters, water when temperatures are above freezing. Follow the general guidelines for fall and winter watering on page 79.

Care
Its strong central leader helps maintain a symmetrical form and therefore should not be pruned or altered; otherwise, its pyramidal growth habit may be lost. The Norway maple tolerates our varied range of soils and is recommended over the soft or silver maple selections, which are noted for chlorosis. Pests and diseases generally do not bother Norway maple.

Landscape Merit
Plant Norway maple as a shade and lawn tree. It needs plenty of space to spread; as it matures, it provides dense shade. Surrounding areas can be underplanted with shade-tolerant perennials.

My Personal Favorite
A cultivar that grows with a straight leader, 'Deborah' has a reddish-purple colored spring leaf that eventually turns dark green.

When, Where, and How to Plant

Plant oak trees in the early spring, and locate them in full sun. Allow plenty of room for them to grow in both height and spread—they are best placed in open areas and allowed to grow into larger specimen trees. Consult pages 76 to 77 for information on soil preparation. Dig the planting hole two to three times as wide as the rootball or container. Place larger, balled-and-burlapped trees in the planting hole; then remove any twine or metal wire wrapped around the roots in the upper portion of the rootball. This step is important in order for the tree to establish good roots. Set the top of the rootball level with the surrounding grade. After transplanting, mulch with a few inches of pine needles or other organic material.

Growing Tips

Water and fertilize oak trees to encourage good establishment and drought endurance. Depending on the variety you select, oaks readily establish if watered on a regular basis. To avoid the accumulation of soluble salts in the root zone, thoroughly water the trees—avoid shallow watering. Use a soaker hose or frog-eye sprinkler to apply enough water, and allow the water to soak down deeply. Applications of granular or powdered chelated iron can help reduce severe iron chlorosis in oaks that are prone to this problem. See watering and fertilizing techniques on pages 78 to 80.

Care

Prune oak trees in late winter or early spring. Some oak species are susceptible to oak gall and aphids, but this is minor and does not cause considerable damage, nor does it affect the health of the trees.

Landscape Merit

Oak trees grow to large, sturdy trees with varied autumn colors. Their strong branch development helps them resist storm damage. Best of all, these majestic trees leave a living legacy for future generations.

My Personal Favorite

The bur oak (*Quercus macrocarpa*) is my favorite. It adapts to varied soil types throughout our region.

Recognized throughout history as symbols of strength and durability, oaks would have more prominence in our landscapes if not for their slow growth rate. Our native Rocky Mountain oak, Quercus gambelii, is noted for its durability and adaptability to dry conditions and alkaline soils. It can be grown as a small tree or large shrub and is hardy to an 8,000 ft. elevation. In autumn, the red-orange, reddish purple-to-maroon foliage accents the golden aspen. Most oaks do not tolerate highly alkaline soils and become chlorotic in soils with poor drainage. Bur oak (Quercus macrocarpa) is one of the best suited for alkaline soils and drier conditions. Swamp white oak (Quercus bicolor) adapts well to heavy clay soils but can become chlorotic if drainage is a problem.

Bloom Period and Seasonal Color

Autumn colors ranging from yellow to orange to maroon-red

Mature Height × Spread

20 to 60 ft. × 15 to 50 ft.

Zones

To zone 3, depending upon species

Ohio Buckeye
Aesculus glabra

One of the showiest trees in spring, the Ohio buckeye has a rounded growth habit and strong, ascending branches that form a dense crown. The blooms resemble yellow trumpets against the dark-green foliage. Ohio buckeye is one of the first trees to leaf out in spring and to drop its leaves in fall. Its autumn color is bright yellow to orange-red. The oak's palmate compound leaves consist of five large leaflets (3 to 6 in. long), with finely toothed edges. The fruit are prickly, reddish tan capsules. When they crack open, they reveal seeds resembling a "buck's eye." I remember, as a child, gathering pocketfuls of these shiny seeds in the park. These fruits are poisonous, though the seed-hoarding squirrels don't seem to mind.

Other Common Name
Fetid buckeye

Bloom Period and Seasonal Color
Greenish yellow flowers in mid-spring; palmate compound leaves turning yellow in the fall

Mature Height × Spread
20 to 35 ft. × 25 to 40 ft.

Zones
To zone 3

When, Where, and How to Plant
The best time to plant Ohio buckeye tree is in the spring as soon as the soil can be worked. Avoid planting in the summer heat—this tree is vulnerable to leaf scorch. Locate Ohio buckeye tree in full sun where it has adequate space to develop and spread. A bit temperamental about heavy-clay, alkaline soils, this tree prefers a richer, loamy soil. It tolerates slightly alkaline soils that are well drained. Take care to find the right location and amend the soil accordingly. Follow the general guidelines for soil improvement and planting on pages 76 to 77. Mulch after planting.

Growing Tips
Check soil moisture weekly by digging down 4 to 6 in. near the edge of the rootball. If the soil is becoming dry, fill the water basin to soak the soil thoroughly. Ohio buckeye tree grows naturally in moist locations, but once established, it does well with occasional deep waterings so it has good drought endurance. During drought, soak the root system every seven to ten days to alleviate leaf scorch. In non-lawn areas, cover the soil beneath the tree out to the drip line with an organic mulch such as pine needles. Refer to pages 78 to 80 for more information on watering and fertilizing techniques.

Care
Leaf scorch occurs if the tree is subjected to continual drought stress, and the tree can then drop it leaves prematurely. The Ohio buckeye fruit can become a nuisance to some from the standpoint of cleanup, but this tree is generally not bothered by pests or diseases. No special pruning is needed. Just prune dead or broken branches in early spring.

Landscape Merit
Its dense shade and relatively small stature make Ohio buckeye tree a good choice for smaller yards. It can be used for screening and in a windbreak. Remember that the seeds are poisonous, but they provide a source of food for squirrels.

I Also Recommend
The common horsechestnut (*Aesculus hippocastanum*) grows larger (50 to 70 ft.) and has wonderful white flowers.

Ornamental Pear

Pyrus calleryana

When, Where, and How to Plant

Plant in early spring as soon as the soil can be worked; plant container-grown trees anytime during the growing season. Ornamental pears perform best in full sun with good air circulation to reduce the onset of powdery mildew disease. Though adapted to a wide range of soils, ornamental pears prefer well-drained soils. For complete details on soil preparation, follow the general planting guidelines on pages 76 to 77.

Growing Tips

Water newly planted trees regularly to encourage healthy growth and strong establishment. Established ornamental pears need a deep soaking weekly throughout the growing season. Consult page 78 for tree watering techniques. Apply 2 to 3 in. of organic mulch over the root zone to help retain soil moisture and to reduce an invasion of annual weeds. To discourage foliage diseases, avoid the use of high-nitrogen fertilizer. Trees planted in lawn areas generally do not need additional fertilizer as they can obtain sufficient nutrients from lawn fertilizer applications.

Care

Most varieties do not need shaping because of their uniform growth habit. When pruning is necessary, remove only broken, damaged, or rubbing branches to aid in good circulation. These trees can occasionally be invaded by small insect pests called aphids and powdery mildew disease on the leaves. Keep trees healthy to discourage pests and diseases. Homemade soap sprays and baking soda can help prevent severe outbreaks. See page 258 for homemade remedies. Protect the trunks of young trees the first few growing seasons to prevent sunscald injury. See page 79 for information on caring for trees in fall and winter.

Landscape Merit

They work well for street planting, small space gardens, and specimens in open lawns and garden areas. If you have space, plant a row along the property boundary for a spectacular effect.

My Personal Favorite

'Autumn Blaze', prized for its glossy green foliage that becomes a dramatic crimson red in the fall, is one of the most cold hardy ornamental pear trees for our region.

Many cultivated varieties of ornamental pear have become major players in the landscape because of their rapid growth, uniform shape, and beautiful white blooms in early spring. Useful in smaller landscapes, these trees make a bold statement, yet they can be used for screening, street plantings, and structural accents. Fall coloration is outstanding, particularly 'Autumn Blaze', whose leaves turn crimson red in autumn and persist for weeks. Once established, ornamental pears are relatively drought tolerant, have good disease resistance, and perform admirably in many types of soils. The most popular is 'Bradford', but it tends to be a bit more brittle and branches are subject to splitting in strong winds and the weight of snow. 'Chanticleer' is an excellent choice where lateral space is limited.

Other Common Name

Callery pear

Bloom Period and Seasonal Color

Bright white flowers in the spring before leaves appear; wonderful crimson-red fall foliage

Mature Height × Spread

30 to 35 ft. × 15 to 20 ft.

Zones

To zone 4

Quaking Aspen
Populus tremuloides

The characteristic smooth white bark and leaves that quake in the breeze, followed by golden-yellow fall foliage, make aspens a Rocky Mountain favorite. Yes, they are native to our region, but there are limitations for their use. Aspen trees do best at elevations of 7,000 ft. and above. When planted at lower elevations, aspen trees are vulnerable to a wide range of problems including insect pests, spider mites, and diseases—this is the most frequently asked question on our radio programs! Because they grow relatively quickly and because of their small ornamental scale, aspens lend themselves for use in foundation plantings to soften the fronts of buildings and entryways. Another species and cultvar, Populus tremula *'Erecta' has a narrower growth habit. It is also less prone to cultural problems.*

Other Common Name
Quaky

Bloom Period and Seasonal Color
Bright-yellow to gold leaves in the fall; white bark

Mature Height × Spread
20 to 30 ft. × 25 to 30 ft.

Zones
To zone 2

When, Where, and How to Plant
The best time to plant aspens is in the spring to allow for good root establishment. The second choice is fall, after the trees have become dormant. Fall planting requires careful monitoring of moisture through the fall and winter. See page 79 for information on winter watering. Aspens do best in full sun and well-drained soils. Choose a location with good air circulation to reduce the incidence of leaf diseases. In their native habitat, aspens grow in soils naturally enriched with lots of humusy leaf mold. When planting these trees in your landscape, amend the soil with a moisture-retentive compost to simulate mountainous conditions. Follow the general guidelines and instructions for soil preparation and planting on pages 76 to 77.

Growing Tips
To maintain vigorous and healthy growth, don't let aspens become stressed. Provide weekly watering throughout the growing season, particularly during long, hot dry spells. These shallow-rooted trees can be easily watered with a frog-eye sprinkler placed at the drip line. Run the sprinkler for fifteen to twenty minutes, then move it to another location until you have completed soaking the root zone. Apply 10-10-10 fertilizer with chelated iron in the spring.

Care
As these trees grow, roots expand into the surrounding area and "suckers" appear everywhere. Skeptical? Just try to pull out those stray sprouts poking through the lawn and flower beds. Prune suckers as needed. Aspen trees bear either male or female flowers—the male tree forms fuzzy catkins while the female forms cottony tassels with seeds. Take this into account when choosing a proper location. Viewing or growing aspens in the mountains may be the most reliable way to enjoy this native. At lower elevations, they are infested with poplar twig gall fly—a pest for which there are no effective controls.

Landscape Merit
Smaller scale and rapid growth make aspens useful for foundation plantings or as temporary screens.

My Personal Favorite
My favorite is still the native quaking aspen (*Populus tremuloides*).

River Birch

Betula nigra

When, Where, and How to Plant

Plant river birch trees in early spring through early summer. Provide ample water during the summer heat for good root establishment. Locate in full sun or partial sun. Single-stem trees can be spaced 15 ft. apart and the canopies allowed to intertwine. Lower branches can be removed to permit foot traffic. Dig the planting hole two to three times wider than the rootball. Once the tree is planted, apply a 2- to 3-in. layer of pine needles or other organic mulch. See page 78 for more details.

Growing Tips

The river birch does best in moist soils but will survive in drier conditions although its growth will slow. Late fall and winter watering are a must to ensure this tree's survival. See the section on fall and winter watering on page 79.

Care

Avoid pruning in early spring as sap will "bleed." The best time to prune is during the summer. Occasionally, leafminer larvae can attack the foliage, devouring the tissue between the upper and lower leaf surfaces and causing the leaves to turn brown. Trees can develop iron chlorosis in highly alkaline soil (pH of 7.8 or higher). Treat this problem in the spring by applying chelated iron.

Landscape Merit

While many trees need adequate space to grow without competition, the river birch can create a dramatic effect in group plantings or as a multi-stemmed specimen. An attractive companion is redtwig dogwood, which also prefers moist soil conditions. The reddish stems and flaking bark of the birch make a nice contrast. During the winter, the river birch tree makes a handsome statement near the evergreen foliage of blue spruce or white fir.

My Personal Favorite

'Heritage' river birch has good resistance to bronze birch borer and appears to tolerate clay soils better than paper birch. The bark starts to exfoliate on smaller trunks and reveals a salmon-white bark that darkens to buckskin as the tree ages.

One of the most interesting and eye-catching characteristics of the river birch is its bark. The young tree has a reddish brown bark, but as the tree matures, it begins to peel and exposes the rich inner bark with colors of buckskin to cinnamon-brown. River birches are very showy during the fall and winter. These trees at maturity can reach 30 to 35 ft. high, with a rounded crown. The fall leaves are a rich yellow. The male tree produces slender, dark-brown catkins that add to its ornamental value. The degree of exfoliating bark varies, so purchase trees that have already started to exhibit showy bark. The river birch is not bothered by bronze birch borers, as the European white birch is.

Bloom Period and Seasonal Color
Handsome exfoliating bark with delicate foliage

Mature Height × Spread
25 to 35 ft. × 20 to 30 ft.

Zones
To zone 3

Serviceberry
Amelanchier alnifolia

Among our native plants, serviceberry grows as a multi-stemmed shrub or small tree in dry conditions; it grows more rapidly and taller in moist, semishaded locations. Serviceberry is an attractive plant with fragrant white flowers and serrated foliage. The blooms appear before leaves fully emerge, but this adds to its landscape interest. Serviceberry is known to produce many sucker shoots, but can be trained into a multitrunk tree. Its sweet blue fruit is treasured by birds and humans alike. In autumn, leaves range from yellow to orange-red. The small size of Amelanchier *makes it perfect for smaller landscapes and for use in patio plantings and as a foundation plant. This tree is definitely wildlife-friendly—birds are drawn in to feast on the tasty fruit.*

Other Common Name
Amelanchier

Bloom Period and Seasonal Color
Early spring clusters of white flowers followed by edible blueberrylike fruit

Mature Height × Spread
18 to 20 ft. × 10 to 15 ft.

Zones
To zone 3

When, Where, and How to Plant
Plant in the spring or early fall. With proper moisture and misting of the foliage, serviceberry can be planted during the summer. Locate in full sun to partial shade. Trees planted in full sun have more blossoms and more intense fall colors. Soils need to be well drained; they benefit from the addition of organic matter. See the section on planting trees on pages 76 to 77. Dig the planting hole two to three times as wide as the rootball. If your soil is heavy clay, make the hole 2 in. shallower than the rootball. In sandy soils, the hole should be no deeper than the rootball. Place backfill into the planting hole and add water slowly to eliminate air pockets. Use some of the extra soil to form a dike or water basin beyond the edge of the planting hole. After planting, mulch with a few inches of shredded pine needles or other organic material.

Growing Tips
Water when the soil begins to dry at 4 to 6 in. deep. Avoid frequent, light waterings, but serviceberry needs regular watering during long, hot, dry periods. Consult pages 78 to 80 for advice on watering and fertilizing techniques. In non-lawn areas, mulch around the root zone to maintain moisture, conserve water, and prevent weeds.

Care
Relatively low maintenance, this small ornamental tree requires periodic pruning of suckers at the base if you intend to keep it as a single or multi-stemmed specimen. Don't fertilize with a high nitrogen formula, which can promote soft growth susceptible to fireblight bacteria.

Landscape Merit
Serviceberry makes an excellent choice for small spaces and is a replacement for diseased or dying aspens. The fleeting, delicate flowers are welcome in the spring, especially with a background of evergreens. The fruit are prized by wild birds.

My Personal Favorite
Amelanchier alnifolia 'Saskatoon Serviceberry' is a mountain native that tolerates dry, alkaline soils in the Rockies. It has lovely yellow-to-red fall foliage.

Thornless Honeylocust
Gleditsia triacanthos var. *inermis*

When, Where, and How to Plant
Plant spring through early fall. Small bare-root nursery stock, available through mail-order sources or locally, transplant easily. Container-grown and balled-and-burlapped trees are widely available and can be planted anytime during the growing season. Locate these trees in full sun. They grow best in well-drained soils. Amend the soil as needed before planting. Consult general planting instructions and soil preparation recommendations on pages 76 to 77.

Growing Tips
Water this tree deeply and infrequently to maintain vigor and prevent shallow root development. If the tree is planted in a lawn, supplemental fertilizer is not necessary. Refer to pages 78 to 80 for more detailed information on watering and fertilizing techniques.

Care
Keep trees healthy to avoid problems with disease and insect outbreaks. Stressed trees are prone to canker disease and will often succumb. Young trees can suffer from "southwest disease"—sunscald of the bark on the south and west sides of the trunk in winter. Protect young trees by wrapping $1^{1}/_{2}$-in. diameter white plastic swimming pool hose around the trunk. Cut the hose to a length equal to the distance between the ground and the first branch. Make a vertical cut the length of the hose, pry it open, and snap the hose around the trunk. Prune in late winter or early spring. Keep grass from growing around the base of the trunk to avoid a condition known as "lawn moweritis"—damaging the bark with a lawn mower or string trimmer.

Landscape Merit
Thornless honeylocust is a good lawn tree and can be used as a street tree. The overall growth form and dappled shade make this an architecturally pleasing tree in any season. The small leaflets generally eliminate any need to rake up leaves.

My Personal Favorites
'Moraine' is a fruitless and thornless tree with dark-green foliage that changes to golden yellow in early fall. 'Halka' has a widely oval form with strong horizontal branches capable of bearing snow loads.

One of the most adaptable trees for Rocky Mountain landscapes is the thornless honeylocust, though it is often overplanted. Noted for its wide-spreading habit and filtered shade, thornless honeylocust tree can be grown successfully in our varied soils. It tolerates alkaline soil conditions and has proven to be tolerant of deicing salt as it grows along streets and highways. Pinnately compound leaves create a feathery foliage that is bright green in the spring and summer and turns bright yellow in early fall. The light shade cast by honeylocust tree's fine-textured foliage allows shade-tolerant turf grasses to grow beneath its canopy. When the leaves drop in the fall, they are small enough to be mowed and mulched, so they don't generally require raking.

Other Common Name
Common honeylocust

Bloom Period and Seasonal Color
Greenish yellow flowers with slight fragrance; bright-yellow fall foliage

Mature Height × Spread
30 to 60 ft. × 25 to 50 ft.

Zones
To zone 4

Weeping Willow

Salix spp.

A diverse group of deciduous trees and shrubs in the Rocky Mountain region, weeping willows are extremely vigorous and grow rapidly under moist conditions. This fast-growing trait makes their wood brittle, so you must take care when locating a planting site in the landscape. Globe willow (Salix matsudana 'Umbraculifera') is common in warmer areas and is noted for its bright-green leaves and globe crown. In contrast, in areas where untimely freezes and frequent temperature fluctuations occur, the globe willow and hybrids will succumb to damage. Willows can be quite effective in moist sites, but allow plenty of room for them to grow. They are known to become messy trees with age since they drop twigs onto the lawn when the wind blows.

Bloom Period and Seasonal Color
Bright yellowish green branches and weeping characteristics, providing contrast in the fall and winter landscape

Mature Height × Spread
35 to 50 ft. × 35 to 40 ft.

Zones
To zone 3

When, Where, and How to Plant
Plant from spring through early fall, but plant bare-root nursery stock in the spring as soon as the soil can be worked. Willows are best adapted to moist sites and loamy soils; locate them in full sun to partial shade. Dig the planting hole two to three times as wide as the rootball or the spread of the roots in bare-root nursery stock. If your soil is heavy, compacted clay, dig the planting hole 2 in. shallower than the rootball. In sandy soils, dig the hole no deeper than the rootball. See page 77 for information on soil preparation. Place backfill into the planting hole, and water slowly to eliminate air pockets. Apply a 2- to 3-in. layer of organic mulch over the root zone to maintain and conserve moisture.

Growing Tips
These moisture-loving trees have extensive root systems. They require additional moisture to maintain health and vigor during extended dry periods—including late fall and winter when there is little or no natural precipitation. Fertilize in early spring; refer to page 79 for more information.

Care
Willows are afflicted by a variety of insect pests and diseases. Stressed trees are predisposed to canker diseases and may be short lived. Aphids can become a problem in late summer because their natural predators are not around. Hose them off with a strong stream of water or use a homemade soap spray. As willows mature, they shed small branches and twigs. These can become a nuisance and require frequent raking of the lawn. Prune in late winter or early spring, as needed.

Landscape Merit
Willows are recommended for areas blessed with plenty of moisture. Their rapid growth and colorful new growth add interest to the landscape.

My Personal Favorite
Globe willow (*Salix matsudana* 'Navajo' or 'Umbraculifera') is praised for its round crown and brilliant green foliage that turns golden in the fall. The distinctive golden bark makes it a handsome tree.

Western Catalpa
Catalpa speciosa

When, Where, and How to Plant
Plant container-grown catalpa trees in spring, summer, or early fall. To enjoy this tree for its unique shape and size, allow it plenty of space in your landscape and locate it in full sun. Western catalpa tree tolerates both wet and dry alkaline soil conditions. Dig the planting hole plenty wide to encourage good root growth during early development. If your soil is heavy clay, dig the planting hole 2 in. shallower than the rootball. In sandy soils, the hole need not be any deeper than the rootball. Follow tree-planting guidelines on pages 76 to 77. Apply a mulch of coarse compost or other organic material to maintain and conserve water during establishment.

Growing Tips
Provide ample water during summer for good root establishment. Water deeply but infrequently to maintain health and vigor. For more rapid establishment, apply fertilizer in early to late spring. Consult pages 78 to 80 for advice on watering and fertilizing techniques.

Care
Western catalpa tree is well adapted throughout the region except where summers are cool. It seems not to be bothered by insect pests or diseases. Prune in late winter or early spring, if needed. The small branches are quite brittle and break off easily in ice and snow storms or during high winds. If a heavy, wet snow threatens, take time to go outdoors and carefully knock the snow off the dropping branches—do not push downward; this causes more breakage. Instead, gently push the branches up to remove heavy snow loads. Avoid planting near sidewalks and driveways since the seedpods can accumulate, and if crushed, they stain concrete surfaces.

Landscape Merit
Western catalpa is a wonderful tree with showy white flower clusters at the onset of hot weather. The tall, narrow growth pattern adds interest to the fall and winter landscape.

My Personal Favorites
The availability of western catalpa tree may be somewhat limited, so check with your local garden retailer early in the season.

One of the most dramatic, large shade trees for the home landscape, the western catalpa grows tall with huge, light-green, heart-shaped leaves. Clusters of bell-shaped flowers in early summer fill the air with a sweet scent. During the winter, the tree's rugged silhouette reveals short, wide-angled branches that carry snow loads quite comfortably. Beanlike seedpods generally persist on the tree throughout the winter. Western catalpa tree's huge leaves and long seedpods can be a nuisance as they require frequent cleanup from patios, sidewalks, and the lawn. Despite this fault, western catalpa is one tree that should be used more frequently in a water-thrifty landscape. It withstands hot, dry conditions and will survive with deep, infrequent waterings once it becomes established.

Other Common Names
Northern catalpa, Indian cigar, Indian bean tree, hardy catalpa

Bloom Period and Seasonal Color
Large white flower clusters with huge bright lime-green leaves in early spring

Mature Height × Spread
40 to 60 ft. × 25 to 30 ft.

Zones
To zone 4

Western Hackberry
Celtis occidentalis

When it comes to survival, the western hackberry is well adapted to our climate extremes and varied soil conditions—it is found growing in clay, sandy, and rocky soils. In favorable growing conditions, hackberry grows quite tall with a large, straight trunk. In less favorable sites, the tree tends to be more open and develops an irregular growth habit with wide, spreading branches. The light-gray bark is noted for its corky knobbed texture. Drying winds don't seem to faze this tough survivor. It is a great selection for the lower elevations of the High Plains and can be grown successfully in the higher elevations of mountain communities. In late summer, hackberry produces small, dark reddish purple berries that persist for several weeks and are favored by wild birds.

Other Common Name
Common hackberry

Bloom Period and Seasonal Color
Thick, leathery leaves turn yellow to golden in the fall; bark with corky ridges provides year-round interest

Mature Height × Spread
40 to 60 ft. × 50 to 60 ft.

Zones
To zone 3

When, Where, and How to Plant
Plant hackberry trees from early spring through early fall. Small bare-root nursery stock can be easily transplanted in the spring. Container-grown and balled-and-burlapped trees can be planted throughout the growing season. Plant in full sun for best growth and development. This tree is very adaptable to our region's alkaline soil conditions. Dig the planting hole two to three times wider than the rootball. Though this tree tolerates a wide range of soils, heavy clay or extremely sandy soils benefit from a soil amendment. Follow the general instructions for soil preparation and planting trees on pages 76 to 77.

Growing Tips
Water hackberry tree deeply every two to three weeks during the growing season and periodically during a dry fall and winter. Small amounts of fertilizer can be applied in early spring if the tree is not planted in a lawn area. Trees situated in lawns generally do not need additional fertilizer because they benefit from the lawn fertilizer, but do *not* apply weed-and-feed fertilizer combinations to your lawn. Refer to page 79 for information on fertilizing trees.

Care
Once it becomes established in a few years, western hackberry is a low-maintenance tree. The light-green, compound leaves are susceptible to hackberry nipple-gall—a primarily cosmetic concern. This nuisance pest lives in a symbiosis with the tree and causes no harmful damage. Therefore, controls are not warranted. Prune hackberry tree in late winter or early spring, if needed.

Landscape Merit
Western hackberry tree is valued for High Plains landscapes because it performs so well under adverse conditions. It has the tenacity to tolerate wind and drought conditions and to withstand city pollution. And it's an excellent tree for the water-thrifty landscape.

My Personal Favorites
The common species of western hackberry tree is probably the best and most adapted choice for Rocky Mountain landscapes. A cultivar called 'Prairie Pride' has nice glossy foliage and is said to be less prone to gall problems.

White Ash

Fraxinus americana

When, Where, and How to Plant

Plant from early spring through early fall, in full sun. If planting in the summer, take care to provide adequate moisture and mulch to conserve water. Allow plenty of space to accommodate white ash's height and open, spreading branches. This tree grows best in well-drained soils. Follow the planting instructions on pages 76 to 77. Dig the planting hole two to three times as wide as the rootball. Larger, balled-and-burlapped trees should have the twine and a good part of the wire basket removed after the tree is placed in the planting hole. It is important to remove this from the upper portion of the rootball to avoid strangling the roots. Be sure the top of the rootball or container root system is planted level with the surrounding grade. If your soil is heavy clay, elevate the rootball so that its top is 2 to 3 in. above the surrounding grade.

Growing Tips

Provide regular moisture during establishment. Water deeply once a week or as the soil dries out. It is important to water in late fall and winter when there is little or no snow cover. See watering and fertilizing techniques for trees on pages 78 to 80. Apply a 2-in. layer of organic mulch around the root zone of newly planted trees to maintain uniform moisture and to conserve water.

Care

When cared for properly, the very adaptable white ash is not bothered by pests and diseases. Frost cracks can be common, but are not generally fatal. Protect young trees by wrapping 1^1/2-in.-diameter white plastic swimming pool hose around the trunk. Cut the hose to a length equal to the distance between the ground and the first branch. Make a vertical cut the length of the hose, and snap the hose around the trunk.

Landscape Merit

White ash makes an excellent shade or street tree. Its straight trunk and long-lasting purple fall color make it a prime choice.

My Personal Favorite

'Autumn Purple' has superior, long-lasting reddish purple to maroon fall color.

White ash offers one of the best examples of the way subtle autumn colors can enhance your home landscape. As fall approaches, its glossy green leaves transform from soft yellow to reddish purple and maroon. Though not as adaptable to heavy soils as green ash is, white ash can be grown on soils improved with a good soil conditioner. Its growth habit is pyramidal when young, but as the tree matures, it develops a well-rounded crown. White ash is unique in maintaining a straight trunk with even distribution of its branches. The handsome gray-brown bark has characteristic diamond furrows and forked ridges. It makes a grand specimen where it has room to grow, but this ash is also an excellent shade or street tree.

Bloom Period and Seasonal Color

Glossy green summer foliage; yellow to reddish purple and maroon in the fall

Mature Height × Spread

50 to 60 ft. × 40 to 50 ft.

Zones

To zone 3

Ground Covers *for the Rockies*

When we talk about ground covers, we refer to a broad category of plants that includes virtually anything that covers the ground quickly. A major advantage of ground covers over grass is that many are ornamental. The varied decorative qualities of ground covers provide pleasing contrasts in color and texture. They may be vines, shrubs, herbaceous perennials, roses, or even annuals that reseed themselves. These plants accomplish their ground-covering feats with specialized growth structures, including underground stolons or rhizomes that explore the soil and send up new shoots, or above-ground runners that do the same thing. Some spread by stems that creep along the ground and root, while others

Periwinkle

ramble along the ground with their long stems. Field bindweed, a creeping perennial and noxious weed throughout the region, is considered a ground cover, but it is extremely invasive and disliked by gardeners and farmers alike.

Location, Location, Location

Like lawn grasses, ground covers are grown both for their ability to hold the soil and for their inviting foliage. After all, who will object to a carpet of blue flowers, such as Turkish veronica? The most desirable attributes of ground cover are that it is low growing, perennial, evergreen, and it requires minimal maintenance. Your mission: Find the right ground cover for your spot. Observe ground covers that are used in your area, in both private and public gardens. When you see ones you like, note their name, height, color, texture, and overall ornamental value. Then consider how much ground cover you need and where it can be obtained.

Most of the herbaceous types are easy to propagate by dividing in the spring. Many are available from local garden retailers or through mail-order nurseries. Choose the appropriate ground cover for your exposure and growing conditions. Plants selected specifically for a site have the best chance of surviving—being healthy, growing vigorously, and creating a dense, weed-free ground cover.

Good News for Gardeners

Ground covers reduce lawn maintenance on steep slopes, where mowing is an arduous chore. But ground covers do require maintenance. They need some attention and an occasional grooming to keep them looking good. The ground cover junipers, *Juniperus horizontalis* and *J. procumbens*, are quite pleasing when planted on a slope or in the area between the street and sidewalk—that hard-to-grow place we call the "hellstrip." In modestly prepared soils, they adapt and thrive without a lot of watering. Ground covers perform other functions, too. Their foliage disguises the ripening foliage of spring-flowering bulbs. Once established, they grow so densely that they are weed-free, which is good news for the lazy gardener. Evergreen ground covers provide year-round greenery even in the dreariest months of winter. With a few exceptions, the procedures for planting ground covers are essentially the same as those for installing a lawn. Ground covers are meant to be permanent plantings that last many years, so soil drainage, exposure, irrigation, and soil preparation are some of the secrets to growing them successfully. Once a ground cover becomes established, it becomes more difficult, and often costly, to alter.

The Lesson to Share

If you have the opportunity before planting a ground cover, prepare the soil in the entire planting area. Remove rubble and trash, thoroughly loosen the soil, and work organic matter deeply into the planting site. Incorporate 25 to 30 percent by volume of compost or aged manure into your native soil; dig or rototill to a depth of 10 in. or more. As monumental as this task may seem, it needn't be. In my landscape, I improved the soil in steps—doing a section of the property at a time. Such soil preparation ensures healthy and long-lived plants. If you are unable to prepare the planting site in this manner, then digging the planting holes and amending the backfill soil do nicely, too. There is one lesson I want to share with you from the school of hard, compacted soils and bent spading forks: Don't skimp in the beginning of the planting process or you will be haunted by sick plants.

Control The Weed Invasion

No matter what kind of ground cover you plant, there will be some competition from weeds—especially those perennial pests. Mulching with shredded bark, pole peelings, and other materials help control most weeds, but hand-to-hand combat is needed to remove some of the more persistent weeds. We know it isn't the easy way—but it's the cowboy way! You can also apply selective pre-emergent herbicides that

prevent the weeds from growing. This must be timed appropriately for the best results. Read and follow label directions carefully. The plants selected for this chapter are easy to grow and, once established, should require little care.

Spotted Deadnettle

Carpet Bugleweed

Ajuga reptans

A great ground cover, bugleweed features glossy, deeply veined leaves that spread quickly to form a rippled carpet of green, purple, bronze, or variegated foliage. It can be grown in sun or shade and adapts well to poor soils. Spikes of blue-purple flowers appear above the low-growing leaves from mid-April to June. The leaves, however, are what make this a desirable ground cover year-round. Use bugleweed in shady areas along sidewalks and driveways, underneath shrubs or vines, and beneath hedges. It works in a shady perennial garden—but it can be somewhat aggressive, so you may have to thin it out periodically. Carpet bugleweed spreads rapidly by runners that root in moist soil, making it appropriate for areas where you desire a vigorous, weed-free ground cover.

Other Common Names
Ajuga, bugleweed

Bloom Period and Seasonal Color
Late spring blooms in blue-purple, pink, or white; colorful foliage year-round

Mature Height × Spread
3 to 8 in. × 12 to 14 in.

Zones
To zone 4

When, Where, and How to Plant

Plant from spring to early fall, but for good root establishment by summer, plant bare-root bugleweed in early spring as soon as the soil can be worked. Ajuga prefers shade to partial shade, but some cultivars grow in partial sun. Bugleweed suffers from leaf scorch in hot locations and damage from winter wind. The soil should be moderately rich in organic matter and hold moisture. A quality soil amendment such as compost or sphagnum peat moss helps retain moisture in sandy soils and improves drainage and porosity in clay. Information on soil preparation is on page 107. Dig the planting hole twice as wide as the rootball, and set the plant at the same level it was growing. Space plants 10 to 12 in. apart.

Growing Tips

Water after planting and during hot, dry periods until the plants are well established. If planted in full sun, bugleweed needs additional water to avoid severe wilt and scorch. Water deeply every week during hot, dry periods. Ajuga tolerates dry shade if the soil has been properly prepared. Mulch young transplants to conserve moisture. In the spring, fertilize with all-purpose 5-10-5 to encourage fresh, new foliage.

Care

Once established, bugleweed is generally low maintenance. The plants can be cleaned up by a light shearing after flowering. Propagate bugleweed by taking divisions—lift the clumps and split them apart. Leafy rosettes that form along the creeping stems called stolons can also be separated and planted. Slugs may devour the foliage but can be controlled by trapping. See remedies on pages 257 to 258.

Companion Planting and Design

Its foliage and low-growth habit make bugleweed useful as a contrast to shrubs, evergreens, hostas, and daylilies. An effective pathway border, it also works well along the edges of a patio, sidewalk, or driveway.

My Personal Favorites

'Bronze Beauty' has glossy bronzy-purple leaves and purplish flowers. 'Rosea' is attractive with green foliage and spikes of pink flowers on 8-in. stems.

Creeping Oregon Grape Holly

Mahonia repens

When, Where, and How to Plant

Plant creeping Oregon grape holly in spring through early summer to allow for strong and healthy establishment. Mahonia grows shorter and fuller in partial sun and prefers some shade during the summer to prevent severe leaf scorch. It is easily established in well-drained soils. An acidic soil is preferred, but creeping Oregon grape holly tolerates most Rocky Mountain soils with some extra soil preparation. Amend with compost or sphagnum peat moss to buffer alkaline conditions and to improve drainage. Soil that is heavy clay or extremely sandy should be conditioned with organic matter to improve drainage or moisture retention. Space the plants 15 to 18 in. apart, depending on how quickly you want a full ground-cover effect. Sprinkle an organic-based granular 5-10-5 fertilizer around the plants, and water thoroughly.

Growing Tips

Water new transplants thoroughly, and mulch with pine needles or compost. Water the plants regularly (every seven to ten days) if rainfall is unreliable or during drought to ensure healthy establishment. Creeping Oregon grape holly can endure periods of drought if you water well every two weeks or so. You may fertilize in the spring; use a slow-release 5-10-5 or 10-10-10 fertilizer around the plants, and water thoroughly.

Care

Once established, creeping mahonia makes a durable, long-lasting ground cover. Pruning is generally not needed; this plant keeps its tidy appearance year after year. Until established, young plants may need some protection from winter sun and drying winds. Occasionally, leaf scorch or leaf rust will strike, or aphids and scale appear. If there is little or no precipitation in the winter, water monthly when temperatures are above freezing.

Companion Planting and Design

Creeping Oregon grape holly is effective in woodland settings, in shrub borders, and for naturalizing beneath trees and shrubs. The spiny foliage provides some traffic control. This plant tolerates dry shade.

My Personal Favorite

Creeping mahonia is the most common and most generally available. Its glossy green hollylike foliage in the summer turns reddish purple in autumn.

One doesn't have to travel far up the mountains to find this handsome ground cover thriving beneath the shade of conifers. Its distinctive foliage resembles true holly or Ilex. Not a true holly, creeping Oregon grape holly is a Mahonia *with characteristic holly-shaped leaves. It thrives in dry shade and moist sites, making it adaptable to a wide range of conditions. As evergreens mature in the landscape and naturally lose their lower branches, consider using creeping Oregon grape holly as a living ground cover. It has attractive reddish purple foliage in the fall and winter. Each spring the plant comes alive with clusters of bright-yellow flowers that are followed by clusters of purple berries. Creeping Oregon grape holly is a good plant for the wildlife-friendly landscape.*

Other Common Name
Creeping mahonia

Bloom Period and Seasonal Color
Spring clusters of yellow blooms followed by purple berries for wildlife

Mature Height × Spread
8 to 24 in. × 18 to 24 in.

Zones
To zone 2

Creeping Phlox
Phlox subulata

One of the highlights in my spring garden is the bright splash of color from creeping phlox spilling over the rock walls and clinging to the dry slopes. It is one of the earliest and showiest flower displays in Rocky Mountain gardens. This semievergreen ground cover features mats of prickly foliage and is known for its brilliant color as it tumbles over rock walls and boulders or creeps along borders. Creeping phlox makes an excellent accent plant in the rock garden and mingles naturally with other perennial flowers. The foliage hugs the ground and provides a dark-green ground cover year-round. Once the plants become established, creeping phlox can withstand shaded dry areas. It is particularly effective planted around rocks or growing over rock walls.

Bloom Period and Seasonal Color
April through June blooms in pink, rose, blue, magenta, or white; year-round evergreen foliage

Mature Height × Spread
4 to 6 in. × 12 to 36 in.

Zones
To zone 3

When, Where, and How to Plant
Plant container-grown creeping phlox in the spring or early fall. Bare-root plants should be planted in early spring. Choose a location that receives full sun. Creeping phlox grows in partial shade, but its flowers are not as abundant. Add a quality soil amendment such as compost or sphagnum peat moss to retain moisture in sandy soils and to improve drainage and porosity in clay soils. Follow the guidelines on page 107. Dig planting holes twice as wide as the rootball, and position the plant at the soil level it was in the container. Space the plants 12 to 15 in. apart. Water well, and apply a mulch of compost, shredded cedar, or other organic material.

Growing Tips
Water new plants weekly to get them off to a healthy and vigorous start. Once creeping phlox is established, it withstands drought and heat. Just water deeply once a week during summer to maintain vigorous growth. A light mulch of compost or other organic material retains soil moisture and reduces weeds. If creeping phlox is planted in a humus-enriched soil, additional fertilizer is usually not needed; otherwise, fertilize with a slow-release granular 5-10-5 product in the spring.

Care
Prune or shear back after blooming to encourage new, fresh growth. As plants get older, they can die out in the center. Lift and divide the plants in early spring or early autumn. Keep new divisions from the outside of the clump. Replant them in soil that has been amended with compost, and water well. Newly set divisions grow quickly. Pests and diseases do not bother this plant.

Companion Planting and Design
Plant creeping phlox in rock walls, on terraces, on slopes, and as edging. It combines well with *Aurinia saxatilis*, basket of gold, and spring-flowering bulbs.

My Personal Favorite
A newer variety with beautiful two-tone flowers is 'Candy Stripes'. Eye-catching pink and white flowers blanket mounds of bright-green foliage in early spring.

Creeping Veronica
Veronica species

When, Where, and How to Plant

Plant creeping veronica in early spring through early summer. Locate it in full to partial sun, though it can tolerate some light afternoon shade. Soil should be well drained; add compost to clay soils to improve drainage and to permit good aeration. Sandy soils need organic matter to retain moisture and improve nutrient-holding capacity. Before planting, incorporate organic matter to a depth of 10 in. or more. Mix in a slow-acting fertilizer during soil preparation to sustain the plants throughout the growing season. Dig the planting holes as deep as and slightly wider than the rootballs so that the plants are set level with the surrounding soil. Space them 12 to 15 in. apart. Backfill with prepared soil, lightly firm the soil around the plants, and water well.

Growing Tips

Water new transplants regularly during the first growing season—weekly, if rain is sparse and especially during droughts. Apply a 2-in. layer of organic mulch to maintain soil moisture and to discourage the germination of annual weeds. Once established, these plants need to be watered deeply just once a week. Applying 5-10-5 slow-release fertilizer in the spring maintains plants throughout the summer.

Care

Established creeping veronica is easy to maintain. It has no significant pest or disease problems, but overwatering causes crown rot. If the plants grow out of bounds, snip back the stems. Shear the plants after bloom to reinvigorate them and to stimulate more blooms.

Companion Planting and Design

Creeping veronica makes an effective edging along sidewalks and driveways, in rock gardens, on rocky slopes, and between steppingstones. It works well as underplantings with botanical tulips and daffodils. Combine with our native yellow stemless sundrop (*Oenothera brachycarpa*). Let its attractive foliage and bright blooms spill over retaining walls.

My Personal Favorites

'Waterperry Blue' (*V. liwanensis*) veronica has beautiful sky-blue flowers and foliage that turns reddish purple in the winter. Turkish veronica has wonderful cobalt-blue flowers with glossy green foliage.

A versatile ground cover, creeping veronica works well in rock gardens, as edging, between steppingstones, and in retaining walls. Some varieties, such as 'Waterperry Blue' (Veronica repens, V. pectinata, or V. prostrata), not only have lovely sky-blue flowers in the summer, but in the autumn and winter, feature attractive reddish purple foliage for winter accents. Creeping veronica's glossy green leaves and stems spread quickly to form a rippled carpet of flowers and foliage over the surface of the soil. The mass of flowers in the spring creates a drift of color that complements spring-blooming bulbs and shrubs. Plant creeping veronica beneath shrub borders as a living mulch, along driveways and sidewalks, in "hell strips," and on slopes. They perform best in well-drained soils from the mountain regions to the High Plains.

Bloom Period and Seasonal Color
April through June blooms in blue, purplish blue, pink, rose, or white; handsome winter foliage

Mature Height × Spread
1 to 6 in. × 12 to 18 in.

Zones
To zone 3

False Rockcress
Aubrieta deltoidea

One of my favorite ground covers is false rockcress. As the weather warms in the spring, this plant's loads of bright blooms always amaze me. It has performed admirably in my landscape over the years, and its low evergreen mats of hairy green foliage add year-round interest. Be sure to plant in well-drained sites. The evergreen, grayish silver, hairy foliage of Aubrieta makes an attractive ground cover for a front border, in a rock garden, or as an underplanting for spring-flowering bulbs. In the spring, small pink to purple blooms cover the plant. Its spreading, mat-forming habit produces a nice compact cover. 'Purple Gem' is a common variety found in many gardens, with small purple flowers held above a dense mat of grayish green leaves.

Bloom Period and Seasonal Color
Spring blooms in rose, purple, bluish purple, or white

Mature Height × Spread
4 to 6 in. × 12 to 18 in.

Zones
To zone 2

When, Where, and How to Plant
Transplant false rockcress from spring through early fall. If you purchase bare-root perennials from a mail-order catalog, plant them in the spring as soon as the soil can be worked. This allows for good root growth before the onset of summer heat. Choose a location with full to partial sun and soil that is well drained. Loosen the soil in the area that is to be planted, then dig the planting hole twice as wide as the container. Add a quality soil amendment such as compost or sphagnum peat moss to retain moisture in sandy soils and to improve drainage and porosity in clay soils. Follow the guidelines for soil preparation on page 107. Set transplants at the same level they were growing in the container. Firm the soil around the roots, and water well. Mulch with compost or shredded cedar. Space plants 12 to 15 in. apart.

Growing Tips
After transplanting, water thoroughly to settle the plants in and allow them to get established. As the soil begins to dry out, water sparingly; check every five to seven days or as needed. If you wish, in early spring apply a low-nitrogen, organic fertilizer such as 5-10-5. Scatter the fertilizer around the plants, and carefully scratch it into the soil. Water well.

Care
A widely adaptable plant, false rockcress needs minimal care. It does best in well-drained sites, so be careful about watering lest the plant succumb to crown rot. After flowering is complete, deadhead false rockcress to keep them tidy and their growth compact. Plants can be divided in the spring and transplanted.

Companion Planting and Design
Plant false rockcress in rock walls for a nice effect. Use it in front of perennial borders and in combination with spring-flowering bulbs.

My Personal Favorites
'Borsch's White' produces white flowers. 'Variegata' has blue flowers contrasted by foliage whose margins are silvery white. 'Gloriosa' has large, soft rose blossoms.

When, Where, and How to Plant

The best time to plant is in early spring as soon as the soil can be worked. This gives the plants a long growing season to establish a vigorous root system. Choose a location with full to partial sun. Loosen the soil. Add a quality soil amendment such as compost or sphagnum peat moss to retain moisture in sandy soils and to improve drainage and porosity in clay soils. Prepare the soil with moisture-retentive compost (30 to 40 percent by volume), and mix uniformly. Dig a hole wide enough to hold the root system. Position the plants at the same depth they were growing. Firm the soil around the roots, and water well. Space plants 12 to 15 in. apart.

Growing Tips

Once transplanted, water hardy iceplant weekly to help it get established. Allow the soil to dry out slightly between waterings. Unlike many other plants in Rocky Mountain landscapes that may benefit from winter watering, it is best to leave hardy iceplant alone. A light application of granular organic-based 5-10-5 fertilizer in spring provides nutrients throughout the growing season.

Care

In highly exposed sites, iceplant can suffer injury from winter desiccation. Provide additional protection by covering the plants with evergreen boughs. If plants become overcrowded, simply dig and divide clumps and transplant sections to other areas. Iceplant is sensitive to heavy snowpack or excessive winter moisture. Overwatering causes crown rot. Iceplant's succulent foliage is rarely browsed by deer. The plant is easy to propagate by taking stem cuttings and rooting them in the soil.

Companion Planting and Design

Hardy iceplant is very effective in rock gardens, planted as edging, and on rocky slopes at higher elevations. Plant it on slopes to reduce erosion and to fill in around other drought-tolerant plants.

My Personal Favorite

Delosperma nubigenum, yellow iceplant, forms a neatly packed mat of succulent lime-green foliage, turning purplish in fall and winter. Yellow blooms appear in early to midsummer.

Though plants have been introduced to the Rocky Mountains for years, the appearance of a ground cover with succulent, glossy green leaves, iridescent flowers, and hardiness is welcome. Durable purple iceplant (Delosperma cooperi) is widely adaptable to our soils. A bright-green species covered with bright-yellow, daisylike flowers, Delosperma nubigenum is perhaps my favorite as its foliage turns reddish purple in winter, adding a touch of contrast to the winter garden. Truly drought tolerant, this ground cover does not tolerate heavy snow cover and winter moisture. Use iceplant along pathways and sidewalks, and in borders, rock gardens, and mass plantings. Combine it with other perennials that have silver or gray foliage. Iceplant is a truly well-adapted, useful plant for our Rocky Mountain landscapes.

Bloom Period and Seasonal Color

May through August blooms in yellow, purple, violet, or white

Mature Height × Spread

2 to 4 in. × 24 to 30 in.

Zones

To zone 4

Heart-leafed Bergenia

Bergenia cordifolia

The heart-leafed bergenias have both handsome foliage and flowers. Large, glossy green foliage resembles cabbage leaves and adds a nice contrast in the shady perennial garden. Later in autumn, the foliage turns burgundy to provide lovely fall coloration. Bergenias grow with thick, creeping rhizomes that spread to produce solid clumps, but the plants are not invasive. Use them under shrubs or trees, along pathways, or in mass plantings. The leaves are bold, glossy, dark green and shaped like paddles. Strong stems bear clusters of waxy flowers in early spring. This ground cover tolerates alkaline soils that have been loosened deeply. Heart-leafed bergenia grows in dry shade where tree or shrub roots grow near the surface. Use this ground cover beneath some of the maturing deciduous trees.

Bloom Period and Seasonal Color
May through June reddish pink blooms

Mature Height × Spread
12 to 15 in. × 12 to 18 in.

Zones
To zone 3

When, Where, and How to Plant

Plant bergenia from spring through fall. If you purchase plants through mail-order catalogs, plant them in the spring as soon as the soil can be worked. This allows bergenia plenty of time to become established before the heat of summer. It prefers partial shade but grows in full shade—and in part sun if the soil is deeply prepared and well drained. The foliage turns burgundy in autumn if grown in a sunny exposure. Add a quality soil amendment such as compost or sphagnum peat moss to retain moisture in sandy soils and to improve drainage and porosity in clay soils. Follow soil preparation guidelines on page 107. Dig the planting hole twice as wide as the container. Position the plant at the same depth it was growing. Space plants 18 to 24 in. apart.

Growing Tips

Water well after transplanting, and mulch with compost or other suitable organic material. The first growing season is critical in getting bergenia established, so keep the weeds out by hand pulling or light cultivation. Mulches help considerably to keep weeds to a minimum. Provide water as needed during dry periods; water deeply every seven to ten days. Overfertilizing results in soft, weak growth and fewer flowers. Apply a slow-release 5-10-5 granular fertilizer around the plants in the spring, and water well.

Care

Bergenia is not invasive and thrives with minimal care. If the plants become too thick and crowded within several years, lift and divide the clumps. Pests and diseases generally do not bother bergenia.

Companion Planting and Design

Use as a border plant near shrubs and hedges, woodland gardens, and other partial shade situations. Some good companion plants include daylilies, Jacob's ladder, ferns, and Siberian irises.

I Also Recommend

Bergenia cordifolia 'Purpurea' has large cabbagelike reddish leaves that become purple in winter. Reddish flower stalks support purple-red blossoms. 'Perfecta' grows taller than the species and has purplish foliage with rosy-red flowers.

Kinnikinick
Arctostaphylos uva-ursi

When, Where, and How to Plant

Plant kinnikinick in the spring as soon as the soil can be worked. Kinnikinick is quite adaptable to sun or shade. It prefers an acidic soil, but tolerates most soils if some extra preparation is done. Amend alkaline soils with compost or sphagnum peat moss to buffer their alkaline conditions and to improve drainage. Prepare the soil with moisture-retentive compost (30 to 40 percent by volume), and mix uniformly with the native soil. Space the plants from 1 to 2 ft. apart, depending on how quickly you want a full ground cover effect; my preference is to set transplants 12 to 15 in. apart. See page 107 for more soil preparation and planting tips.

Growing Tips

Water kinnikinick thoroughly, and mulch new transplants with pine needles or compost. Water weekly during the first season for good establishment. Kinnikinick can endure drought if you provide a good watering every two weeks or so. It requires little or no fertilizer. If fertilizer is needed, apply a light sprinkling of an all-purpose slow-release 5-10-5 granular fertilizer, and water thoroughly.

Care

Young plants may need some protection from winter sun and drying winds until they become established. Once established, though, kinnikinick is a durable and long-lasting ground cover. Pruning is generally not needed. Kinnikinick keeps its tidy appearance year after year. Pests and diseases do not bother it.

Companion Planting and Design

The year-round glossy evergreen foliage of kinnikinick is one of its best features. Let this ground cover naturalize in rock gardens, on slopes, or underneath evergreen trees. Its tolerance to shade makes it very adapted to woodland gardens.

My Personal Favorites

The native kinnikinick is the most adapted, but look at some cultivars, including 'Point Reyes', which has more rounded leaves and pink flowers.

With its handsome glossy, bright-green foliage, kinnikinick is one of my favorite low-growing native evergreen ground covers. It is an excellent choice to plant beneath pines and spruce; its broadleaf evergreen leaves contrast nicely with the evergreen needles. Light pink flowers appear in the spring and are followed by small, red berries in the fall. Kinnikinick makes a nice accent plant in the rock garden. It is a great choice for planting in a larger area and is drought enduring once the plants become established. The glossy green foliage turns bronze to reddish in the fall and winter. Indians used this plant for medicine, tea, and as a type of tobacco and to cure skin problems. Early settlers used the berries for cider and jelly.

Other Common Name
Bearberry

Bloom Period and Seasonal Color
Spring to late-spring blooms in white and pink

Mature Height × Spread
6 to 12 in. × 18 to 24 in.

Zones
To zone 2

Lily-of-the-Valley

Convallaria majalis

The sweet fragrance emitting from the nodding, bell-shaped flowers of lily-of-the-valley is unforgettable. This plant grows into an excellent ground cover in well-drained soil and partial shade. As the spring bulbs are blooming, the sturdy green shoots of lily-of-the-valley are pushing their way up through the soil. By mid-May, dainty stalks arch over the foliage and bear racemes of white buds. As the buds open, lily-of-the-valley releases a delicious fragrance, which some gardeners claim is the essence of spring. This plant is an easy-to-grow ground cover and spreads quickly by underground stems or rhizomes. At times, lily-of-the-valley grows so strongly that it is considered invasive. Put it to work beneath shrubs to create a living mulch, or keep it within bounds with metal edging.

Bloom Period and Seasonal Color
Pure white or pink spring blooms

Mature Height × Spread
6 to 12 in. × 18 to 24 in.

Zones
To zone 3

When, Where, and How to Plant

Plant divisions of lily-of-the-valley rhizomes or underground stems with two to three pips (the "eyes" or shoots) in early spring. Lily-of-the-valley likes humus-rich soils and moist conditions in full to partial shade. Prepare soil with a moisture-retentive compost; be sure the soil is well drained. This rapidly spreading ground cover does best in shaded areas that do not receive foot traffic. Space plants 8 to 12 in. apart. Set them at the same level they were growing in their original containers. Gently firm the soil around the roots, and water well. Divisions can be set 6 in. apart 1 to $1^{1}/_{2}$ in. deep.

Growing Tips

After transplanting, water lily-of-the-valley thoroughly to settle it and to ensure healthy establishment. Water during hot, dry periods to prolong the life of the leaves. Mulch with compost to maintain uniform moisture and to keep the soil cool. A light application of organic-based 5-10-5 granular fertilizer in the spring helps maintain the plants through the summer. In autumn, top-dress the plants with well-aged manure or compost.

Care

Once established, lily-of-the-valley is relatively carefree. In late summer, the foliage begins to look ratty, especially if the plants are grown in the sun. Pull out mature foliage to keep the area tidy. If you plant lily-of-the-valley beneath trees, the plants benefit from additional water and occasional fertilizer (5-10-5). Slugs often riddle the foliage. See remedies on pages 257 to 258.

Companion Planting and Design

Plant lily-of-the-valley on the north side of the house and in woodland settings and shade gardens; use it to cover north- or northeast-facing slopes to prevent erosion. Combine with hostas, ferns, and astilbes. Lily-of-the-valley makes a good cut flower; pick a bouquet of stems, and enjoy these cute, fragrant blossoms indoors. **Caution:** All parts are toxic, including the red-orange berries.

My Personal Favorites

The old-fashioned white lily-of-the-valley is the hardiest to grow and combines well with *C. majalis* var. *rosea*, which produces soft, lavender-pink flowers.

Periwinkle
Vinca minor

When, Where, and How to Plant

Plant rooted cuttings or divisions in early spring through early summer. Transplant container-grown plants anytime. Vinca grows in partial sun to shade. When grown in shady locations, vinca has darker green foliage and a slower growth rate. Once established, it tolerates dry shade. Vinca prefers a well-drained soil, but will grow in any type of soil enriched with compost. Loosen the soil to a depth of 8 in. or more, and mix in a granular slow-release fertilizer to maintain the plants through the growing season. Dig planting holes twice as wide as the original root system, and set the plants so that they are growing at soil level. Backfill with prepared soil, lightly firm the soil around them, and water well. Space plants 12 in. apart. Mulch between new transplants to maintain moisture and to help control germination of annual weeds.

Growing Tips

Water new transplants well during the first growing season; as the soil dries out to a depth of 2 in., water deeply. Once vinca is established, water every five to seven days; pay particular attention to this plant during dry spells. Water monthly during drought periods in the fall and winter. Apply a slow-release granular 5-10-5 fertilizer in the spring.

Care

Once established, vinca is amazingly drought enduring. It has no significant pest or disease problems. Vinca is easy to maintain, requiring only an occasional trimming to keep it in bounds. To increase plant density, prune stems back to 4 in. in early spring. If slugs devour the foliage, consult the controls on pages 257 to 258.

Companion Planting and Design

Use vinca in spring-flowering bulb beds to help camouflage the ripening foliage after bulbs bloom. Plant it as a living mulch beneath the canopy of deciduous trees and large shrubs. Its attractive foliage and trailing growth habit add accent in container gardens and hanging baskets.

My Personal Favorite

'Bowles' is a variety with lovely lavender-blue flowers.

Periwinkle is perhaps one of the most reliable and adaptable ground covers. Its small, glossy, dark-green foliage provides a distinctive refinement beneath the filtered shade of large shade trees. Graceful arching low stems that often root along the way sets vinca apart from other coarser plants. In spring, delicate, lovely five-petaled blue flowers lighten the garden. Some varieties produce rose, red, or white blooms. It is not uncommon for a single plant to send out multiple stems in its haste to grow. This is desirable, especially when you want to cover an area quickly. Vinca's shallow roots make this plant easy to pull up when it gets overcrowded. Variegated leaf forms are available—now foliage color can be added to periwinkle's list of virtues.

Other Common Name
Vinca

Bloom Period and Seasonal Color
April into May blooms in purplish blue, white, or red; some varieties have variegated foliage

Mature Height × Spread
6 to 8 in. × 24 to 36 in.

Zones
To zone 4

Pussytoes
Antennaria parvifolia

Pussytoes is one of the native plants in our landscape, found growing contentedly in grassy stretches with cactuses, buffalograss, and blue grama. It is one of the few broadleaf ground covers that remains evergreen year-round. The silvery-gray leaves are made up of many tight small rosettes that grow into a handsome mat. The furry clusters of flowers are borne on shortened stalks and resemble the toes of a cat. This is a great ground cover for low-water zones because it reliably forms an attractive drought-tolerant, ornamental carpet. Use it along pathways, sidewalks, and driveways or tuck it among rocks in gritty soil. It is very appealing when planted between paving stones in a garden pathway. Pussytoes is particularly useful to control erosion on rocky slopes.

Bloom Period and Seasonal Color
Early summer small blooms in white, buff, or pink

Mature Height × Spread
2 to 6 in. × 18 to 24 in.

Zones
To zone 2

When, Where, and How to Plant
Plant container-grown plants from spring through early summer. Because pussytoes self-sows readily, you may end up with many seedlings. Those seedlings can be transplanted in the spring as soon as the soil can be worked. Choose a sunny site, and be sure the soil is well drained. Loosen the soil in the area to be planted. Follow the soil preparation tips on page 107. Set the plant in the hole at the same level it was growing in its container. Space pussytoes 10 to 12 in. apart.

Growing Tips
After transplanting, water pussytoes well and lightly mulch with pine needles or coarse compost. During extended dry periods or drought, a light watering ($3/4$ in. to 1 in.) every few weeks is beneficial. As a native, pussytoes can survive on natural precipitation once the plant becomes established in your garden. Pussytoes do not need additional fertilizer.

Care
Antennaria species are easy to grow and require very little care. During long, hot spells, pussytoes may go dormant after it flowers. This can be prevented by supplying a little extra water and picking off ("deadheading") the spent flowers. Pussytoes are not bothered by pests or diseases.

Companion Planting and Design
Use pussytoes as a border planting or a mass planting, or plant it among rocks and slight slopes. It works nicely when planted between flagstones or other paving stones. Pussytoes combines well with other ground covers including 'Dragon's Blood' sedum and hen and chicks (*Sempervivum*). The blooms make nice cut flowers for drying.

I Also Recommend
Antennaria dioica 'Rubra' has furry, pink flowers borne above a low carpet of small, woolly, silvery spoonlike foliage. *Antennaria plantaginifolia* has green leaves that are silvery underneath and has a growth habit that forms neat, small turflike patches. *Antennaria rosea* (4 to 12 in.) has flowers that are predominantly pink.

Snow-in-Summer

Cerastium tomentosum

When, Where, and How to Plant

Plant new transplants in spring to early fall. Take divisions from older clumps in early spring, and transplant them to new locations or use them to fill in spots. Snow-in-summer reseeds; young seedlings can be transplanted in early spring or fall. Locate the plant in full sun with plenty of space to spread. Loosen the soil in the area to be planted; snow-in-summer requires good drainage and aeration. Add a quality soil amendment such as compost or sphagnum peat moss to retain moisture in sandy soils and to improve drainage and porosity in clay soils. Follow soil preparation guidelines on page 107. Dig the planting hole twice as wide as the rootball. Space plants 18 in. apart. Water well, and mulch with suitable organic material.

Growing Tips

Once established, *Cerastium* tolerates drought. Water as the soil becomes dry to maintain vigor, but allow the soil to dry out slightly between waterings. Avoid using high-nitrogen plant food, which encourages weak, spindly growth and fewer flowers. Apply a slow-release 5-10-5 granular fertilizer in early spring, and water well.

Care

Easy to grow, snow-in-summer spreads rapidly. Shear off the faded flowers to keep the plant growing with a neat mat of fuzzy silvery-white leaves for the rest of the growing season. Overwatering results in leggy growth and possible crown rot. Slugs occasionally hide beneath the thick foliage but can be controlled. See remedies on pages 257 to 258.

Companion Planting and Design

Snow-in-summer can become aggressive. It is an effective border plant along sidewalks, pathways, and driveways or used as an accent in rock gardens. It is effective on rocky slopes and provides good erosion control. Choose less-invasive cultivars for the rock garden or perennial border.

I Also Recommend

The compact *Cerastium biebersteinii* (4 in. tall) produces larger flowers arranged in cymes of three to five. *C. tomentosum* var. *columnae* has a more refined growth habit for accent planting; it forms 4-in. mounds of silver-white foliage.

The silvery carpet of snow-in-summer's foliage provides an attractive year-round mat. From late spring to early summer, this ground cover is covered with an abundance of snowy-white flowers. It has become a favorite in my garden, merely because it has done so well in dry, infertile soils and taken the heat. After snow-in-summer has finished flowering, I've been known to take the lawnmower to it to shear it back and keep it neat. This has helped to rejuvenate the plants so that they produced fresh foliage and a denser mat growth. If you have a difficult site in your landscape, snow-in-summer is a good candidate and works well in larger areas. It makes a good accent plant in rock gardens.

Bloom Period and Seasonal Color
Spring mass of white, daisylike blooms; year-round silvery-gray foliage

Mature Height × Spread
6 to 12 in. × 24 to 36 in.

Zones
To zone 2

Spotted Dead Nettle
Lamium maculatum

The effect of dappled light created by spotted dead nettle's mat of variegated foliage enhances the shade garden with a sense of movement. Leaves marked with a stroke, splash, or almost complete coat of silver lighten dim parts of the garden. In partial shade and moist, well-drained soils, spotted dead nettle grows quickly and fills in open spots. It readily roots at its leaf joints to form a tidy ground cover. The short spikes of hooded flowers, although not the main attraction, also create an attractive display. Blooms appear from May to early June on short spikes and are typically pink, but some cultivars feature rose-pink or white flowers. Use spotted dead nettle in containers and hanging baskets to accent annual flowers.

Other Common Name
Dead nettle

Bloom Period and Seasonal Color
May through June blooms in pink, rose pink, or white

Mature Height × Spread
6 to 8 in. × 12 to 36 in.

Zones
To zone 3

When, Where, and How to Plant
Plant spotted dead nettle from spring through fall. Keep the soil moist if plants are set out in summer. Spotted dead nettle does best in moist, well-drained soils. Partial shade to full shade suit this ground cover just fine. It can become straggly in dry shade where tree roots compete for moisture. Consult page 107 for details on preparing the soil for ground covers. Plant spotted dead nettle 12 to 18 in. apart. Dig the planting holes large enough to accommodate the root system. Position the plant so that the soil level is the same as it was in the container. Gently firm the soil around the roots, and water well.

Growing Tips
Water weekly early in the season to help the plants establish. Provide regular watering during dry spells and especially under trees where there is competition from the tree roots. Mulch to conserve moisture. A light application of a granular slow-release 5-10-5 fertilizer can be applied in the spring; water well. In average soils and shade gardens, *Lamium* usually does not need more fertilizer than that applied in the spring.

Care
Shear back after flowering to keep the plants compact and neat. They can be dug and divided in the spring or early summer. Lift sections, and separate plants. Replant, and keep the new divisions moist until they become established. Dead nettle suffers from no serious pests or diseases.

Companion Planting and Design
Use spotted dead nettle as a ground cover under trees and shrubs, on shaded slopes, and in shade gardens and as a cover for bulb gardens. It combines well with shade-loving *Astilbe* and the coarse heart-shaped leaves of Siberian bugloss.

My Personal Favorites
'White Nancy' has handsome silver-gray leaves, edged greenish gray, that look fresh most of the summer. Pure white flowers appear in June to bring out the sheen of the foliage. 'Beacon's Silver' has rose-purple flowers and a center stripe of silver.

Stonecrop
Sedum spp.

When, Where, and How to Plant

Plant sedum from spring through early fall. The plants are easy to start from cuttings anytime of the year. Choose locations that have full to partial sun and well-drained soils. If the soil is too fertile, the plants tend to grow weaker and are more prone to breakage. Add a quality soil amendment such as compost or sphagnum peat moss to retain moisture in sandy soils and to improve drainage and porosity in clay soils. Position the plant so that the soil level is the same as it was in the container. Gently firm the soil around the roots, and water well. Space plants 12 to 15 in. apart. Also refer to page 107 for more planting advice.

Growing Tips

Sedums are carefree and do best in well-drained soils. An occasional watering when the soil gets dry will sustain the plants. If you want to apply a fertilizer, use a granular organic-based 5-10-5 once in the spring and water well. Avoid fertilizing with high nitrogen products as this makes the plants weak and prone to rot.

Care

Stonecrops need very little input from the gardener. They quickly spread to form a dense ground cover. Stonecrops can be propagated by dividing the plants in the spring, early summer, or early fall. Transplant divisions in open spaces, and water well. But then water sparingly to avoid rotting the plants. They are not generally bothered by pests and diseases.

Companion Planting and Design

Stonecrop is heat and drought enduring. Use it in perennial borders, dry gardens, and mass plantings. Sedum works well in rock gardens, on rocky slopes, and between steppingstones and terracing. Some are particularly effective planted around rocks, along pathways, or tucked into rock walls.

My Personal Favorite

King's crown roseroot (*Sedum rosea* var. *integrifolium*) is a native with attractive green columns that elongate to produce a flat head of 2-in.-deep red blooms from May through June.

Sedums comprise a diverse group of ground covers that will tolerate poor soil conditions and reward the gardener with an abundance of blooms and attractive foliage. The fleshy, succulent leaves remain attractive for months, and if sedum is planted in a somewhat protected site, the foliage may remain evergreen, adding winter interest. Goldmoss stonecrop (Sedum acre) has a creeping growth habit with its tiny, bright evergreen leaves forming a dense mat over the ground. The flowers are borne in terminal clusters of shortened spikes or flattened heads. Sedum lanceolatum is a drought-enduring native. Use sedum in rock gardens and in mass plantings; it works well in-between steppingstones and terracing. This drought-tolerant ground cover is well adapted to sunny exposures and thrives in heat.

Other Common Name
Sedum

Bloom Period and Seasonal Color
May through September blooms in white, yellow, red, or pink; succulent foliage year-round

Mature Height × Spread
2 to 4 in. × as allowed

Zones
To zone 2

Sweet Woodruff
Galium odoratum

One tough ground cover, sweet woodruff adapts to a wide range of conditions, including dry shade. It produces fragrant white blossoms that rise above the bright-green foliage. The tiny, pure white, star-shaped flowers cluster into loosely branched cymes. Though it prefers damp, slightly acidic conditions, woodruff tolerates Rocky Mountain soils that have been enriched with humus. Once it becomes established, it makes a nice ground cover for dry, shady locations, including beneath pines and junipers and around deciduous shrubs and hedges. In my garden, it has retained its foliage year-round in the semi-protected locations. Once you get woodruff started, it can spread to other areas, so have a shovel handy to dig it out of areas where it is not wanted and put it to use in other spots.

Bloom Period and Seasonal Color
April through June fragrant white flowers

Mature Height × Spread
6 to 8 in. × 18 to 24 in.

Zones
To zone 3

When, Where, and How to Plant
Plant from early spring through early fall. Sweet woodruff grows more rapidly if planted in full sun, but it is very well adapted to partial shade conditions. The soil should be well drained; amend the soil with compost or sphagnum peat before planting. Loosen the soil in the area where this ground cover is to be planted. Add a quality soil amendment such as compost or sphagnum peat moss to retain moisture in sandy soils and to improve drainage and porosity in clay soils. Follow the guidelines for soil preparation on page 107. Space plants 12 to 15 in. apart. Water thoroughly, and mulch with pine needles or coarse compost.

Growing Tips
Water new plants each week to ensure healthy growth and establishment. Sweet woodruff tolerates dry partial shade once it has become established. Water it as the soil becomes dry. In the spring, a light application of granular 5-10-5 slow-release fertilizer can be added around the plants. Then water well, and this will maintain the plants throughout the growing season.

Care
If the foliage is damaged by winter desiccation or winter sunburn, shear back the plants in the spring and new growth will eagerly return. Sweet woodruff is generally not bothered by pests or diseases.

Companion Planting and Design
Sweet woodruff is a very durable ground cover to grow beneath trees and shrubs. It spreads rather quickly and provides a nice mass grouping. The leaves have a mild, pleasant fragrance that can be used when making potpourris. The white, star-shaped flowers contrast nicely with evergreen foliage. Use sweet woodruff on slopes to control erosion and in areas where it doesn't need to be confined.

My Personal Favorite
The most common selection of sweet woodruff is *Galium odoratum.* Once you get it started, you will have plenty of small plant divisions to share with friends.

Woolly Thyme

Thymus pseudolanuginosus

When, Where, and How to Plant

Transplant woolly thyme from early spring to early fall. Sow seed in early spring. It grows readily from seed, plant divisions, or cuttings. Full to partial sun and well-drained soil are its prime requirements. Add a quality soil amendment such as compost or sphagnum peat moss to retain moisture in sandy soils and to improve drainage and porosity in clay soils. Prepare the soil with moisture-retentive compost (30 to 40 percent by volume), and mix uniformly with native soil. Dig the planting hole twice as wide as the rootball, and position the plant so that the soil level is the same as it was in the container. Gently firm the soil around the roots, and water well. Space plants 12 to 15 in. apart, depending on how fast you want to cover an area.

Growing Tips

Keep the soil evenly moist until the plants become established. Thyme is easy to establish—as long as you don't overwater and cause the plants to rot. Water when the soil becomes dry. Fertilize with a slow-release 5-10-5 plant food in the spring.

Care

In the spring, remedy semiwoody stems by cutting the plants back. Prune back to live wood to promote more compact growth. As plants become old, they may start to die out in the center; lift the clumps, and divide them in early spring. Keep healthy divisions from the outer section of the clump, and transplant the new divisions at the same depth they were growing. They start growing quickly to fill in bare spots. There are no pests to bother woolly thyme; overwatering is the bigger danger.

Companion Planting and Design

Thyme is great for bordering walks and in crevices of rock walls where it can spill downward. Use it to fill in between flagstones and steppingstones. Underplant with pasque flowers, botanical tulips, dwarf irises, or other spring-flowering bulbs for a dramatic spring display.

I Also Recommend

Mother-of-thyme (*Thymus praecox* ssp. *arcticus*) 'Coccineus' has attractive reddish purple blooms on dark-green stems and foliage. Its leaves become bronzy in winter.

Woolly thyme is one of the most useful creeping and mat-forming evergreen ground covers. Its leathery, aromatic, gray-green leaves form a dense surface. Since it tolerates being walked on, woolly thyme works well when planted among steppingstones. When the plant leaves are brushed or trod upon, an invigorating fragrance is released into the air. I had it planted between pavers; when my sheltie walked the pathway, the thyme was not damaged by the light paw traffic. His tiptoeing through it left a pleasant scent on his paws. As a ground cover, it even tolerates being mowed to keep the plant neat. Rose-pink to magenta flowers rise above the foliage in late spring and are beloved by bees. Woolly thyme is a truly drought-enduring ground cover.

Other Common Name
Creeping thyme

Bloom Period and Seasonal Color
Late spring to early summer blooms in rose pink, pink, or white; silvery foliage all season

Mature Height × Spread
1 to 4 in. × 10 to 12 in.

Zones
To zone 3

Lawns *for the Rockies*

Rocky Mountain residents take great pride in their lawns. A healthy carpet of soft, green turf is both attractive and functional. Your lawn is a soft, cool area on which to throw out a blanket; enjoy a picnic; read a book; play catch, croquet, or football; toss a Frisbee®; or just relax and appreciate the beauty of the world around you.

When selecting a turfgrass species for your lawn, consider how much time you want to dedicate to maintaining your lawn and what type of maintenance you're willing to provide. You may prefer pulling weeds from flower beds, hoeing, deadheading spent flowers, and maintaining perennials to watering, fertilizing, and mowing a lawn.

Live to Mow Another Day

With proper planning, you can have your lawn and enjoy it, too! The Rocky Mountain Sod Growers Association has put together some helpful questions for you to answer when selecting the right turf for your landscaping situation.

1. How will the turf be used? For recreation? Aesthetics? Ground cover? Near a house or a heavily used building? For outlying areas?
2. How much water do you want the lawn to consume? What is the cost of water in your area?
3. How much traffic will the lawn bear, and what wear tolerance do you need?
4. What are the mowing requirements?
5. How long do you want it to stay green?

Perennial Ryegrass Lawn

6. What are the fertilizer requirements?

7. Will it be in shaded or sunny areas—or both?

8. How is the soil? Clay? Sandy? Salty?

9. How much time do you want to spend on lawn maintenance?

Turf Choices

Throughout most areas of our region, cool-season grasses such as Kentucky bluegrasses, turf-type fescues, and perennial ryegrasses are planted for home lawns, parks, and athletic fields. Seed germination is best at soil temperatures of 60 to 80 degrees Fahrenheit and the optimum growth temperature is between 60 and 75 degrees F. The best growth quality for cool-season grasses occurs in the spring and fall; these grasses become dormant in summer when temperatures rise and drought periods come. But full dormancy rarely occurs if you continue to water and fertilize the lawn. Kentucky bluegrass (*Poa pratensis*), which has a rhizomatous root system, is one of the most drought-tolerant lawn grasses that goes dormant in summer without irrigation; it starts growth again in autumn as cool temperatures and moisture return.

Conversely, clump-forming turf-type tall fescue (*Festuca arundinacea*) grasses do not have this recuperative quality. Once stressed from long dry periods, they cannot recover and will eventually die. In deep, rich soils, fescue can develop a deep root system that draws on deeper water resources, resulting in some drought tolerance. But on compacted, clay soils, fescue grasses do not develop that miracle root system.

Perennial ryegrass (*Lolium perenne*) is used widely in grass mixtures because it germinates quickly from seed. The leaf texture and color are compatible with bluegrass. Perennial ryegrass has good heat and wear tolerance and, if planted in deep, well-prepared soil, goes dormant in extreme heat and short periods of drought. It is important to have a sharp mower blade when mowing perennial ryegrasses; a dull blade results in a ragged look. The presence of endophytic fungi in ryegrass improves the grasses' ability to resist some insect species, such as billbugs, cutworms, sod webworms, and possibly white grubs.

Fine fescue (*Festuca* spp.) grasses are best adapted to shady conditions where trees mature and cast shadows over lawn areas. They are drought resistant and cold tolerant and grow in soils of poor-to-average fertility. In extreme heat and drought periods, fine fescue goes dormant and rests until moisture becomes available. Fescues are well adapted for high-country lawns. Red, chewings, hard, or sheep fescues are typical fine fescues with fine, narrow grass blades.

Warm-season grasses that can be planted as lawns include buffalograss and blue grama. Seed germination is best when temperatures are between 70 to 90 degrees Fahrenheit, with their optimum growth occurs between 80 and 95 degrees F.

Buffalograss

Blue grama (*Bouteloua gracilis*) is a clump-forming grass that grows 10 to 16 in. tall. Buffalograss and blue grama are very drought-tolerant. Blue grama needs little fertilizer and only infrequent mowing. Left unmowed, it can grow to 15 in. and produces attractive seedheads. Blue grama cannot tolerate high traffic or shady areas, nor does it perform well in elevations above 6,500 ft. In native stands, blue grama is found growing in association with buffalograss in short and mid-grass prairies. I recommend combining the two in landscape uses.

Buffalograss (*Buchloe dactyloides*) is a true sod-forming grass that grows 6 in. tall, can be left unmowed, and can be maintained on 1 to $1^3/4$ in. of water every two to three weeks during the summer—a low-maintenance, water-thrifty grass. It is green to grayish green only between May and October, and a handsome straw color at other times of the year. Buffalograss does not tolerate shade or heavy traffic; if overwatered or overfertilized, it thins out and weeds invade. It is not recommended for elevations above 6,500 ft. A vigorous sod-former that spreads by runners and stolons, buffalograss requires periodic edging along driveways, sidewalks, and shrub and flower beds to keep the persistent runners in check. It can be planted from seed, sod, or plugs. "Vegetative" cultivars are available as sod or plugs and include '609', '315', 'Highlight', 'Buffalawn', and 'Prairie'. Other varieties can be planted from seed and include 'Plains', 'Topgun', 'Bison', and 'Sharp's Improved'.

Wheatgrasses (whose botanical names are synonymous to *Agropyron*), include crested (*Agropyron desertorum*), western (*Pascopyrum smithii*), thickspike, (*Elymus lanceolatus*), and streambank (*Agropyron riparium*). They are coarse-textured and bunch-type grasses adapted to tolerate precipitation as low as 10 in. per year; this suits them well for a water-thrifty landscape. During dry spells, wheatgrass goes dormant, but makes a rapid recovery when moisture returns. It is a cool-season bunchgrass and is recommended for dryland lawn situations.

Smooth brome (*Bromus inermis*) is a cold- and drought-tolerant pasture grass with wide leaf blades. It greens up in early spring, needs minimal water, and requires little fertilizer. When maintained as a lawn, smooth brome loses some of its density. It can be used alone or combined with crested wheatgrass and western wheatgrass for soil-erosion control, a water-thrifty lawn, or a mountain lawn. Some available cultivars include 'Bromar', 'Lincoln', and 'Manchar'.

Site Preparation

Proper soil preparation is especially important in establishing a drought-enduring lawn. Subsoil from basement excavation or "contractor dirt" that has been spread out around the home and then compacted by heavy equipment is not suitable for lawn establishment. A soil test will determine what nutrients your soil needs before you start a new lawn. Your state university's soil-testing laboratory or a local soil-testing lab can help you prepare a soil sample for analysis.

Organic matter improves the soil's ability to drain, as well as its capacity to retain moisture. If the organic content of the soil is less than 5 percent, incorporate 3 to 6 cubic yards of well-aged manure or compost per 1,000 sq. ft., depending on grass selection. Mix the organic amendment into the existing soil to a depth of 8 to 10 in. Rake the surface smooth before seeding or sodding.

Planting and Caring for Your Lawn

The best time to start cool-season grasses from seed is in late summer to late September. By this time, the nighttime temperatures are cooling down, the days are still warm, and weeds are less competitive. These conditions are ideal for the germination of grass seed and its establishment. If you are unable to seed your lawn at these times, the second-best time to sow grass is in early spring.

Warm-season grasses such as buffalograss and blue grama should be sown in May or June because they need warm soils to germinate successfully.

Starting a lawn from seed is economical, but requires more frequent watering and takes longer to achieve good results. Sod, while initially more costly, provides an "instant lawn." You can install sod from spring through late fall as long as the soil has been properly prepared and depending upon the availability of the sod from the sod farm. Whether you choose to seed or sod your new lawn, the key to success is proper soil preparation.

Before planting a lawn from seed or installing sod, it's a good idea to eliminate any weeds, especially the difficult perennial weeds, such as Canada thistle, bindweed, quackgrass and bermudagrass. The best way to achieve this is by spraying the actively growing weeds with a herbicide that has no soil residual, such as glyphosate, and allow the herbicide to fully translocate and kill the weeds before you cultivate. Read and follow label directions.

After the organic matter has been thoroughly incorporated into the soil, install an in-ground automatic sprinkler system, if your budget allows. This is the most efficient way to water larger lawn areas and saves you time. Plan your automatic sprinkler system so that turf zones are separate from zones that water flowers, shrubs, and trees. Remember that shaded areas generally need less water than those with full sun exposure.

Seeding a New Lawn

Prepare the area with quality organic matter as previously discussed, and rake the surface smooth in preparation for seed or sod. Apply 5 lb. of a starter fertilizer such as diammonium phosphate (18-46-0) per 1,000 sq. ft. of lawn by raking it into the soil surface. The soil should be left firm but not packed. If walking over the prepared soil leaves footprints more than 1-in. deep, the soil can be firmed with a roller. Spread the grass seed in two directions at right angles, distributing one half of the seed each direction. After planting, lightly rake or roll the area to make sure the seed is in contact with the soil. Water, and then cover the surface with a light mulch, such as clean wheat straw or

An Inviting Lawn

pulverized compost, to conserve moisture. Water lightly and frequently to keep the soil surface moist during the germination process. This may mean watering three to five times daily until the seeds have germinated—here's where an automatic sprinkler is most effective and efficient.

Once the grass seed has germinated and the seedlings begin to develop a deeper root system, begin to water the lawn less frequently, but increase the amount of water applied each time you water. Deeper, less frequent watering encourages the development of a deeper root system, which makes lawn grasses more drought tolerant during the heat of summer. Young, tender grass seedlings can easily be damaged by weed killers. Although it can be frustrating to have weeds pop up in a newly seeded lawn, this is common and should not discourage you. If you did proper preplanting weed control, most weeds that sprout in a new lawn are eliminated after the grass is mowed several times and the lawn thickens. Mow your newly seeded lawn when it grows to a height of 3 in. Cut the grass to remove no more than $^1/_2$ in. off the new grass plants.

Mow cool-season grasses high—2, $2^1/_2$, or even 3 in. tall. With more surface area, grass can manufacture more food energy to nourish the roots and stems. Also, longer grass blades shade the soil surface, making it harder for annual weed seeds to germinate.

Lawns should be mowed frequently enough so that no more than a third of the grass blade is clipped off. This may mean mowing every four to five days when the lawn is growing fast in the spring. The lawn looks better and undergoes less stress, and the amount of clippings is smaller so they drop back into the lawn more easily. When clippings are returned to the lawn, nitrogen and other nutrients are recycled in an organic, slow-release form that promotes a healthier lawn. It is a myth that grass clippings cause thatch. Thatch is actually the compacted, brown, spongy, organic layer of living and dead grass stems and roots that accumulates above the soil surface. It is usually a result of poor lawn management practices. As thatch layers thicken, the lawn is predisposed to drought stress, insect, disease, and weed problems.

Watering Established Lawns

Soil type, weather conditions, turfgrass species, and the desired quality of lawn influence how much water you should apply and how often. Turf-type fescue lawns require as much or more water as the typical bluegrass lawn. Buffalograss and blue grama lawns survive and look good for weeks without watering.

Root Growth

When you water, thoroughly wet the soil to the depth of the lawn's root system. Don't water again until it becomes dry at that depth. Deeper, infrequent watering promotes a deeper root system and drought endurance—and conserves water. Rocky Mountain soils vary in how they accept water. Sandy soils require less water more often than loam and clay soils. Grasses growing in shade generally require less water, but more water is needed where tree roots compete with the lawn.

To avoid runoff and wasting water, practice "cycling" or "interval watering." Rather than trying to apply water all at one time, water an area to the point of runoff (fifteen to twenty minutes), then shut off the water and allow it to soak in for thirty minutes or more. Repeat the watering cycle in the same area to allow deeper percolation into clay soils. This technique is helpful for watering sloped areas where water naturally runs downhill.

Thatch

Thatch is a persistent problem in lawns throughout our area. Although some believe thatch is an accumulation of grass clippings in the lawn, it is actually a tightly intermingled layer of partially decomposed stems, roots, and some leaves sloughing off the crown between the actively growing grass blades and the soil surface.

Thatch should not be allowed to accumulate in lawns because it restricts the movement of water, oxygen, and nutrients into the soil. Because it also becomes resistant to wetting, drought stress occurs. Core aeration is a lawn management technique that aids in water infiltration by reducing compaction and breaking through the thatch layer.

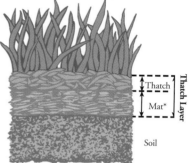

Grass with Thatch Layer

Thatch
Mat*

Thatch Layer

Soil

*Old thatch and soil

Core Aeration

One of the most beneficial ways to reduce soil compaction while controlling thatch accumulation is by core aeration. Plugs or cores of soil and thatch, 2 to 3 in. long, are removed by a mechanical aerating machine and deposited on the lawn's surface. The holes left from aeration permit water, air, and nutrients to enter the soil and create a healthier root zone environment. You can either rake the plugs off the lawn after aeration or leave them to disintegrate and filter back down into the lawn. It may take several days to weeks before the plugs dissolve, depending on your soil type. Mowing over the plugs with a rotary lawn mower can break them down more rapidly, but this will dull the mower blade. The cores of thatch and soil can be collected and put into the compost pile.

Fertilizing the Home Lawn

One of the most frequently asked questions on my radio and television shows is how often to fertilize the lawn. This gets us back to what kind of lawn you want. A low-maintenance or utility lawn won't look as uniform or deeply green as a higher maintenance lawn, but it won't need as much fertilizer, watering, or mowing, either.

Nitrogen is the most important nutrient for lawn grasses to maintain growth and good color; but don't overstimulate your lawn with excess nitrogen, particularly during the spring and summer. This can contribute to thatch accumulation and disease problems and will certainly increase mowing frequency.

Cool-season grasses such as Kentucky bluegrass, turf-type fescues, and perennial ryegrass need nitrogen fertilizer to produce an attractive and dense turf. Apply the equivalent of 1 lb. of available nitrogen per 1,000 sq. ft. of lawn, per application every six weeks, depending on the quality of lawn you desire. Three to four applications are usually sufficient. The amount

Tall Fescue Lawn

of product to use can be determined by dividing 100 by the nitrogen number (the first number on the fertilizer bag). For example, if you choose a regional formula of 20-10-5, you will need 5 pounds of fertilizer to equal 1 pound of actual nitrogen. Time your fertilizer applications around the following holidays: Memorial Day, Fourth of July, Labor Day, and Halloween.

Iron chlorosis (yellowing of the grass blades) is a common problem in our region. Our alkaline soils are the reason for this chlorosis because iron, while present in the soil, is not in a form available to turf grasses. To keep the lawn green, apply an appropriate lawn fertilizer containing iron or a separate iron supplement.

How Lawn Fertilizers Stack Up

The type of fertilizer you decide to apply is a matter of personal choice. Remember that nitrogen is the most important nutrient in lawn fertilizers. Organic fertilizers, which are composed of natural products such as animal manures or plant components, are not as concentrated, so more fertilizer is needed to achieve the recommended rate of nitrogen. The nitrogen content is usually 5 to 15 percent on a weight basis. The lower concentration, however, means less danger of pollution from runoff. Also, organic fertilizers have a lower potential to "burn" the grass if overapplied or applied under warm conditions. Organic and organic-based lawn fertilizers release nutrients slowly in conjunction with soil microorganisms. This reduces the growth surge that can occur when a straight chemical fertilizer is used, providing long-term green, without stimulating excessive top growth.

Nonorganic or so-called chemical fertilizers can be categorized into two types: synthetic organic fertilizers—which contain carbon—and the inorganic types that are nutrients mined from the earth but which contain no carbon. Synthetic organic fertilizers include urea, sulfur-coated urea, ureaform and IBDU®. These fertilizers are broken down by soil microbes to release nitrogen, carbon dioxide, and water. Most of the potassium, phosphorus, sulfur, and iron components are mined from the earth. Some fertilizers contain phosphorus derived from bone meal.

Weeds in the Home Lawn

Weed control in your lawn begins with the proper identification of the weed. Lawn weeds are classified as grassy types (crabgrass, tall fescue, quackgrass) or broadleaf (dandelion, plantain, spurge). Once you've determined the weed, find out whether it's an annual that grows from seed each year or a perennial that grows back from its roots year after year. Knowing what kinds of weeds you are dealing with helps you determine the correct way to control them. You may decide whether you want to use a chemical weed killer or just pull or dig the weeds by hand—"the cowboy way."

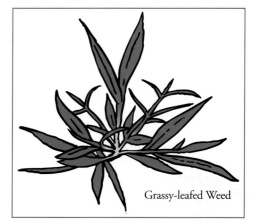
Grassy-leafed Weed

Broadleaf Weed

Before applying weed killers over the entire lawn, analyze the extent of the weed problem. It may be possible to deal with weeds on a spot basis rather than treating the whole lawn, which may not need it. If perennial weeds such as dandelions are a concern, dig them out with a long dandelion digger, pull by hand, or if desired, spot treat them individually with an appropriate herbicide.

The easiest way to control annual weeds is with pre-emergent herbicides that prevent weed seed germination and rooting. Of course, timing is important—these materials must be applied before the seeds are allowed to germinate. To control annual weeds that begin to grow in late spring or early summer (crabgrass, spurge, purslane), apply a pre-emergent in mid- to late April, before warm weather causes the seeds to germinate. Some annual weeds also germinate in late summer (annual bluegrass, cheatgrass, chickweed); apply a pre-emergent to those in late August. Read product labels carefully to make sure the product will control the weeds you are battling.

Perennial weeds such as Canada thistle, bindweed, plantain, and buckhorn grow from their roots each year and spread from both seeds and underground roots. To control them, use a post-emergent herbicide after the weed leaves have emerged. Know whether the weed is a grassy or broadleaf plant. Certain herbicides kill broadleaf weeds but are ineffective on grassy weeds, and vice versa. Read the product label to determine whether it will do the job you desire.

When in Drought

Some years, naturally occurring droughts can have a major impact on lawn care in the Rockies. These conditions often result in water restrictions. In most situations, to sustain your lawn in a dormant or semidormant state, you can reduce watering to a third as much as you normally would. Following are some lawn maintenance tips to help your lawn stay alive and healthy when water is scarce:

- Reduce lawn fertilizer applications to decrease a lot of top growth. Avoid fast-release, high-nitrogen fertilizers. Use slow-release, organic-based lawn fertilizers that work in harmony with nature.
- Keep your lawnmower blade sharpened to provide a cleaner cut; this also reduces water loss from the leaf blades.
- Raise the mowing height of the grass to shade the roots and soil. This helps reduce soil moisture evaporation.
- Return grass clippings to the lawn by mowing often. Finely ground grass clippings help provide a natural mulch to the roots and help retain soil moisture.
- Reduce traffic on the lawn to prevent soil compaction and stress to the grass plants. Compacted soils have decreased water absorption.

To avoid runoff and wasting water, practice "cycling" or "interval watering."

The Benefits of Lawns

Lawns do much more than consume water and grow. Properly chosen and maintained, a lawn contributes to the quality of our life. Unlike gravel, concrete, asphalt, or bare dirt, the lawn cools the surrounding area. Temperatures are 10 to 15 degrees F. cooler around a lawn, and this ultimately reduces water consumption of nearby plants. A 2,000-sq. ft. lawn provides enough oxygen for a family of four—every day. Turf areas reduce noise, air, and water pollution and provide excellent dust control. Well-established turf areas, with extensive root systems, control soil erosion and reduce glare. And the properly selected lawn is one of the safest and softest natural playing surfaces for children, adults, and pets.

Ornamental Grasses *for the Rockies*

Ornamental grasses have increased in popularity and are becoming an important component of Rocky Mountain landscapes. Their beauty is natural, never contrived, and they provide a unique textural contrast in the garden. When selected and sited correctly, ornamental grasses add a unique beauty and grace to the garden. They are worth growing for the sounds they make when the slightest breeze blows. The gentle rustling of the leaves and seedheads evokes sounds of the prairie. Plant ornamental grasses in drifts, swathes, or as accent plants in the shrub or perennial flower garden, where the fine textures create dramatic contrasts.

Standing Tall

When other landscape plants are winding down or killed by autumn frosts, ornamental grasses stand tall, displaying shades of tan, russet, brown, gold, or red, providing color and form for winter interest. The foliage and flowers are usually finer and more delicate than other plants. Their small, unobtrusive flowers create a cloudlike effect.

Planted in groups throughout the landscape, ornamental grasses provide a unifying element in flower beds and borders. Specimen grasses combine well with asters, rudbeckia, coneflower, liatris, Joe-pye weed, helianthus, and goldenrod. The larger dramatic grasses such as big bluestem look good with flowers on

Fountain Grass

long stems such as daylilies, hibiscus, and cannas. Russian sage and yarrows make natural grass companions. The beauty of ornamental grasses in the fall garden can be accented with *Sedum* 'Autumn Joy', *Zauschneria arizonica* (hummingbird trumpet), obedient plant, and hyssop.

Making Good Choices

To select the right kind of grass for your garden, understand its growth habit. Most ornamental grasses are perennials and grow in two different ways. Those classified as running grasses generally spread quickly by vigorous underground stems or rhizomes. These must be contained so they won't become invasive in the flower garden. Others are clump-formers and increase in size more slowly. They grow in bunches and produce new buds at the base of the clump near the crown. Their growing buds are close to ground level, thus naturally protected from climatic extremes. Their dense, fibrous root systems are quick to rejuvenate.

Most ornamental grasses do best in full sun, but some do just fine in light shade. Those are available at garden retailers and through mail-order sources. Plant them in the spring or early summer. If you wait to plant in the fall, grasses can be damaged when alternate freezes and thaws heave them out of the soil. Take precautions to apply a winter mulch over fall-planted grasses after the soil freezes.

Variegated Miscanthus

Ornamental grasses are not fussy about soil conditions, as long as they are well drained. In poor soils, amend with 25 to 30 percent by volume of compost, aged manure, sphagnum peat moss, or a combination of those organic materials. Incorporate organic amendments to a depth of 18 in. or more to encourage strong root development and drought endurance. In early spring, a light application of organic-based granular 10-10-10 fertilizer can be scattered around the grass plants and watered in well. Space ornamental grasses as far apart as their height at maturity. Planting them closer together in mass plantings creates a sea of grass. Spacing them farther apart emphasizes the form of the individual plant.

Low Maintenance Design

Ornamental grasses are not maintenance-free, but they come pretty darn close. They grow in poorer soils than many other plants, and once established, they rarely need watering. Cutting back the foliage is the most important maintenance activity, but since ornamental grasses transcend each season, don't cut them back right away. Instead, leave the foliage to dry and ripen in the winter sun. Layers of frost and snow on the stems and seedheads silhouetted against a backdrop of snow ensure another season of pleasure.

Cut back the faded stalks in March or April when spring fever demands that you get outdoors and exercise that itching green thumb. Remove the dead foliage close to ground level as soon as the new shoots start emerging in order to give them more light and room to grow.

Spring is a good time to rejuvenate old clumps, too. Dig up the clump with a spading fork, and divide it by cutting or tearing out rooted sections. This technique also renews an occasional clump of grass that is "running out" or dying back in the center. Keep the most vigorous divisions, and discard the old center portion. Replant the new clumps, and water well. Provide ample moisture as needed until they show new growth.

Adding Another Dimension

Ornamental grasses add a special dimension to your landscape. Their handsome foliage, tiny flowers, fruits, growth habits, textures, autumn colors, and winter form are attributes worthy of consideration.

Blue Fescue
Festuca glauca

The blue fescue grasses are among the most attractive and tame ornamental grasses. When planted in groups, blue fescue's growth habit resembles an army of symmetrical bluish gray hedgehogs. Dwarf blue fescue is valued for its delicate, light, silvery-blue foliage that retains good color year-round. This grass is ideal for the cool conditions in the Rockies. Plant them in groups in well-drained soils on rocky slopes and as accent plants in rock gardens. In heavy clay soils, the plants are more prone to dying out in the center and are short lived. Festuca glauca 'Sea Urchin' is a clump-forming ornamental grass with light-blue foliage. It grows to a height of 12 to 15 in.; an individual clump can get 12 to 15 in. wide.

Bloom Period and Seasonal Color
Silvery-blue foliage year-round; light-green flowers turn tan in the summer

Mature Height × Spread
6 to 18 in. × 10 to 15 in.

Zones
To zone 4

When, Where, and How to Plant
Blue fescue can be planted from spring through fall, but planting early in spring when temperatures are cooler allows plants to become well established before summer. Do not plant in heavily shaded areas—the colors appear faded. This grass tolerates a wide range of soils, but good drainage is essential. Rocky slopes, sandy loam, or well-loosened clay soils amended with compost create favorable conditions. In heavy clay soil, till 2 in. of quality compost into the top 6 in. of soil. Adding organic matter helps sandy soils retain moisture and nutrients. Dig planting holes wide enough to accommodate the root system without crowding. Space 12 to 15 in. apart. Position the plants so they are growing at the same level as in their containers. Lightly firm the soil around the roots, and water thoroughly.

Growing Tips
Water new transplants every five to seven days. Mulch with pine needles or shredded cedar to conserve moisture. Even though it is drought tolerant, blue fescue needs moisture, especially during extended droughts. Water deeply once a week or as the soil dries out. Avoid watering too often in clay soils; otherwise, the plants die out in the center and are short lived. Work slow-acting organic fertilizer into the soil at planting to provide nutrients for the growing season. In early spring, fertilize lightly with 10-10-10.

Care
Blue fescue is relatively free of insect pests and diseases. Each spring, cut off the old foliage to tidy up the plant and stimulate new colorful growth.

Companion Planting and Design
Blue fescue is a clump grass that adds year-round interest. The grass is excellent for rock gardens, in the foreground of perennials, as specimen planting, and as ground cover. A delightful ornamental grass, blue fescue can be grown successfully in large containers to create a special effect on a deck or patio.

I Also Recommend
Besides the standard species, I recommend the cultivar 'Elijah Blue'. Sheep's fescue, *Festuca ovina*, is another good choice.

Blue Oat Grass
Helictotrichon sempervirens

When, Where, and How to Plant

Plant blue oat grass in well-drained soil and full sun from spring to early fall. The grass will grow in light shade for part of the day. It tolerates a wide range of soils, but avoid heavy, wet soil. Space the plants 2½ to 3 ft. apart. Dig the planting hole wide enough to accommodate the roots without crowding. Position the plant so that the soil level is the same as in the container. If the plants are root-bound, gently loosen the roots. Add backfill soil, and lightly firm around the roots.

Growing Tips

Water plants thoroughly and keep them moist until established. A light application of slow-acting organic fertilizer at planting time provides nutrients for the growing season. Thereafter, apply a complete slow-release 10-10-10 fertilizer in the spring. Mulch to maintain and conserve moisture. Once established, blue oat grass is drought resistant, but water deeply each week during prolonged droughts or as the soil dries out.

Care

Blue oat grass needs some grooming, but not the severe pruning given to other ornamental grasses. Cut only the top of the clump in early winter. Keep the plants tidy; clean out dead foliage in the spring by lightly tugging it. Remove flowering stems when they are no longer appealing, usually mid- to late summer. As plants mature, they may need division in the spring. Lift out the clump with a heavy-duty spading fork, and divide it into sections with a sharp spade or knife. Pests and diseases do not bother this grass.

Companion Planting and Design

Planted in the foreground of a flower bed, the tall flowering stems of blue oat grass add height, but their delicacy allows you to see through the plant. Try this grass with Russian sage or smokebush. Other companions are spring-flowering bulbs such as ornamental onion and white or lavender tulips.

My Personal Favorite

My favorite is 'Sapphire Fountain', for its attractive bright-blue leaves.

With its silvery-blue metallic leaves and beige oatlike seedheads that rise on arching, silvery-gray stems 1 to 2½ ft. above the foliage, blue oat grass is one of my favorites. As a cool-season grass, blue oat gets a head start on the season, producing its handsome foliage in early spring. Blue oat grass forms clumps of spiky foliage 18 to 24 in. tall. The spiky tufts of steel-blue leaf blades augment pink, purple, and magenta flowers in late spring and early summer. They arrive early and wave in the spring breezes. Blue oat seedheads persist for winter interest. Blue oat grass can be planted in groups or used alone as an accent grass among perennials or shrubs.

Other Common Name
Blue avena

Bloom Period and Seasonal Color
Silvery-blue foliage throughout the growing season; bluish gray flowers turn tan in the summer

Mature Height × Spread
2 to 3 ft. × 2½ ft.

Zones
To zone 4

Feather Reed Grass
Calamagrostis × acutiflora

The wheatlike look of feather reed grass makes it one of the showiest ornamental grasses, and its attractive, changing display lasts almost ten months of the year, placing it among the most popular grasses for home garden use. This cool-season grass quickly forms a fresh green clump that matures at about 3 ft. In late spring and early summer, when other ornamental grasses are just getting started, feather reed grass sends out greenish flower spikes with a purple tinge. Later, the plumes transform to coppery tones, then a golden wheat color, and stiffen into a handsome vertical form. As late fall arrives, the foliage turns orange to yellow and persists into winter. This well-behaved ornamental grass is sterile and does not self-seed.

Bloom Period and Seasonal Color
Purplish green flowers changing to coppery tones in early summer; attractive foliage spring to late winter

Mature Height × Spread
5 to 6 ft. × 2 to 2½ ft.

Zones
To zone 4

When, Where, and How to Plant
Plant feather reed grass in the spring so it can establish roots before summer. If planting in summer, provide ample moisture to help it establish in hot weather. Feather reed grass tolerates some shade, but choose a sunny location. Too much shade causes the clumps to flop over. It prefers moderately moist to medium-dry soils. Improve sandy or clay soils by adding compost to improve drainage and retain moisture. Plant 2½ to 3 ft. apart. Dig the planting hole wide enough to accommodate the roots without crowding. Position the plant so that the soil level is the same as in the container. If the plants are rootbound, gently loosen the roots. Add backfill soil, and lightly firm some soil around the roots.

Growing Tips
Water new plants thoroughly, and keep them moist until established. Mulch to maintain and conserve moisture. Once the plants are established, water deeply each week or as the soil begins to dry out. A light application of slow-acting organic-based 10-10-10 fertilizer can be applied around them at planting time and again each spring. Water in well.

Care
This grass requires little care. Cut clumps back to within 6 in. from the ground in mid- to late winter. Feather reed grass starts to grow earlier than warm-season grasses. It doesn't need frequent division, but clumps can be split in the spring to increase your collection. Lift older clumps with a heavy-duty spading fork and separate them. Discard the woody unproductive center, and replant the vigorous, healthy sections. Pests don't bother this grass.

Companion Planting and Design
For a stately effect, use feather reed as a background grass. Single-specimen plants add a vertical architectural accent. Combine with perennials, in drifts or as a screen, with shrubs, or with other grasses and perennials in meadowlike mass plantings.

My Personal Favorites
'Karl Foerster' is one of the best. If you have limited garden space, I suggest *Calamagrostis × acutiflora* 'Overdam'.

Fountain Grass
Pennisetum alopecuroides

When, Where, and How to Plant
Plant in the spring so roots can develop before summer. Choose a sunny location with well-drained soil. Though adapted to a wide range of soils, fountain grass benefits from the addition of organic matter to improve drainage and to retain moisture in sandy or gravelly soils. Space plants at least 3 to 4 ft. apart. For a meadow effect or when planting dwarf cultivars, space plants closer. Dig the hole wide enough to accommodate the roots without crowding. Position the plant so that the soil level is the same as it was growing previously. If it's rootbound, gently loosen the roots.

Growing Tips
Water thoroughly, and keep the plants moist until established. Mulch to maintain and conserve moisture. Once established, water them weekly or when the soil begins to dry out. Fertilize in the spring with a slow-acting organic fertilizer such as 10-10-10 to provide nutrients for the entire season.

Care
Cut fountain grass back in early spring to several inches from the ground. For larger mass plantings, this is easily accomplished with a hedge trimmer. Mature clumps eventually die out in the center and split open. Lift and divide old clumps in the spring after new foliage appears. Dig the clump with a heavy-duty spading fork and split with an ax or pruning saw. Discard the woody center portion. Divide the remaining healthy sections. This grass is known to self-sow; volunteer seedlings can be thinned and relocated. Fountain grass is not completely hardy in many Rocky Mountain gardens. Winter mulching after the ground freezes offers some protection. Fountain grass has no particular pest or disease problems.

Companion Planting and Design
Use fountain grass to contrast with more coarse-looking plants such as tall sedums and 'Goldsturm' black-eyed Susan and many annual flowers. Specimen plants soften a corner or accent pathways.

I Also Recommend
Purple fountain grass (*Pennisetum setaceum* 'Rubrum') is a tender annual grass with burgundy foliage and purplish red plumes. It grows 2 to 3 ft. and works well in containers.

When backlit by the sun, fountain grass resembles a sparkling fountain. Its glossy, narrow leaves and pinkish foxtail flowers create a pleasing loose-cascade effect. Even though this warm-season grass may freeze out in the coldest winters, it's worth planting. When tulips are emerging, fountain grass begins to grow; its graceful green clumps provide a nice contrast in the garden. Buff-colored flower heads with pink, maroon, or magenta tones appear in midsummer. Leaves bleach tan by late fall and persist to catch the snow and add excitement to the winter scene. Dwarf cultivars such as 'Hameln', 'Little Bunny', and 'Moudry' (2^1/2 to 3 ft.) are excellent choices for limited spaces. They are not as dramatic as the species, but they are hardier for our area.

Other Common Name
Pennisetum

Bloom Period and Seasonal Color
Feathery spikes in shades of bronze to tan; finely textured arching foliage through late fall

Mature Height × Spread
3 to 4 ft. × 2 to 3 ft.

Zones
To zone 4

Hardy Pampas Grass

Saccharum ravennae

If you yearn to grow pampas grass in your garden, but are stifled by cold temperatures, your wish is granted with Saccharum ravennae (whose genus was formerly Erianthus), hardy pampas grass. It grows into large mounds of cascading foliage; abundant and spectacular 10- to 12-ft. tall late-summer flower stalks feature a pink tinge when they first open. The foliage turns handsome tan to orange in late summer. As autumn approaches, flowers transform into fluffy, lustrous silvery plumes that resemble true pampas grass. Harvest some of the flower stalks before they fully expand to use in fresh floral arrangements or in dried displays. Standing tall and persisting into winter, this grass adds lovely vertical accents to the winter garden. It is drought tolerant once established.

Other Common Name
Ravenna grass

Bloom Period and Seasonal Color
Silvery to bronze plumes in late summer through winter; handsome gray-green foliage in summer

Mature Height × Spread
9 to 12 ft. × 3 to 5 ft.

Zones
To zone 5

When, Where, and How to Plant

Plant hardy pampas grass in the spring to allow it time to establish. Divisions can be transplanted in early spring. Locate in full sun. It can grow in a wide range of soils, but heavy soils should be conditioned with compost to improve drainage. Consult page 135 for details on soil preparation. Space 3 to 6 ft. apart, depending on the mature height and width of the cultivar and what you are trying to achieve. If you want the area to fill in faster and provide more cover, space the plants closer. Dig the planting hole wide enough to accommodate the roots without cramping, and position the plant at the same level it was growing. Gently firm the soil around the roots, and water thoroughly.

Growing Tips

Keep the soil moist until the plant is established. Apply organic mulch to conserve water. Water weekly or as the soil dries out during drought. Overwatering makes the plant grow weak and leggy stems that fall outward to the ground unless staked. Do not use high-nitrogen fertilizer; this weakens the plants, which then blow over. Apply slow-acting organic 10-10-10 granular fertilizer at planting time to provide nutrients for the growing season.

Care

This grass grows with minimal maintenance. In early spring, cut clumps to several inches from ground level. Use hedge trimmers or pruning loppers to make this task easier. If the clumps begin to die out in the center, renew them by lifting in the spring and transplanting outside divisions. It is free from pests and diseases.

Companion Planting and Design

Use it as a specimen plant near evergreens or deciduous shrubs, or plant near water features. Ravenna grass combines nicely with fall-blooming perennials, including asters, Japanese anemone, goldenrod, and chrysanthemums. This grass does in a single season what it takes years for hedges to do.

My Personal Favorite

Saccharum ravennae, the species, is one of the most stunning ornamental grasses for year-round interest.

Little Bluestem
Schizachyrium scoparium

When, Where, and How to Plant

Plant little bluestem grass in the spring so that the plants establish before summer. They prefer full sun and dry soil; avoid soils that stay wet or mucky. Space little bluestem grass plants $1^1/_2$ to 2 ft. apart, depending on the effect you seek. If you want the grasses to fill in faster and provide more cover, space them closer. Dig the planting hole wide enough to hold the root system without crowding it. If the plants are rootbound, gently loosen the roots. Position the plant so that the soil level is the same as it was in the container. Add backfill soil to the planting hole, and lightly firm the soil.

Growing Tips

Water new plants thoroughly, and keep them moist until they become established. Mulch to conserve moisture and prevent weeds. During dry, hot spells, water periodically—once a week or as the soil begins to dry out—but avoid overwatering. Apply a slow-release 10-10-10 fertilizer in the spring, and water thoroughly.

Care

Cut back clumps in early spring before the new growth expands—it's much easier to cut straight across the old blades than around and among new shoots. For larger mass plantings, use hedge trimmers or a weed trimmer to cut the grasses back to within a few inches of the ground. Pests and diseases generally do not bother this grass.

Companion Planting and Design

Plant little bluestem grass in groups to provide a unifying element in beds and borders. The upright clumps contrast nicely with spring-flowering bulbs and draw attention away from the slowly maturing foliage of bulbs. Little bluestem grass makes a good companion to irises, poppies, and other taller perennials. This grass is also often used to reduce erosion and stabilize roadbanks.

My Personal Favorite

Among my favorites is 'The Blues' with its handsome fine bluish green leaves. It's great for prairie gardens or as an accent in the perennial border.

A native American prairie grass with outstanding drought and cold tolerance, little bluestem is well suited for the Rockies. This ornamental grass has fabulous winter characteristics as the fiery-orange to russet-red foliage accents the landscape. The handsome growth habit, adaptability, autumn color, fluffy white plumes, and winter presence make this grass worth growing. Little bluestem grass grows in almost any soil, especially dry and rocky sites, and prefers full sun. It is particularly attractive in a naturalized garden as the fluffy white seed plumes wave in the breeze. Medium-textured foliage ranges from green to blue-green to blue. Another outstanding species is the 4- to 6-ft. tall big bluestem (Andropogon gerardii), with bluish foliage that turns to shades of bronze and seedheads that look like a turkey's foot.

Bloom Period and Seasonal Color
Bluish foliage through summer turning shades of red and orange in the fall

Mature Height × Spread
2 to 3 ft. × 2 ft.

Zones
To zone 3

Maiden Grass
Miscanthus sinensis

Maiden grass, with its long, arching fine leaves, has the noble bearing of a garden aristocrat. Cultivated in Japan for centuries and used in American gardens in the early twentieth century, maiden grass is back in vogue. Its handsome growth habit, adaptability, fall color, silvery plumes, and winter presence make it worth growing. Many cultivars are available, so be sure to choose ones that are hardy for your area—earlier flowering types are recommended for our region. 'Purpurascens', often called flame grass, is a good selection. It grows more compactly (to 5 ft.), flowers in August, and is strikingly reddish orange in the fall beginning as early as September. The attractive fluffy plumes catch the snow, and the plant remains attractive until spring.

Other Common Names
Japanese silver grass, miscanthus grass

Bloom Period and Seasonal Color
Feathery pinkish bronze flower spikes changing to silver white in late summer and fall; graceful gray-green summer foliage

Mature Height × Spread
3 to 8 ft. × 2 to 5 ft.

Zones
To zone 4

When, Where, and How to Plant
Spring is the time to plant maiden grass. Locate it in full sun, where it grows best. Maiden grass will take some light shade, but in too much shade, the clumps sprawl open and need to be staked. Moist, average-to-rich soil is ideal to make this plant quickly grow tall and wide, but maiden grass tolerates a wide range of soils from moist to dry. Space the plants 3 to 6 ft. apart, depending on the cultivar. If you want the area to fill in faster and provide more cover, space the plants closer. Dig the planting hole wide enough to accommodate the roots without cramping. Position the plant at the same level it was growing. Gently firm the soil around the roots, and water thoroughly.

Growing Tips
Keep the soil moist until the plant is established. Water deeply once a week or as the soil dries out. When the grass needs watering, the leaf blades roll, indicating stress. Mulch to conserve water. High-nitrogen fertilizer weakens the plants, which then become spindly. Fertilize maiden grass each spring with a slow-release or organic fertilizer low in nitrogen such as 10-10-10. Water in thoroughly.

Care
In early spring, cut crowded clumps to several inches from ground level. Hedge trimmers or pruning loppers make this easier. Be sure to wear long sleeves and gloves because maiden grass leaves are sharp and can irritate your skin. Divide older clumps in the spring, and transplant them. Pests and diseases do not bother this ornamental grass.

Companion Planting and Design
Use this grass as a specimen plant near evergreens, or plant it near a water feature. Combine maiden grass with fall-blooming perennials, including asters, chrysanthemums, helenium, rudbeckia, and goldenrod.

My Personal Favorites
My favorite is 'Morning Light' (5 to 6 ft.), with finely variegated leaves that appear silvery. 'Variegatus' (5 to 7 ft.) has wider variegated foliage and an almost white effect.

When, Where, and How to Plant

Plant northern sea oats in the spring to allow for good root growth before summer. If you plant later, provide adequate moisture for proper establishment. This ornamental grass prefers moist, well-drained soils and partial shade associated with shade gardens. With adequate moisture, northern sea oats grows in sun, but the foliage may be lighter green. Amend with a 2- to 3-in. layer of compost in the planting area, and mix uniformly to a depth of 6 in. or more. Space 1 1/2 to 2 1/2 ft. apart. Dig the planting hole wide enough to hold the root system without crowding it. If the plants are rootbound, gently loosen the roots. Plant so that the soil level is the same as it was in the container. Add backfill soil, and lightly firm the soil around the roots.

Growing Tips

Water new plants thoroughly, and keep them moist until established. Mulch to add moisture and to reduce weeds. Apply a slow-release 10-10-10 fertilizer each spring. If northern sea oats is located in full sun, be sure to water regularly during dry, hot periods. Once the plants are established, water deeply every five to seven days or as the soil begins to dry out.

Care

As new growth emerges in the spring, cut back clumps to the ground. Divide older clumps in the spring. Dig with a strong spading fork, and split apart with a sharp shovel or knife. Remove the old woody parts, and replant the vigorous, healthy ones. This grass self-sows. Volunteer plants can be transplanted or shared with friends. There are no pests or diseases to bother it.

Companion Planting and Design

Plant in moisture-retentive or semishady perennial beds; by streams, ponds, or water features; as an accent grass; and in woodland settings. Northern sea oats makes wonderful dried arrangements. If stems are cut while still young, they keep a greenish cast and later the stalks turn coppery brown.

My Personal Favorite

My favorite is the common northern sea oats.

With its wide, green leaf blades held roughly perpendicular to the stems, northern sea oats is quite appealing. It resembles a small 2- to 3-ft. bamboo, giving the garden a somewhat tropical appearance. A native woodland origin makes northern sea oats one of the few ornamental grasses that will grow in partial shade. A warm-season grass, wild oats begins its growth cycle when warm temperatures return in spring. By early summer, the flower stalks arise, and as they mature, threadlike wire stems barely support the 1-in. flattened spikelets, creating a nodding habit. The flowers start out green and gradually transform to a coppery tan. Northern sea oats is particularly effective when its coppery-tan spikelets are backlit by sunshine. This grass offers diversity and accent in the perennial garden.

Other Common Name
Wild oats

Bloom Period and Seasonal Color
Wide green to bronze foliage; pendulous, flattened coppery-brown spikelets that hold well into winter

Mature Height × Spread
2 to 3 ft. × 2 ft.

Zones
To Zone 4

Prairie Dropseed
Sporobolus heterolepis

Native to the prairies, prairie dropseed is one of the most delicate and elegant of the ornamental grasses. The simple beauty of its upright arching stems produces a fountain of shimmering emerald-green foliage in the landscape. In late summer, cloudlike flowers push above the foliage on graceful stems. Backlit by the sun and trembling in a breeze, mass plantings of prairie dropseed create a glowing translucent veil against rudbeckia, asters, and other perennials. When in bloom, the flowers emit a sweet crushed cilantro fragrance that can be detected from a distance. The foliage transforms to beautiful gold to reddish orange hues in autumn. The seeds attract birds and other wildlife. Mass plantings make an effective tall ground cover. This drought-tolerant ornamental grass deserves more attention.

Bloom Period and Seasonal Color
Sweetly fragrant, tannish brown flowers in late summer; fine textured emerald-green foliage in summer turning orange-red in the fall

Mature Height × Spread
18 to 24 in. × 2 ft.

Zones
To zone 4

When, Where, and How to Plant
Plant prairie dropseed in the spring in full sun. It tolerates some light shade, but tends to grow leggy and flop open. Tolerant of most soils, including heavy clay, prairie dropseed does best in well-drained soils. Condition the site with compost before planting to improve drainage in clay and to help sandy soils retain moisture. Space plants 18 to 24 in. apart to allow them to develop their true form and airiness. Spacing too closely obscures their natural growing form. A small amount of slow-acting organic 10-10-10 fertilizer can be applied at planting time; water in thoroughly.

Growing Tips
Water new transplants regularly to ensure good establishment. Be patient; prairie dropseed tends to be slow to get established, and clumps may take two to three years to grow to their full effect. A light application of slow-release organic 10-10-10 fertilizer in the spring sustains the plants through the summer. Once established, this grass is drought resistant, but during extended dry periods, it requires watering weekly or as the soil dries out.

Care
Once established, prairie dropseed is deep rooted and drought and heat tolerant. It is long-lived and not bothered by insects or diseases. It rarely suffers from center dieback and therefore does not need spring renewal like many other ornamental grasses. Prairie dropseed is simple to maintain; cut back faded clumps in early winter to about 3 in. from the ground.

Companion Planting and Design
Prairie dropseed is excellent for edgings or ground cover. Use it as an accent in sunny perennial beds or in a naturalistic prairie garden. It is especially nice with fall-blooming perennials, including asters and goldenrod. Plant it in the foreground of flower beds so the delicate flowers create a "see-through veil" while the foliage adds contrast to many perennials.

My Personal Favorite
Prairie dropseed is a wonderful native that should be used more often in Rocky Mountain landscapes.

Switchgrass
Panicum virgatum

When, Where, and How to Plant

Plant in the spring so roots have time to develop before summer. This adaptable plant tolerates soil extremes. It does best and grows rapidly in full sun and moist, fertile soils, but will grow in both dry and moist sites. In very dry areas, the grass will be stunted. Space the plants 3 to 4 ft. apart. Dig the planting hole wide enough to accommodate the roots without crowding. Plant so that the soil level is the same as in the container. If the plants are rootbound, gently loosen the roots. Add backfill soil, and lightly firm around the roots. Water thoroughly.

Growing Tips

Water new plants every five to seven days until established. Then water deeply each week or as the soil dries out. Don't water so much that the soil stays soggy. Mulch to maintain moisture and reduce weeds. A light application of slow-acting organic 10-10-10 fertilizer at planting provides nutrients for the season. When established, fertilize this grass in the spring with slow-release 10-10-10.

Care

Cut back switchgrass in late winter or early spring to within 4 in. of the ground. If the plants split open in late summer, divide the clumps the following spring as leaves emerge. Lift clumps out of the ground, and split them apart with a sharp knife or pruning saw. Discard the spent center, and replant healthy sections from the outside of the clump at the same level they were growing. Switchgrass is not bothered by many pests or diseases; grasshoppers occasionally attack, so take appropriate measures.

Companion Planting and Design

To create a prairie-style garden, use switchgrass in sweeps with yellow coneflower, purple coneflower, blazing star, or Russian sage. Use it in combination with many fall-blooming perennials including Japanese anemone and asters.

My Personal Favorites

Among my favorites is 'Rotstrahlbusch' (4 ft.) with burgundy foliage in late summer. 'Strictum' (4 to 5 ft.) grows more upright and is orange to purplish red in the fall.

Native to the tallgrass prairie, switchgrass tolerates our various soil extremes. This warm-season grass starts slowly in the spring, but eventually it forms clumps of leaves that are 3 to 4 ft. tall. By late summer, the hazy cloud of flowers rises another foot or two over the foliage. The species varies in height, habit, and fall color; it is best used in prairie-style gardens or naturescapes for wildlife cover. Switchgrass's early autumn colors of yellow, orange, and purplish red add an incendiary glow to the landscape. The plant persists into the winter, with bleached leaves turning straw-colored and the sturdy stems contributing a visual silhouette to the winter landscape. Look for cultivars with compact growth habits, upright forms, and attractive autumn colors.

Bloom Period and Seasonal Color

Airy clusters of pinkish green to burgundy flower heads in midsummer; green foliage turning tan to bronze in the fall

Mature Height × Spread

4 to 6 ft. × 3 to 4 ft.

Zones

To zone 4

Perennials *for the Rockies*

Planting a flower garden that will thrive for years is a growing passion among Rocky Mountain gardeners. A perennial garden brings to mind a popular definition of a perennial that says a perennial "is any herbaceous plant that, had it lived, would have come back year after year." While this definition may bring a smile to veteran gardeners, it often misrepresents perennials as temperamental and challenging to grow. The perennials represented in this chapter are among some of my favorites that thrive in almost any Rocky Mountain garden.

If you long for flowers with attributes of permanence in your garden, plant perennials—the plants that return year after year.

The word *perennial* comes from Latin and means "enduring" or "perpetual," a plant that will survive several growing seasons. Although the top portion of many herbaceous perennials dies back in winter, the roots remain alive and the plants awaken when conditions are suitable for growth (that is, unless your perennial acts like a "perannual" and refuses to survive cold winters and fluctuating climatic conditions).

Something for Everyone

Perennials offer gardeners tremendous variety in color, height, bloom time, shape, size, flower form, and foliage color. Don't be intimidated by the vast numbers of varieties. Create your own flower garden by first concentrating on tried-and-true plants to build your gardening confidence. Later you can branch out into some of the more exotic offerings. Perennials tend to have fairly short blooming times, so if you want a garden that flowers from spring through fall, take care to choose plants that succeed each other in blooming times.

Peony 'Mitama'

This chapter introduces you to a group of perennials that are "herbaceous," which means that their stems are green and soft, and the top growth dies back in the fall. But in the spring, the crown and roots start growing again. Signs of life all over the perennial garden awaken your spirits as the little green shoots and buds emerge from the earth. Some perennials may remain evergreen all year-round. Others, like the hellebores, brave the cold days of winter with a show of unique blooms.

Part of the pleasure of gardening with perennials comes from orchestrating a garden

Coreopsis 'Sunray' with Lobelia

for all-season color and interest, and planning seasonal combinations of flowers, as well as foliage. Attractive leaves develop the charm and texture of a well-planned perennial garden and become the unifying ribbon that ties the garden together.

Perennials are a hardy bunch and grow in a wide range of conditions. It's a good thing that perennials are so adaptive, because we have such diverse conditions—from the High Plains to the High Country. We are blessed with quality sunshine and low humidity in our region, so we can grow perennials without a high incidence of plant diseases, which often occur in the more humid parts of the United States. Perennials are generally long lived and also adapt to our various soil types. They have few, if any, insect pests and diseases when planted in the right location and if properly maintained. As with all plants, the secret to growing perennials successfully is having the right soil for the right plant. In most cases, soil preparation is especially important since perennials are meant to remain in one location for many years. They may outlive the gardener who plants them! So before planting, get to know a little about the plant and amend the soil as needed.

Selecting Perennials

When choosing perennials for your landscape, consider what they look like even when they're not blooming. Many bloom for a week or a few weeks, but their foliage can be an important element in the garden all season long. Hostas, for example, are grown more for their leaves than for their flowers. And you're not limited to growing perennials in sunny borders, since many perennials thrive in partial to full shade. With so many new and interesting plants coming into our region all the time, it's tempting to want to grow one of each. Certain qualities can help you determine which ones will be hardy and reliable in your garden. If you're looking for plants that require the least amount of maintenance, be sure to choose varieties that don't require staking—or site the plants so that other plants help support them.

There are those of us who grow perennials for sheer pleasure, and we don't care about low maintenance. We're looking for plants that offer a wide range of diversity and experimentation. It's fun, and in many ways relaxing, to embark on the adventure of growing some of the more unique varieties— that is, if the pocket gophers, rabbits, deer, elk, chipmunks, or other critters don't get them first!

Artemisia
Artemisia spp. and hybrids

In the wild, silver and gray foliage dots the landscape to punctuate the greens and browns. This is the role of artemisias in the home garden; their distinctive silvery leaves help to calm bright colors. Artemisias provide textural interest, and their spreading habit is quite useful to create a backdrop of silver that helps to tie other plantings together. Two popular cultivars, 'Silver Queen' and 'Silver King', are commonly available. 'Silver King' grows to about 3 ft. tall and has slender stems and fine-textured narrow silver leaves. 'Silver Queen' is a bit more variable, growing to 2 ft. tall, with wider leaves that have jagged edges. Artemisias can withstand drought and heat, and they grow well in light, sandy soils.

Other Common Names
Wormwood, white sage

Bloom Period and Seasonal Color
July through September inconspicuous whitish to green flowers; primarily grown for silvery foliage spring through fall

Mature Height × Spread
2 to 3 ft. × as permitted

Zones
To zone 4

When, Where, and How to Plant
Plant from spring through early fall. For the most effective growth and display, locate artemisias in full to partial sun—the more sun, the better. They tolerate a wide variety of soil types, but spread more rapidly in sandy loam. Plant 2 to 3 ft. apart to allow for spreading growth. Dig the planting hole twice as wide as the container. Position the plant so that the soil level is the same as it was in the container. Fill in with soil around the root system about halfway up, gently firm, and water well. After the water soaks in, add more soil to completely fill in the hole.

Growing Tips
Water regularly until the plants establish. These water-thrifty plants should not be overwatered or overfertilized. Avoid high-nitrogen fertilizers; they make these plants grow soft and leggy. Artemisias tolerate heat and drought, so mulch is generally not necessary.

Care
Each spring, evaluate the plantings and remove unwanted sections to tidy up the garden. Underground roots spread several feet from the main plant, so cut down with a sharp spade to sever all roots. Then pull and remove the plants. As older clumps die in the centers, dig them up and replant the vigorous sections from the outside edges. To control spread, grow artemisia much like mint, in a bottomless 5-gallon bucket, to keep its underground root system in check. They are pest and disease free.

Companion Planting and Design
Plant in informal areas where the spreading growth habit is welcome as part of a large, sweeping display. Artemisias make good companion plants with yellow yarrow and violet-blue salvia. Cut and dry the plants; then use them as fillers in arrangements and herbal wreaths.

My Personal Favorites
The upright, well-branched subshrub common wormwood (*Artemisia absinthium*) features stems and leaves coated with silky hairs. The readily available 'Lambrook Silver' is one of the best ferny silver plants for the perennial garden.

When, Where, and How to Plant

Plant asters in spring or early summer. They like full to partial sun in well-drained soils kept moderately moist. Plant New England asters 2 to 3 ft. apart. Other varieties can be spaced 15 to 18 in. apart. Avoid overcrowding; asters do best with good air circulation. Dig the planting hole twice as wide as the container or root system. Position the plant in the hole so that the soil level is the same as it was in the container. Fill in with soil around the root system about halfway up, gently firm the soil, and water well. After the water has soaked in, completely fill the hole with soil.

Growing Tips

Until they become well established, water new transplants regularly as the soil begins to dry out. Asters are drought-enduring, but do best in moderately moist locations. Water regularly during dry periods. Avoid wetting the foliage; it creates a favorable environment for leaf diseases. A slow-release 5-10-5 organic fertilizer can be applied at planting time and monthly until mid-August.

Care

Divide older plants every three years to keep the plant vigorous. Lift and divide clumps in the spring. To keep asters from becoming too tall and flopping over, pinch in late spring to encourage bushier, more compact growth. Taller varieties may need to be staked. Mildew can be a recurring problem, so improve air circulation by thinning the plants if they become overcrowded.

Companion Planting and Design

Asters make excellent perennials for the back of a border and in mixed plantings, rock gardens, cutting gardens, and meadow or prairie-style gardens. Combine asters with ornamental grasses, coneflowers, goldenrod, Joe-pye weed and sedums for a spectacular display.

My Personal Favorite

Another one of my favorites is alpine aster (*Aster alpinus*), which has a compact growth habit (6 to 12 in.). It is ideal for rock gardens and blooms early (in May and June) in white, blue, lavender, purple, or pink.

Asters are a familiar sight along roadsides and open fields from the plains to the High Country. The Aster genus represents a large group of plants with many new hybrids available. They are adapted to a wide range of soils from moist to dry, but prefer lean soils low in fertility. Some varieties reach only a few inches in height, while others may tower above other perennials, reaching 3 ft. or more. One of my favorites is New England aster (Aster novae-angliae), with its bold profusion of blooms from late summer to frost. The bright-purple, daisylike flowers provide lots of bloom to liven the garden when annuals are losing their gusto. Asters are tough, colorful plants that provide vivid color until frost.

Bloom Period and Seasonal Color
Late summer to frost blooms in lavender, blue, pink, or white

Mature Height × Spread
18 in. to 4 ft. × 16 to 24 in.

Zones
To zone 3

Blanket Flower
Gaillardia × grandiflora

Your summer garden will rejoice if you plant blanket flowers. Their bright and dazzling daisylike flowers offer a mixture of reds and yellows like an Indian blanket laid on the grassy plains. Gaillardia is a hardy soul, withstanding the heat and dryness of summer. Cutting back leggy growth and spent flowers only encourages the plants to regrow and put on another display of late blooms. In heavy clay soils, blanket flower is a short-lived perennial, but you'd never know it since the plant reseeds so freely that new plants take over the ones that don't survive through the winter. Blanket flowers also make good cut flowers. They are excellent when planted in a meadow garden and work well as a border planting.

Other Common Name
Gaillardia

Bloom Period and Seasonal Color
June through September blooms in red, yellow, or gold

Mature Height × Spread
8 in. to 3 ft. × 12 to 24 in.

Zones
To zone 4

When, Where, and How to Plant
Plant container-grown blanket flowers spring through fall. Seedlings started indoors in late winter should be ready to transplant into the garden in eight weeks. Transplant root cuttings from older plants in early spring. For best growth and flowering, site blanket flower in a sunny location. Soils should be well drained. In hard, compact clay soil, blanket flowers tend to be short-lived. Sandy soils yield compact plants with lots of blooms. Dig the planting hole twice as wide as the container or the spread of the root system. Position the plant so that the soil level is the same as it was in the container. Add backfill, gently firm around the plant, and water well.

Growing Tips
Blanket flowers are easy to establish with minimal care; water them regularly as the soil begins to dry out. To reduce weed invasions in new plantings and to conserve water, apply a 2-in. mulch. Give blanket flowers a healthy start by applying a slow-release 5-10-5 fertilizer at planting. Apply the same formula each spring to give the plants a boost for continuous summer flowering.

Care
Once established, blanket flowers need little care. These tough plants thrive in the heat and are generally not bothered by pests or diseases. Remove the spent flowers, and the plants continue producing flowers well into autumn. *Gaillardia* species are self-sowing and distribute seed freely. These seed-grown plants vary, but do produce some interesting color combinations. Cultivars remain true only through asexual propagation, such as root cuttings or plant divisions taken in the spring.

Companion Planting and Design
Essential to prairie and meadow gardens, blanket flowers combine well with shorter ornamental grasses, in perennial borders, and in xeriscape gardens. Plant some in the cutting garden, too.

My Personal Favorites
The compact 'Goblin' (12 in.) produces large, dark-red flowers with wide, irregular yellow borders. 'Burgundy' grows 2- to 3-ft. tall and has large 3-in. wine-red flowers.

Blazing Star

Liatris spicata

When, Where, and How to Plant

Transplant potted blazing star spring through early fall. Plant bare-root divisions or corms in early spring. Blazing star does best in a sunny location. For vigorous plants, grow in humus-enriched, well-drained soil. Amend the soil with compost before planting to make sure the soil retains moisture through the summer. Plant 18 to 24 in. apart. Dig the planting hole twice as wide as the container. Position the plant so that the soil level is the same as it was in the container. Fill in with soil around the root system about halfway up, gently firm, and water well. After the water has soaked in, add more soil to completely fill the hole. Place bare-root plants so that the pinkish corms are 1 to 2 in. below the soil surface. Firm the soil gently, and water well.

Growing Tips

Keep new plants moist during hot, dry weather. Water occasionally during the summer, especially during extended dry, hot periods. Although the plants endure drought, they prefer moist soils. Moisture-retentive organic amendments at the initial planting are crucial. Mulch to conserve water and to discourage weeds. Avoid high-nitrogen fertilizers; they can make the plants floppy.

Care

To increase your collection of this easy-to-grow perennial, lift established plants in the spring and divide the corms. Deadhead flower spikes as they fade to keep the garden neat. Otherwise, in a naturalized setting leave the seedheads for wild birds. Tall varieties may need to be staked in windy sites, or just plant shorter cultivars to avoid this inconvenience. There are no serious pest problems for blazing star.

Companion Planting and Design

Blazing star is at home in a prairie or meadow planting where stems are supported by grasses and other summer flowers. Some good companions include Russian sage, coneflowers, rudbeckias, and ornamental grasses.

I Also Recommend

The rough blazing star (*Liatris aspera*), 4 to 5 ft., is particularly drought tolerant and prefers dry, sandy soils. It is an excellent choice for a prairie garden.

The truly spectacular blazing star features long, plump spikes of rosy-purple flowers above handsome narrow foliage. You may often see it used in florists' arrangements, but it is more at home on the prairie. The flowers open from top to bottom and attract butterflies to your garden. Blazing star is at its best in prairie and meadow plantings where the tall stems (up to 3½ ft.) are supported by the grasses and other meadow flowers. In the open garden, the tall spires may need to be staked, especially in windy areas. The cultivar 'Kobold' (15 to 18 in.), also called 'Gnome', has a compact growth habit, which eliminates the need for staking. Bright red-violet flower spikes stand out in the garden.

Other Common Name
Gayfeather

Bloom Period and Seasonal Color
July through August blooms in mauve, purple, rosy-purple, or white

Mature Height × Spread
18 in. to 3 ft. × 18 in. to 2 ft.

Zones
To zone 4

Bleeding Heart
Dicentra spectabilis

One of my favorite old-fashioned perennials, bleeding heart evokes memories of Grandma's shade garden. It can naturalize in a woodland setting, as well. Bleeding heart's graceful arching growth habit and handsome, fernlike leaves add a special touch of class to the perennial border. If you meet a few simple requirements, these long-lived plants thrive. Soil enriched with humus and partial shade make this perennial flourish. It is programmed to cope with heat and drought by dying back in summer, storing water and nutrients in its deep tuberous roots. In the spring, bleeding heart awakens with distinctive heart-shaped, rosy-pink and white lockets. Combine with ferns, hostas, spring bulbs, and shade-loving ground covers to make up for this plant's lack of foliage in late summer.

Other Common Name
Dutchman's breeches

Bloom Period and Seasonal Color
May through June blooms in rose-pink and white, or white

Mature Height × Spread
2 to 3 ft. × 2 to 3 ft.

Zones
To zone 3

When, Where, and How to Plant
Transplant potted plants in the spring. Plant bare-root plants in early spring to allow good establishment before summer. Choose a location with partial sun to shade where the soil has been enriched. Bleeding hearts grow best in evenly moist, but well-drained, soils with a relatively high organic content. Avoid hot, dry, or windy locations. Bleeding heart tolerates some sun, as long as you provide adequate moisture. Too much sun makes the foliage die back prematurely and shortens the blooming season. Space 18 to 24 in. apart. Dig the planting hole twice as wide as the container or wide enough to accommodate bare roots without cramping. Position the plant so that the soil level is the same as it was in the container. Fill in with soil around the root system about halfway up, and water well. After the water has soaked in, add more soil to complete the planting.

Growing Tips
Water regularly until the plants are established. Apply a 2-in. organic mulch to maintain even moisture, keep the soil cool, and conserve water. Also, organic mulches add humus as they break down over time. Once the plants are established, keep the soil moist by watering deeply each week, especially if spring rains are sparse. Use a slow-release 5-10-5 granular fertilizer each spring.

Care
Winter mulch helps protect plants from frost heave. Divide older plants in early spring to yield more plants. Lift the clump before the brittle stems elongate. Transplant into prepared soil, and water well. Slugs may attack the foliage but they can be trapped; follow the tips on pages 257 to 258.

Companion Planting and Design
Bleeding heart combines well with most shade-loving perennials, particularly hostas, ferns, hardy geraniums, forget-me-nots, ajugas, and sweet woodruffs.

I Also Recommend
Common bleeding heart has the showiest blooms and is long lived. Fringed bleeding heart (*Dicentra eximia*) has mounds of blue-gray, finely dissected leaves with a more compact growth habit (10 to 18 in.).

Blue False Indigo
Baptisia australis

When, Where, and How to Plant

Plant blue false indigo in the spring through early fall. Newly planted transplants should be protected with a winter mulch for the first year. As is common in members of the pea family, baptisia doesn't like root disturbance. Too much shade causes plants to grow open and flop. Choose sites that receive full to partial sun with moist, well-drained soil. Average to fertile soil will do. In compacted soils, loosen and work in a moisture-retentive organic amendment such as compost or well-aged manure. Allow plenty of room; space 3 to 4 ft. apart. Dig the planting hole twice as wide as the container. Position the plant so that the soil level is the same as it was in the container. Fill in with soil around the root system about halfway up, gently firm, and water well. After the water has soaked in, add more soil to completely fill the hole.

Growing Tips

Water new transplants well until established. After that, blue false indigo is drought enduring. To provide nutrients through the growing season, apply a slow-release 5-10-5 organic fertilizer in the spring.

Care

Though it's a bit slow to start, blue false indigo lives a long time and is not invasive. It requires little care once established and is not generally bothered by pests or diseases. Be patient after planting blue false indigo; it takes several years for the plant to reach maturity—but it's worth the wait. **Caution:** Blue false indigo is toxic, so don't plant it where grazing animals might get to it.

Companion Planting and Design

Use blue false indigo as a background in perennial beds, for foundation plantings, or in island beds; the smooth bluish green foliage is attractive. Combine it with peonies, hardy geraniums, Siberian irises, hybrid anemones, and ornamental grasses.

I Also Recommend

For a shorter version, plant *Baptisia australis* var. *minor*. Prairie false indigo (*Baptisia lactea*) features white flowers tinged with purple.

Blue false indigo adorns the garden in late spring with blue-violet pealike flowers on 3- to 5-ft. stems. The attractive smooth gray-green foliage provides a beautiful background to other perennials. The growth of blue false indigo emerges quickly in the spring garden and beckons for attention when combined with the majestic blooms of peonies. Later in the summer, swollen 2-in. dark-purple to blackish seedpods appear. The stems of the blue false indigo grow rapidly in the spring, and in June the intense blue flowers open on the tall stalks. For the remainder of the season, the three-lobed cloverlike leaves add a smooth, soft texture to the garden. The inflated, almost blackish purple seedpods of the blue false indigo work well when used in dried arrangements.

Other Common Names
Baptisia, false indigo

Bloom Period and Seasonal Color
Late spring blooms of blue-violet

Mature Height × Spread
3 to 4 ft. × 3 ft.

Zones
To zone 3

Butterfly Weed

Asclepias tuberosa

With a splash of bright orange, butterfly weed brightens the perennial garden in the summer. Once established, this plant is easy to care for—though it may take a season or two before the plants bloom freely. Butterfly weed's deep taproot makes it sensitive to disturbance, so handle the plant carefully. Because they emerge late in the spring, be sure not to disturb the area where they are planted. When in bloom, butterfly weed beckons butterflies in profusion. This milkweed doesn't have a milky sap. The orange flowers are produced in clusters on upright stems with handsome linear leaves. Later in the season, tapered seedpods (4 to 6 in.) appear and are quite ornamental as they open to release typical milkweed seeds with the fun fluffy parachutes.

Bloom Period and Seasonal Color
June through July blooms of orange, red, or yellow (depending on the species or cultivar)

Mature Height × Spread
18 to 24 in. × 18 in.

Zones
To zone 4

When, Where, and How to Plant
Plant in spring through early fall. These temperamental plants have brittle tuberous roots, so handle them carefully to prevent transplant shock and slow establishment. Locate in full sun and in average, well-drained garden soil. Sandy loam is ideal, but clay soils are fine if drainage is good. Space 1½ to 2 ft. apart. Dig the planting hole at least twice as wide as the container. Position the plant so that the soil level is the same as it was in the container. Fill in with soil around the root system halfway up, and water well. Add more soil after the water has soaked in to complete the planting.

Growing Tips
Water regularly when the soil dries out until the plants are well established. Then water deeply once every seven to ten days. To provide a boost for the growing season, apply slow-acting organic 5-10-5 fertilizer at planting.

Care
Once established, butterfly weed needs little care. The deep tuberous roots resent disturbance, so allow the plants to develop into mature clumps for several years. Division is seldom needed. Plants self-sow if seedheads are allowed to disperse. Deadheading encourages an additional flush of later blooms. Butterfly weed emerges late in the spring; it is easy to damage the plant when weeding or overplanting annuals. Mark the plant with a label, or when cutting it back, leave 6 in. of stems to remind you of its location. Aphids may attack in late summer or early fall; control them by hosing off the plants.

Companion Planting and Design
These plants thrive in a meadow garden or naturescape. Plant butterfly weed with lavender, rosy-purple spires of verbena, or ornamental grasses. Just one plant creates an eye-catching focal point and brings in butterflies.

My Personal Favorite
The Gay Butterflies series includes colors of red, pink, and yellow. All make fine cut flowers, and the ornamental seedheads can be used in dried arrangements.

When, Where, and How to Plant

The best time to plant is early spring as soon as the soil can be worked. Avoid summer planting; this perennial takes a rest when it gets dry and hot. Chiming bells prefers shade to partial shade and moist, well-drained soil. The soil should be rich in humus, like the forest floor. If necessary, amend the soil with compost or leaf mold. Space plants 15 to 18 in. apart. Dig the planting hole at the same depth as the plant was growing in the container. Add backfill soil around the roots, gently firm with your hands, and water slowly. Apply a mulch of shredded leaves or shredded wood chips to maintain uniform moisture and discourage weed seed germination.

Growing Tips

Keep the plants mulched to maintain even moisture; this delays summer dieback. Mulch with chopped leaves; they eventually break down and release nutrients for healthy plant growth. Water plants deeply once a week or as the soil dries out. A slow release 5-10-5 fertilizer can be applied each spring.

Care

To rejuvenate an older plant that has lost vigor, dig the clump as the foliage dies down in late summer and divide it into sections. The foliage of chiming bells must remain on the plant after flowering, eventually turning yellow and tan. It is during this time that the plant is storing nutrients. As with many other native forest plants, chiming bells thrive in a shady site with well-drained, but moist and fertile, soils. Provide those conditions in your shade garden, and chiming bells will spread, frequently self-sowing. Cut back old growth in late fall. Chiming bells suffers from no serious pest problems.

Companion Planting and Design

Chiming bells are a natural for a woodland garden. Combine with other shade-loving perennials such as bleeding heart, bloodroot, hosta, bergenia, and woodland fern.

My Personal Favorite

Although Virginia bluebell (*Mertensia virginica*) is more widely grown in perennial gardens, our native species, *M. ciliata*, is well worth the effort.

One glimpse of the pinkish blue nodding clusters opening with dainty blue flowers will make you want to include this native perennial in your shade garden. Mountain bluebells spring from the forest floor at subalpine and montane zones in early spring and form a bluish green clump of foliage. Taller stems emerge bearing smaller leaves and ending with a hanging cluster of pink buds that open to light blue flowers and are a welcome addition to a woodland garden. Blossoms remain attractive for several weeks, taking on a pinkish blush as they fade. If your neighborhood is older, with lots of shade trees, plant chiming bells beneath deciduous trees where they receive sun at the beginning of the season and shade after the trees leaf out.

Other Common Name
Mountain bluebell

Bloom Period and Seasonal Color
Late spring to summer blooms in pinkish blue, blue, or bluish purple

Mature Height × Spread
12 to 24 in. × 2 ft.

Zones
To zone 3

Coneflower
Rudbeckia spp.

The yellow and orange daisy-petals and chocolate-brown centers of Rudbeckia provide flamboyant color to the perennial garden from summer till frost. These easy-care perennials are long lived if planted in well-drained soils. The familiar black-eyed Susan (R. hirta) is a short-lived perennial, but there are many other cultivars available that bloom for weeks and last for years. Rudbeckia fulgida var. sullivantii 'Goldsturm' is one of the most popular coneflowers. It produces masses of 2- to 3-in. yellow-orange flowers with dark centers over coarse, deep green foliage from midsummer until frost. When in full bloom, it adds a sunny meadow feeling to the landscape. Flowers continue to proliferate for two to three months. The brown center cones remain attractive even into the winter.

Other Common Names
Black-eyed Susan, rudbeckia

Bloom Period and Seasonal Color
Mid- to late summer through September blooms in gold, yellow, or orange-yellow with chocolate-brown centers

Mature Height × Spread
18 in. to 4 ft. × 18 in. to 2 ft.

Zones
To zone 3

When, Where, and How to Plant
Transplant potted plants of rudbeckia in the spring through early fall. If you plant in the heat of summer, provide ample water for good plant establishment. Rudbeckias are at their best in open, full- to partial-sun locations. They prefer soil of average fertility; too rich a soil results in soft, floppy growth. Good drainage is essential. Space the plants 18 in. to 2 ft. apart. Dig the planting hole twice as wide as the container. Position the plant so that the soil level is the same as it was in the container. Backfill, gently firm the soil, and water well.

Growing Tips
Water regularly until the plants are established. Keep rudbeckia well watered during hot, dry spells; though the plants tolerate heat, they need water during extended dry periods. A light application of 5-10-5 fertilizer in the spring gives the plants a boost to start the growing season. Additional fertilizer is not necessary.

Care
Most rudbeckias are vigorous growers; clumps can be divided every three to four years as the centers die out. Lift the old clumps, and amend the soil in which the plants were growing with compost or rotted manure. Separate the clumps with a sharp knife, and discard the spent center section. Replant the new divisions at the same level they were growing, and water well. New transplants usually bloom the first season. Blooming can be extended by regularly deadheading the spent flowers. The raised brown cones in the center of the flowers do provide winter interest. Occasionally, aphids or whiteflies bother it, but not seriously.

Companion Planting and Design
Use rudbeckias in perennial borders, island beds, and mixed plantings. Combine 'Goldsturm' with *Sedum* 'Autumn Joy' and ornamental grasses. Experiment with different combinations using coneflowers with blue asters and prairie dropseed.

My Personal Favorite
Cutleaf coneflower (*Rudbeckia laciniata*) has deeply cut, dark-green leaves. The smooth, branched stems support large flower heads with olive-green raised disks and drooping golden-yellow 1- to 2-in. rays.

Coral Bells

Heuchera spp. and hybrids

When, Where, and How to Plant

Plant coral bells in the spring through summer. Their shallow roots are subject to frost heaving. Spring planting allows enough time for the plants to develop a strong root system. Coral bells grow in full sun to shade. They flower more abundantly in the sun, but need ample moisture. Coral bells prefer moist, well-drained soils that have been enriched with moisture-retentive compost. Avoid locations that are heat traps and are poorly drained. Plant coral bells 12 to 15 in. apart. Dig the planting hole twice as wide as the root system. Position the plant so that the soil level is the same as it was in the container or at the same depth the plants were originally growing.

Growing Tips

Water new transplants regularly as the soil dries out so they become well established. Apply a 2-in. mulch around the plants to maintain moisture and to discourage weed invasions. Coral bells need additional water during dry spells to perform at their best. Water deeply at least once a week or as the soil begins to dry out. A slow-release fertilizer applied at planting provides nutrients through the growing season and each spring thereafter.

Care

Deadheading ensures continued bloom. Do not remove the foliage in autumn—it often remains evergreen and attractive over the winter. You can apply a winter mulch of evergreen boughs or pine needles after the ground freezes to prevent the roots from heaving. A thick cover of snow provides excellent insulation. If slugs become a problem, use the remedies on pages 257 to 258.

Companion Planting and Design

Plant these old-fashioned favorites in perennial beds or drifts in the lightly shaded woodland garden. Coral bells are effective choices for edging pathways and flower beds. Plant them with columbines and hardy geraniums.

My Personal Favorite

Heuchera micrantha var. *diversifolia* 'Palace Purple' has maplelike leaves that are bronze-red and beet-red beneath. It makes a superior ground cover.

Sprays of dainty bell-shaped flowers held high above handsome foliage make coral bells a beautiful addition to the garden. The foliage—dark green with scalloped, lobed, or wavy edges—remains evergreen most of the year. We now have the luxury of choosing from several varieties of this tough and versatile plant. Some of these plants boast striking foliage with bronze, purple, and silver hues. 'Palace Purple' has purplish leaves. In early June, slender stalks support a profusion of bright-red flowers that appear to form a cloud of brilliant red. Coral bells invite hummingbirds to your garden as those hovering jewels migrate from the High Country. The remarkably hardy coral bells resist pests; they tolerate both shade and drought. Coral bells make good cut flowers, too.

Other Common Names

Alum root, heuchera

Bloom Period and Seasonal Color

June through September blooms in pink, coral, red, green, or white

Mature Height × Spread

1 to 2 ft. × 12 to 15 in.

Zones

To zone 3

Coreopsis
Coreopsis spp.

Some of the most carefree perennials are Coreopsis species. The name thread-leaf coreopsis (Coreopsis verticillata) mainly describes that plant's finely cut foliage, but one of this perennial's finest features is its long blooming season. 'Moonbeam' blooms from early summer into autumn, with peak bloom in midsummer. The pale-yellow, daisylike flowers blend nicely with purple-, blue-, and white-flowering perennials without distracting. The finely textured foliage and growth habit give the plant an airy look that is quite attractive. Coreopsis grandiflora features varieties with semidouble and double flowers. The scientific name Coreopsis comes from the Greek words koris, meaning bug, and opis, which indicates the resemblance of seed ticks. Leave the stems uncut for the fall and winter; the small, dark-brown, buttonlike seedheads provide winter interest.

Other Common Name
Tickseed

Bloom Period and Seasonal Color
June through October blooms in yellow, gold, or pink

Mature Height × Spread
10 in. to 3 ft. × 12 to 15 in.

Zones
To zone 3

When, Where, and How to Plant
Plant in the spring or early summer. Coreopsis can be divided in the spring and the new divisions transplanted at the same level they were originally growing. It does best in full to partial sun and moderately moist, but well-drained soils. Plant 2 to 3 ft. apart. Dig the planting hole twice as wide as the container or the root system. Position the plant so that the soil level is the same as it was in the container. Fill in with soil around the roots about halfway up, gently firm, and water well. Once the water has soaked in, add more soil to completely fill the hole.

Growing Tips
Water new transplants well as the soil becomes dry to a depth of 3 to 4 in. Water established plants deeply each week. Mulch to conserve water and to discourage weed germination. Once established, this plant endures drought well. Apply slow-acting 5-10-5 fertilizer at planting to provide nutrients for the growing season.

Care
Coreopsis needs little care. In light, sandy soils and full sun, it spreads quickly. After several years, plants die out in the middle, flower less profusely, or spread into areas where they're not wanted. Divide and conquer in the spring! When the flowering wanes, shear back the plants to encourage a new crop of leaves and to promote more blooms. But the plant doesn't have to be cut back; it will continue to bloom on and off and develop seedheads. Coreopsis is another plant remarkably free from pests.

Companion Planting and Design
Use coreopsis for perennial borders, for mass plantings, and as edging ground cover, or combine it with ornamental grasses. It is a natural for meadow and wildflower gardens. Plant in rock gardens and in containers. Good companions for 'Moonbeam' include salvia 'May Night' or 'Butterfly Blue' pincushion flower.

My Personal Favorites
'Moonbeam' forms a nice mound of dark-green foliage and pastel-yellow blossoms. Pink coreopsis (*Coreopsis rosea*) is a pink-flowering form similar to 'Moonbeam'.

When, Where, and How to Plant

Plant anytime from spring through fall. If planting in hot weather, just be sure to provide ample water. For the best flowering, plant daylilies in full sun to light shade. Intense afternoon sun can "scorch" the flowers. The ideal soil is well drained with average fertility. Loosen the soil in areas that are to be planted, and add compost. On steep or erosion-prone areas, the tough root system of daylilies helps control soil erosion. Space plants 2 to 3 ft. apart. Dig the planting hole twice as wide as the root system, and position the plant so that the soil level is the same as it was in the container. Set bare-root plants no deeper than 1 to 1 1/2 in. below the soil surface. Add backfill soil, gently firm around the plant, and water thoroughly.

Growing Tips

Water transplants regularly until they become established. Use organic mulch to conserve water and to prevent weed invasions. Water deeply each week during dry spells to maintain healthy foliage and to encourage flowering. A slow-release 5-10-5 fertilizer can be worked into the soil at planting. A single application of slow-release fertilizer in the spring carries the plants through the growing season.

Care

These long-lived, tough plants seem to prosper even if neglected, and once established, they tolerate drought well. Deadhead old flowers to keep the plants neat. Check periodically for aphids, mites, and slugs. Early detection and control will prevent severe damage.

Companion Planting and Design

Plant in drifts of three or more. Daylilies are an attractive foil for other perennials. They are wonderful in mixed plantings, perennial borders, or island beds. Use them as ground covers to reduce soil erosion. Combine with finely textured plants such as catmint, coreopsis, and Russian sage.

My Personal Favorites

There are hundreds of daylilies from which to choose. Among my favorites are these cultivars: 'Stella de Oro', 'Condilla', 'Happy Returns', 'Hyperion', 'Jason Salter'm and 'Jolyene Nichole'.

Among the most popular and easy-to-grow perennials, daylilies grow rapidly and propagate so easily that within a few years the thick foliage crowds out any competing weeds. A display of daylilies is as close as you can come to a "plant-it-and-forget-it" garden. The only frustration is choosing which varieties to grow. Its strong flower stalks, called "scapes," produce several flowers that bloom for only twenty-four hours, a trait that Carolus Linnaeus took into account when he named this genus Hemerocallis, *which translated from Greek means "beautiful for a day." The plants produce many flowers over several weeks. Daylilies are attractive when teamed with finer textured plants such as Russian sage and 'Moonbeam' coreopsis. Daylilies are an outstanding perennial for a naturescape, water-thrifty garden, or xeriscape.*

Bloom Period and Seasonal Color

July through August blooms in orange, yellow, red, pink, maroon, lavender, or bicolor

Mature Height × Spread

1 to 4 ft. × 2 to 3 ft.

Zones

To zone 3

Evening Primrose
Oenothera macrocarpa

Every evening and morning, the welcome flower known as evening primrose blooms, illuminating the perennial garden with cheery yellow flowers. Glossy, narrow foliage, with a distinguishable white midrib, are positioned alternately on reddish tinged, hairy stems. The flowers are pleasantly scented, delicate looking, and yellow with red spotted sepals. They open in the evening and last through the next morning. Mexican evening primrose (O. speciosa) is a daytime bloomer with white and pink flowers; it produces an impressive ground cover in dry, poor soils. Thriving on the rocky, dry slopes at lower elevations, our native yellow stemless evening primrose (Oenothera brachycarpa) lights up the early morning and evening landscape with luminous lemon-yellow blooms. Collect seeds from this beauty and introduce them into your water-thrifty garden.

Other Common Names
Ozark sundrop, sundrops

Bloom Period and Seasonal Color
Summer to September fragrant yellow blooms

Mature Height × Spread
6 to 12 in. × 1 to 4 ft.

Zones
To zone 3

When, Where, and How to Plant
Plant potted evening primrose in early spring. Start seeds indoors in late winter using a sterile seed-starting mix. Keep them at 70 degrees Fahrenheit for germination in fifteen to twenty days, and keep the mix moist, but not soggy. Locate these plants in full sun for the best bloom and growth. Evening primrose can be grown at higher elevations, to 8,000 ft., if located in a sunny, well-drained exposure. It performs best in well-drained soils; average soils are fine, but amend heavy clay soils with a combination of compost and scoria (crushed volcanic rock) to improve drainage and to add porosity. Plant transplants at the same level they were growing in their containers; space the plants 18 to 24 in. apart.

Growing Tips
Water new transplants regularly to help them establish, but allow the soil to dry out between waterings. Do not mulch; it can keep the soil too moist and cause crown and root rot. Once established, evening primrose develops a large taproot, which allows it to withstand drought with ease. Do not overwater or fertilize with high-nitrogen plant foods or the plants grow leggy with poor flowering. A light application (half the recommended label rate) of slow-release granular 5-10-5 fertilizer in the spring can give them a boost.

Care
Evening primrose is self-sufficient and should be treated accordingly. To prolong the flowering season, deadhead the spent flowers regularly; you'll enjoy blooms from early summer to frost. Pests and diseases do not bother this plant.

Companion Planting and Design
Use evening primrose in rock gardens, wildflower settings, and perennial beds. Plant it as ground cover on rocky slopes and informal borders adjacent to sidewalks and driveways. It is an excellent perennial for the water-thrifty garden as it weaves among Russian sage, lamb's ears, and ornamental grasses.

I Also Recommend
Our native Rocky Mountain yellow stemless sundrop (*Oenothera brachycarpa*) has darker green, narrow foliage. The blooms are delicately lemon-yellow colored.

Gentian
Gentiana spp.

When, Where, and How to Plant

Plant gentians in early spring to allow them plenty of time to root in. Spring is also the time to divide older plants. Locate gentian in full to partial sun to ensure the plants grow vigorously and show off their spectacular flowers. Most gentians perform at their best in sandy loam or gravelly loam soil, such as a rock garden or other well-drained area with humus-enriched soil. Amend heavy clay soils with a quality compost or sphagnum peat moss. Sand- and rock-based soils benefit from the addition of organic matter. Dig planting holes, and position the plants so that the soil is the same level as it was in the container.

Growing Tips

Water thoroughly after planting, and water weekly during extended dry periods. Apply a mulch, such as old pine needles or shredded cedar, to help the plants stay moist during establishment. If given the humus-rich soil they prefer, gentians generally don't need fertilizer.

Care

Rarely bothered by pests and diseases, gentian may be nibbled by rabbits and other wildlife. Leave plantings undisturbed for years to allow them to develop to their maximum size and for prolific flowering. The foliage is attractive when the plant is not flowering and should be well maintained. During spring cleanup, be careful not to damage emerging foliage and shoots. This is when the plant is storing nutrients for future energy and blooming stems.

Companion Planting and Design

Plant in rock gardens, in mountain perennial gardens, and near rock features. Combine with other woodland wildflowers, such as wild geraniums, in alpine rock gardens and in the front of perennial borders, where the blooms are best displayed. They contrast well with ornamental grasses, such as blue fescue.

My Personal Favorites

My favorite is everyman's gentian, with its intense blue trumpet flowers that can wind their way up and around a mossy rock. Large, bright-blue goblet-shaped flowers make Parry gentian (*Gentiana parryi*) a stunning species.

Once you see the blooms of gentian, you won't forget this wonderful alpine plant. The blue of the flowers is so intense and distinct that it competes for attention with a clear blue Rocky Mountain sky. There are many species of gentians, but they are usually low growing and suitable only for the alpine rock garden. My favorite, everyman's gentian (Gentiana septemfida), can be grown in just about everyone's home garden. Gentian can thrive in a sunny location, but also does well in partial sun. The blue trumpet flowers are borne on a shorter plant, reaching 8 to 12 in. tall, but gentian is still worth planting in the front of a perennial border or tucked near a specimen rock where it can be appreciated from July through August.

Bloom Period and Seasonal Color
July through August blooms of stunning blue trumpets

Mature Height × Spread
8 to 12 in. × 10 to 15 in.

Zones
To zone 4

Goldenrod
Solidago spp. and hybrids

Goldenrod has suffered an unjustified bad rap. It is thought by many to cause hay fever, but its pollen is much too heavy and waxy to float in the wind. The plant relies on bees and butterflies, rather than wind-borne pollen, to pollinate it. Goldenrod gets the blame, but the prime cause of sneezing and runny noses is ragweed, which blooms inconspicuously at the same time as goldenrod and releases clouds of tiny, airborne pollen grains. Goldenrod tolerates clay and sandy soils, and it thrives in sun or partial shade. There are compact forms with showy plumed clusters of golden yellow from late summer into autumn. Native goldenrod species are fit for garden use. Some are well behaved, but others can be aggressive.

Bloom Period and Seasonal Color
Midsummer through fall blooms in gold or yellow

Mature Height × Spread
18 in. to 4 ft. × 18 in. to 4 ft.

Zones
To zone 3

When, Where, and How to Plant
Plant potted goldenrod plants in the spring through fall. Plant rooted divisions in early spring. Choose a site with full to partial sun and average, well-drained soil. Goldenrod prefers sandy or loamy soils. Soils that are too rich result in floppy growth. Space plants 18 to 36 in. apart, depending on the species or cultivar. Dig the planting hole twice as wide as the container. Position the plant so that the soil level is the same as it was in the container. Backfill, gently firm the soil, and water thoroughly.

Growing Tips
Water goldenrod until it is established. Once established, it is very drought tolerant. Avoid excessive watering and fertilizing, which results in soft, weak growth and plants that require staking to stay upright. Water deeply once every seven to ten days during hot, dry periods. Mulch to discourage weed competition. In the spring, incorporate a slow-release 5-10-5 granular fertilizer into the soil and water well.

Care
Once goldenrod is well established, it needs no special care. Many goldenrods produce self-sown seedlings, which can be weeded out in the spring. Deadheading after blooming reduces some of this seed dispersal. New plants can be started by division in the spring or early fall. Lift the clump, and split it into pieces with a sharp knife. Replant the vigorous pieces from the outside of the clumps, and toss the unproductive middle. Powdery mildew can become a problem on the foliage of goldenrod. To reduce this situation, grow plants where there is good air circulation.

Companion Planting and Design
Use goldenrod in perennial borders, meadow and prairie gardens, and naturalized areas or with ornamental grasses. Lavender-blue *Aster frikartii* makes an ideal foil for goldenrod. Burgundy, orange, and red mums and black-eyed Susans are good companion plants.

My Personal Favorite
Solidago sphacelata 'Golden Fleece' is a highly ornamental variety (18 in. tall) that produces compact, horizontal trusses of bright-yellow flowers.

Hardy Chrysanthemum

Chrysanthemum × grandiflorum

When, Where, and How to Plant

Spring-planted mums, whether container grown, bare root, or plant divisions, have a better survival rate when it comes to overwintering. Hardy mums do best in humus-enriched, well-drained soils. They prefer full sun, but tolerate partial shade. Too much shade causes leggy growth and fewer flowers. Space 18 to 24 in. apart. Dig in compost, sphagnum peat moss, or well-rotted manure for moisture retention and to improve drainage. Dig the planting hole twice as wide as the container or root system. Position the plant so that the soil level is the same as it was in the container or at the same depth the plants were originally growing. Backfill, gently firm around the roots, and water well.

Growing Tips

Water regularly as the soil dries out until established. Once established, water deeply each week. An organic mulch helps retain moisture and prevent weed invasions. Apply a slow-release 5-10-5 fertilizer at planting time for a vigorous and healthy start. Fertilize hardy mums in early spring, mid-spring, and summer using a 5-10-5 granular fertilizer.

Care

You don't need to cut down the plants in the fall. Apply a winter mulch around Thanksgiving. The dried stems add winter interest and catch snow to provide additional protection. Pinch mums back during the spring and summer to encourage lateral branching and a sturdier, more compact plant. Unpinched mums tend to be more open and have fewer flowers. Pinch as soon as the new shoots are 4 in. long. Be aware of these possible pest and disease concerns: aphids, spider mites, leaf miners, and mildew. Take action when necessary.

Companion Planting and Design

Hardy mums combine well with perennials that bloom in late summer and fall, including 'Moonbeam' coreopsis and *Aster frikartii*, either 'Mönch' or 'Wonder of Staffa', and *Sedum* 'Autumn Joy'. Plant in containers to extend the garden season.

My Personal Favorites

Some of the most dependable hardy mums include 'Clara Curtis' (pink flowers), 'Mary Stoker' (buff-yellow daisy flowers), 'Sheffield Pink' (salmon-pink blooms), and 'Grenadine' (coppery-pink, plus a red selection).

As the days of summer shorten and other flowers have faded, hardy chrysanthemums burst into bloom to brighten the fall garden. In warm shades of russet, deep-red, purple, soft pink and lavender, or glowing gold, hardy garden mums complement the changing foliage of autumn. The National Chrysanthemum Society has divided this vast and varied group of plants into thirteen classifications according to flower types. It can be a challenge to find plants that are dependable for the Rockies, especially when considering varieties that overwinter in colder regions. So visit with gardener friends to find out which ones have been reliable for them over the years. Mums are the traditional backbone of the autumn garden, but they can be planted in containers as well.

Other Common Names
Garden chrysanthemum, cushion mum, florist's chrysanthemum

Bloom Period and Seasonal Color
August to October blooms in red, copper, pink, lavender, bronze, orange, or white

Mature Height × Spread
1 to 3 ft. × 2 to 3 ft.

Zone
To zone 4

Hardy Geranium
Geranium spp.

Among the most versatile perennials, hardy geraniums thrive from the plains to the High Country. Blooms range from white to shades of pink, rose, lavender, or violet-blue. The simple, symmetrical, open-faced and five-petaled flowers measure ¹/₂ to 2 in. in diameter; some have delicate venation. The finely cut or deeply lobed foliage remains attractive even when plants are not blooming. Low mounds of spreading foliage, ripening to scarlet and bronze in autumn, add texture to the garden. Younger leaves remain semievergreen. These are good filler plants with other perennials, including Rocky Mountain columbine, the yellow-green blooms of lady's mantle, and blue and white perennials. A weaving growth habit moves them through the garden, making them an effective ground cover or accent plant around taller perennials.

Other Common Name
Cranesbill

Bloom Period and Seasonal Color
Spring to fall blooms in white, pink, blue, violet, or magenta; colorful fall foliage

Mature Height × Spread
6 to 24 in. × 18 to 24 in.

Zones
To zone 2

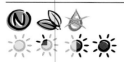

When, Where, and How to Plant
Plant spring to early summer. Hardy geraniums thrive best in moist, well-drained soils. Add a moisture-retentive compost to improve soil conditions before planting. Full sun with adequate moisture is ideal, but some species tolerate shadier conditions. Growth tends to be more open in shade. Once established, they are drought enduring because of their fleshy root system that stores moisture. Space 1¹/₂ to 2 ft. apart. Dig the planting hole twice as wide as the container. Position the plant so that the soil level is the same as it was in the container. Fill in with soil around the root system about halfway up, and water well. After the water has soaked in, add more soil to complete the planting.

Growing Tips
Hardy geraniums are easy to grow. Water regularly until established. During the summer heat or in drought conditions, water deeply each week. Mulch to conserve water and to prevent weed invasions. Slow-acting organic 10-10-10 fertilizer can be scattered lightly around plants during the planting process to provide nutrients for the growing season and can then be applied each spring.

Care
If plants are deadheaded after the flowers fade, additional blooms develop in late summer. Hardy geraniums rarely need division, but in tight situations, lifting a crowded plant in the spring and dividing it curtails its spread. Separate clumps into smaller sections, and replant. If plants become too straggly and shabby after flowering, cut them back to promote a new flush of growth.

Companion Planting and Design
Hardy geraniums are ideal with daffodils and other spring-flowering bulbs; the leaves expand to mask the bulbs' dying foliage. Plant them in rock gardens, on slopes, and in perennial beds.

My Personal Favorite
Geranium sanguineum var. *striatum* blooms with outstanding pink flowers delicately etched with dark-rose veins. The common name, cranesbill, comes from the long, narrow fruit capsules that split open when dry. Seeds are dispersed far and wide.

When, Where, and How to Plant

Plant container-grown hostas from spring through early fall. Plant bare-root hostas in the spring as soon as the soil can be worked. Hostas thrive in moist, well-drained soils in partial to full shade. Amend soil with moisture-retentive compost to add fertility and to improve drainage. Smaller hostas can be spaced 1 1/2 to 2 ft. apart. Avoid planting too close; the plants will spread. Dig the planting hole twice as wide as the container. Position the plant so that the soil level is the same as it was in the container. Fill in with soil around the roots about halfway up, firm gently, and water well. After the water has soaked in, add more soil to complete the planting.

Growing Tips

Water new plants regularly as the soil dries out to ensure vigorous establishment. Be sure to water during drought—leaves easily scorch from heat. Water deeply once a week. Apply a 2-in. mulch to conserve moisture and to keep the soil cool. Apply a slow-acting fertilizer (10-10-10) each spring.

Care

Once established, hostas require little care. Divide older plants in the spring before the leaves are fully expanded. Dig out the clump, and separate it into pieces with a sharp knife. Replant new divisions at the same level they were growing. Slugs can be a problem in moist, shaded areas. At dusk, hunt down and destroy these pests before they shred the foliage. See pages 257 to 258 for other slug remedies.

Companion Planting and Design

Hostas are excellent additions to shady gardens, edges of ponds, foundation beds, and woodland gardens. Try them as a ground cover under a specimen tree or shrub.

My Personal Favorites

A classic with large bluish green leaves, *Hosta sieboldiana* var. 'Elegans' forms clumps 2 to 3 ft. across and grows 18 to 24 in. tall. 'Gold Standard' (18 to 22 in.) features golden leaves with green edges. It grows in full and partial shade.

Hostas are dependable perennials for shade gardens. Although they produce attractive, sometimes fragrant flowers on taller stems, hostas are prized for their colorful foliage. They add textural interest and color to shady areas. Leaves vary from green to chartreuse, blue, or variegated. Some leaves have interesting textures—appearing puckered or veined so that they look quilted. Leaf edges may be smooth or wavy. Hostas make a bold statement in the perennial garden. They form clumps ranging from several inches to several feet wide. Use hostas under trees, along a shady pathway, or around a patio or deck. The plants are hardy and handsome from late spring through fall, when they often turn golden. For light-colored accents in the shade garden, select variegated forms.

Other Common Name

Plantain lily

Bloom Period and Seasonal Color

July through September blooms in lavender, purple, or white

Mature Height × Spread

6 to 36 in. × 1 to 3 ft.

Zones

To zone 3

Hyssop
Agastache spp.

Hummingbirds cherish the delicately fragrant flowers of double bubble mint (Agastache cana). Long-lived perennials in the mint family, hyssops are not as invasive as the mints. The tubular flowers have a fragrance like Dubble Bubble® bubblegum. Tiny, mintlike, gray-green leaves give this plant a soft appearance; the foliage has a different odor from the flowers. Plants are prolific bloomers in midsummer; spikes of pink, mauve, or orange flowers are a magnet for hummingbirds, butterflies, and hawkmoths. Agastache foeniculum grows to 3 ft. and has bluish purple flowers from June through September with the fragrance of aniseed. A. barberi grows even taller, to 4 ft., with rose-purple blooms above mauve-tinted foliage. Hyssops are excellent plants for the water-thrifty flower garden. Deer don't seem to bother them.

Other Common Name
Hummingbird mint

Bloom Period and Seasonal Color
July through mid-October blooms in pink, mauve, bluish purple, or orange

Mature Height × Spread
18 in. to 3 ft. × 12 to 24 in.

Zones
To zone 4

When, Where, and How to Plant
Plant potted hyssops in the spring to early fall. For the most prolific bloom, hyssops prefer well-drained soils and full sun. Avoid heavy clay soils; too much water can make the plants succumb to root rot. Loosen the soil, and amend clay soils with coarse gravel or scoria (crushed volcanic rock) to improve drainage. Add up to one-third by volume of compost or sphagnum peat moss to your native soil. Space plants 15 to 18 in. apart. Set transplants at the same level they were growing in their containers. Backfill with soil, gently firm the soil around the plant, and water well.

Growing Tips
Water new plants periodically throughout the growing season, but avoid frequent light watering. Between waterings, dig down around the root zone to check whether the soil is drying out. Once established, hyssop is long lived and should be watered sparingly, but water every two weeks during drought periods to sustain the plants. Slow-release granular 5-10-5 fertilizer can be lightly applied in the spring to provide nutrients through the growing season. No organic mulch is needed; it can keep the soil too moist. Try using pea gravel or crushed granite as a decorative mulch to highlight the plant.

Care
Deadhead old flower spikes to extend the flowering season. Don't overwater—the plant succumbs easily to root rot. Hyssops are not generally bothered by pests or diseases.

Companion Planting and Design
Plant hyssop in a mixed perennial garden, in perennial borders, and on rocky slopes. The soft foliage and spikes of flowers combine well with other perennials, including Russian sage, ice plants, tall sedums, and especially ornamental grasses.

My Personal Favorite
Agastache rupestris 'Sunset Hyssop' features luminous orange flowers on plants that grow to 3 ft. tall. I particularly like to plant this selection in the foreground of the ornamental grass *Miscanthus sinensis*.

Japanese Anemone

Anemone × hybrida

When, Where, and How to Plant

Plant Japanese anemones from spring to early summer. They prefer sun or light shade but don't like really hot, dry sites. Enrich the soil with a moisture-retentive compost. Japanese anemones tolerate a heavier soil if it's amended to improve drainage. Plant 2 ft. apart. Dig the planting hole twice as wide as the container or clump of roots. Position the plant so that the soil level is the same as it was in the container. Fill in with soil around the root system about halfway up, gently firm, and water well. Once the water has soaked in, add more soil to complete the planting.

Growing Tips

Water regularly until the plants establish. To get the most from Japanese anemones, water deeply once a week during dry spells. Spread an organic mulch at the base of the plants to maintain moisture and to conserve water. A light application of an all-purpose, slow-release fertilizer such as 5-10-5 or 10-10-10 in the spring helps the plants get started.

Care

Apply a winter mulch to help overwinter and protect the plants in colder areas. The late-blooming period of some cultivars can be tricky—an early frost may curtail the magnificent flower display. Spring is also a good time to control any plants that may have spread into unwanted areas. Dig clumps, and make divisions for transplanting or giving to friends. Pests and diseases are not a bother.

Companion Planting and Design

Anemones work well in perennial borders, in mixed plantings, and for background effect. The white variety 'Honorine Jobert' combines well with ornamental grasses and the pink 'Clara Curtis' chrysanthemum.

I Also Recommend

The pasqueflower (*Anemone pulsatilla*) has a short growth habit (12 in.) and blooms April through May. The 2- to 2¹/₂-in. purple or red-purple flowers glisten in the morning sun. Pasqueflower makes an excellent spring plant then matures, with feathery seedheads persisting into summer.

A prized late-summer- and autumn-blooming perennial, Japanese anemone spends most of the growing season as a low clump of handsome foliage. Then as the garden is slowing down, hybrid anemones burst on the scene with a multitude of delicate springlike flowers in shades of rose, pink, and white. The attractive, durable divided leaves present a nice texture to the garden, reaching a height of 1 to 1¹/₂ ft. By late summer, the plant is 3 to 4 ft. tall and branching stems push upward, topped with round silvery-furred buds. These buds open to reveal simple, yet delicate, flowers with pink or white petals surrounding a green button and yellow stamens. The blooms sway in the breeze from late summer until frost.

Other Common Name
Hybrid anemone

Bloom Period and Seasonal Color
Late summer to early fall blooms in white, pink, or rose

Mature Height × Spread
3 to 4¹/₂ ft. × 2 ft.

Zones
To zone 4

Joe-pye Weed
Eupatorium purpureum

For a bold architectural statement in a perennial garden, consider Joe-pye weed, which can grow to 6 ft. tall and 4 ft. wide. The large, lanceolate leaves are produced in whorls, usually with three to five leaves at each node. Strong, hollow, canelike green stems are often marked with purple where the leaves attach. Very showy and large rose-pink to purplish flower heads, up to 18 in. across, remain attractive for weeks beginning in late summer. Use this tall perennial for naturalizing in the landscape where there is lots of water, as a backdrop for perennial borders, or as a focal point in the fall garden. Joe-pye weed attracts butterflies and bees as its big masses of flowers sway in the breeze.

Bloom Period and Seasonal Color
Late summer through fall blooms in white or rose-pink to purplish

Mature Height × Spread
4 to 6 ft. × 3 to 4 ft.

Zones
To zone 3

When, Where, and How to Plant
Plant Joe-pye weed in the spring through early summer so the plant can establish a strong root system. Locate in full sun to partial shade and in a relatively moist area. Space 2¹/₂ to 4 ft. apart. Dig the planting hole twice as wide as the container or spreading root system. Position the plant so that the soil level is the same as it was in the container. Fill in with soil around the rootball about halfway up, gently firm, and water well. After the water soaks in, fill the hole with soil.

Growing Tips
Water new plants well as the soil dries out, until they establish. After the first growing season, Joe-pye weed tolerates dry conditions, but water weekly during extended droughts. Water as needed to prevent stress. Apply a 2-in. layer of mulch to maintain an even supply of moisture and to reduce weeds. In the spring, apply a slow-release granular fertilizer such as 5-10-5 to provide nutrients through the growing season.

Care
Cool nights, bright sun, and a constant supply of water allow this tall perennial to thrive. Cut back old stalks in late spring to achieve a more compact plant. Joe-pye weed spreads quickly in moist soils, but is less aggressive under drier conditions. It may need staking in windy areas. Older plants benefit from division every three to four years. If it gets too dry, the foliage becomes scorched and wilted in the heat of summer. Pests and diseases generally don't bother this plant.

Companion Planting and Design
Joe-pye weed needs plenty of space; use it as a background accent or in a naturalized planting near a stream or water source. It makes a superb specimen plant in island beds, the perennial border, and background planting. Joe-pye weed combines wonderfully with ornamental grasses and Russian sage.

I Also Recommend
Eupatorium maculatum has attractive reddish purple blooms and stems speckled with purple.

Lamb's Ears
Stachys byzantina

When, Where, and How to Plant

Plant container-grown lamb's ears in the spring to early fall. Also in the spring, lift and separate the old clumps and then transplant the divisions. Lamb's ears do best in full to partial sun. They prefer well-drained soil with average to low fertility; excess fertilizer and water promote soft, weak growth that will rot. Space lamb's ears 18 to 24 in. apart. Dig the planting hole twice as wide as the container or root system. Position the plant so that the soil level is the same as it was in the container or at the same depth as the plants were originally growing. Backfill with soil, gently firm, and water thoroughly.

Growing Tips

Water new transplants regularly, but allow the soil to dry out between waterings. Lamb's ears tolerate drought. They should not be overwatered. Additional fertilizer is generally not required, but you can give the plants a boost in the spring by lightly applying a low-nitrogen 5-10-5 granular fertilizer.

Care

Avoid getting water on the leaves; constant moisture on the foliage tends to promote foliar diseases and crown rot. Deadhead old flower stalks to prevent self-seeding. Older plants eventually die out in the center and should be divided in the spring. Dig up the old clumps, and separate them into pieces. Then replant the vigorous outer portions of the plant and discard the spent centers. Set the plants at the same level as they were growing, and water well. Pests do not bother lamb's ears, and these plants generally do not attract deer.

Companion Planting and Design

Plant lamb's ears in dryland gardens, in perennial beds, and as edging. Combine with Russian sage and catmint.

I Also Recommend

The nonflowering cultivar 'Silver Carpet' forms a dense, feltlike silver carpet. Big betony (*Stachys macrantha*) grows 1 to 2 ft. tall and features upright spikes with whorls of purple, pink, or white flowers offset by rough dark-green foliage.

My children can't resist petting the fuzzy silver leaves of lamb's ears. This perennial forms dense mats of silvery-white, woolly leaves that make it ideal for edging and ground cover. Lamb's ears spreads by creeping fibrous-rooted rhizomes and helps hold the soil on slopes and terraces. Its foliage remains attractive all season although it is brightest in the spring. As summer approaches, the flowering stalks bear rosy-purple flowers in furry clusters. Tall stems can become floppy, so prune them off, if you desire. Some cultivars do not produce flowering stems. Look for the many varieties and species that are suited to your landscape. Use lamb's ears with such other perennials as Russian sage, salvia, creeping thyme, hybrid yarrows, catmint, and ornamental grasses.

Bloom Period and Seasonal Color
Late spring to early summer blooms in purplish red; silvery foliage year-round

Mature Height × Spread
12 to 15 in. × 12 to 18 in.

Zones
To zone 4

Lenten Rose

Helleborus orientalis

In late winter, gardeners watch and wait for the first signs of spring, and one of the plants that greets us, even in midwinter, is the lenten rose. In February and early March, brush the snow off the evergreen leaves of hellebores to discover the thick flower buds patiently waiting to open in warmer temperatures. Soon the flowers emerge as nodding waxy blooms pushing their way up from the crown. Flowers range from cream to rose to purple and are often stippled with maroon. This plant blooms over an extended period and remains attractive even after the petals and stamens have dropped. Cool spring air prolongs the blooming time. Plants are somewhat slow to establish, but once they do, they thrive, even in a dry shade garden.

Other Common Name
Hellebore

Bloom Period and Seasonal Color
February through May blooms of purple, rose, pink, maroon, cream, or speckled

Mature Height × Spread
15 to 18 in. × 12 to 15 in.

Zones
To zone 4

When, Where, and How to Plant

It's best to plant potted hellebores in early spring or early fall. Starting them from seed is difficult and requires patience. Sow fresh seed about 1/4 in. deep in a shady spot, and mulch with a light layer of compost or shredded leaves. Germination may occur during the next year or two. Plant in partial to full shade in soil that is rich in organic matter and drains well. Since the roots resent disturbance, don't skimp on the initial soil preparation. Space plants 1 1/2 to 2 ft. apart. Dig the planting hole twice as wide as the container. Position the plant so that the soil level is the same as it was in the container. Fill in with soil around the root system, gently firm, and water well.

Growing Tips

Water regularly until the plants are well established. During extended dry periods, be sure to provide ample water to lenten roses. Water deeply at least once a week. In late spring, apply a slow-release 10-10-10 organic granular fertilizer to provide nutrients for health and vigor.

Care

Remove any brown leaves in early spring to allow for the development of new growth. Avoid damaging the flower buds that rest close to the ground. It takes lenten rose two to three years to develop an impressive clump of evergreen foliage, but the wait is worth it. Because of this, they are not good candidates for transplanting. A 2-in. mulch of compost each fall helps keep the soil rich and retain fall and winter moisture. **Caution:** All parts of hellebores are poisonous to humans and animals.

Companion Planting and Design

Use lenten roses in shady borders, foundation plantings, woodland gardens, and shade gardens. Tuck them under shrubs and small flowering trees where they will get noticed. Lenten roses are valued not only for their early flowers, but for their persistent foliage as well.

I Also Recommend

My favorite is the Christmas rose (*Helleborus niger*), with its pristine white flowers that mature to a bluish pink. The foliage persists year-round.

When, Where, and How to Plant

Plant container-grown lupines in the spring. Seeds can be started indoors in the winter and then transplanted outside in the spring. Lupines prefer full to partial sun, but benefit from afternoon shade. Good air circulation and well-drained soils are essential. Amend soil by adding compost to retain moisture and to improve drainage. Space 18 to 24 in. apart. Dig the planting hole twice as wide as the container or root system. Position the plant so that the soil level is the same as it was in the container or at the same depth the plants were originally growing. Fill in with soil around the roots about halfway, gently firm, and water well. After the water soaks in, complete filling in the hole with soil.

Growing Tips

Water new transplants well as the soil dries out to allow for good establishment. In hot weather, water plants deeply. Mulch to conserve water and to keep the soil cooler. Apply a slow-release 5-10-5 fertilizer in the spring to provide a supply of nutrients through the growing season.

Care

Deadhead flower spikes to encourage more blooms later into the season. This also reduces prolific self-seeding. Hybrid lupines produce rather large heavy blooms that may need staking. Hybrid strains also tend to be short lived; replace them periodically. Provide winter protection by mulching with shredded leaves or cedar shavings in late fall or early winter. Aphids love lupines, so be prepared to go to war when they invade. Gently washing them off with a stream of water can reduce their populations.

Companion Planting and Design

Use lupines in perennial borders, mixed plantings, and island gardens. Plant some in the cut flower garden, too.

My Personal Favorite

One of our natives, silvery lupine (*Lupinus argenteus*) features light bluish lavender to purple blossoms (12 to 30 in. tall). It can be seen growing throughout the mountains in open meadows and forests, and along roadsides.

Since they prefer cooler conditions, lupines are among the most dependable plants in the higher elevations, but I have grown them successfully in the High Plains when they are sited properly. The Russell hybrids are among the showiest for the perennial garden, but they require a richer, well-drained soil. Some of our native species tolerate drought better and can thrive under less than average soil conditions, but they are not as showy as the hybrids. When choosing which lupines to plant, remember that beauty is in the eye of the beholder. Lupines form large mounds of palmately compound leaves that add exceptional interest and contrast to the perennial bed. The showy pealike flowers are borne on columnar racemes in a great variety of colors, both solid and bicolors.

Bloom Period and Seasonal Color
May through July blooms in blue, purple, red, pink, white, or bicolored

Mature Height × Spread
18 in. to 3 ft. × 2 to 3 ft.

Zones
To zone 3

Oriental Poppy
Papaver orientale

Oriental poppies are the quintessential perennial for the early-summer perennial flower garden, and they're drought resistant. Huge flower buds, bristly and nodding, are held high above the coarse, hairy foliage that grows in a massive clump. What a joy to see these buds open into 5- to 6-in. globe-shaped flowers with thin, crepe paper petals and a showy boss of purple-black stamens. When in bloom, they dominate the garden. The foliage dies back during midsummer when the plant is in its dormant and water-conserving mode. Plant other water-efficient perennials, such as pitcher salvia, rudbeckia, coreopsis, or butterfly weed, to fill in the gap created by the "missing" poppy. After blooming, a showy seed pod is produced that can be used in dried floral arrangements.

Bloom Period and Seasonal Color
June to early July blooms in white, red, pink, orange, or bicolored

Mature Height × Spread
2 to 4 ft. × 2 to 4 ft.

Zones
To zone 3

When, Where, and How to Plant
Transplant potted oriental poppies in early spring or fall. They are notorious for not transplanting well, but 4- to 6-in. root cuttings can be taken in summer and replanted with success. Sow seeds in the fall or early spring. Locate in full sun. Well-drained soil is essential for their drought tolerance and winter survival. Soils that are too rich in organic matter and nutrients result in rank, weak growth and fewer flowers. Plant container-grown poppies so that the top of the rootball is level with the surrounding soil grade. Backfill, gently firm the soil around the plant, and water well.

Growing Tips
Water new plants regularly until they become well established; dig down 4 in. to check that the soil is drying out slightly between waterings. Once established, oriental poppies resist drought and need to be watered only once every seven to ten days. Water deeply, but infrequently. A light mulch of compost or well-aged manure can be spread around the plants in early fall or spring. In the spring, apply a slow-release fertilizer (5-10-5) to give the plants a boost for their growing season.

Care
Oriental poppies die back in midsummer, and new growth appears in early fall as the nights turn cool again. Carefully prune away ripened foliage. To prevent flower damage, water poppies at ground level when they are in bloom; don't use overhead sprinklers. These plants are generally not bothered by pests, but spider mites may attack during a hot, dry summer.

Companion Planting and Design
Use poppies as specimen plants or in a flower border, mass plantings, and the cut flower garden. Since oriental poppies steal the show in early summer, combine with softer, less striking companion plants such as yarrow, coreopsis, pitcher sage, or asters.

My Personal Favorites
'Allegro' is a beautiful scarlet with a dark basal blotch. 'Brilliant' produces fiery red blooms that are wonderful when backlit by a clear blue sky.

Penstemon
Penstemon spp. and hybrids

When, Where, and How to Plant
Transplant potted plants in the spring through early summer. Penstemons do best in full sun and well-drained soils. Well-drained soil of low to average fertility is fine. Do not add too much organic amendment, or you encourage crown rot. Penstemons are subject to rot if they are too wet in the winter, so site them on a rocky slope or raised bed. Loosen the soil in areas to be planted. Dig the planting hole twice as wide as the container or root system. Position the plant so that the soil level is the same as it was in the container or at the same depth the plants were originally growing. Backfill, firm soil gently, and water well. Space 12 to 18 in. apart.

Growing Tips
Water new plants regularly to permit them to become well established, but allow the soil to dry out between waterings. Scarlet bugler and other penstemons are drought-tolerant perennials and resent soggy conditions. In fact, once penstemons are established, it is best to leave them alone. There is no need to apply additional fertilizer since they prefer it "lean and dry." With less water and little care, plants bloom longer than plants placed in more formal, frequently watered flower beds.

Care
Increase the longevity of penstemons by not over-watering and by cutting the seedheads after bloom. Penstemons tend to reseed readily. Pests and diseases do not generally bother them.

Companion Planting and Design
Use penstemons in rock gardens, informal borders, or mixed dryland gardens. Combine with sages such as *Artemisia frigida*, ornamental grasses, and other water-thrifty perennials. Tall-growing varieties make excellent cut flowers.

My Personal Favorites
I like pineleaf penstemon (*P. pinifolius*). It has compact growth (1 ft.) with shrubby needlelike foliage and small, bright-scarlet flowers from June to early September. Rocky Mountain penstemon (*P. strictus*), 2 to 3 ft., is a striking plant with shiny foliage and deep-blue to purple flowers.

Plant penstemons in your garden, and if it's hummingbirds you want, it's hummingbirds you'll get! Scarlet bugler (Penstemon barbatus) and its panicles of bright-scarlet trumpet blooms bring these flying jewels into your garden. Butterflies and sphinx moths also find these flowers. This native penstemon thrives in rocky or gravelly soils and tolerates heat and drought. Orchid beard tongue (P. secundiflorus) is one of my favorite early blooming species. Penstemons are short lived if you overwater them; good drainage is essential. Because scarlet bugler is so long lived, this species is popular for hybridization and has been crossed with other penstemons to develop some exceptional varieties. One such cultivar is 'Prairie Dusk', with rich rose-purple flowers on 12- to 18-in. stems. 'Prairie Fire' has vermilion blossoms on 2-ft.-tall stems.

Other Common Name
Beard tongue

Bloom Period and Seasonal Color
Late spring to early summer blooms in blue, purple, pink, red, scarlet, or white

Mature Height × Spread
18 to 36 in. × 18 to 24 in.

Zones
To zone 3

Peony
Paeonia lactiflora and hybrids

Other perennials may come and go, but peonies last a lifetime. The "Queen of Garden Flowers," peonies are beloved by gardeners and nongardeners alike. When I was a child, my family and I brought bouquets of fragrant peony blooms to the cemetery on Memorial Day. Flowers range from 3 in. to 10 in. wide and may be single, double, or semidouble. Peonies contribute more to the garden than stunning flowers in spring. The foliage camouflages ripening spring-bulb foliage and bare-ankled perennials. As herbaceous perennials, peonies die back to the ground each winter. Tree peonies are somewhat different; even after herbaceous peonies have finished blooming, the tree peony's glossy green leaves remain handsome into fall. The vigorous woody plants grow into mounds 18 to 36 in. tall and wide.

Bloom Period and Seasonal Color
Late spring to early summer blooms in red, rose, pink, white, yellow, or bicolored

Mature Height × Spread
2 to 4 ft. × 3 ft.

Zones
To zone 3

When, Where, and How to Plant
Transplant potted peonies in the spring through early fall. Plant bare-root peonies in early spring. Ideally, locate them in well-drained soil with full to partial sun. Prepare the planting hole 24 to 36 in. across and at least 18 in. deep. Add a generous supply of compost, along with a handful of 5-10-5 granular fertilizer, and mix well. Gently firm the soil in the bottom of the hole so the peony won't settle too deeply. Place the crown of the plant so that the buds or "eyes" point upward. Planting depth is one of the secrets to success with peonies. The buds should be barely 1 in. below the soil's surface. If peonies are either planted or settle too deeply, they do not flower. Backfill, firm the soil around the roots, and water well. Space 2 to 3 ft. apart.

Growing Tips
Water plants well, particularly when buds are forming. Peonies may use up to an inch of water each week during the growing season. In the spring, apply a slow-release organic 10-10-10 granular fertilizer.

Care
I turn sturdy tomato cages upside down around young plants in the spring to prevent their flopping over. (Be careful about the sharp ends.) Be sure to remove ripened foliage in late fall or early winter. For winter protection, spread a layer of mulch over the crown in late fall. Peonies fail to bloom for several reasons—lack of moisture during plant development, unusually cool spring weather, too much shade, lack of nutrients, and plants that have settled too deeply. Ants visit peony buds in the spring, seeking the sweet secretions of nectar on the buds, or they may be "farming aphids." Just ignore them.

Companion Planting and Design
Use peonies as specimens or as an informal herbaceous hedge, or integrate them into perennial flower beds.

My Personal Favorite
Old-reliable 'Festiva Maxima' has fragrant, full double-white blooms flecked with dark red. Strong stems support the huge flowers.

When, Where, and How to Plant

Plant container-grown perennial flax in the spring through early fall. Seedlings can be lifted and replanted in early spring. Perennial flax prefers full sun, but tolerates some light shade. Too much shade causes the plants to grow leggy and produce fewer flowers. Perennial flax prefers well-drained clay soils. Allow room for plants to self-sow and fill in bare spots; space 15 to 18 in. apart. Dig the planting hole twice as wide as the root system. Position the plant so that the soil level is the same as it was in the container or at the same depth the plants were originally growing. Fill in with soil around the roots about halfway, gently firm, and water well. After the water soaks in, finish filling the hole with soil.

Growing Tips

As the soil dries out, water new transplants well to allow for healthy establishment. To conserve and maintain moisture, apply 2 in. of organic mulch around the plants. Once established, water the plants deeply each week. Perennial flax does well in soils of poor to average fertility. Avoid fertilizing with high-nitrogen plant foods, which results in tall, weak growth and few flowers. An application of a 5-10-5 fertilizer in early spring is all that's needed.

Care

Perennial flax needs little care and is not bothered by pests. To prevent frost heave, mulch plants in the winter after the ground freezes. Deadhead developing seedheads to encourage flax to rebloom in late summer. Cut the plants back by half to tidy up the garden and induce new growth. Leave some seeds if you want new seedlings to grow and fill in open areas.

Companion Planting and Design

Perennial flax is at its best in prairie and meadow plantings with grasses and other native wildflowers. Use in borders, mixed perennial beds, and rock gardens.

I Also Recommend

A western native, prairie flax (*Linum lewisii*), 2 to 3 ft., sports sky-blue flowers and tolerates partial shade.

Perennial flax is one of my favorites. Its narrow bluish green leaves provide an airy appearance among the foliage of other perennials. The wiry, often arching, stems support a profusion of delicate, simple blue flowers. White and dwarf cultivars are available. Individual flowers open on sunny days, but generally close by late afternoon and drop to the ground. New flowers are produced every day, so you won't even notice this natural thinning. Perennial flax self-sows in abundance and can fill in a large area within a few years. I allow the new seedlings to grow every year; this keeps the planting vigorous. You can transplant seedlings in the spring to share with friends. Perennial flax resists heat and tolerates drought—good for a water-thrifty garden or xeriscape.

Other Common Name
Blue flax

Bloom Period and Seasonal Color
May through June blooms in delicate blue or white

Mature Height × Spread
1 to 2 ft. × 12 to 15 in.

Zones
To zone 3

Perennial Salvia
Salvia × superba

Perennial hybrid salvia, or violet sage, provides months of purple-blue blooms on sturdy upright spikes. Salvia nemerosa 'East Friesland' has purple flowers and grows to 2 ft.; S. sylvestris 'May Night' has darker violet-blue flowers. 'Lubeca' has a shorter growth habit (15 to 18 in.) and rich purple flowers. There are pink- and white-flowering hybrids, too. Numerous dense spikes of flowers are held above handsome mounds of grayish green foliage. The spikes remain effective even after the flowers drop; they retain their reddish purple bracts for added contrast. Pitcher sage (Salvia azurea var. grandiflora) is a long-lived perennial with light-blue flower clusters cherished by bees, butterflies, and moths; it is well suited for a water-thrifty garden or xeriscape. Colorful and long-lasting blooms make this plant a favorite. It generally is not appealing to deer.

Other Common Name
Violet sage

Bloom Period and Seasonal Color
Late spring through September blooms in blue, purple, rose, violet-blue, pink, or white

Mature Height × Spread
18 to 24 in. × 18 to 36 in.

Zones
To zone 4

When, Where, and How to Plant
Plant potted perennial salvia in the spring through summer. The earlier you plant, the better to establish strong roots before winter. For optimum growth and flowering, locate salvia in full to partial sun and in well-drained soil. Too much shade results in sprawling plants with few flowers. Plant perennial salvia 1½ to 2 ft. apart. Dig the planting hole at least twice as wide as the container. Set the plant in the hole so that the soil level is the same as it was in the container. Backfill, gently firm the soil, and water well.

Growing Tips
Water regularly until the plants are well established. Once established, perennial salvia tolerates drought conditions with minimal watering, but during extended dry periods, water deeply every seven to ten days. A slow-release granular 5-10-5 fertilizer can be applied in the spring to provide nutrients throughout the summer. Perennial salvia is quick to grow and generally blooms well the first growing season.

Care
Plants that are properly located need minimal care. Remove the spent flower stalks to keep the planting tidy and to promote new, vigorous sturdy growth. Deadheading also encourages a second flush of bloom. Older plantings can be rejuvenated by dividing the clumps in the spring; carefully split the clumps with a spading fork or sharp knife. Mulch the plants in late fall or early winter with pine needles or evergreen boughs. This prevents severe desiccation and possible "winter kill." Pests do not generally bother perennial salvia.

Companion Planting and Design
Use perennial salvia in rock gardens and perennial borders, for edging, and in island gardens. The rich blue and violet blooms combine well with hardy geraniums, dianthus, pale daylilies, the silvery leaves of lamb's ears, and artemisias.

I Also Recommend
Upside-down sage (*Salvia jurisicii*) is a truly drought-tolerant perennial in the sunny flower garden. It blooms profusely with spikes of bluish lavender flowers above handsome gray-green foliage.

Purple Coneflower
Echinacea purpurea

When, Where, and How to Plant

Transplant potted plants in early spring through early fall. You can order bare-root plants by mail. Plant these as soon as the soil can be worked in the spring. This hardy perennial tolerates a wide range of soils, including heavy clay, crushed granite, and extremely sandy soil. Moderately moist, well-drained soils are ideal. Full sun is best although the coneflower tolerates partial shade in the late afternoon. Space 1 1/2 to 2 ft. apart. Dig the planting hole twice as wide as the container or spread of the roots. Position the plant so that the soil level is the same as it was in the container. Fill in with soil around the root system about halfway up, gently firm around the roots, and water well. Add more soil to complete the planting.

Growing Tips

Until the plants are established, water regularly as the soil dries out. A slow-release 5-10-5 granular fertilizer applied at planting provides nutrients through the growing season. Coneflower withstands heat and drought. Water deeply once a week during dry periods.

Care

This easy-to-grow plant is generally an undemanding favorite. Deadhead spent flowers to prolong the blooming season. As late summer approaches, leave some flowers to form seedheads for winter interest; wild birds love the seeds. Purple coneflower self-sows seeds that germinate throughout the garden. These seedlings bloom the second or third year, but may not be identical to the parent plant. This works well for a naturescape or meadow garden. If you desire a more formal garden, weed out the seedlings.

Companion Planting and Design

Use in the perennial flower bed, mixed plantings, the cutting garden, the meadow garden, and especially a naturescape setting. Coneflower combines well with ornamental grasses, black-eyed Susans, asters, and sedums.

My Personal Favorites

'Bright Star' has rosy-pink flower rays with maroon disks; its petals tend to be more horizontal. 'White Swan' is a compact white form (24 to 36 in.) with copper-orange cones.

A favorite plant for butterflies who seek its nectar and for flower arrangers who love the long-lasting blooms and dried cone heads, the purple coneflower is also a favorite in my garden. This perennial is easy to care for and thrives in a sunny border or meadow garden. Native Americans have long used the purple coneflower and its relatives for medicine, and today Echinacea has renewed popularity as a treatment to prevent the common cold. If you've ever touched the cone of the flower, it comes as no surprise that Echinacea comes from the Greek echinos, which means "hedgehog," giving it the common name hedgehog coneflower. But coneflower is a bright and durable addition to the perennial garden.

Other Common Names
Coneflower, purple echinacea

Bloom Period and Seasonal Color
July to August blooms in deep-pink, rose, or white

Mature Height × Spread
2 to 4 ft. × 18 to 24 in.

Zones
To zone 3

Rocky Mountain Columbine

Aquilegia caerulea and hybrids

Rocky Mountain columbine produces an abundance of long-spurred flowers from mid-May through June with repeat blooms in August if the plants are deadheaded soon after flowering. The delicate 2½-in. flowers have bluish purple sepals and white petals. Both foliage and flowers make charming additions to the perennial garden. Rocky Mountain columbine prefers cool, moist locations; High Plains gardens are often too hot, but this plant is a perfect choice in the foothills and High Country. The secret to success with columbines is to realize that the plants are short-lived perennials. They should be replanted every three to four years if you want to keep the original varieties. Allow Rocky Mountain columbines to go to seed; they sow themselves in a multitude of colors.

Other Common Name
Columbine

Bloom Period and Seasonal Color
Mid-May to August blooms in bluish purple, lavender, yellow, and red

Mature Height × Spread
2 to 4 ft. × 10 to 12 in.

Zones
To zone 2

When, Where, and How to Plant

Plant from spring through fall. Collect and scatter the small, jet-black seeds while they are still fresh in late summer to early fall. These seed-grown plants generally flower the following year. New seedlings from hybrids vary considerably in flower color, but are more muted than the parents. Columbine prefers well-drained, light, humus-enriched soils. It also grows well in sandy or rocky spots. Locate in full sun to partial shade in an area with good air circulation. Good drainage is essential. Position container-grown plants at the same depth as they were growing. Space the plants 12 to 15 in. apart. Mulch after transplanting to maintain and conserve moisture and to keep the roots cool.

Growing Tips

Water regularly until the plants are established, then keep them watered during drought. Water deeply each week during extended dry periods. Scatter a slow-release organic 5-10-5 granular fertilizer around the plants in the spring to provide nutrients through the growing season.

Care

Columbines thrive for several years when established in well-drained soils with sufficient humus. To encourage secondary bloom, deadhead spent flowers routinely (unless you intend to collect the seeds). Since individual columbines are short lived, allow plants to reseed to keep the population stocked. Dig up hybrid columbines when they begin to lose their vigor, and replace them with new plants. Leaf miners can become a nuisance; the damage created as they tunnel through the leaves is unattractive, but doesn't kill the plant. Remove and destroy infested leaves. The plant sends out new growth to sustain it through the season. Powdery mildew can appear in late summer and early fall. Snip off and dispose of infected leaves.

Companion Planting and Design

Columbines combine well with cranebills, coral bells, and lady's mantle. The scalloped foliage creates a nice accent in the perennial garden.

My Personal Favorite

Among those in the Songbird Series, I prefer 'Blue Jay'.

Russian Sage

Perovskia atriplicifolia

When, Where, and How to Plant

Transplant potted plants in the spring through early fall. Don't wait too long; roots need time to establish before winter. Bare-root plants can be planted in early spring. Locate in full sun for optimum growth and flowering. These plants tolerate some shade, but lean toward the light and sprawl. Good drainage is necessary; amend heavy clay soils with compost or sphagnum peat moss. Space 1 1/2 to 2 ft. apart. Dig the planting hole at least twice as wide as the container or root system. Position the plant so that the soil level is the same as it was in the container. Fill in with soil around the rootball about halfway, gently firm the soil, and water well. After the water soaks in, finish filling in the hole with backfill.

Growing Tips

Water new transplants regularly to help them become established, but allow the soil to dry out between waterings. Once established, Russian sage is quite drought enduring. Plants prefer soil on the lean side, so don't fertilize too often and avoid high-nitrogen plant fertilizer. A light application of all-purpose 5-10-5 in early spring is all that's needed.

Care

This tough and long-lived perennial has no serious insect pests or disease problems. Classified as a subshrub, Russian sage doesn't die back completely. Leave the silvery-white stems over the winter to add interest to the landscape. Prune in the spring as new growth reappears. At that time, you can cut the plant down to the ground or remove dead and weak branches and cut remaining branches back, leaving five to seven vigorous buds.

Companion Planting and Design

Russian sage has a blooming period among the longest of any perennial. Use it in many plant combinations, including daylilies, purple coneflowers, rudbeckias, and asters. Use in perennial borders, backdrops, mixed plantings, and cutting gardens. Bees love it.

My Personal Favorite

'Filagran' has all the virtues of the species, but more delicate foliage and an upright growth habit.

Russian sage is a graceful, aromatic perennial clothed in silvery, grayish green foliage topped with beautiful lavender-blue blossoms that are beloved by bees. The flowering effect lasts for months; combined with ornamental grasses in late summer, it makes quite an elegant statement in the landscape. With its light and airy appearance, Russian sage works nicely as a backdrop for daylilies and 'Autumn Joy' sedum, and it combines well with purple coneflower. The dissected foliage has a noticeable odor when crushed, similar to the culinary sage. But Russian sage is not used in the kitchen unless in a floral arrangement. It makes a nice cut flower, so you can include it in the cutting garden. Russian sage is one of the few perennials that is deer-resistant.

Bloom Period and Seasonal Color
Early summer to fall spikes of lavender-blue blooms

Mature Height × Spread
3 to 5 ft. × 4 ft.

Zones
To zone 4

Sedum 'Autumn Joy'

Sedum 'Autumn Joy'

If you're looking for a dependable perennial, one of the top ten is Sedum 'Autumn Joy'. The attractive, fleshy light-green leaves add texture to the flower garden from spring through fall. When this plant forms flower buds, the chunky heads resemble broccoli. As the flowers open, the tight clusters reveal vivid, near-iridescent pink blooms in the sunlight, which beckons honeybees, bumblebees, and a variety of butterflies to the flower garden. In late summer to early fall, the pink flowers transform into a mellow deep rose and open wider to mature into a richer mahogany that remains upright throughout the fall and winter, unless an early, heavy, and wet snow buries them. Although some believe sedum is often overplanted, it is a durable and long-lasting water-thrifty perennial.

Other Common Name
Showy stonecrop

Bloom Period and Seasonal Color
August to frost blooms in vivid pink, maturing to red or copper

Mature Height × Spread
18 to 36 in. × 12 to 24 in.

Zones
To zone 3

When, Where, and How to Plant
Plant potted *Sedum* 'Autumn Joy' from spring through fall. To get the best growth and lots of blooms, locate the plants in full sun and average well-drained soil. Avoid soils that are too rich; they make plants leggy and cause the large flower heads to flop over unless you provide support. Tall sedums are highly tolerant of heat and drought conditions. Space from 1¹/₂ to 2 ft. apart. Dig the planting hole twice as wide as the pot in which it was grown. Position the plant so that the soil level is the same as it was in the container. Backfill, gently firm the soil, and water thoroughly.

Growing Tips
Until the plants are well established, water regularly as the soil becomes dry. Water thoroughly during summer, but not too frequently. Allow the soil to dry out. A light application of all-purpose 5-10-5 fertilizer in early spring helps the plant get off to a hardy start. Avoid high-nitrogen fertilizer; it promotes leafy growth and weak stems.

Care
Sedum 'Autumn Joy' grows with almost no input from the gardener. As older clumps become crowded and begin to split open in the center, divide the plant. In early May, lift the clumps with a spading fork and remove the unproductive center. Replant healthy, vigorous divisions from the outside of the clump. The presence of aphids isn't a significant problem, but keep them in check by washing them off with a spray of water. To tidy the garden in the spring, cut back the dried seedheads to make way for a burst of fresh new growth.

Companion Planting and Design
Good companions are purple coneflower, *Aster frikartii*, black-eyed Susan, and ornamental grasses. Plant in island gardens, perennial borders, and mixed plantings with other water-thrifty perennials and as an accent plant in a rock garden.

I Also Recommend
S. telephium ssp. *maximum* 'Atropurpureum' has purple to maroon, lightly toothed leaves with clusters of small pink flowers.

Shasta Daisy
Leucanthemum × superbum

When, Where, and How to Plant

Plant shasta daisies in the spring to enjoy the current season of bloom. Plant in groups of three or more; mass plantings create a more natural effect. Most prefer full sun, but newer varieties seem to do best with afternoon shade to reduce scorch to the flowers. Shasta daisies grow best in well-drained soils that are moist and fertile. Space plants 18 to 24 in. apart. Position the rootball so its top is level with the surrounding soil grade. Backfill with soil, firm gently around the roots, and water thoroughly.

Growing Tips

Water new transplants regularly as the soil dries out. Shasta daisies need ample water during their blooming and growing season, so don't skimp or the flowers may be sparse. Water deeply each week or as the soil begins to dry out. A year-round 2-in. layer of mulch helps keep the soil moist and cool, and discourages weed growth. Incorporate a slow-release 5-10-5 granular fertilizer into the soil at planting. Fertilize in the spring with a slow-acting 5-10-5 granular plant food to provide nutrients through the growing season.

Care

Deadheading encourages rebloom and extends the flowering season. Occasionally, the foliage and stems may be attacked by aphids. These are easily controlled by handpicking, washing off with a stream of water, or using a homemade soap spray. You can also invite ladybugs into the garden to devour these critters. Shasta daisies can be fairly short-lived, so be prepared to divide or replace them every three years or so.

Companion Planting and Design

Shasta daisies are perfect plants to use when naturalizing into a meadow garden, and they work well in formal flower beds or the cutting garden. Combine with daylilies, yarrow, phlox, and anemones. Dwarf varieties are useful for edging and can be planted in containers.

My Personal Favorites

There are many wonderful varieties and hybrids available. 'Alaska' and 'Polaris' have large, single, pure-white blooms. 'White Knight Hybrid' has 4-inch-wide blooms on sturdy 20-in. stems.

For a brilliant and fun summer display, a drift of Shasta daisies is hard to surpass. Butterflies love to perch on the blooms, diligently sipping nectar stored in the hundreds of miniature yellow florets that are compacted into the golden centers of each flower head. The pure-white rays, or petals, are held stiffly on naked stems above clumps of dark-green, coarsely toothed, linear leaves. Besides the simple flower forms, some varieties have frilled, crested, or double flowers. Shasta daisies put on their best show in full sun, but appreciate some afternoon shade. During their blooming and growing season, they need ample water, but will tolerate drought for a short time. 'Alaska' and 'Polaris' varieties produce large single flowers in profusion.

Bloom Period and Seasonal Color
June through September blooms in white

Mature Height × Spread
1 to 3 ft. × 2 ft.

Zones
To zone 4

Siberian Iris
Iris sibirica

Siberian irises are durable perennials and hardy at higher elevations. Their flowers have the same elements of bearded irises—three spreading outer petals called "falls" and three upright petals called "standards"—but they are smaller and more open, lacking the furry strips or beards on the falls. The falls on Siberian irises often have intricate veining and a marking called a "blaze." Their light, airy flowers dance like butterflies atop slender, upright stalks of grasslike leaves. The elegant blooms come in blue, purple, red-violet, or white and are truly stunning under a clear blue sky. Siberian iris's handsome arching foliage provides vertical lift to the perennial garden all summer long. As the name suggests, Siberian irises are very cold hardy and can survive even the coldest winters.

Bloom Period and Seasonal Color
Late spring to early summer blooms in blue, purple, red-violet, or white

Mature Height × Spread
18 in. to 4 ft. × 24 in.

Zones
To zone 3

When, Where, and How to Plant
Plant container-grown plants from spring through early fall. Plant rhizomes in the spring to ensure good establishment. Siberian irises do best in well-drained soils rich in humus. Choose a site with full sun to partial shade. These plants don't like to dry out; if the soil has not been prepared, add 3 to 4 in. of compost to retain moisture and improve drainage, especially in sandy soils. Space 1 1/2 to 2 ft. apart. Set rhizomes 2 in. deep, and water well. Place container-grown plants in a hole twice as wide as the container. Position the plant so that the soil level is the same as in the container. Fill in with soil around the roots about halfway, gently firm, and water well. After the water soaks in, add more soil to complete the planting, and water again.

Growing Tips
Provide ample water for the first month or so, until the leaves emerge. Apply a 2-in. layer of mulch to conserve water and to discourage weed invasions. Water Siberian irises regularly during the summer. Fertilize with a slow-release 10-10-10 plant food in the spring.

Care
Deadhead spent flower stalks after flowering. Though they don't need frequent division, if clumps of Siberian iris die out in the center and produce fewer flowers, lift and divide the clump in the spring. Split the clump in pieces with a pruning saw or sharp knife. Discard the woody center, and replant the vigorous portions from the outside of the clump. New divisions may take two years to put on a show. There is no need to be concerned about pests or problems.

Companion Planting and Design
Use Siberian irises as accents among peonies, poppies, coreopsis, hardy geraniums, and other perennials. The foliage makes a graceful screen, and the blooms paint a cloud of color near water features.

My Personal Favorites
'Caesar's Brother' is a deep purple with graceful blooms. 'Ruffled Velvet' has velvety, reddish purple flowers with falls that roll under at the edges.

Sneezeweed
Helenium autumnale

When, Where, and How to Plant

Plant container-grown sneezeweed from spring through fall. Locate in full sun and well-drained soil. A deep soil enriched with moisture-retentive compost keeps the plants from drying out in summer's heat. Space 18 to 24 in. apart. Dig the planting hole twice as wide as the container. Position the plant so that the soil level is the same as it was in the container. Fill in with soil around the root system about halfway up, gently firm, and water well. After the water soaks in, add more soil to completely fill the hole.

Growing Tips

Water new transplants regularly until establishment. Mulch to retain moisture and to prevent weeds. Provide ample water during extended dry, hot spells, watering deeply once a week. A slow-release 5-10-5 organic fertilizer can be applied at planting and annually to provide nutrients through the growing season and each spring thereafter.

Care

If sited properly, sneezeweed thrives and blooms profusely. To encourage more flowers, deadhead old flowering stems after the first flush of blooms. Tall leggy growth results if the plant is in too much shade or the soil is too rich or overfertilized. Every four to five years as the plants mature and the clumps die out, lift and divide in the spring. Dig old clumps, and split the fibrous root system into several sections. Replant the most vigorous sections taken from the outside of the clump at the same level the plant was originally growing, and water well.

Companion Planting and Design

Use in sunny perennial beds, borders, moist areas, and naturalized plantings. Combine with 'Coronation Gold' yarrow or 'Moonbeam' coreopsis for a nice effect. It works well with butterfly bush, perennial sage, and verbena.

My Personal Favorites

An old favorite, 'Moerheim Beauty' (3 ft. tall) features rich reddish brown flowers that fade to burnt orange. 'Wyndley' (2 to 2$\frac{1}{2}$ ft.) has copper-orange flowers; 'The Bishop' (2 to 2$\frac{1}{2}$ ft.), with yellow flowers, has more compact growth.

Indispensable in the summer and early fall garden, sneezeweed lights up the flower border. Daisylike flowers feature a prominent raised and rounded knob of disk florets, surrounded by wedge-shaped, notched, and reflexed petals. Sneezeweed has become a favored plant because of its heat tolerance and long blooming season. Among the best known are 'Butterpat', with long-blooming yellow flowers, and 'Bruno', which has reddish bronze flowers. With a name like sneezeweed, it's easy to understand why this plant has a hard time achieving fame. Many years ago, the leaves were dried and ground up to produce a type of snuff. Today, this perennial is among the best for intense summer colors and ease of care. It seldom needs staking and quickly fills in an area.

Other Common Name
Helen's flower

Bloom Period and Seasonal Color
August through September daisylike blooms in orange-red or yellow

Mature Height × Spread
3 to 5 ft. × 2 ft.

Zones
To zone 3

Sweet William

Dianthus barbatus

The clove-scented flowers of this old-fashioned beauty evoke memories of a parent's or grandparent's flower garden. It is a member of the Dianthus genus, which includes pinks and carnations. Unfortunately, many of the new cultivars have lost the intoxicating fragrance of flowers from times past. Sweet Williams are considered biennial, but the plants live much longer: They self-sow so readily that they appear to persist almost indefinitely. Cottage pink (Dianthus plumarius) is an excellent mat-forming (6 to 12 in.) species with flowers 1/2 to 1 1/2 in. across in red, pink, white, and bicolors. The foliage is usually gray-green and often evergreen, which provides a contrast to the foliage of other plants even in winter. Use in front of borders, in rock gardens, and as accent plants.

Other Common Name
Dianthus

Bloom Period and Seasonal Color
Late spring to summer red, pink, purple-red, or multicolored fragrant flowers

Mature Height × Spread
6 to 18 in. × 12 to 24 in.

Zones
To zone 3

When, Where, and How to Plant
Plant from early spring through early fall. Bare-root stock is best planted in early spring. *Dianthus* species prefer well-drained soils and full to partial sun. Heavy soils should be thoroughly loosened and amended with compost to improve drainage. Space plants 18 in. to 2 ft. apart, depending on the species. Dig the planting hole twice as wide as the container or the root system. Position the plant so that the soil level is the same as it was in the container. Fill in with soil around the roots about halfway, gently firm, and water well. After the water soaks in, finish filling in the hole with soil.

Growing Tips
Water new transplants regularly as the soil dries out. Apply an organic mulch to maintain and conserve moisture. Sweet William and other *Dianthus* species do best in cool weather, but tolerate drought if watered regularly. Avoid overwatering, especially in winter—the plants rot if kept too wet. Slow-acting 5-10-5 organic granular fertilizer applied at planting and annually in the spring provides nutrients through the growing season. Do not use high-nitrogen fertilizers; they promote weak growth, leaving the plant susceptible to breakage and rot.

Care
Deadhead when the plants finish flowering; this promotes reblooming and keeps the plants tidy. Garden slugs are fond of *Dianthus* species but can be deterred by applying a collar of wood ashes around the plants; also see page 258. If powdery mildew attacks in the summer, use the homemade remedy for prevention on page 258.

Companion Planting and Design
Plant Sweet William and other *Dianthus* species in borders, in rock gardens, or as specimen plants. Cottage pinks, with their soft mats of gray-green foliage, accent rock walls, garden pathways, and rocky slopes.

I Also Recommend
With its mat-forming, bright-green foliage, *D. deltoides* 'Brilliant', maiden pink, makes a nice ground cover (6 to 8 in.). Double, bright-crimson blossoms appear for several weeks in the summer. 'Tiny Rubies' (4 in. tall) features deep-pink blooms; use it in rock gardens.

Veronica
Veronica spicata

When, Where, and How to Plant

Transplant potted veronicas in the spring through early fall. Choose a location in full to partial sun with average, well-drained soil. Good drainage is a must. Loosen the soil well, and augment it with compost for moisture retention and to improve soil porosity. Space spiked speedwell 18 to 20 in. apart. Dig the planting hole twice as wide as the container or root system. Position the plant so that the soil level is the same as it was in the container or at the same depth the plants were originally growing. Backfill with soil, gently firm the soil, and water thoroughly.

Growing Tips

Water regularly as the soil dries out. Veronica appreciates a deep watering each week during drought periods. Mulch to conserve water, to keep the soil cool, and to discourage weed competition. Apply a low-nitrogen, slow-release 5-10-5 fertilizer in the spring, but avoid high-nitrogen fertilizers; they result in floppy plants.

Care

When planted in full sun and well-drained soil, veronica is durable and resists pests. To promote rebloom, deadhead the spent flowering spikes. Older plants can be divided for rejuvenation—this should be done in the spring. Dig the clumps, and split them apart with a sharp knife. Replant the vigorous sections taken from the outside of the clumps. Water new divisions well until established. Taller species of veronica make good cut flowers. Divide old plants every three to four years to keep the plants vigorous and compact.

Companion Planting and Design

Use veronica in mixed plantings of lady's mantle, dianthus, and 'Moonbeam' coreopsis, and plant it with hardy geraniums. Some veronicas form tight mounds for a rock garden; others are easy-care ground covers. The taller species are superior for the perennial bed or border.

I Also Recommend

Woolly veronica (*V. incana*), 12 to 24 in., is a wonderful plant with silvery foliage and an ocean of navy-blue flowers. Use it to border a pathway or driveway.

Spiked speedwell is a superior garden perennial that provides vertical lift to the mound and mat shapes of the garden foreground. It brings a refreshing spiky contrast to an abundance of rounded plants. Veronica's tapering spikes of light-blue to lavender blossoms tower above neat clumps of green foliage. Some cultivars, such as 'Blue Fox', can be fairly tall (at 24 in.) and are suitable for the center of an island garden. 'Red Fox' sports 8- to 12-in. spikes of red-violet blooms from a low clump of foliage. 'Icicle' has clean white flowers with contrasting dark-green foliage that blooms most of the summer. With their showy spikes and variety of growth habits, veronicas are truly the elite of the perennial garden.

Other Common Name
Spiked speedwell

Bloom Period and Seasonal Color
May through August blooms in blue, pink, rose, or white

Mature Height × Spread
12 in. to 2 ft. × 18 to 24 in.

Zones
To zone 3

Roses *for the Rockies*

As a child, I was always fascinated by the old shrub rose 'Harison's Yellow' growing along the fence row, not far from the irrigation ditch. Without fail, it bloomed every year, filling the air with its unforgettable fragrance. Though this old rose bush would bloom only once, over three to four weeks, there were hundreds of scented blooms. Today's modern roses, particularly hybrid tea roses, are much more tame; they bloom from summer till a hard frost in autumn. Perhaps we've become spoiled: Developing a long bloom period has become a driving force in modern rose breeding. We haven't come to expect this from the spring-blooming daffodils, tulips, and peonies. Each season has many other flowering plants for us to enjoy.

Fortunately, there are rose bushes for all tastes. Growing them in the Rockies is different, so let us briefly explore rose gardening as it pertains to our climate and soil.

The Secret to Successful Rose Gardening

Most of us instinctively love roses. But loving roses and knowing how to grow them are often two different matters. To be successful in the art of rose gardening in the Rockies, one must not forget about the practicalities. Roses pose a particular challenge for Rocky Mountain gardeners since many of the modern types cannot endure the cold and fluctuating winter conditions. How much coddling do you want to give to rose bushes in your landscape? Not only is it disappointing to buy roses each spring, only to have them die after the first winter, but it's hard on the pocketbook. So if you stumble upon an old variety that has stood the test of time, it deserves consideration. Though that old shrub rose from yesteryear was remarkably water thrifty and adaptable, it roots deeply and requires deep digging before planting. So don't expect a rose to do well if you just dig a hole, stick the bush in, and water it now and then. It takes some planning to find the logical location for specific rose varieties, and it takes time to properly prepare the soil.

The Who's Who Among Roses

With so many roses to choose from, it's a good idea to gain a basic understanding of how roses are classified. The American Rose Society (ARS) lists over fifty categories. This can become quite confusing, even a bit intimidating. Rose aficionados are very serious about rose classification. That may be fine for them, but for average gardeners, growing roses should be fun and rewarding. In this chapter, you find brief descriptions of some of the more popular groups of roses that can be grown successfully in our region. You can even grow roses in pots if you have limited gardening space.

What Roses Like

Most roses perform best in full sun, but you can expect excellent results if they are planted in a spot where they receive six to eight hours of sun daily. The location should have good air circulation—avoid a "heat trap" where afternoon sun stresses the plants. Too much shade yields few flowers and early attacks from powdery mildew disease. Good soil drainage is essential to grow roses successfully. Poorly drained sites or locations where water accumulates result in short-lived rose bushes.

To test your soil's drainage, dig several holes 18 in. deep in scattered locations where you intend to plant. Fill each hole with water. After twelve to twenty-four hours, fill the holes with water again. If the water drains away in eight hours or less, your soil is adequately permeable to air and water and will support plant life. Soils that drain as fast as the water enters are too permeable (sandy); soils that do not drain in eight hours are not permeable enough (clay) and will result in oxygen starvation to plant roots. The solution to both problems is similar—add a quality organic material such as compost, aged manure, sphagnum peat moss, or a combination of these materials. Organic matter helps hold moisture in sandy, fast-draining soils and helps open up clay soils to improve drainage and provide oxygen.

Making a Good Investment

Roses grow in a wide range of soil types, from heavy clay and crushed granite to sandy conditions. But take the time to build a good soil; you'll grow more vigorous plants with more prolific blossoms. Even the ugliest soil can be improved by adding quality organic matter, plus loosening and aerating it. If the planting location is new, infertile, compacted, and in need of improvement, dig the planting hole 2 to 3 ft. wide and 18 to 24 in. deep. The subsoil in the bottom of the hole should be thoroughly loosened. To your native soil, add one-third to one-half organic matter by volume and mix well. If your soil does not require such extensive treatment, it can be improved by spreading a 2 to 3 in. layer of compost over the soil surface and working it in to a depth of 10 to 12 inches. Then dig the appropriate-sized planting hole.

Selecting Roses

Rose bushes are available as bare-root plants, potted, and in packages. Mail-order nurseries usually send out bare-root dormant plants. Local garden and nursery retailers sell container-grown roses. Department and grocery stores may offer both packaged and potted roses. Experience has shown that bare-root,

Hybrid Tea Rose
'Double Delight'

dormant plants are excellent choices when planted in early spring. They successfully acclimate and adapt to local soil conditions. Potted roses are a good choice if the nursery has practiced good cultural practices in potting and growing the plants.

Bush and Climbing Roses in Garden

Packaged roses should be purchased before they send out long shoots or before they have had a chance to dry out in storage.

Planting Tips

The preferred time to plant roses in the Rockies is spring, though container-grown plants can be planted successfully from spring through early fall. The earlier you plant, the greater chance the plant has to develop a strong, vigorous root system before the heat of summer or before the soil freezes. Prepare your planting location before buying the plants. If bare-root roses and packaged roses have dry roots when they arrive, put them in a 5-gallon bucket of tepid water to soak overnight. Avoid soaking the roots longer than twenty-four hours.

Bring the rose to the planting hole and prepare it for planting. Prune away any damaged or broken roots. Position the bush in the hole so that the graft or bud union (swollen knot or knob) is an inch below ground level. If needed, mound backfill soil in the center of the hole to position the bush properly. Gently add the prepared backfill soil around the roots and firm it with your hands. When you have filled the hole in halfway, stop and water thoroughly. After the water has soaked in, finish adding the remaining soil and water again.

When planting is complete, the top of the bush can be pruned. To keep the center of the bush open for light and air circulation, prune the canes to an outward-facing bud. Pruning cuts should be made at a 30 to 45 degree slant above a bud, leaving 6 to 8 in. of the cane.

Next, cover the newly planted and pruned rose bush with a mound of the loose, prepared backfill soil. This prevents the canes from desiccation while the root system becomes established. In early spring, this technique protects the emerging shoots from frost damage. To prevent damaging the tender new growth, take care when removing the soil from around the stems.

Potted roses can be planted throughout the growing season. Dig the planting hole wide enough to accommodate the root system without crowding and deep enough to position the bud union 1 in. below ground level. If the roots have become rootbound, carefully loosen and spread them out into the planting hole or lightly score the rootball to encourage root development. Fill in with backfill soil, and water thoroughly.

Watering Tips

To grow vigorously and produce lots of blooms, roses need plenty of water. Dig into the top 2 to 4 in. of soil; if the soil is dry, it's time to water. Roses growing in clay soils require less watering than roses in sandy soils. Newly planted roses may need to be watered twice a week until they become well established. When you water, water thoroughly and deeply. To reduce leaf diseases, water roses from the bottom rather than sprinkling overhead. To maintain soil moisture and conserve water—mulch. Pine needles, coarse compost, shredded cedar, and pole peelings are good choices for mulching roses.

With fluctuating weather conditions in late fall and winter, dry air and long periods without rain or snow, it is important to drag out the hose occasionally and water. Extended dry spells during fall and winter can result in the death of the root system. Water when air temperatures are above freezing and when the soil is not frozen solid. Water early in the day so the liquid has time to soak in before nightfall. Fall and winter watering may be needed every four to five weeks, depending on weather and soil conditions.

Fertilizing Tips

Today's modern roses need several applications of fertilizer to keep growing vigorously and blooming. Apply an appropriate rose fertilizer monthly beginning in mid-May and ending by mid-August. My favorite is an organic-based granular that can be applied monthly through mid-August. Follow label directions on the rose fertilizer package. Avoid the old adage: "If a little fertilizer is good, a bunch more will be even better." To reduce the chance of stressing the plant roots, water the soil the day before fertilizing.

Pruning Tips

Roses need to be pruned to maintain vigor and health and, in some cases, to keep the bush in bounds. Depending on the effect you want, roses can be pruned in a variety of ways. In the Rockies, don't prune roses back severely in the fall. They need all the stored food energy possible to sustain themselves in our fluctuating climate. Some general guidelines for pruning established roses: Prune hybrid teas, grandifloras, floribundas, and polyanthas in the spring; climbing roses should be pruned after flowering. Prune the nonproductive old heavy canes of climbing roses to ground level in early spring. Remember that roses are resilient and will benefit from proper pruning.

The Most Wanted List

Luckily, our semiarid climate and higher altitude translates to relatively few pest problems on roses. But as we become more urbanized, pests soon follow. Early spring visitors may include aphids; these small and voracious pests cluster on the buds and young tender growth to feed on the juices of the plant. They may be green, red, tan, or black and are easily banished by smashing them between your fingers and rinsing with clear water from the hose. If you prefer, Neem oil, homemade soap sprays, or insecticides can be used. Read and follow label directions.

Summer insects may include the curculio beetle, which drills holes in rose buds; if spotted, it drops from the bud to the ground and scurries away. If you're quick, hand picking keeps them at bay.

Spider mites are minuscule pests found on the undersides of the leaves; their feeding causes the foliage to develop a "salt and pepper" or stippled appearance. They can be kept under control by a forceful spray of water from the garden hose directed to the underside of the leaves on a weekly basis. Watering from the bottom of the bush is also effective in thwarting other pests.

Thrips affect the buds and blossoms of roses and can be found at the base of the flower petals. They seem to prefer light colored blossoms, and damage can be detected by discoloration of the flower petals. Some buds may not open normally because of their presence. Systemic insecticides should be used if thrips pose a threat in your rose garden.

The rose midge is perhaps the worst enemy; it causes the tips and buds to wither, blacken, and die. If rose midge becomes a problem, soil insecticide treatments are recommended, plus periodic insecticide applications to the plant.

Powdery mildew, blackspot, rust, anthracnose, and verticillium wilt are some common diseases that may attack stressed or weakened roses.

Providing proper growing conditions, well-drained soil, and good air circulation, along with the good cultural practices of watering, fertilizing, and pruning; removing yellow and diseased leaves; maintaining clean mulch around the plants; and inspecting the rose bushes weekly helps reduce the incidence of major disease and pest outbreaks.

Winter Care

Some of the most popular roses, including hybrid teas, grandifloras, floribundas, and many climbing types, cannot endure cold and fluctuating weather conditions. After the first hard freeze, these types can be protected by applying a layer of loose soil at the base of each rose. Form a 6 to 12 in. cone-shaped mound around the bases of the canes. For additional protection, you can add evergreen boughs or straw on top of these mounds to protect the upper portions of the canes. Here's a Green Thumb Tip: Place an inverted tomato cage over the rose bush to hold the loose mulch materials in place. Tie the loose canes with soft twine to prevent wind damage. Climbing roses can be laid on the ground and protected with shredded wood mulches or a covering of evergreen boughs. Don't forget to water if the weather has been dry and windy.

Not So Needy

I admit to being a lazy gardener. With the size of my landscape and so many other things to grow, there isn't time to lavish a lot of care on needy rose bushes. If I could have it my way, none of my roses would receive special treatment. Over the years I have learned that roses are less demanding than many of the rose gardening books make them out to be. Roses don't need an inordinate amount of care, just a little care on a regular basis. Well-drained soil, adequate moisture, occasional fertilizing, and regular maintenance make your roses thrive.

'Iceberg' Border

Climbing Rose

Rosa

When trained to a trellis, fence, wall, pillar, or arbor, climbing roses can raise your landscape to new heights. Often included in the group known as "ramblers," climbing roses generally bloom once in late spring to early summer. They have mixed parentage and vary in color, growth rate, hardiness, and fragrance. It is best to select the hardier cultivars, as fluctuating winter weather can readily kill exposed and unprotected canes. Climbers generally bloom on a cane from the previous year's growth and need extra protection to prevent their freezing. Since climbers require different care than other roses, be prepared to devote some extra time to growing and caring for them. The Canadian Explorer Series promise hardier climbing varieties for our region.

Other Common Name
Rambling rose

Bloom Period and Seasonal Color
Mid-May to frost; blooms in all colors except blue

Mature Length
6 to 20 ft.

Zones
To zone 5

When, Where, and How to Plant
Plant bare-root climbing roses in early spring; healthy container-grown plants can be planted anytime from spring to early fall. Locate the plants in full to partial sun, preferably with an eastern or southern exposure, with shelter from prevailing winds. Good drainage is essential; prepare the soil well in advance of planting. Consult page 187 for details on soil preparation. Dig the planting hole 2 to 3 ft. wide to a depth of 2 ft. and amend with compost and a handful of 5-10-5 fertilizer. Have the rose support in place before planting.

Growing Tips
Water climbing roses regularly throughout the growing season, and apply an organic mulch to maintain moisture. Water every four to five weeks during prolonged drought in fall and winter. If planted near the foundation, take care to water them deeply. Consult page 189 for more details on watering. Fertilize monthly with an organic-based, slow-release rose food; stop fertilizing by mid-August.

Care
Climbers almost always bloom on laterals (side branches) off the main cane. Training canes laterally encourages more and better blooms. After blooming, prune the bloom stem down, leaving two leaves above the main stem. This causes a new bloom to come from the same lateral. Shape the bush and thin canes anytime during the growing season. Spring pruning consists of taking out small or nonblooming branches and removing dead wood. Every three years, remove one-third of the oldest basal canes to maintain a climber that renews itself. Refer to page 190 for information on pests and diseases.

Companion Planting and Design
Climbers may be used as an architectural feature in your landscape, as the center of a mixed bed of other rose types, or as a sprawling mound in a large rock garden.

My Personal Favorites
'Improved Blaze' is a reliable climber with medium red blooms in spring and occasionally later in the season. My new favorite is 'Fourth of July' with cream-and-white striped semidouble blooms in huge clusters on a vigorous plant to about 9 ft. tall.

Floribunda Rose

Rosa

When, Where, and How to Plant

Plant bare-root floribundas in early spring. Container-grown rose bushes can be planted from spring to early fall. Plant in a sunny location and in well-drained and fertile soil. Plant them in a prepared garden bed, or dig individual planting holes at least 18 in. deep and 24 in. wide. Add some of the prepared backfill soil into the hole to form a cone of soil in the center. Spread the roots of the bare-root plant over the mound, and position the plant at the proper depth. The bud or graft union should be at least 1 in. below ground level. Set container-grown plants at the same level they were growing in their pots, but check for the graft union and position accordingly. Backfill with prepared soil; gently firm the soil, and water thoroughly.

Growing Tips

Watering roses properly requires careful observation to see what works best for your soil and climate. Floribundas grow best in soil kept evenly moist, but not soggy. Since soils differ, devise your own watering schedule. Dig down into the soil (2 to 4 in.) and feel whether the soil is dry. Water the soil thoroughly, as needed. This may be once or twice a week. Apply 2 to 3 in. of clean organic mulch to maintain and conserve moisture. Fertilize with an organic-based rose food starting in mid-May and continue monthly through mid-August.

Care

Inspect bushes periodically for pests. Consult page 190 for information on pest and disease controls. Floribunda roses are pruned differently than hybrid teas; clip the faded blooms just below the flower clusters. New growth will resume to provide repeat blooms.

Companion Planting and Design

Floribundas are versatile roses and can be planted as a border, to edge walkways and driveways, in groups, or for informal hedging.

My Personal Favorite

A real show stopper is 'Betty Boop', a yellow-and-red bicolor consisting of twelve to fifteen petals. It is a vigorous grower and has excellent hardiness.

Floribunda roses are the result of crossing hybrid teas with polyanthas. As their name implies, these rose bushes produce flowers in abundance and are among the most popular for landscaping. Blossoms are borne in clusters like polyanthas, but with larger flowers, which come in all forms from double to five-petaled singles; some are fragrant. The floribunda rosebush generally grows 2 to 5 ft. and is a prolific bloomer from early summer through autumn. Polyantha, the smaller parent of the floribunda, is also a good landscape rose. The multipetaled flowers are always small and borne in clusters. Only a few varieties are available; 'The Fairy' is the most popular and easy to grow polyantha rose. It does well in containers or in beds with other roses or perennials.

Bloom Period and Seasonal Color
Mid-May to frost; blooms in all colors except blue

Mature Height × Spread
2 to 5 ft. × 3 to 4 ft.

Zones
To zone 4

Grandiflora Rose

Rosa

The grandiflora rose is a cross between a hybrid tea and a floribunda rose. It has the best traits of its parents. Larger than those of floribundas, the flowers may be borne singly or in clusters. The blossoms and long stems come from the hybrid tea parentage, while the vigor and continuous, abundant blooming comes from the floribunda parent. This continuous abundant bloom and vigorous growth make grandifloras excellent background plants. Use them for hedging, screens, and backdrops to other roses in a border. 'Queen Elizabeth' is a popular grandiflora variety with fragrant, soft-pink blossoms. The rugged, vigorous bush produces profuse blooms and repeats flowering throughout the summer. The long-stemmed blooms of the grandiflora rosebush are excellent for cut flowers and floral arrangements.

Bloom Period and Seasonal Color
Mid-May to frost; blooms in all colors except blue

Mature Height × Spread
3 to 6 ft. × 3 ft.

Zones
To zone 4

When, Where, and How to Plant
Plant bare-root grandiflora roses in early spring. Container-grown bushes can be planted from spring through fall. It is best to plant before the heat of summer. Grandifloras prefer sunny exposures, with at least six hours of full sun per day. Soil should be well drained and fertile; prepare soil as recommended on page 187. Plant grandifloras in prepared garden beds, or dig individual planting holes as described at the beginning of this chapter. Position the graft or bud union about 1 in. below the ground level. Backfill with prepared soil, gently firm the soil around the bush, and water thoroughly. Mulch with compost or shredded cedar to maintain moisture while the bush is becoming established.

Growing Tips
As do hybrid tea roses, grandifloras need ample water and nutrients to grow vigorously and repeat blooming. Water rosebushes thoroughly when the soil begins to dry out a few inches below the surface. Check your soil conditions to determine how frequently you should water. Sandy soils require more attention, while clay soils do not need to be watered as often. Fertilize with an organic-based rose food monthly beginning in mid-May and continue through mid-August.

Care
Use clean organic mulches around your roses to conserve and maintain moisture and to keep the roots cool. Prune in mid- to late spring as the new growth is emerging. Roses thrive in bright sunshine. Provide good air circulation with proper pruning, and disease problems should be minimal. See page 190 for information on pests and diseases.

Companion Planting and Design
The versatile grandifloras add to the landscape. They can be used for screening, hedges, and backdrops and can be grown as specimen plants.

My Personal Favorites
Among my favorites are 'Queen Elizabeth', with soft-pink, fragrant blooms. 'Love' is a beautiful red with white on the underside of the petals. 'Gold Medal' produces soft-gold flowers with red blushes in cooler weather. It is prolific, with nice individual flowers.

Hybrid Tea Rose

Rosa

When, Where, and How to Plant

Plant bare-root hybrid tea roses in early spring; container-grown plants from spring through early fall. They should be located in full sun for the best blooms and healthiest, disease-free foliage. The beds in which they grow should be of deeply prepared organic soil with excellent drainage. See page 187 for details on planting.

Growing Tips

Care must be taken to maintain moisture at least two inches down from the soil surface. This is made much easier by spreading 2 in. of organic mulch around the bush. Apply fertilizer monthly through mid-August. Also see page 189 for more water and fertilizer details.

Care

Hybrid teas performs better by cutting long-stemmed blooms down to a strong five leaflet on the growing cane. This encourages a new blooming stem at that point. General pruning is addressed on page 190. Spray for diseases and pests on a regular basis; they seem to need this treatment more often than some other types of roses, but the extra effort pays off with long-stemmed, perfect rose blooms for your pleasure. Some common diseases are blackspot and powdery mildew; these are worse on neglected or poorly watered plants. Refer to page 190 for more information on diseases and pests.

Companion Planting and Design

Hybrid teas make striking specimen plants and should be featured in places where they can be seen and the fragrance enjoyed close up. Smaller annuals and perennials growing as borders for rose beds are an attractive way to cover hybrid teas' long green stems. Take care that the plants chosen as companions have the same cultural needs as the rose (moisture, fertilizer, and light requirements)—such as dianthus, alyssum, pansies, wax begonias, or smaller petunias. Avoid marigolds; they serve as hosts for red spider mite.

My Personal Favorites

'Secret' is a pale-pink blend known for outstanding fragrance and delicate beauty. For vigor, health, and long-lasting showy blooms, grow 'Olympiad', a medium-sized, bright-red hybrid tea.

Perhaps the most popular, illustrated, written about, and photographed roses, hybrid teas feature the classic rose form with attractive buds and large flowers. Most blooms are produced one bloom to a long stem rather than in clusters. If you want big, fragrant blooms for a bud vase, this is the rose for you. Most blooms are composed of many petals and are generally fragrant; they flower throughout the entire growing season. One of my favorites, 'Dainty Bess' does not have multiple petals, but has flat, single soft pink blossoms. Hybrid teas come in a wide variety of colors, sizes, and shapes. They have in past years had some of the fragrance bred out in favor of more disease resistance and better qualities, but contemporary breeders offer very fragrant varieties.

Other Common Name
Tea rose

Bloom Period and Seasonal Color
Mid-May to frost; blooms in all colors except blue

Mature Height × Spread
3 to 5 ft. × 3 to 4 ft.

Zones
To zone 3

Miniature Rose

Rosa

If you think you don't have the room to grow roses or the patience for all the spraying and pruning, miniature roses are perfect for your garden. They are your garden's little jewels, possessing the same characteristics of many of the larger roses, only in miniature. Available in a rainbow of colors, miniature roses feature tiny pointed buds, fully formed blooms (some fragrant), delicate foliage, and a compact growth habit. Small in stature, but covered with hundreds of tiny, perfectly formed blooms, they deliver more "bang for your gardening buck" than any other plant you tend. Miniature roses grow equally well in outdoor pots or in beds and are perfectly hardy in all situations. The exciting color choices feature some lovely lavender and purple shades, striking bicolors, and smoky russets.

Other Common Names
Mini rose, mini-flora rose

Bloom Period and Seasonal Color
Mid-May to frost; blooms in all colors except blue

Mature Height × Spread
6 to 8 in. × 2 to 3 ft.

Zones
To zone 3

When, Where, and How to Plant
Miniature rosebushes can be planted from spring through early fall. Plant them where they receive full to partial sun. As with other roses, the soil should be well drained. Consult page 187 for information on soil preparation and planting tips. Plant these roses at the same level as they were growing in their containers.

Growing Tips
Water new plants regularly to ensure establishment. Apply an organic mulch around the plants to maintain moisture. Fertilize miniature roses monthly through the growing season with an organic-based, slow-release rose fertilizer. If you grow the plants in containers, you may need to fertilize every two to three weeks to sustain them.

Care
Although perfectly hardy and capable of maintaining most of their branches during winter, miniature roses perform best if pruned heavily in the spring. Leave a few inches of major canes, and prune all the smaller twigs and crossing branches. After a bloom cycle, prune spent blooms to fresh stems, fertilize them lightly, and keep the moisture constant. They are generally much hardier than other roses and usually don't need extensive winter protection, just a light mulching to help retain moisture. Blackspot and powdery mildew may attack the foliage in some years. Refer to page 190 for more details about pest controls.

Companion Planting and Design
Miniature roses may be used as bedding plants with tiny companions such as pansies, alyssum, herbs, and small grasses. They are very attractive in a rock garden, but can also be grown in containers and brought indoors for winter if you have a sunny and cool location.

My Personal Favorites
The vigorous miniature climber 'Jeanne Lajoie' is a light pink that grows to 8 ft. tall and 6 ft. wide. It looks wonderful on a small trellis. No other climbing miniature blooms as well. For bedding and cut flowers, 'Rainbow's End', 'Minnie Pearl', 'Old Glory', and 'Snowbride' are some of my favorites.

Modern Shrub Rose

Rosa

When, Where, and How to Plant

Plant bare-root bushes in early spring. Container-grown plants can be planted from spring to early fall. Put them where they receive full sun; although afternoon shade is acceptable. For instructions on soil preparation and planting, refer to page 187.

Growing Tips

Water new transplants well to ensure vigorous and healthy establishment. Apply organic mulch to maintain soil moisture and prevent weeds. Shrubs are vigorous growers and need sufficient fertilizer and water to encourage and maintain good growth. Consult page 189 for general information on watering and fertilizing roses. Bloom increases with monthly fertilization; use an organic-based granular rose fertilizer that has a higher phosphate content, such as 18-46-0. Read and follow label directions.

Care

Spent blooms should be cut back to encourage future flowering. Some shrubs benefit from a reduction in bush size after the initial bloom. Cut back blooming canes by a third of their length. Prune ground cover types heavily in late winter or early spring before growth starts. Spring pruning of other types consists of removing dead wood, crossing canes, and diseased or older wood back to about two-thirds the size of the bush. Modern shrubs are resistant to disease and should need little spraying. The few insects may be controlled with a spray of water or homemade soap sprays. Consult page 190 for more information about rose pests.

Companion Planting and Design

Modern shrub roses are effective for shrub borders, foundation plantings, barrier plantings, focal points, accents, and ground covers. Some varieties do well in containers. They make excellent cutting roses.

My Personal Favorites

For sheer quantity of eye-catching blooms, pick 'Sally Holmes', a vigorous grower with glossy dark foliage and large clusters of peach buds that open to single ivory white flowers. The deep-crimson 'L.D. Braithwaite' is a fantastic addition to borders and blooms all summer. 'Heritage' is a favorite English rose that blooms all summer with quartered shell pink blooms and powerful fragrance.

If P.T. Barnum had been a rose breeder, he would have introduced this category of roses—you have to see them to believe them! The modern shrub rose is an enormous and highly popular category of roses. Advances in breeding have brought about hundreds of new and exciting varieties to use in landscaping and modern gardens. Modern shrub roses are bred using the hardiness of old garden roses and the colors and repeat-blooming characteristics of hybrid teas and floribundas. They have beautiful foliage, along with the fragrance essential to many rose gardeners. Modern shrub roses range in height from a few inches, which are used as ground cover, to shrubs tall enough to be trained as climbers on a fence or trellis.

Other Common Names

English rose, Renaissance rose, cottage rose, shrub rose, ground cover rose, landscape rose

Bloom Period and Seasonal Color

Mid-May to frost; blooms in all colors except blue

Mature Height × Spread

6 in. to 12 ft. × as permitted

Zones

To zone 4 with protection

Old Garden Rose
Rosa spp.

In 1966 the American Rose Society defined old garden roses as those that existed before 1867, the year hybrid teas were introduced. Within this generic definition lies a world of rose history. These are the roses of your grandmother's garden. These hardy, disease-resistant and low-maintenance plants make ideal candidates for Rocky Mountain gardens. Most take more room to grow than their modern counterparts, and this fact must be considered when selecting a planting site. They are broken down in sub-classes distinguished by their parentage and include alba, centifolia, damask, gallica, moss, tea, hybrid perpetual, bourbon, china, noisette, and Portland. They offer a range of rose fragrance from light "tea" to heavy musk. Most bloom heavily once in early summer; companion plantings should provide for color throughout the season.

Other Common Names
Antique rose, heritage rose

Bloom Period and Seasonal Color
Heavy mid-May through June, with occasional blooms later according to variety; blooms in all colors except blue

Mature Height × Spread
3 to 9 ft. × as permitted

Zones
To zone 3

When, Where, and How to Plant
Plant bare-root plants in early spring. Container-grown plants may be planted anytime through late summer, but the bush may not bloom until the next summer. Plant in a location that receives full sun all day; some afternoon shade is acceptable. General soil preparation and planting instructions can be found on page 187. This class of rose needs time to grow into a mature plant to support the heavy bloom; it may be several seasons before their beauty is fully appreciated.

Growing Tips
Mulch old garden roses heavily, and spread an inch of aged manure around the bushes in late winter or early spring. One application of a slow-release rose fertilizer is all they require in the spring. Water deeply and thoroughly on a weekly basis to sustain their extensive root system. If you wish, apply an organic mulch around the bushes to maintain soil moisture and reduce weed invasions.

Care
Prune lightly in early spring to shape the bush and cut back dead wood. Summer pruning should remove spent blooms and keep the bush in bounds. After several years, older woody canes may be removed to encourage new growth from the base of the plant. Most need no spraying, and some are actually "allergic" to spray material and defoliate if sprayed even a little bit. Nearly all insect problems can be taken care of with soap and water spray. See pest information on page 190.

Companion Planting and Design
Old garden roses are spectacular as specimen plants in early spring gardens. Spring bulbs, other spring blooming shrubs, perennials, and herbs make perfect companions. Some have spectacular autumn foliage color and make a nice background for asters and chrysanthemums.

My Personal Favorites
'Mme Hardy' is a hardy and dependable white damask with blooms of many petals, a green button eye, and a nice fragrance. 'Marchesa Bocella' is a hybrid perpetual with light-pink double flowers and a lovely fragrance.

When, Where, and How to Plant

Plant bare-root bushes in early spring before the canes break into leaf. Container-grown plants can be planted from spring to early fall. Species roses should be located where they receive maximum sun. In natural situations, they are planted by birds and generally survive best in well-drained, even rocky soil. Water new plants until they become established. If your soil is poor, condition it with organic matter before planting. Consult page 187 for more information on soil preparation and planting instructions.

Growing Tips

Keep newly planted bushes well watered weekly during the first growing season to ensure healthy and strong establishment. Once the plants are established, water deeply and infrequently to allow them to acclimate to natural conditions and become drought tolerant. Fertilize in spring with an organic rose food, and water well.

Care

Species roses are generally carefree. Do not prune after blooming; doing so removes the fertilized flowers and inhibits rose hip formation. Little pruning is needed, except to direct new growth or remove dead or old canes. Remove older and heavy canes at the base in late winter or early spring to encourage young vigorous cane growth. Do not spray with chemicals of any kind.

Companion Planting and Design

Species are perfect for a large rock garden, xeriscape plantings, vacation homes at higher altitudes, and remote plantings in rural situations. They look good along long driveways and work well in locations where watering is impractical. Species roses are lovely when planted with grasses of various heights and with wildflowers.

My Personal Favorites

Among my favorites are *Rosa hugonis*, 'Father Hugo's Rose'. This hardy and vigorous shrub is a prolific spring bloomer with fragrant, yellow, double flowers. Its flowers are followed by attractive maroon rose hips and beautiful orange-bronze fall foliage. The fern-like foliage of *Rosa spinosissima*, draped with pure white, single blooms in spring, makes it an outstanding specimen rosebush. I have one located near my office window.

Species roses are those that exist in nature. Tough, disease resistant, and winter hardy, these roses thrive in a wide range of soils and are good for the High Country. Most of the species roses bloom once, early in spring. Although modest, the blossoms are beautiful, and most are fragrant. After flowering, brightly colored seed hips develop; these add landscape interest and provide a food source for wild birds or a supplement for homemade jellies or beverages. I consider this class of roses low maintenance; pests rarely bother them, and they require no special winter protection. One of my favorites is Rosa glauca, with simple, single pink blossoms, handsome silvery foliage overlain in hues of maroon, and reddish orange hips late summer through fall.

Other Common Name
Wild rose

Bloom Period and Seasonal Color
Early to late May; blooms in red, pink, yellow, white, or bicolored

Mature Spread × Height
3 to 12 ft. × 5 to 12 ft.

Zones
To zone 3

Shrubs *for the Rockies*

At one time shrubs were simply those plants that homeowners automatically planted around the foundation just because every other house in the neighborhood used them that way. But you don't have to continue to install shrubs in this antiquated fashion. There is an extensive array of shrub choices now. Shrubs are as diverse as the gardeners who grow them, and they can serve several different functions. They provide a solid background for perennial and annual flower beds. Many shrubs have unique flowers, handsome bark, or fruit that add color and texture to the landscape.

Smaller Trees

Generally speaking, the classification *shrub* refers to that group of plants that are woody, like trees, but smaller in stature. Some are deciduous, losing their leaves in winter, while others are evergreen. Some shrubs are grown for their flowers and some for their berries; others, such as burning bush, are noted for their brilliant autumn color. Among the many pleasures of growing shrubs is discovering ways to combine different kinds so that they complement the other plants in the landscape.

Many shrubs live to a ripe old age, so allow them space in which to grow and spread their branches. Unless you're planting a hedge, keep in mind the shrub's mature landscape size when choosing its location.

Adaptable Shrubs

Shrubs are among the most adaptable and easy-to-care-for landscape plants. Like trees, most shrubs develop root systems that help them endure during periods of drought, yet their small size allows them to be movable if needed. Growing shrubs successfully begins with making the right choices—be sure to select a shrub whose needs match the special growing

Lilac Border

conditions in your area. Most shrubs are relatively resistant to insects and diseases. If a problem develops, it's generally the fault of the gardener, not of the shrub. The presence of spider mites on an euonymus probably indicates that the shrub's natural defense system is stressed from being planted too close to a house, fence, or other "heat trap."

Less Is More

As with most plants, shrubs thrive in well-drained soils that have been enriched with compost or other quality organic matter. Most soils throughout the Rocky Mountain region are both alkaline (high pH) and low in organic matter, but don't overamend the soil with too much organic matter. When it comes to supplementing the backfill soil, less is better. If your soil is of poor quality, you can mix 25 to 30 percent by volume of compost to the native soil and blend it in uniformly. Adding excessive amounts of organic amendments or fertilizer to the planting hole creates a "bathtub" effect—the roots of a newly planted shrub may decide to remain within the planting hole and never explore the surrounding native soil. Roots grow and move into soil that contains a balance of oxygen and moisture, so the best advice is to dig the planting hole wide rather than deep and to thoroughly loosen the soil.

A Tip on Planting

Container-grown shrubs that have a tight mass of roots encircling the rootball, with no soil visible, are considered extremely rootbound. In these situations, use the "split ball" or "butterfly" root pruning technique. Laying the plant on its side, slice through the rootball vertically from the bottom about halfway to the top. Spread the two halves, like butterfly wings, over a mound of soil in the planting hole. Add the backfill soil, and water slowly. With this technique, you bring the roots, which had grown to the bottom of the container, nearer the surface where soil conditions are more favorable for vigorous root

Firethorn

development. **Caution:** Don't use this technique on larger balled-and-burlapped shrubs, newly potted specimens, or containerized plants where the roots are not rootbound.

Fertilizing Shrubs

After their first growing season, shrubs can be fertilized in spring as growth resumes. Use an organic-based granular 5-10-5 or 10-10-10 fertilizer at the rate of 1/4 cup per each foot of the shrub's height. Use a crowbar or metal rod to make a series of holes, 8 to 10 in. deep and 12 in. apart, around the shrub's drip line. Broadcast the fertilizer in the area where the holes were made, and water thoroughly.

Pruning With a Purpose

While many trees never need pruning once they reach a mature shape, shrubs benefit from regular pruning. Prune to achieve specific results: to keep the shrub the proper size and shape, to help it produce more flowers, or to rejuvenate a tired, old shrub into youthful vigor. Pruning can simply mean removing three to five of the oldest stems each year almost to ground level (leaving stubs of only 3 to 4 in.). New buds on the stubs then become activated to grow into new, vigorous stems. Such "renewal" pruning keeps the shrub youthful with healthy stems that produce more flowers. Pruning to limit a shrub's size is generally reserved for those plants that have outgrown their space. It may be a result of having selected the wrong shrub to fit the planting site. Make the pruning cuts just beyond a healthy bud or small branch that you want to preserve on the shrub. Use a sharp pair of bypass hand pruners. If larger stems need to be cut off, a long-handled lopper makes this task a breeze. Forget about those electric hedge trimmers—the problems they cause usually outweigh their benefits. Shearing the tops of shrubs with trimmers and clippers turns your favorite shrubs into "green meatballs." The resulting dense shell of green foliage on the top and outside of the shrub causes the inside to be dark, dead, and lifeless. You always get the best results and maintain the shrub's natural shape by using hand tools.

Prune flowering shrubs to promote more blooms. Those shrubs that bloom on last season's growth, such as lilacs and forsythia, should be pruned right after they flower. Pruning them in the fall or winter removes next spring's flower buds!

Those that bloom on the current season's growth, such as butterfly bush, blue mist spirea, summer spirea, and potentilla, should be pruned in early spring. Many of these perform at their best if cut back to the ground in March.

Treasured Memories

Shrubs can provide privacy, screen out unsightly views, or even serve as a windbreak to protect some of our more tender and vulnerable plant selections. They can provide shelter and food to attract wild birds, an important asset for those of us who believe that the landscape should be heard as well as seen. The sweet fragrance of Grandma's lilacs at the back door is a treasured memory. With the right planning, shrubs offer beauty and versatility in our landscapes in every season for many years. The shrubs chosen in this chapter are among the best for our region, but many more can be used here. Experiment to discover the ones that may soon become your favorites.

Cotoneaster 'Coral Beauty'

American Plum

Prunus americana

A common native plant, American plum is frequently seen growing and thriving along the roadsides from the High Plains to the Foothills. It is a harbinger of spring, blooming profusely before the leaves emerge; bees are busily gathering nectar and pollen from the fragrant blossoms. You can harvest the fruit to make jam and jelly—that is, if the birds and other wildlife don't get to it first! American plum is a tough, widely adaptable shrub that endures drought conditions quite well. Keep it pruned to maintain a more formal look, or let it grow in its natural form for a naturescape or wildlife-friendly garden. Unlike many other of the Prunus species, native American plum is resistant to pests known as crown borers.

Other Common Name
Wild plum

Bloom Period and Seasonal Color
Loads of fragrant white blooms in early spring

Mature Height × Spread
10 to 20 ft. × 8 to 12 ft.

Zones
To zone 3

When, Where, and How to Plant
Plant container-grown shrubs in the spring through early fall. Transplant bare-root plants in early spring. This shrub does best in full sun and well-drained soils. Dig the planting hole two to three times wider than the rootball. Add compost (25 to 30 percent by volume), and loosen the soil thoroughly. Plant container-grown shrubs according to instructions on page 201. Water thoroughly.

Growing Tips
Water new transplants regularly when the soil begins to dry out to ensure healthy establishment. Once established, water them deeply every seven to ten days or as the soil becomes dry. Avoid overwatering; plants suffer in poorly drained soils and become more vulnerable to pests. Mulch year-round with a 2-in. layer of organic material to conserve moisture and discourage weed invasions; do not allow mulch to touch the stems. In the spring, apply a slow-release granular fertilizer to provide nutrients through the growing season.

Care
Once American plum becomes established, it should be a permanent fixture. It can tend to sucker and spread; periodic pruning helps keep the plant in bounds. Watch for leaf spot fungi, powdery mildew, and aphids. Early detection and control can prevent any severe problems. Another common summer pest is the pear slug. An infestation of this pest causes the leaves to skeletonize. One of the safest ways to control pear slugs is to dust the foliage with wood ashes. This turns these pests into "crispy critters."

Companion Planting and Design
American plum can be used in naturalized settings or to attract wildlife. Use it as a backdrop or informal hedge, or in windbreaks.

I Also Recommend
One of the more drought-resistant species that deserves more use is western sandcherry (*Prunus besseyi*), a low-growing shrub (about 3 ft. tall) with masses of white flowers in May. The quite showy, glossy, silver-green leaves turn burgundy-red in the fall. The 3/4-in. black cherries are edible—if the birds don't get them first.

Apache Plume

Fallugia paradoxa

When, Where, and How to Plant

Plant container-grown Apache plume in the spring. Choose a location with well-drained soil that receives full sun. This plant is an excellent choice for open, dry, sunny locations. Loosen compacted soils, and amend with scoria (crushed volcanic rock) or pea gravel to add porosity and to improve drainage. A small amount of compost (20 to 25 percent by volume) can be mixed with the backfill soil. Dig the planting hole to accommodate the root system, and loosen the soil well beyond the hole. It may take two growing seasons for the plant to establish, so add a mulch of pine needles or pea gravel to conserve natural moisture, reduce soil compaction, and prevent weeds.

Growing Tips

Water deeply, but infrequently. This shrub does not tolerate "wet feet," so be careful not to overwater. Allow the soil to dry out before watering. Apache plume often succumbs in wet winter situations where drainage is poor. Shrubs planted in hot, dry locations must be thoroughly and deeply watered several times during spring and summer to sustain growth and flowering. These shrubs require additional fertilizer.

Care

Insect pests and diseases do not bother Apache plume. It is one of the few carefree shrubs that can survive on its own. Pruning is generally not recommended—Apache plume looks best when allowed to grow and cascade naturally. Once the plant establishes, a few suckers may appear; they can be dug and transplanted. Periodically cut older stems to ground level to encourage new growth. Native Americans used the stems to make brooms and arrow shafts.

Companion Planting and Design

Use Apache plume on rocky slopes to control erosion. It's a great plant for mass plantings, accents in rock gardens, and xeriscapes. It combines well with Russian sage (*Perovskia atriplicifolia*). The exfoliating, whitish bark adds winter interest.

My Personal Favorite

The common Apache plume (*Fallugia paradoxa*) is the most widely available and very hardy.

Apache plume grows as an arching, lacy shrub with finely dissected leaves. It is drought enduring and can be planted in dry, sunny locations. Attractive single, white, roselike flowers appear during early summer and continue through late summer. As the flowers mature, feathery silver-pink rounded seedheads develop. These seed plumes are quite decorative on the shrub, particularly when backlit by sunlight. They also add fall and winter interest to the garden. Consider this shrub for a xeriscape. It is also effective as a single specimen plant, or use it as a shrub border. Its ability to survive the semiarid climate and hot, dry summers makes Apache plume a must for water-thrifty landscapes.

Bloom Period and Seasonal Color
Late spring simple, white roselike blooms; followed by feathery, silver-pink seedheads in summer

Mature Height × Spread
3 to 6 ft. × 3 to 6 ft.

Zones
To zone 3

Barberry
Berberis spp.

A popular, upright-growing shrub, barberry is used for hedging, for mass planting, or as an accent plant. Most species are deciduous, though some varieties are semievergreen with dense foliage that persists into winter. Its wood is yellow, with leaves that grow in small clusters and turn a brilliant orange, red, or yellow in autumn. Barberry produces a multitude of arching branches with thorns. This shrub is not noted for its flowers, but each spring small yellow or red ones appear, followed by red berries in late summer. There are many selections that can be used in the landscape. Barberry is a good choice for color contrast and can be used for screening or as an impenetrable barrier. Japanese barberry (B. thunbergii var. atropurpurea) is a commonly available species.

Bloom Period and Seasonal Color
Grown for its wine-red, yellow, variegated, or green foliage (depending on species) throughout the growing season

Mature Height × Spread
18 to 24 in. × 2 to 3 ft.

Zones
To zone 4

When, Where, and How to Plant
Plant potted shrubs spring through fall and bare-root plants in early spring. To get the most intense leaf color, plant barberry in full sun, though some varieties tolerate partial shade. Most are adapted to Rocky Mountain soils, though Japanese barberry is notorious for chlorosis (yellowing leaves) in highly alkaline soils. Dig the planting hole two to three times wider than the rootball. If the soil is compacted and poorly drained, amend it with compost before planting to help maintain soil fertility and moisture. Consult page 201 for more detailed information on soil preparation and shrub planting techniques. When planting a hedge, space plants 2 ft. apart; space 5 to 6 ft. apart for mass plantings.

Growing Tips
To ensure healthy establishment, water new transplants well each week or as the soil dries out. Once barberry becomes established (within a few years), it has good drought resistance. This shrub is sensitive to excess moisture, so avoid frequent watering in lawn areas. A slow-release 5-10-5 granular fertilizer can be lightly applied at planting time to provide nutrients through the growing season.

Care
As individual plants start to become ragged, prune out the oldest canes to ground level. This technique rejuvenates the shrub to grow fresh, colorful stems and brightly colored leaves. If iron chlorosis (yellowing of the leaves) occurs due to the lack of available iron, apply a chelated iron nutrient in the spring. Pests and diseases do not generally bother this plant.

Companion Planting and Design
Use barberry as a barrier plant, an informal hedge, or an accent shrub in rock gardens. Plant low-growing varieties as a ground cover. Barberry's growth habit and thorns make it a good foundation plant to thwart would-be burglars or stray animals.

My Personal Favorite
Berberis thunbergii var. *atropurpurea* 'Crimson Pygmy' is a low-growing form with deep-red foliage. At a height of 18 to 24 in., it makes a nice background or accent plant.

Beauty Bush

Kolkwitzia amabilis

When, Where, and How to Plant

Plant container-grown shrubs from spring through early fall and bare-root plants in early spring as soon as the soil can be worked. Locate in an open, sunny exposure with plenty of space to grow. Beauty bush tolerates a wide range of soils and is easily transplanted. Dig the planting hole three times wider than the rootball. As long as the soil has been broken up and is not severely compacted, no amendment is necessary. However, sandy soils benefit from some compost to help retain moisture. When planting bare-root plants, spread the roots out in the planting hole without crowding them. Consult page 201 for general information on soil preparation and planting techniques. Once the shrub is in place, add backfill soil into the planting hole and water slowly.

Growing Tips

Water regularly and deeply throughout the growing season. Spread an organic mulch around the base of the shrub to conserve moisture and to discourage weed growth. Once the plant is established, water deeply (6 to 8 in.) each week or as the soil dries out. Apply a granular, slow-release 5-10-5 fertilizer in the spring, and water well.

Care

Beauty bush endures with little care once it becomes established. Renew older, overgrown shrubs by pruning them completely to the ground in the spring. To keep this shrub in bounds and to shape, thin out the oldest stems to ground level; that also helps it maintain vigor after flowering. New growth emerges from the base. Beauty bush is not generally prone to pests or diseases.

Companion Planting and Design

Plant in shrub borders, foundation plantings, informal hedging, or windbreaks. Use as a backdrop to a perennial border for contrast. Beauty bush also provides a nice contrast to evergreen plantings.

My Personal Favorites

The very hardy species is the most common, but a few selections have improved flower color. Look for 'Pink Cloud' and 'Rosea', which produce blossoms of deeper pink than those of the species.

A hardy, old-fashioned shrub that has withstood the test of time, beauty bush can survive years of utter neglect. Its bloom is spectacular, with bright-pink, yellow-throated, tubular flowers in early June. Clusters of feathery brown seeds follow the flowers and persist into winter. The gray-brown bark exfoliates on the older canes, giving this shrub an interesting winter texture. Upright and arching branches make beauty bush somewhat leggy, so give it plenty of room to grow. You will appreciate the beauty of this shrub when it stands alone or planted in an open area where it can naturalize in a naturescape for wildlife. The foliage has a nice reddish color in autumn. I have planted a few in my windbreak to provide contrast to the evergreens.

Bloom Period and Seasonal Color
Early summer pink tubular flowers

Mature Height × Spread
6 to 12 ft. × 8 to 12 ft.

Zones
To zone 3

Blue Mist Spirea

Caryopteris incana

The blue mist spirea is not a true Spiraea, but its long arching branches give this shrub a similar appearance. The foliage is bluish green above with silvery undersides and has a spicy aroma when bruised. When few other shrubs are in bloom, light- to dark-blue blossoms emerge on blue mist spirea in late summer. The flowers are a favorite of bees, so it might be a good idea to avoid planting near entryways. This is a versatile shrub that will find a natural spot in the landscape combined with perennial flowers or as a single specimen plant for accent. It looks great with ornamental grasses, and the foliage and flowers are attractive combined with fall-blooming magenta and pink asters and Sedum 'Autumn Joy'.

Other Common Name
Bluebeard

Bloom Period and Seasonal Color
July through August blooms in light blue or dark blue

Mature Height × Spread
2 to 4 ft. × 2 to 3 ft.

Zones
To zone 4

When, Where, and How to Plant

Plant container-grown shrubs from spring to early fall and bare-root plants in early spring. Choose a location with full to partial sun for the best foliage effect and for prolific flowering. Avoid areas that are too wet or poorly drained or crown rot will result. The fibrous root system makes blue mist spirea easy to transplant and establish. Do not overamend the soil with organic matter; doing so causes rank growth with few flowers. Refer to the general planting information on page 201. After positioning the shrub, add backfill soil and water slowly to eliminate any air pockets under the roots. Mulch with shredded cedar or other organic material to maintain and conserve moisture during the heat of summer.

Growing Tips

Water new transplants regularly to promote healthy establishment. This shrub is adapted to dry conditions, but can suffer severe wilt in the heat of summer. Water thoroughly, but infrequently. As soon as growth appears in the spring, broadcast an all-purpose 5-10-5 fertilizer according to the manufacturer's recommendations. Water fertilizer in well. Additional applications of fertilizer are not needed.

Care

Each year, the branches die back to the woody center or crown of the plant. Cut the shrub back to near ground level in early spring before growth begins. Seedlings are common and can be removed or transplanted to other areas. Butterflies and bees love this shrub's late-season blooms. Pests and diseases do not bother this shrub.

Companion Planting and Design

Its silvery-gray foliage makes blue mist spirea a good choice in shrub or perennial borders. This shrub is a delightful foil for yellow- and white-flowering potentillas, as well as many ornamental grasses and the late-flowering Japanese anemone. Use as accent plants in a mixed perennial garden with coneflowers, daylilies, and liatris.

I Also Recommend

'Blue Mist' has striking powder-blue flowers. *Caryopteris* × *clandonensis* 'Dark Knight' has a darker gray-green foliage and darker blue-purple flowers.

When, Where, and How to Plant

Plant burning bush from spring through fall. If planting in the summer, water well—a stressed burning bush is susceptible to spider mites. This shrub does well in partial shade to full sun, but to get the best fall color, avoid full shade. Burning bush performs best in well-drained soils, so amend the soil with compost to improve soil porosity and drainage. Refer to page 201 for specific information on soil preparation and planting instructions. Set the plant in the planting hole; keep the top of the rootball level with the surrounding soil grade. Water thoroughly, and apply a few inches of pine needles or cedar mulch.

Growing Tips

Water new transplants regularly to ensure strong and healthy establishment. Once burning bush is established, water deeply and infrequently. Keep a layer of mulch around the shrub to retain moisture and to keep the soil cool during the summer. A light application of an all-purpose 5-10-5 fertilizer in early spring is helpful to get the shrub off to a healthy start.

Care

Burning bush grows in somewhat horizontal tiers, which gives it a flat-topped look. Pruning is generally not recommended; when done improperly, frequent pruning or shearing destroys this plant's natural shape. In the summer, spider mites can become a nuisance; control by washing them off with a strong stream of water or setting a "frog-eye" sprinkler under the shrub periodically to eliminate these pests.

Companion Planting and Design

Plant burning bush in mass plantings or as a background shrub, informal hedge, screening, or foundation planting. The autumn display of this shrub is so intense that a single specimen planting is also desirable.

I Also Recommend

European spindle tree (*Euonymus europaeus*) is one of my favorites; it grows to a height of 18 ft. The foliage changes to handsome red tones in the fall, and in late summer or early fall, this shrub produces unique red-pink fruits.

Leaves that turn fire-red in autumn give this shrub its common name: burning bush. Only our native sumac (Rhus glabra) comes close to matching burning bush's brilliant fall color display. Plant a burning bush near a water garden; the brilliant scarlet foliage reflects on the water for a spectacular show. During spring and summer, the foliage is dark green. Burning bush's unique stems feature corky ridges called wings all along them. In winter, these winged stems collect snow to create an interesting plant sculpture for the winter garden. 'Compactus' is a dwarf form that grows to 5 ft. with crimson fall foliage. E. nanus var. turkestanicus has narrow, bluish green foliage that transforms to red in autumn and is hardy to zone 2.

Other Common Names

Euonymous, winged euonymous

Bloom Period and Seasonal Color

In spring, inconspicuous greenish yellow flowers; grown primarily for its autumn foliage

Mature Height × Spread

8 to 15 ft. × 10 to 12 ft.

Zones

To zone 3

Butterfly Bush

Buddleia davidii

Do you want to create a naturescape or wildlife-friendly garden that attracts butterflies? Buddleia should be at the top of the list for shrubs. It has earned a reputation for vigorous growth in a single season. This easy-to-care-for shrub has a long season of bloom and tolerates drought well. It has arching branches with willowlike gray-green or bluish green leaves. A profusion of white, pink, red, purple, or lavender flowers, borne in racemes, graces the plant in the summer. The woodsy and sweet fragrance of its blossoms is certain to draw the butterflies to your yard. Buddleia davidii is the most recognized, with such varieties as 'Black Knight', with dark-purple blooms; 'Charming' with pink flowers; and 'Harlequin' with variegated foliage and magenta flowers.

Other Common Name
Summer lilac

Bloom Period and Seasonal Color
June through September blooms in purple, lavender, pink, rose, or white

Mature Height × Spread
4 to 6 ft. × 3 to 4 ft.

Zones
To zone 4

When, Where, and How to Plant
Container-grown plants are readily available. Plant them in early spring through summer. Set out bare-root plants in early spring, too. Locate the shrub in full to partial sun so it grows vigorously and produces an abundance of blossoms. A butterfly bush growing in the shade soon becomes leggy and has few, if any, flowers. Dig the planting hole two to three times wider than the rootball of the plant. Consult page 201 for more detailed information on soil preparation and shrub planting techniques. Water thoroughly, and spread an organic mulch under the plant. The mulch helps maintain moisture and discourage annual weed invasions.

Growing Tips
Keep the soil evenly moist for several weeks to ensure strong and healthy establishment. To encourage vigor and an abundance of blossoms, water during the heat of summer. Lightly apply a slow-release 5-10-5 granular fertilizer in the spring to give these plants a boost through the growing season. Butterfly bushes are adapted to poor soil conditions. Be sure not to overfertilize them, or leggy growth and fewer blooms result.

Care
During most winters, the plants die back to the ground, but the roots survive. Cut the shrub back to the ground in the spring, and new growth emerges. Butterfly bush's foliage can be attacked by spider mites during hot, dry summers. The symptoms are foliage that appears mottled and twisted. Hosing down the bottoms of the leaves with water helps reduce mite infestations.

Companion Planting and Design
Plant butterfly bush as specimen shrubs in mixed borders and as accent shrubs in the landscape. Butterfly bushes can be used as temporary summer hedges. This shrub is a must for the butterfly-friendly garden.

I Also Recommend
Butterfly bush's arching stems of flowers are delightful in early summer. The flowers of *Buddleia davidii* 'Black Knight' are dark purple. One of the hardiest species is fountain butterfly bush (*Buddleia alternifolia*), which features silvery foliage and bark.

Common Ninebark
Physocarpus opulifolius

When, Where, and How to Plant

Plant container-grown shrubs from spring through fall. If you purchase bare-root plants, plant them in early spring. Common ninebark can become leggy over time, so locate this shrub in full sun to partial shade. It prefers moderately fertile, well-drained soil, but this shrub tolerates dry situations. Dig the planting hole twice as wide as the rootball. Loosen the soil deeply, and add 25 to 30 percent by volume of compost to your native soil. Consult page 201 for more details on soil preparation and general shrub planting techniques. Set the shrub so that the top of the rootball is level with the surrounding grade. Add backfill soil, and water slowly to eliminate any air pockets beneath the roots. Mulch with pine needles or shredded wood chips.

Growing Tips

To ensure strong establishment, water new transplants regularly the first growing season. Allow the soil to dry out between waterings. Once established, common ninebark requires only periodic watering. Maintain an organic mulch at the base of the plant to conserve moisture and to discourage weed encroachment. In the spring, apply a slow-release 5-10-5 granular fertilizer.

Care

Prune established plants to thin out branches that die back. Renew an older shrub by cutting it to the ground in late winter or early spring. After a hard pruning, apply a slow-release granular 5-10-5 fertilizer to supply nutrients through the growing season. This extremely hardy plant resists pests and diseases. Common ninebark is a long-lived shrub that dares to go where no shrub has gone before.

Companion Planting and Design

Plant common ninebark as an informal hedge, for screening, or in windbreaks. Use it for background plantings or to soften walls or fences.

My Personal Favorites

Physocarpus opulifolius 'Dart's Gold' features attractive lime-green leaves and flowers that open in late spring. Plant it against evergreens for a nice contrast. Dwarf ninebark (*Physocarpus opulifolius* 'Nana') is a compact bush that works well for hedging.

A hardy deciduous shrub whose growth habit resembles that of spirea, common ninebark grows upright, arching somewhat. As it matures, it becomes open and leggy. In the spring, this shrub produces masses of white flowers; its attractive, green, toothed leaves feature three to five lobes. Common ninebark's flowers are very showy, and are followed by purple fruit that birds savor. As the shrub's bark matures on the stems, it exfoliates in thin, coarse sheets that add winter interest to the landscape. Common ninebark is a rugged, well-adapted shrub for the Rocky Mountain region. Some selections have golden to lime-green foliage that provides a wonderful accent in the landscape. Mountain ninebark (*Physocarpus monogynus*) is especially useful for mass planting and as a low, informal hedge.

Bloom Period and Seasonal Color
Early summer blooms in white

Mature Height × Spread
4 to 10 ft. × 3 to 6 ft.

Zones
To zone 2

Cotoneaster

Cotoneaster spp.

The lustrous dark-green foliage of cotoneaster makes this a versatile shrub in the landscape. Hedge cotoneaster (Cotoneaster lucidus) is ideal for pruning into topiaries or a formal hedge. But cotoneaster is best left unpruned and allowed to grow and spread naturally. Small pinkish white flowers appear in late spring followed by black berries that persist into winter, providing food for wild birds. Hedge cotoneaster puts on a beautiful display with red-orange foliage in autumn. Cranberry cotoneaster (C. apiculatus) has small glossy foliage on arching branches; it is one of my favorites to use as ground cover or allow to cascade over walls and rocks. Rock cotoneaster (C. horizontalis) has stiff, fanning branches that grow in a herringbone pattern; it is excellent for rock gardens.

Bloom Period and Seasonal Color
May through June blooms in white, pinkish white, or pink, followed by colorful berries

Mature Height × Spread
2 to 8 ft. × 5 to 8 ft.

Zones
To zone 2

When, Where, and How to Plant

Get bare-root plants into the ground in early spring as soon as the soil can be worked. Container-grown plants can be planted anytime. This shrub thrives in full sun to partial shade. It grows in almost any garden soil that is well drained. Dig the planting hole two to three times wider than the rootball. When planting bare-root plants, spread the roots in the planting hole without cramping them. Refer to page 201 for specifics on soil preparation and shrub planting techniques. Water thoroughly after planting, and add a 2-in. layer of mulch around the plants.

Growing Tips

Water new transplants regularly during the first growing season to ensure healthy and strong establishment. To maintain vigor and plant health, deep soak the plants weekly or as the soil dries out in the heat of summer. Incorporate a 5-10-5 organic fertilizer at planting time.

Care

Thin overcrowded shrubs in the spring to tidy up the plants and increase air circulation. Pests known as pear slugs, which skeletonize the leaves, often attack the foliage of cotoneaster. The damage is merely cosmetic and not harmful. Hose the slimy creatures off, or dust the infested leaves with wood ashes and they turn into "crispy critters."

Companion Planting and Design

Plant cotoneaster as an informal or formal hedge, screen, background, or accent. There are several species of cotoneaster that are well adapted to temperature fluctuations and various soil conditions.

My Personal Favorites

Cotoneaster comes in a wide range of varieties, including tall to medium shrubs and ground covers. Cranberry cotoneaster (*C. apiculatus*) is an attractive 2- to 3-ft. tall shrub with glossy green leaves and large red berries borne on cascading branches. *Cotoneaster dammeri* 'Coral Beauty' and 'Lowfast' grow as semievergreen, low-spreading shrubs (1 to 2 ft. tall with a spread to 6 ft. or more). They are good choices if you want your cotoneaster to cascade over retaining walls or rocks.

When, Where, and How to Plant

Plant container-grown shrubs from spring through early fall, and plant bare-root currants in early spring. These shrubs transplant easily. Locate them in full sun to partial shade. Currants do well in almost any garden soil that is well drained. Dig the planting hole plenty wide to accommodate the root system. Loosen the soil in the planting area, and add compost if the soil is extremely clay or sandy. Position container-grown plants so that the top of the rootball is level with the surrounding soil. Backfill, gently firm the soil around the plant, and water well.

Growing Tips

Water new transplants regularly for the first growing season to make sure they establish. Once established, these plants tolerate drought, but water when the soil dries out. Maintain a 2-in. layer of mulch over the root zone to conserve water and to discourage weed competition. In the spring, apply a slow-release 5-10-5 granular fertilizer around the root zone, then water. Avoid overfertilizing—it leads to lanky, weak growth.

Care

These widely adaptable shrubs are easy to maintain. Trim out the oldest canes after flowering to keep the shrub growing vigorously. Prune currant in the spring to shape and to keep the plant in bounds for hedge purposes. Caterpillars may forage on the foliage and berries, but they can be controlled with biological insecticides.

Companion Planting and Design

Use alpine currant for a shrub border or background, or in mass plantings. Wild birds love the fruit, so be sure to include this in a wildlife garden.

My Personal Favorites

Our native golden currant (*Ribes aureum*) features spicy, clove-scented blooms that are followed by edible black berries in late summer. The foliage is a striking scarlet-red in autumn. *R. odoratum* is similar, but young stems are pubescent. Wax currant (*R. cereum*) is a low-growing native (2 to 4 ft.) with grayish-green foliage and bright-red berries. It's useful for mass plantings and in a naturalized area.

It's easy to see why this old-fashioned shrub was beloved by our ancestors. Hardy alpine currant (Ribes alpinum) tolerates most garden soils, and thrives in sun or partial shade. Its compact growth habit makes it a good choice for small hedges or an informal shrub border, or as a backdrop for the flower garden. It needs very little pruning to keep its neat and tidy appearance. The greenish yellow flowers are inconspicuous and then followed by juicy reddish black berries for wildlife. Our native buffalo currant (Ribes aureum) has fragrant yellow blooms, followed by black teardrop-shaped edible fruit. Currants are excellent shrubs for naturescapes and will surely attract wildlife. If you live in the High Country, this shrub is a must.

Bloom Period and Seasonal Color
In spring, greenish yellow flowers, followed by reddish black berries in summer

Mature Height × Spread
3 to 6 ft. × 3 to 6 ft.

Zones
To zone 2

Daphne
Daphne spp.

If you're looking for a highly fragrant shrub to plant beneath a window, include daphne on your list. The sweet fragrance from the spring blossoms permeates the air. It is a beautiful small to medium shrub with dense clusters of white, pink, or lilac blossoms that appear in late May and early June. The star-shaped flowers measure about $^{1}/_{2}$ in. diameter, and have a waxy, somewhat artificial appearance. Besides its fragrant flowers, daphne has handsome foliage throughout the year. Daphne × burkwoodii 'Carol Mackie' has rich green leaves with creamy white or yellow margins and sports clusters of light-pink flowers that are pleasantly fragrant during late spring. While lilacs may be damaged by late spring frosts, daphnes bloom later and generally survive fickle spring weather.

Other Common Name
Garland flower

Bloom Period and Seasonal Color
April through early June blooms in white, pink, or rose

Mature Height × Spread
3 to 4 ft. × 2 to 5 ft.

Zones
To zone 4

When, Where, and How to Plant
Plant early spring through early fall. Locate in full sun to partial shade. This shrub does best in well-drained soils—it does not tolerate wet feet. Avoid planting near roof lines where snow and ice loads might fall on the fragile stems and branches. Dig the planting hole three times wider than the rootball and as deep as the container in which it was growing. Add a quality soil amendment such as compost or sphagnum peat moss. Consult page 201 for more details. Container-grown plants transplant easily, but avoid disturbing the root system. Set the plant in the center of the planting hole level with the ground. Add backfill soil, lightly firm around the roots, and water thoroughly. Mulch to conserve water and to discourage weed competition. To reduce stem rot, pull the mulch 3 to 4 in. back from the stems and lower branches.

Growing Tips
Water new transplants weekly or as the soil begins to dry out—but allow the soil to dry out slightly between waterings. This helps ensure strong, healthy establishment. To keep the soil uniformly moist, apply the mulch and, during summer, regularly check soil moisture. Avoid excessive use of high-nitrogen fertilizer. In the spring and again in midsummer, apply a slow-release 5-10-5 fertilizer at the rate of 1 tablespoon per foot of the plant's height.

Care
Established daphnes need little maintenance. An occasional pruning in the spring to thin out crowded stems keeps the shrub tidy. Pests and diseases are seldom a problem.

Companion Planting and Design
Daphne works well as foundation plants or for specimen planting. Combine with low-growing evergreens, or plant in a perennial flower garden or a shrub border backed by evergreens.

My Personal Favorite
Rose daphne (*Daphne cneorum*), my favorite rock garden shrub, grows 6 to 12 in. tall and develops into an attractive ground cover. In mid- to late spring, a profusion of rosy-pink flowers accents the dark-green foliage.

Dwarf Arctic Willow

Salix purpurea

When, Where, and How to Plant

Plant bare-root willows in early spring and container-grown willows from spring to early fall. Locate in sun to partial shade. Willow prefers moist soil, so amend heavy clay, sandy, or gravelly soils with a moisture-retentive compost, sphagnum peat moss, or a combination of the two to help retain moisture. Dig the planting hole two to three times wider than the rootball. Bare-root plants should have enough space so the roots spread into the hole without cramping. Consult page 201 for specific information on soil preparation and shrub planting. Position the rootball so its top is level with the surrounding soil, add backfill soil, and water slowly. Mulch after planting to maintain moisture and to keep the soil cool.

Growing Tips

Water new transplants regularly during the first growing season to ensure healthy establishment. Once established, water them once or twice a week to prevent stress and leaf scorch. Water monthly during drought in fall and winter; consult page 79 for details. Willows can be temperamental and need proper moisture to grow and look good. Extreme periods of drought cause them to perish. Mulching around the plants can conserve and maintain moisture. In the spring, apply a slow-release 10-10-10 granular fertilizer, and water well.

Care

Arctic willow requires uniform moisture to maintain its natural growth habit and cannot tolerate extended drought periods. Don't be afraid to prune these fast growers heavily to keep the shrubs growing vigorously with bright and insect-free stems.

Companion Planting and Design

A good choice for wet sites, dwarf arctic willow can be used for informal hedging or screening.

I Also Recommend

The graceful arching branches of blue fountain willow (*Salix purpurea* 'Pendula') are a showy purplish gray. Bluestem willow (*Salix irrorata*) is a more upright growing shrub with handsome fuzzy gray catkins that emerge from jet-black calyxes in the spring. The taller coyote willow (*Salix exigua*), 6 to 12 ft., features slender, golden-yellow branches that mature to ash-gray.

Many of us have a difficult wet site in our landscapes. Luckily, dwarf artic willows can come to our rescue. The unique dwarf arctic willow features a dense growth of slender, gray-green leaves on handsome purplish branches. Another harbinger of spring, its yellow-green catkins appear before the leaves. This shrub can be planted near the downspout of the house in foundation plantings and thrive there. The compact growth habit and fine-textured stems make this a good shrub for wet areas. The blue-green foliage provides a nice contrast. The colorful stems provide winter interest. Just be sure to keep it moist during extended dry periods in the fall and winter. Cut some branches in late winter and early spring to use in arrangements.

Other Common Names
Arctic willow, blue stem willow

Bloom Period and Seasonal Color
Early spring yellowish green catkins

Mature Height × Spread
6 to 8 ft. × 6 to 10 ft.

Zones
To zone 3

Firethorn

Pyracantha coccinea

A desirable broadleaf evergreen shrub, firethorn features showy white blooms in the spring and bright-red to orange fruit in autumn. Lustrous dark-green leaves make it a desirable shrub as an informal hedge, barrier planting, or screen. The stems are noted for thorns, which makes the shrub a good barrier plant, yet birds use this shrub for nesting and find the fruit a good food source. You can train firethorn on a trellis or for espaliers on walls. It tolerates heat, drought, and alkaline soils. It is adaptable to full sun or partial shade conditions. There are many cultivars in the nursery trade, so be sure to read the plant tags to make sure the selection is cold hardy for your particular location.

Other Common Name
Scarlet firethorn

Bloom Period and Seasonal Color
Early summer clusters of white flowers, followed by bright-red to orange berries in fall

Mature Height × Spread
4 to 8 ft. × 4 to 10 ft.

Zones
To zone 4

When, Where, and How to Plant
Plant container-grown nursery firethorn from early spring to early fall. Choose a site in full sun to partial shade. Be sure the site is both large enough to allow this shrub to grow and spread and permanent—firethorn is difficult to move once it becomes established. Refer to page 201 for information on soil preparation. Dig the planting hole two to three times wider than the rootball. Position the rootball so its top is level with the surrounding soil. Backfill, firm the soil gently around the plant, and water thoroughly.

Growing Tips
Water regularly for the first growing season to ensure healthy and strong establishment. Once established, water firethorn deeply once a week or as the soil becomes dry. This shrub tolerates dry conditions well but will succumb to root rot if watered too heavily in clay soils. Water as the soil begins to dry out. Mulch the root zone with organic material to conserve water and discourage weed invasions, and to set off the glossy foliage and brightly colored berries. In the spring, apply a slow-release granular fertilizer to provide nutrients through the growing season.

Care
Thorns make pruning somewhat difficult, but if necessary, prune firethorn shortly after flowering. This shrub is prone to fireblight disease. A bacterial disease, fireblight is difficult to control; prune out infected stems in late winter. Pests include aphids and spider mites; scale can be a problem. Early detection and control prevent severe problems.

Companion Planting and Design
Firethorn works well as a barrier shrub under windows and around foundations or as informal hedges along property lines. It can be trained as espalier on a trellis, fence, or wall.

My Personal Favorites
'Fiery Cascade' is one of the hardier, disease-resistant selections, with small, glossy leaves and abundant reddish orange berries. 'Pauciflora' is a more compact-growing rounded shrub with orange-red berries. 'Wyatti' grows more upright to a height of 6 ft. or more.

Forsythia

Forsythia × intermedia

When, Where, and How to Plant

Plant container-grown forsythia from spring to early fall and bare-root plants in early spring. Choose a site that allows plenty of room for the arching branches. For a screen or hedge, space 2 to 3 ft. apart. In mass plantings, space 9 to 12 ft. apart. For the most prolific and best blossoms, plant in full to partial sun. Dig the planting hole two to three times wider than the rootball. If the soil is compacted, add 1/3 compost to the planting area. Rootbound container-grown plants benefit if you lightly score or prune the roots—or unwind the longest ones and spread them in the planting hole. Add backfill soil around the plant, and water thoroughly.

Growing Tips

Water regularly to help forsythia establish. Mulch can be applied at planting, but as this shrub matures, the arching branches cover the ground and additional mulching is not needed. Water deeply and thoroughly in the summer to avoid severe drought stress and leaf scorch. Fertilize with a slow-release granular 5-10-5 formula in the spring to provide nutrients for the season.

Care

As it matures, prune forsythia every few years to maintain plant health and prolific blossoms. Selectively remove older stems, cutting them back to ground level. New young stems arise and flower within a few years. Flower buds can be killed when temperatures drop below -15 degrees Fahrenheit. Pests and diseases do not generally bother forsythia; occasionally, rabbits chew the stems.

Companion Planting and Design

Plant on banks for soil stabilization and as a shrub border. The brilliant-yellow flowers show up well against a dark-evergreen backdrop. Combine with spring flowering bulbs.

My Personal Favorites

One of the hardiest, *Forsythia* 'Meadowlark' features flower buds that withstand -35 degrees Fahrenheit. Bright-yellow flowers appear in early April before the foliage. The smaller 'Northern Gold' (6 to 8 ft.) sports outstanding yellow blossoms and excellent flower bud hardiness. 'Arnold Dwarf' is a drought-enduring, pest-resistant and low-growing plant.

Standing tall above the flowering spring bulbs, the bright-yellow blossoms of this shrub are eager harbingers of spring. The impatient gardener who just can't wait can easily coax forsythia branches into bloom indoors in late January and February. This shrub features a multitude of spreading, arching branches in an upright growth habit. Left unpruned, forsythia can become unruly, so it is a good idea to thin out the older stems and renew this shrub every three years to maintain healthy stems and encourage more prolific blooming. Masses of bell-shaped flowers grace the tannish gray arching branches in early spring. While forsythia may lose its appeal in summer, its bright-green foliage means that it works well as a foundation planting or screening.

Bloom Period and Seasonal Color
Early spring bright-yellow blossoms

Mature Height × Spread
6 to 9 ft. × 6 to 12 ft.

Zones
To zone 3

Glossy Buckthorn
Rhamnus frangula

One of the most attractive fast-growing screen or hedge plants for Rocky Mountain landscapes, glossy buckthorn features lustrous foliage that grows densely from near ground level to the top of the plant. This shrub is strongly columnar, which makes it an excellent choice for landscapes with limited space. Tallhedge (Rhamnus frangula 'Columnaris') has a dense growth habit and works well as a screen for privacy. Glossy buckthorn withstands sun and partial shade. The dark-green glossy leaves make this shrub a nice background plant for perennials or low-growing evergreens. Creamy-white flower clusters are followed by red berries that turn a purplish black as they mature. I have found this shrub very useful in limited space, and it makes an excellent plant to attract wildlife.

Bloom Period and Seasonal Color
In spring, inconspicuous greenish white flowers, followed by purple-black berries

Mature Height × Spread
8 to 12 ft. × 3 to 5 ft.

Zones
To zone 2

When, Where, and How to Plant
Plant container-grown shrubs from spring through early fall. Bare-root plants are available in early spring. Though this shrub tolerates a wide range of soils, it does not do well in heavily compacted soils. Glossy buckthorn prefers a moderately rich, organic soil that is well drained. It needs plenty of water to become established. Buckthorn transplants readily. Locate this shrub in full sun to partial shade. Dig the planting hole twice as wide as the rootball. Position the roots or rootball so the top is level with the surrounding soil. Backfill, firm soil gently around the plant, and water well. Spread a 2-in. layer of organic mulch beneath the plant to conserve moisture.

Growing Tips
Water regularly once a week or as needed during the first year for good establishment. Once established, water buckthorn deeply (6 to 8 in.) and thoroughly each week during the summer to maintain vigorous growth and to prevent leaf scorch. To conserve water and discourage weed invasions, mulch around the root zone. In the spring, apply a slow-release granular fertilizer (5-10-5) to provide nutrients through the growing season.

Care
Once well established, buckthorn requires minimal care. Prune this shrub in the spring to thin out crisscrossing branches or broken limbs. Pests do not generally bother buckthorn—birds frequent the plant for berries and take care of any visible critters.

Companion Planting and Design
Glossy buckthorn is excellent for a narrow privacy screen or hedge, or in windbreaks. Use it in a naturescape or wildlife-friendly garden.

I Also Recommend
The selection *Rhamnus frangula* 'Asplenifolia' has a finer texture than the species, with narrow, irregularly margined leaves that give this shrub a fernlike appearance. *Rhamnus smithii,* Smith's buckthorn, develops into a more rounded form, spreading outward to 6 ft. or more. The common buckthorn (*Rhamnus cathartica*) grows to 20 ft., with comparable spread, and makes a good, dense background shrub. Birds love the berries and help to spread the seeds.

Honeysuckle
Lonicera spp.

When, Where, and How to Plant

Plant container-grown shrubs from spring through early fall and bare-root plants in early spring. Honeysuckle is easy to transplant and quick to establish. It prefers full sun, but adapts to partial shade. It does best in well-drained, loamy soils with moderate moisture. Dig the planting hole two to three times wider than the rootball. Set the rootball so that it is at ground level, add backfill soil, and water slowly. Apply a 2-in. layer of mulch to maintain uniform moisture during the first growing season.

Growing Tips

Water new transplants well to ensure healthy establishment. Once established, honeysuckle is very drought enduring. Avoid overwatering—water deeply and infrequently during the summer. Apply a slow-release granular 5-10-5 fertilizer in the spring to provide nutrients throughout the growing season. Water in well.

Care

To maintain vigor, prune honeysuckle after it flowers. Remove the oldest canes to ground level to rejuvenate older shrubs. Some varieties are susceptible to honeysuckle aphids, but this varies by geographical areas. The distorted growth caused by honeysuckle aphids can be pruned off as it appears.

Companion Planting and Design

Honeysuckle is useful for borders, informal hedges, or specimen plants.

My Personal Favorites

Blueleaf honeysuckle (*Lonicera korolkowii*) features gray-blue leaves and rose-pink blossoms. It bears bright-red berries in late summer and is not bothered by aphids. Twinberry honeysuckle (*Lonicera involucrata*) is a compact oval shrub (3 to 6 ft.) with pairs of yellow flowers in late spring to early summer. Hardy to elevations of 11,000 ft., tiny trumpet honeysuckle (*Lonicera syringantha*) sports arching branches and small, strongly fragrant, pale-violet, trumpetlike flowers in late spring. Its bluish green leaves contrast nicely with newer red stems. Amur honeysuckle (*Lonicera maackii*) has an upright growing habit with leaves that are medium to dark green. Fragrant white flowers are borne in clusters May to June, followed by bright-red fruits that are beloved by birds. Honeysuckle aphids do not affect it.

The tubular flowers of honeysuckle possess a fragrance that evokes memories of Grandma's garden. She planted 'Zabelii', a variety that has since become severely plagued by the honeysuckle aphid. These pests cause a "witches broom" or distorted growth on the terminals, primarily affecting tender new growth. The leaves become stunted and develop into distorted bunches. Despite this invasion, honeysuckle still flowers prolifically. Ornamental berries follow flowering. The fruit is a favorite of robins and vanishes quickly. One of the better cultivars is Lonicera tatarica 'Arnold Red', with characteristic pinkish red blossoms in late spring followed by glossy red berries that robins consume in mass quantities. Another favorite is blue velvet honeysuckle (Lonicera korolkowii 'Floribunda'), with pest-resistant, blue-gray foliage and prolific pink blooms.

Other Common Name
Shrub honeysuckle

Bloom Period and Seasonal Color
Spring through early summer fragrant red blooms

Mature Height × Spread
8 to 10 ft. × 6 to 8 ft.

Zones
To zone 2

Hydrangea
Hydrangea spp.

Hydrangea arborescens *'Annabelle'*, Hydrangea paniculata *Pee Gee hydrangea, and* Hydrangea quercifolia
*oakleaf hydrangea, are good shrubs for the shade garden.
In mid- to late summer, a season when color is lacking,
hydrangeas come to the rescue with the cooling effect of
their light-colored panicles. One of my favorites is the
oakleaf hydrangea, with lobed leaves that resemble those
of oaks. They emerge a grayish green with felt undersides
in the spring and transform to a striking wine-purple by
fall. Flowers are a creamy beige tinged with pink.
'Annabelle' is a smaller, yet dense shrub with large to
medium green leaves and stout stems that provide a
coarse texture. Huge, 12-in.-wide globe-shaped clusters of
flowers open pale-green and mature to white from July
through September.*

Bloom Period and Seasonal Color
July through August blooms in white

Mature Height × Spread
3 to 10 ft. × 3 to 8 ft., depending upon variety

Zones
To zone 3

When, Where, and How to Plant
Plant hydrangeas in the spring to allow for vigorous
growth and flowers in late summer. Container-
grown hydrangeas transplant without difficulty.
Locate this shrub in partial shade to shade. It
prefers moist, well-drained soils, but adapts to average soils. Refer to page 201 for more details on soil
preparation and shrub planting techniques.

Growing Tips
Hydrangeas appreciate regular watering during dry,
hot periods. Water thoroughly during drought.
Maintain a 2- to 3-in. layer of organic mulch on
the soil to retain moisture and to discourage weed
competition. Apply slow-release fertilizer over the
mulch for these acid-loving plants, and water well.
An application of fertilizer in the spring sustains the
plants for the growing season, but there is no need
for subsequent feedings.

Care
Hydrangeas are generally free of pests and diseases.
Powdery mildew may appear on the foliage; prune
dense growth to improve air circulation and to discourage leaf diseases. Hydrangeas also need
periodic pruning to keep the shrubs tidy and
blooming. Prune the panicle hydrangea in the
winter or early spring, because it forms flower buds
on new growth each season. Prune oakleaf
hydrangea after flowering to control shrub height
and spread. Don't wait too long since flower buds
for next season's bloom form shortly after the
blooming cycle. Neglected hydrangea shrubs can
be pruned in early spring; cut old stems to the
ground to stimulate denser new growth.

Companion Planting and Design
Plant hydrangeas to brighten shady gardens, as
specimen shrubs against north walls, or as elements of a shrub border. They are at home in a
shady woodland garden. Interplant with Oregon
grape holly, viburnums, and hardy rhododendrons
such as 'Ramapo'.

My Personal Favorites
Oakleaf hydrangea (*H. quercifolia*) features lacy
clusters of creamy beige flowers with a pinkish
tinge. Its autumn foliage coloration is a wonderful
reddish purple. *H. arborescens* 'Annabelle' produces
huge, 12-in.-wide panicles that open pale-green
and mature to white.

When, Where, and How to Plant

Plant leadplant from spring through fall. Bare-root stock is available and should be planted in early spring; container-grown plants can be planted anytime. Leadplant prefers full sun and soils that are well drained. It also prefers dry conditions; this shrub suffers in conditions that are too wet. It tolerates alkaline soils well. Plant leadplant in dry, sandy soils, and it prospers with minimal care. Space plants 2 to 3 ft. apart. Dig the planting hole twice as wide as the root system. Soil amendments may be needed in heavy clay, pure sand, or gravel-based soils. For general information on soil preparation and shrub planting techniques, consult page 201.

Growing Tips

Water new transplants weekly to allow for healthy establishment. Once established, water leadplant thoroughly, but infrequently. This drought-enduring plant withstands both wind and heat. Before summer, apply a layer of shredded cedar shavings or pine needles to conserve moisture. A light application of slow-release 5-10-5 granular fertilizer in late spring provides nutrients to start the growing season, but leadplant fixes nitrogen from the atmosphere, so it generally does not need additional fertilizer.

Care

Once leadplant is established, it is a virtually no-maintenance shrub, needing only a periodic pruning in late winter to clean up the garden. This plant may die back from a harsh winter, or from being browsed on by deer, but leadplant can be cut to ground level in early spring to tidy up the plant. It grows back readily. Pests and diseases do not bother this shrub.

Companion Planting and Design

With its silvery foliage, leadplant integrates well into a dryland garden. Plant it as an accent in group plantings, informal edgings, or shrub borders.

I Also Recommend

Indigobush (*Amorpha fruticosa*) has a taller growth habit (6 to 12 ft., with a spread of up to 10 ft.) and features bright-green foliage. It grows even in poor soils and resists drought well.

This native of the mixed-grass and tallgrass prairies is a truly drought-resistant shrub. Leadplant's broad, flat-topped growth habit and arching stems make an attractive, fine-textured landscape shrub. Fifteen to forty-five grayish, inch-long leaflets comprise the foliage, giving this shrub an airy texture. Silvery-gray hairs on the leaves create a grayish green appearance that is quite attractive in the summer landscape. Spikes of purple flowers appear in summer on dense 6-in. terminal racemes and contrast nicely with the silvery foliage. This shrub's small stature helps its silvery-gray foliage blend well into perennial gardens. Leadplant is also effective in group plantings or as accent plants in a mixed-shrub planting. It tolerates heat and drought, which makes it an ideal shrub for water-thrifty or xeric gardens.

Other Common Name
Leadwort

Bloom Period and Seasonal Color
June through July spikes of purple flowers

Mature Height × Spread
2 to 4 ft. × 3 to 4 ft.

Zones
To zone 4

Lilac
Syringa spp.

Undeniably one of the most enduring flowering shrubs throughout our region, lilac is often found surviving in long-abandoned home sites. The sweet smell of this familiar shrub in the spring evokes memories of Grandma's garden. The common lilac species have purple flowers borne in 4- to 8-in. terminal panicles. Today, many species, hybrids, and cultivars are available, ranging in size from the compact shrub 'Miss Kim' to larger shrub forms. Flowers come in white, blue, violet, lilac, magenta, pink, reddish purple, and deep purple. One of my favorites is the bicolored variety 'Sensation', with dark-purple petals edged in white. In a good growing season, you can enjoy fragrant flowers for up to eight weeks if you plant different species with varied blooming times.

Bloom Period and Seasonal Color
Late April through early June blooms in purple, lilac, white, pink, rose, or reddish purple

Mature Height × Spread
6 to 15 ft. × 5 to 12 ft.

Zones
To zone 2

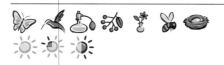

When, Where, and How to Plant
Plant from spring through early fall; plant bare-root lilac in early spring. Locate in full sun or partial shade with plenty of space for good air circulation. This reduces the development of powdery mildew, a disease that thrives in shady, wind-protected locations. Plant in well-drained soil with a good complement of compost worked into it. Dig the hole plenty wide so the root system of bare-root plants can be spread out fully. Once planted, water thoroughly.

Growing Tips
Water new transplants regularly the first growing season to ensure strong and healthy establishment. Deep soak the soil periodically during hot, dry weather, but avoid overwatering; this encourages diseases. Apply an organic mulch around the root zone to maintain moisture and to discourage weed competition. In the spring, apply a slow-release granular 5-10-5 fertilizer. Also see page 202.

Care
Lilacs can require three years to establish, but once firmly rooted, they are easy to maintain. Powdery mildew, leaf blights, and wilt may attack stressed plants. Maintain shrubs well to reduce the onset of such problems. Removing spent flowers isn't necessary, unless you find them unattractive. The seeds provide food for wild birds. If you deadhead old flowers, be careful not to remove next year's flower buds; they develop on the same branch just below the dead flower heads. Rejuvenate older plants that have become too thick by removing the old stems to ground level. New growth then comes from the base.

Companion Planting and Design
Use for an informal hedge, as a privacy screen, and along fence rows. Single specimen plantings can anchor flower beds and foundation plantings and make a spectacular display when in bloom.

My Personal Favorites
Favorites include *Syringa vulgaris* 'Charles Joly', with double, reddish purple flowers; 'Sensation', which sports large purple florets edged in white; 'Wedgewood Blue', with lilac-pink buds that open to blue with a sweet fragrance; and 'President Lincoln', with long panicles of single, blue florets.

When, Where, and How to Plant

Plant container-grown nursery plants from spring through fall and bare-root plants in early spring. Choose a site with full to partial sun for best growth and prolific flowering. This shrub needs plenty of space to grow and spread. Though it tolerates a wide range of soils, mockorange performs best in well-drained locations. Consult page 201 for information on soil preparation and shrub planting techniques. Dig the planting hole two to three times wider than the rootball. Set the plant so the top of the rootball is level with the surrounding grade. After adding the backfill soil to the hole, water thoroughly. Mulch with shredded cedar or pine needles.

Growing Tips

Water new transplants regularly to ensure they become well established. Dig down to a depth of 4 in. near the rootball; if the soil feels dry, give the shrub a deep soaking. This plant is drought enduring after it becomes well established in three to five years. Apply a slow-release granular 5-10-5 fertilizer each spring to provide nutrients for the growing season.

Care

Once established, mockorange is a dependable shrub that provides years of fragrant blossoms. If it becomes overcrowded, prune out the oldest stems to rejuvenate the shrub and induce new growth from the base. This ensures a continuous supply of flowering wood for future blooms. Remove as much as 30 percent of the older wood every two to three years. These shrubs are seldom bothered by insects or diseases.

Companion Planting and Design

Mockorange is an excellent shrub for background plantings, fitting in with evergreens and other deciduous shrubs. Plant near a window, patio, or entryway, where its fragrance can waft into your home.

My Personal Favorites

Littleleaf mockorange (*Philadelphus microphyllus*) is a slower growing species that can reach a height of 6 ft. Its star-shaped flowers bloom in June and are pleasantly fragrant. *Philadelphus* 'Miniature Snowflake' has a more compact growth habit and double white blooms.

The sweet fragrance that permeates the air in June reminds us the mockorange is in bloom. The common mockorange (Philadelphus coronarius) is an old-fashioned favorite that is underused in Rocky Mountain landscapes. This shrub has remarkable ability to withstand heat, drought, and poor soil conditions. Philadelphus lewisii, Lewis mockorange, is among the only shrubs that continue to thrive and bloom at the Cheyenne Research Station in Wyoming. Native to the western United States, it can be grown at higher elevations and develops into a rounded, upright shrub. Once established, mockorange produces an abundance of 1- to 1¹⁄₄-in. pure white flowers in early summer. Plant this shrub beneath a window or near a pathway where you can enjoy the sweet fragrance of the blooms.

Bloom Period and Seasonal Color
June through July sweetly fragrant blooms in white

Mature Height × Spread
6 to 10 ft. × 5 to 8 ft.

Zones
To zone 4

Mountain Mahogany
Cercocarpus montanus

One of the most drought-resistant shrubs for a water-thrifty landscape is mountain mahogany. Its thick and leathery wedge-shaped leaves curl under slightly around the edges. This adaptation helps the plant reduce exposure to the sun's hot rays and drying winds. Once established, mountain mahogany survives dry, arid conditions. Even the curled seeds have a purpose: Once the seed falls to the ground, damp conditions make the seed coil up, but when it becomes dry, the seed straightens out. This adaptation helps to work the seed into the ground so that it germinates successfully. Mountain mahogany's foliage, though sparse, is a handsome gray-green and usually evergreen. The tiny yellow flowers in mid-spring are followed by fuzzy, twisted seed tails that add an interesting texture.

Bloom Period and Seasonal Color
Inconspicuous yellow flowers in early spring; grown for its semievergreen gray-green foliage

Mature Height × Spread
3 to 10 ft. × 4 to 6 ft.

Zones
To zone 2

When, Where, and How to Plant
Plant mountain mahogany in the spring. Choose a sunny site with well-drained soil. Soil preparation is generally not required, but break up any areas of compacted soil to help improve drainage. If adding compost, add only 25 percent by volume. Do not add too much organic matter—doing so can make the soil too rich and result in poor establishment. Set the rootball at the same level it was growing in the pot. Water thoroughly. Apply a mulch of pine needles, shredded leaves, or shredded wood chips to conserve moisture. Mountain mahogany grows slowly, so be patient.

Growing Tips
Keep new transplants moderately moist during the first growing season to help them get off to a strong start. Once established, mountain mahogany endures drought and can survive without supplemental irrigation, except during long, hot periods. Water deeply every two weeks, and this shrub will endure. It needs no supplemental fertilizer.

Care
Once mountain mahogany is established, it requires little care. Occasional pruning in late winter or early spring keeps the plant in bounds. Pests and diseases do not bother this shrub.

Companion Planting and Design
Its resistance to drought makes mountain mahogany very useful as a foundation plant. The shrub's open and spreading growth habit lends itself well to use as an informal hedge or screen. One of the best features of mountain mahogany is its evergreen nature in the winter. In the summer, its white feathery plumes are quite attractive. Mulch with pea gravel to set off the interesting foliage and seed tails.

I Also Recommend
Curlleaf mahogany (*Cercocarpus ledifolius*) is a larger shrub or small tree (10- to 20-ft. tall, with a spread of 8 to 12 ft.). The leathery, lance-shaped leaves are dark green with edges that curl under, giving the plant its common name; it has excellent drought resistance and retains its leaves through the fall and winter with fuzzy seed tails for winter interest.

Oregon Grape

Mahonia aquifolium

When, Where, and How to Plant

Plant container-grown plants in early spring. If you plant during summer, provide ample moisture for good root establishment. Oregon grape does best in partial sun to shady locations. It needs protection from winter wind and sun to avoid leaf scorch. Plant in soil that is moderately fertile and well drained, with slightly acidic organic matter. Dig the hole two to three times wider than the rootball. Prepare the soil with compost or sphagnum peat moss before planting to improve water retention and bring down the pH. Add up to 50 percent by volume of soil amendment, and mix uniformly with the native soil. Work the soil conditioner into the planting hole, as well. Set transplants level with the ground, and water thoroughly. Mulch with pine needles.

Growing Tips

Water new transplants well and regularly for the first growing season to ensure healthy and strong establishment. Oregon grape prefers evenly moist conditions, but should not be overwatered. Since it spreads by underground roots, this plant creates a natural living mulch over time. Apply a slow release 5-10-5 fertilizer in the spring.

Care

If the plant becomes straggly, renew it by pruning after flowering to maintain height and spread. Protect from intense winter sun and wind by constructing a screen of burlap on the windward exposures. Pests and diseases do not generally bother this shrub.

Companion Planting and Design

Plant Oregon grape in shady locations on the north and northeast sides of buildings. Enjoy the glossy new foliage in the spring and the bluish purple fruit in late summer and fall.

I Also Recommend

Our Rocky Mountain native, creeping mahonia (*Mahonia repens*), makes a useful woody ground cover with handsome foliage, flowers, and fruit. It resists drought, has excellent red fall foliage, and is a good choice to plant beneath evergreens. *Mahonia aquifolium* 'Compacta' has a compact growth habit (2 to 3 ft.) and works well as a foundation plant in shady locations.

Oregon grape is one of the few, upright-growing and broadleaf evergreen shrubs. It is especially useful as a foundation plant in a north or east exposure, and it can be planted as a shrub border or specimen. The glossy, leathery leaves are highlighted by bright-yellow flowers in May, followed in late summer by clusters of deep-blue berries. The hollylike leaves are spiny and remain evergreen through the seasons, but turn a purplish bronze with the onset of cold weather. If exposed to persistent wind and sun, the leaves tend to develop scorch and turn tannish brown. This somewhat aggressive grower spreads by underground stems and, over time, forms irregular colonies. The foliage has nice color variations in autumn—from dull-red to orange and yellow.

Bloom Period and Seasonal Color
Early spring clusters of yellow flowers followed by bluish purple fruit

Mature Height × Spread
3 to 6 ft. × 3 to 5 ft.

Zones
To zone 3

Potentilla
Potentilla fruticosa

Potentillas have become a mainstay in many Rocky Mountain landscapes. Our native shrubby cinquefoil has an open habit and becomes woody as it matures. Bright-yellow blooms grow from 1 to 1¹/2 in. wide and are complemented by fine-textured grayish green leaves. Cinquefoil grows into a dense shrub with soft, slender, upright branches. Some varieties have arching branches that make them effective for use in informal hedge or barrier plantings. A flush of bloom occurs in May, with flowers continuing until frost. This shrub tolerates alkaline soils, and once established, it endures drought conditions for short periods. It makes an excellent small shrub, thriving from the lower elevations of the High Plains all the way up to the higher elevations of the High Country.

Other Common Names
Shrubby cinquefoil, bush cinquefoil

Bloom Period and Seasonal Color
Summer blooms in yellow, orange, white, or pinkish white

Zones
To zone 2

When, Where, and How to Plant
Plant potentilla from early spring through early fall. Locate this shrub in a sunny site with good air circulation. Potentilla prefers soil with good drainage, so if your soil is heavy clay, amend it with a good source of compost. These plants quickly develop a strong fibrous root system when grown in containers, which makes them easy to transplant. Dig the planting hole wider than the rootball to encourage a strong and vigorous root system. Refer to page 201 for more details on soil preparation and shrub planting techniques.

Growing Tips
Water new transplants regularly during the first growing season to ensure a healthy establishment. Potentilla shrubs are very hardy and drought enduring once established. Organic mulch conserves soil moisture and discourages weed invasions; cedar mulch sets off the clean, bluish green foliage and brilliant flowers. Apply a slow-release granular 5-10-5 fertilizer in the spring to provide nutrients through the growing season.

Care
If your potentilla plants become unkempt, prune to renew them by removing one-third of the oldest stems each year. After that, new growth will emerge with fresh blooms. For total rejuvenation, cut older shrubs to ground level in late winter or early spring. Spider mites can become a problem in hot, dry exposures. Control them by hosing potentillas off with a strong stream of water on a regular basis. Chlorosis can also become a problem in some areas but can be corrected by applying a wettable powder of chelated iron in the spring.

Companion Planting and Design
Potentillas are useful for low shrub hedges, for accent shrubs in mixed plantings, and for foundation plantings. Use on rocky slopes to help stabilize the soil and to provide colorful accents.

My Personal Favorites
My favorites include 'Goldfinger', which features an upright growth habit and golden-yellow blossoms, and 'Katherine Dykes', which has a wider spreading habit and sports greenish gray foliage with a heavy spring bloom of pale-yellow flowers.

Redtwig Dogwood
Cornus sericea

When, Where, and How to Plant

Plant container-grown redtwig dogwood shrubs from spring through early fall. Bare-root stock, if available, is best planted in early spring. This shrub thrives in full sun or partial shade, but too much shade makes the plant leggy and decreases flowering. Plant redtwig dogwood in well-drained soil. Dig the planting hole much wider than the rootball. Spread the roots of bare-root plants into the planting hole so that they are not cramped. Redtwig dogwoods are quick to establish. For complete details on soil preparation and shrub planting techniques, refer to page 201.

Growing Tips

To ensure good establishment, water new transplants thoroughly every five to seven days for the first month after planting. Water thoroughly and deeply during the heat of summer to prevent severe leaf scorch. Although native dogwood does best in moist soils, it tolerates dry conditions if properly mulched with shredded cedar shavings or other organic material. Mulching helps conserve soil moisture, keep the soil from baking, and discourage annual weed invasions. Apply a complete all-purpose 5-10-5 fertilizer in early spring.

Care

To keep the shrub vigorous and to promote brightly colored stems, prune out one-fourth to one-third of the oldest canes each year. Remove these canes to ground level, and new growth will emerge from the base. An insect pest known as oystershell scale can become a problem on older stems, but this can be remedied by pruning out infested canes to ground level.

Companion Planting and Design

Redtwig dogwood makes an effective informal hedge or summer screen. It is attractive as a backdrop for the perennial bed or as an accent against fencing. The variety *C. coloradensis* 'Cheyenne' has blood-red stems, but doesn't grow too tall.

I Also Recommend

'Cardinal' has bright, cherry-red stems and nice fall foliage color. For a different accent, plant 'Flaviramea', with its yellow twigs and reddish purple fall foliage. The quite unusual *Cornus alba* 'Argenteomarginata' features variegated white and green leaves.

Redtwig dogwood is widely adaptable to the diverse climate and soil conditions of the Rocky Mountains. It prefers moist conditions, but grows successfully in moderately dry conditions once it becomes established. Maintain soil moisture by keeping a layer of organic mulch over the root zone, and this shrub thrives. Both redtwig and yellowtwig dogwood bear clusters of small, fragrant, creamy-white flowers in the spring, followed by clusters of white fruit in late summer. This shrub is a good choice for a wildlife-friendly garden and provides a source of both food and shelter for birds. The dark-green leaves change to a beautiful wine-red in autumn. One of redtwig dogwood's most striking features is its glossy red stems, which are especially attractive when framed in winter snow.

Other Common Name
Red-osier dogwood

Bloom Period and Seasonal Color
Late spring creamy white blooms followed by white fruits; vivid winter stem coloration

Mature Height × Spread
6 to 8 ft. × 8 to 10 ft.

Zones
To zone 2

Rock Spirea
Holodiscus dumosus

A Rocky Mountain native, rock spirea features handsome sprays of white to pink flowers in late June. This plant's wispy, colorful sprays of blossoms brighten rocky canyon walls from late spring through early summer. As the flowers mature, they transform and deepen to russet in the fall and then persist through the winter. Rock spirea features fine-textured foliage that is quite attractive during the summer, but is even more magnificent when it turns reddish in the fall. If you should rub up against the leaves or crush some with your fingers, you will discover that they produce a spicy scent. Rock spirea tolerates both heat and drought. This plant makes an excellent, upright-spreading shrub for a water-thrifty or xeric garden.

Other Common Names
Rockspray, mountain spray

Bloom Period and Seasonal Color
June sprays of white to pink flowers

Mature Height × Spread
3 to 4 ft. × 3 to 4 ft.

Zones
To zone 4

When, Where, and How to Plant
Plant potted rock spirea shrubs in the spring to allow them to become fully established before fall arrives. This native shrub performs best when located in areas that receive full to partial sun. It can even thrive in partial sun exposures, as it does in native stands with ponderosa pine communities up in the spruce and fir zones of our region. Rock spirea is not fussy about soils as long as they are well drained. Heavy clay soils can be amended with organic matter to improve drainage and porosity. Consult page 201 for more information on soil preparation and shrub planting techniques.

Growing Tips
Water new rock spirea transplants each week to ensure a strong and healthy establishment. Allow the soil to dry out between waterings; to determine soil moisture, dig down around the rootball to a depth of 4 in. If the soil feels dry it is time to give the shrub a good drink, but avoid overwatering. Once it becomes established, rock spirea tolerates drought very well. During extended drought periods, water this shrub periodically (once every two to three weeks). A slow-acting 5-10-5 fertilizer can be applied in late spring to give rock spirea a boost for the growing season. Once established, rock spirea does not need extra fertilizer.

Care
Once it becomes established, rock spirea is a relatively carefree shrub that needs only periodic pruning. Prune dead or dying branches in early spring to allow for good air circulation and to maintain the natural shape of the shrub. Pests and diseases do not generally bother rock spirea.

Companion Planting and Design
Plant rock spirea as an informal border, on rocky slopes, and in xeriscape settings. It can be used as an accent shrub in rock gardens or mixed plantings.

My Personal Favorite
The native Rocky Mountain rock spirea is the only available species. It is a wonderful shrub with attractive blooms, and it endures drought.

Rose-of-Sharon

Hibiscus syriacus

When, Where, and How to Plant

Plant container-grown shrubs from spring through early fall and bare-root plants in early spring as soon as the soil can be worked. Rose-of-Sharon tolerates light shade, but choose a site with full sun. Avoid wet or poorly drained soils. Consult page 201 for general information on soil preparation and planting. Dig the planting hole two to three times wider than the rootball. With bare-root plants, spread the roots into the planting hole without cramping them. Add backfill soil, and water slowly to eliminate any air pockets beneath the roots. Spread a 2-in. layer of mulch under the shrub.

Growing Tips

Keep the soil evenly moist for at least one month. Water new plants regularly the first season to ensure good establishment, then water regularly during the summer. Rose-of-Sharon experiences drought stress in extremely dry sites or sandy soils. Mulch to maintain moisture and to discourage weeds. Apply ¹/₄ cup of 5-10-5 all-purpose granular fertilizer per foot of shrub height in the spring and again in midsummer.

Care

Rigorous pruning in late spring to thin out crowded branches encourages vigorous and floriferous stems. Each spring, prune the previous season's growth to two or three buds for fewer but larger flowers. Rose-of-Sharon is slow to start in the spring, so be patient for the leaves to emerge. Pests and diseases do not generally bother this plant.

Companion Planting and Design

Use rose-of-Sharon in mixed plantings or shrub borders, or as a specimen shrub. Place it against a garden shed or garage to hide a bare wall and provide a showy display of flowers summer through frost.

My Personal Favorites

A triploid variety, 'Diana' features large 4-in. flowers and doesn't produce seed. You won't have to weed hibiscus seedlings each summer. 'Bluebird' has beautiful sky-blue, single flowers. 'Aphrodite' is especially attractive; its large 4- to 5-in., dark-pink flowers feature a prominent dark-red eye. 'Collie Mullens' bears large, double lavender-purple flowers in late summer.

Rose-of-Sharon, also known as shrub althea, is one of my favorite old-fashioned shrubs. Its eye-catching blossoms appear in late summer when other shrubs start to wane. Depending on the variety, flowers range from 2¹/₂ to 4 in. and can be single, semidouble, or double. Rose-of-Sharon makes an excellent focal specimen in the landscape, but it also works well when planted as a group in a shrub border. Though this shrub is known to die back to ground level in the winter, it endures erratic climatic conditions very well and grows new, vigorous stems the following spring. Such "Nature's pruning" results in a smaller shrub, but much bigger flowers. If you prefer, you can selectively prune the shrub to maintain shape, height, and flower development.

Other Common Name
Shrub althea

Bloom Period and Seasonal Color
Late summer to early fall single or double blooms in white, pink, red, purple, or lavender

Mature Height × Spread
8 to 12 ft. × 6 to 10 ft.

Zones
To zone 4 (with protection)

Saucer Magnolia
Magnolia × soulangiana

Who said you can't grow magnolias in the Rockies? The saucer magnolia, hybridized from Japanese and Chinese magnolias, defies the critics. Its stunning 5- to 8-in.-wide, fragrant, pure-white saucer-shaped blooms are preceded by plump buds with a pink or purplish blush underneath. For all its beauty, this early blooming shrub has limitations in Rocky Mountain landscapes. Engaging in an annual battle to outwit Mother Nature, many flower buds are killed by a hard frost. But if the saucer magnolia wins the battle, your rewards are absolutely stunning: Flowers cover the shrub before its leaves emerge. Proper siting of this shrub increases the odds that you can experience its radiant blooms. This cold-hardy version of magnolia is easy to establish and blooms when young.

Bloom Period and Seasonal Color
Early spring blooms in white with pink

Mature Height × Spread
6 to 12 ft. × 4 to 10 ft.

Zones
To zone 4 (with protection)

When, Where, and How to Plant
Plant container-grown magnolias in the spring. Handle their temperamental, thick, fleshy roots with care; be careful not to break them. Smaller, potted plants transplant best. Plant saucer magnolia in full to partial sun, but avoid sites with a warm southern or western exposure or the buds open early and risk death to frost. A northern or northeastern exposure helps keep the buds tight and delays emergence until the danger of frost has passed. Saucer magnolia does best in well-drained soil enriched with sphagnum peat and compost to buffer alkaline conditions. Incorporate 40 percent by volume of sphagnum peat moss with native soil, and mix uniformly. Dig the planting hole twice as wide and only as deep as the rootball. Position the shrub so that the top of the rootball is level with the surrounding ground, but no deeper. Backfill with prepared soil, gently firm it around the shrub, and water thoroughly.

Growing Tips
Water saucer magnolia well during the first growing season. Once the plant becomes established, water weekly or as the soil dries out. Mulch the root zone with a layer of pine needles to keep the soil moist and cool, and to prevent weeds. Fertilize with an acid-based formula in the spring and again in early summer.

Care
Prune for size and shape in late spring after flowering—new buds form over the summer for the next season's bloom. To encourage this shrub's natural growth habit and ensure the best display, avoid pruning lower branches. Remove crisscrossing branches, water sprouts, or broken branches anytime. Pests and diseases do not generally bother this magnolia.

Companion Planting and Design
Saucer magnolia is an effective specimen shrub that is worth trying. Underplanted with hardy, spring-flowering bulbs, its huge pure-white saucer blooms are sure to provide a spectacular spring display.

My Personal Favorite
Magnolia 'Galaxy' tends to bloom later in the spring so its dark-pink flowers usually escape early spring frosts.

Scotch Broom

Cytisus scoparius

When, Where, and How to Plant

Plant in the spring to give the plants a full season to become established before winter. Brooms do best in full sun and well-drained soils. Container-grown plants transplant easily. Though brooms tolerate infertile, sandy soils, it is beneficial to add organic amendments to heavy clay soils to improve drainage. In sandy soils, add compost to help retain moisture during extended dry periods. Refer to page 201 for complete information on soil preparation and planting techniques. Dig the planting hole two times wider than the rootball. Add backfill soil, and water slowly to eliminate any air pockets beneath the roots. Apply a mulch of pea gravel or shredded wood chips to conserve moisture.

Growing Tips

Water new transplants regularly the first growing season to ensure strong and healthy development. Then water deeply and infrequently throughout subsequent growing seasons. Check the soil moisture by digging down 4 to 6 in.; if the soil is drying out, give the shrub a good drink. A slow-release 5-10-5 fertilizer can be applied lightly in the spring to supply some nutrients. Bacteria on the roots fix atmospheric nitrogen, so additional fertilizer is generally not required.

Care

Established brooms need little maintenance. Young shrubs can be pinched for shaping, but older shrubs don't respond well to pruning. Allow broom to grow in its natural form. Pests and diseases do not generally bother it.

Companion Planting and Design

When scotch broom is in bloom, its profusion of flowers is stunning. Use it along pathways and driveways, or in a shrub border. Smaller species such as *C. decumbens* and *C. hirsutus* make handsome accent plants in rock gardens, berms, and island gardens.

I Also Recommend

Cytisus scoparius 'Moonlight', a nice rounded shrub, features nodding branches peppered with narrow, bright-green leaves. Creamy-yellow flowers create a showy display in late spring. Prostrate broom (*Cytisus decumbens*) is a favorite ground cover, with a summer sea of bright-yellow blooms.

The unique linear leaves of scotch broom give this shrub a leafless appearance, and the adaptation allows it to withstand windy, dry conditions. The bright, pealike, golden-yellow flowers bloom profusely, creating a very showy display in late spring. Scotch broom's long arching stems remain green to yellow-green year-round, presenting a nice texture in all seasons. Because it can fix nitrogen from the atmosphere, this plant thrives even in infertile soils. Scotch brooms are attractive in xeric or water-thrifty gardens. They need additional protection from direct winter sun and desiccating winds. Cytisus purgans 'Spanish Gold Broom' has a compact growth habit (2 to 3 ft. × 4 ft.) with bright-yellow blooms. It is extremely hardy and grows in a wide range of soil types.

Other Common Name

Common broom

Bloom Period and Seasonal Color

Late spring to summer blooms in yellow, red, orange, and some bicolors

Mature Height × Spread

4 to 5 ft. × 4 to 6 ft.

Zones

To zone 4

Sea Buckthorn

Hippophae rhamnoides

Excellent for the water-thrifty or xeric landscape, sea buckthorn features spiny stems and linear, silvery foliage that provide a nice contrast in the landscape. This shrub is great for planting in a naturescape to attract wildlife. It produces yellowish flowers in early spring before the leaves emerge. The showy orange berries on the female plants persist into the winter and have a very high vitamin C content. Both male and female plants are needed to produce berries. The growth habit can be somewhat varied from the more upright male plants to a spreading, irregular rounded form in female plants. Sea buckthorn seems to do best in infertile soils rather than soils too rich in organic matter. Once established, this reliable, water-thrifty shrub provides year-round interest.

Bloom Period and Seasonal Color
Early spring yellow flowers before leaves emerge, then bright-orange berries on female shrubs

Mature Height × Spread
12 to 18 ft. × 10 to 15 ft.

Zones
To zone 3

When, Where, and How to Plant
Container-grown shrubs can be planted from early spring through fall. Locate them in a sunny, open area. As long as the soil has been broken up and is not lumpy, no soil conditioner is necessary. If you are planting in hard clay compacted soils, refer to page 201 for tips on soil preparation. Dig the planting hole three times wider than the rootball. Set the shrub in the planting hole so that the rootball is level with the ground. Add backfill soil to the planting hole, and water slowly.

Growing Tips
Water new plants each week during the first growing season to ensure good establishment. Mulch with shredded wood chips, cedar shavings, or other organic mulch. Once the sea buckthorn becomes established, it is a true survivor. Water when the soil dries out 4 to 6 in. deep; apply water thoroughly with a soaker hose or drip irrigation system. Avoid light, frequent waterings. Sea buckthorn is a nitrogen-fixing plant, so supplemental fertilizer is generally not required.

Care
For sea buckthorn to produce berries, both male and female plants are needed. It has been suggested that a ratio of six female plants to one male is sufficient for good pollination. I enjoy growing this plant on the High Plains, where it has endured the ever-changing climatic conditions of heat and drought. Insects and diseases do not bother sea buckthorn. Prune in the spring to remove crisscrossing branches.

Companion Planting and Design
Plant sea buckthorn as an informal hedge or a privacy screen, or as an accent plant in the background. It is a desirable selection for roadside and street plantings where salts are used for winter deicing. Sea buckthorn provides year-round interest.

My Personal Favorite
Sea buckthorn is the only species available to date. I have planted several in my windbreak and have found this plant, with its attractive silvery foliage and bright fruits, to be a rugged, yet interesting landscape shrub.

Siberian Pea Shrub

Caragana arborescens

When, Where, and How to Plant
Plant container-grown pea shrubs from early spring through fall and bare-root plants in early spring as soon as the soil can be worked. This allows good root establishment before the heat of summer. Siberian pea shrub grows in most well-drained soils, but prefers sandy soil and full sun. If the soil is compacted, loosen it thoroughly to encourage good root development. Dig the planting hole two times wider than the rootball. No soil conditioner is needed as long as the soil has been broken up. In sandy soils, add some compost or well-rotted manure to help retain moisture. Consult page 201 for more information on soil and planting techniques. Water thoroughly after planting. For hedging, plant 2 to 3 ft. apart.

Growing Tips
Water new transplants regularly the first growing season to ensure healthy establishment. Apply 1 to 2 in. of water each week. A 2-in. layer of mulch helps to conserve water and discourage weed growth. A slow-release 5-10-5 fertilizer can be applied in the spring to provide nutrients through the growing season, although pea shrub does not require fertilizer since it fixes nitrogen from the atmosphere.

Care
Once established, this shrub requires little care. Pruning encourages denser growth. Remove the previous season's growth by one-third to one-half after the shrub has finished blooming. Cut older shrubs back to ground level in early spring to rejuvenate. Siberian pea shrub resists most pests, but is occasionally attacked by leafhoppers, blister beetles, and leaf cutter bees. No controls are warranted.

Companion Planting and Design
Siberian pea shrub makes a hardy windbreak or privacy screen. It is an effective specimen shrub when used in a water-thrifty or xeric garden.

My Personal Favorites
The weeping Siberian pea shrub (*Caragana arborescens* 'Pendula') is an unusual ornamental with weeping branches that give the shrub the shape of an umbrella. The threadlike leaflets of 'Lorbergii' give the plant a ferny appearance with narrower flowers.

Siberian pea shrub hails originally from the cold and windy regions of northern Asia, and that makes this shrub widely adaptable in our region, from the plains to the mountains. A valuable screen, hedge, or windbreak, Siberian pea shrub works well where growing conditions are difficult because this plant tolerates winter temperature extremes and withstands wind, heat, and dry conditions. Its charming clusters of fragrant yellow pealike flowers in late spring are followed by small slender pods in the summer. The eight to twelve leaflets on its pinnately compound foliage resemble feathers. Siberian pea shrub's stems are yellow-green and have pale horizontal lenticels in the bark. This is a truly effective shrub for naturescapes, water-thrifty gardens, or difficult spots in your landscape.

Other Common Names
Peashrub, Siberian pea tree

Bloom Period and Seasonal Color
May through June showy yellow, pealike blooms followed by pealike pods

Mature Height × Spread
10 to 15 ft. × 6 to 12 ft.

Zones
To zone 2

Silver Buffaloberry

Shepherdia argentea

Leathery silvery-green leaves make silver buffaloberry a handsome addition to the Rocky Mountain landscape. One of the most drought-resistant plants, this shrub tolerates conditions that other shrubs will not survive. The dense, upright, rounded growth habit of this shrub provides a good screen, informal hedge, or mass planting for a windbreak. Silver buffaloberry's silvery-gray, fuzzy stems contrast nicely with its foliage. The ends of the branches have 1- to 2-in. thorns. This extremely drought- and cold-tolerant shrub will grow in alkaline soils. It is an excellent naturescape plant with orange-red berries favored by wildlife. Both male and female plants are required to produce fruit. Silver buffaloberry is one of my favorites in a naturalized setting and provides an attractive shelter for birds.

Other Common Names
Buffaloberry, silverberry, rabbit berry

Bloom Period and Seasonal Color
Tiny yellow flowers in spring, followed by edible orange-red berries

Mature Height × Spread
8 to 15 ft. × 6 to 12 ft.

Zones
To zone 2

When, Where, and How to Plant

Container-grown silver buffaloberry shrubs can be planted from spring to early fall. If you purchase bare-root plants, plant them in early spring. Place these plants in a sunny, open exposure. This shrub is very useful in dry, alkaline soil conditions. Dig the planting hole two to three times wider than the rootball. No soil amendment needs to be added as long as the soil has been broken up to relieve soil compaction. When planting bare-root plants, spread the roots into the planting hole without cramping them. Position the rootball so that the top is level with the surrounding soil; add backfill, gently firm the soil around the plant, and water well. For more details on shrub planting, consult page 201.

Growing Tips

Water new transplants regularly during the first season to ensure their healthy development. Add a 2-in. layer of organic mulch to maintain soil moisture, conserve water, and discourage weed competition. Water when the soil dries out 4 to 6 in. deep. Water thoroughly, but not frequently—water to a depth of 6 to 8 in. every ten to fourteen days. Silvery buffaloberry fixes atmospheric nitrogen, so it generally does not need additional fertilizer.

Care

Once it becomes established, silver buffaloberry is an extremely durable and hardy shrub. Prune out dead wood in early spring, or shape the plant to remove any branches that may be crisscrossing. Insects and diseases do not bother this plant.

Companion Planting and Design

Use silver buffaloberry for informal hedges, screening, and background planting. It is very effective in windbreaks to contrast with evergreens.

I Also Recommend

Russet buffaloberry (*Shepherdia canadensis*) is a native of rocky slopes that grows as a loosely, rounded shrub to a height of 6 ft. or more, with a comparable spread. Its dark-green leaves have silvery undersides and a "gritty" texture. The yellowish red and bitter fruit is borne on the female plants.

Snowberry
Symphoricarpos albus

When, Where, and How to Plant

Plant container-grown snowberry from spring through early fall. If you purchase bare-root plants, plant them in early spring. These shrubs adapt to the varied soil conditions throughout our area. They can grow in almost any light situation, from full sun to shade. Dig the planting hole twice as wide as the rootball. If the soil is hard and compacted, add organic matter to the planting area. Consult page 201 for more specific information on soil preparation and planting techniques. Once the plants are positioned in the planting hole, add backfill soil, and water slowly.

Growing Tips

For the first season, water new transplants regularly (each week or as the soil dries out) to ensure healthy establishment. Once established, water snowberry deeply once a week. In the spring, apply a slow-release 5-10-5 granular fertilizer and water well. Mulch is helpful during establishment, but is not necessary once the shrub matures as its stems and branches naturally cover the ground.

Care

Once established, snowberry grows and thrives. It benefits from a periodic pruning in early spring to keep the plant in bounds or for minor shaping. If flowers are lacking, prune in the spring to encourage the current season's growth to produce blossoms. In late summer and early fall, powdery mildew is common. But it can be prevented with proper pruning to increase air circulation and by applying a homemade mildew control. See page 258.

Companion Planting and Design

Plant in mass plantings or informal edgings, as foundation plants, or as an accent shrub in a corner. Snowberry can be used as underplanting among evergreens and deciduous trees in a woodland setting.

I Also Recommend

The attractive low-growing chenault coralberry (*Symphoricarpos × chenaultii* 'Hancock') makes an effective ground cover. Pink flowers are followed by fruit that is pink or white and tinged pink. Red coralberry (*Symphoricarpos orbiculatus*) has handsome green leaves with clusters of 1/4-in. coral-red berries that last all winter.

The bright blue-green foliage of snowberry is quick to produce a bushy, rounded shrub in most types of soil throughout our Rocky Mountain region. Widely adapted to sunny exposures, snowberry is also useful in shaded conditions for underplanting in a woodland setting. Its tiny pink blossoms contrast nicely against its leaves in early summer. Showy 3/4-in. berries soon follow and persist into winter, providing food for the birds. Snowberry's spreading growth habit makes it useful for planting on steep slopes or in other problem locations. This shrub has a tendency to sucker profusely, which makes it useful as a ground cover to help stabilize the soil. Snowberry's arching, spreading branches grow 3 to 5 ft. high; the bright-green foliage makes this shrub quite attractive.

Bloom Period and Seasonal Color

Late spring blooms in pink or pale-pink, followed by white or red berries, depending on variety

Mature Height × Spread

3 to 5 ft. × 3 to 10 ft.

Zones

To zone 3

Spirea

Spiraea spp. and hybrids

Drive through any neighborhood in the spring, and you find the arching branches of bridal wreath spirea (Spiraea × vanhouttei), laden with fragrant clusters of small white blooms. It is a testimonial to the adaptability of this plant that our ancestors brought cuttings of it on their move west. Today, there are many species and cultivars, ranging in size from 18 in. tall to 6 ft. or more. The profuse clusters of blossoms in early spring and summer are sure to provide weeks of enjoyment for gardeners who want an easy-to-grow shrub. Spiraea × bumalda 'Gold Mound' is a wonderful mounding shrub with yellow-gold foliage throughout the summer; it provides a nice accent in perennial borders or foundation plantings. Once established, spireas endure drought, resist disease, and are pest free.

Bloom Period and Seasonal Color
Spring or summer (depending on species) blooms in white, rose, or pink

Mature Height × Spread
18 in. to 6 ft. × 2 to 6 ft.

Zones
To zone 3

When, Where, and How to Plant
Plant container-grown spirea from spring through early fall, and plant bare-root spirea in early spring. Locate this shrub in full sun to partial shade. Spireas do best in well-drained soils, but tolerate many soil conditions. Avoid areas that tend to stay wet; spireas don't like wet feet. Dig the planting hole two to three times as wide as the rootball. Add compost to soil that is extremely sandy or has poor drainage. Loosen the soil throughout the area where spirea is to be grown. Refer to page 201 for more details on soil preparation and shrub planting techniques. Position the rootball so it is level with the surrounding soil, add backfill, firm the soil around the plant, and water well.

Growing Tips
Keep the soil evenly moist for the first month to ensure healthy establishment. Once established, these shrubs are easy to maintain and most endure drought well. Water deeply and thoroughly during the summer if you want more prolific flowering. Apply an organic mulch around the plants to maintain moisture and to discourage weed invasion. In the spring, apply a slow-release granular 5-10-5 fertilizer to provide nutrients through the growing season.

Care
After the flowers fade, use hedge clippers or hand pruners to remove 6 in. of the foliage from all around the plant. The new growth usually provides a second flush of flowers later in the summer. Prune older shrubs every three years by removing the oldest canes to ground level. This encourages new growth from the base and renews the shrub. There are no pest problems to speak of.

Companion Planting and Design
Useful for foundation plantings, mass plantings, informal hedges, borders, background plantings for flower beds, or accent plants in mixed beds.

My Personal Favorite
A true survivor here, *S. nipponica maxim* var. *tosaensis* 'Cheyenne Snowmound' features profuse clusters of pure-white flowers in May. It has lived over forty-five years at the Hildreth-Howard Arboretum at the USDA High Plains Research Station in Cheyenne, Wyoming.

Sumac

Rhus spp.

When, Where, and How to Plant

Plant from early spring through early fall. Locate in a sunny, open area where the shrubs can grow naturally. Avoid shade or this shrub becomes straggly and leggy. Sumacs do well in average, well-drained garden soil. Dig the planting hole twice as wide as the rootball. For details on shrub planting, refer to page 201. Position the rootball so its top is level with the surrounding soil. Backfill, gently firm the soil around the plant, and water well.

Growing Tips

Water new transplants weekly to help them establish. Once established, water them once a week or as the soil becomes dry. Sumac adapts well to dry conditions but does not tolerate or survive extremely wet sites. Mulch with shredded wood or pine needles to conserve water, discourage weed invasions, and set off the colorful autumn foliage. In the spring, sprinkle a slow-release granular 5-10-5 fertilizer around the root zone and water well.

Care

Occasionally temper this shrub's vigorous growth by cutting it back to ground level in early spring. New growth soon results, allowing the plant to reestablish its territorial hold. Sumac is generally not bothered by pests, but can suffer from wilt diseases if the plant becomes stressed or weakened.

Companion Planting and Design

Do not use sumac as a foundation plant because it will soon consume the area and become a nuisance. Locate sumac where it will not become invasive. It is a tough, resilient shrub for problem spots, such as rocky slopes or areas where soil needs to be stabilized.

My Personal Favorites

Staghorn sumac (*Rhus typhina*) features stout terminal twigs covered with a fine brown velvet coating that resembles the covering on deer antlers. Another native, three-leaf sumac (*Rhus trilobata*) has three-lobed leaves that turn reddish orange in the fall. Its upright and spreading habit (6 to 8 ft.) makes it an excellent choice for an informal hedge. The sticky red berries are a favorite of wild birds.

We often relegate some of our finest native shrubs to the "plant thugs" category because of their rampant growth and wild characteristics. As more become available in the nursery trade, we should look again at the possibilities they offer. Desirable qualities include drought resistance, an ability to tolerate most soils, and beautiful foliage and texture. The native Rocky Mountain sumac is considered an "untamed" shrub due to its tendency to sucker, but its fine attributes as a ground cover make it an excellent choice for the water-thrifty landscape. Compound leaves provide a fernlike appearance; bright green in the summer, they turn brilliant scarlet in autumn. If you find golden aspens beautiful, Rocky Mountain sumac's intense scarlet autumn coloration will take your breath away.

Bloom Period and Seasonal Color
Grown for its brilliant autumn foliage; some with interesting fruit

Mature Height × Spread
3 to 6 ft. × 3 to 10 ft.

Zones
To zone 3

Viburnum

Viburnum spp.

Viburnums comprise a large group of adaptable and valuable shrubs that feature handsome foliage and attractive flowers. These easy-to-grow plants tolerate most soils throughout the Rocky Mountain region. The berrylike fruits of viburnum are a favorite food for wild birds. Viburnum × rhytidophylloides 'Alleghany' has shown excellent adaptability and thrives in hot dry conditions, as well as in fertile cool soils near evergreens. The flowers are showy white flat panicles that produce handsome red berries in late summer and fall. Viburnum lantana 'Mohican' has a compact growth habit, to 8 ft., and handsome red-orange fruits in July that persist for weeks. With so many species and cultivars available, you are certain to find one or more viburnums to plant in your landscape.

Bloom Period and Seasonal Color
Spring blooms in white or pinkish white

Mature Height × Spread
4 to 12 ft. × 3 to 10 ft.

Zones
To zone 2

When, Where, and How to Plant
Plant from spring through early fall; plant bare-root plants in early spring. Viburnums do best in well-drained soils but tolerate varied soil conditions in the Rockies. Locate this shrub in full sun to partial shade. Dig the planting hole two to three times as wide as the rootball. Since viburnums prefer moist soils, amend the soil with compost at the rate of 30 percent by volume to the native soil. Refer to page 201 for general information on soil preparation and planting techniques. Position the rootball level with the surrounding soil, add soil, firm gently around the plant, and water well.

Growing Tips
Water newly planted shrubs well for the first growing season to ensure healthy establishment. Generally, deep watering once a week suffices, but check the soil to a depth of 4 in. and water as soon as it begins to dry out. Water throughout the summer to prevent scorch or severe wilting. In the spring, apply a slow-release granular 5-10-5 fertilizer. Mulch to conserve moisture and to discourage weed invasions.

Care
Once established, these easy-to-maintain shrubs need only minor pruning to keep them in shape; prune after flowering. Aphids frequently attack the European cranberry bush (*Viburnum opulus*). Early detection and control helps prevent a severe problem. Powdery mildew can be a problem in shaded areas or in sites with poor air circulation.

Companion Planting and Design
Viburnum's glossy green foliage makes these shrubs excellent choices for mass plantings, hedges, foundation plantings, or shrub borders. Use them to soften perennial borders, and fences or walls.

My Personal Favorites
Mapleleaf viburnum (*Viburnum acerifolium*) is a low-growing shrub (4 to 6 ft.) with bright-green foliage that turns reddish purple in the fall. It withstands shade and dry to moist soils. The glossy green leaves of *Viburnum × burkwoodii* become beautiful wine-red in autumn. Koreanspice viburnum (*Viburnum carlesii*) is valued for its fragrant pinkish white flowers and crimson fall foliage.

When, Where, and How to Plant

Transplant container-grown shrubs from spring through early fall. Locate in full sun to partial shade in areas with well-drained soils rich in organic matter. Witchhazel prefers a slightly acidic soil; use a combination of sphagnum peat moss and compost (50/50) at the rate of 40 percent by volume mixed with native soil. Prepare the planting hole as deep as the rootball and twice as wide. Position the rootball level with the surrounding ground. Hybrid varieties are grafted; be careful not to damage the graft union or set it too deep. Backfill with the prepared soil, gently firm around the plant, and water thoroughly. For more planting tips, turn to page 201.

Growing Tips

Keep the soil moist to allow for healthy establishment. Water every four to five days, and maintain a decomposing 2-in. layer of organic mulch (pine needles or leaf mold) around the root zone to maintain moisture and to keep the soil cool. Once established, water witchhazel to a depth of 6 in. or more weekly or as the soil begins to dry out. Fertilize in the spring, and again in early summer, with an acidic formula to provide nutrients for the growing season.

Care

Witchhazels are generally pest- and disease free. Their growth habit develops into a strong and handsome framework that doesn't usually require annual pruning. The rootstock of grafted plants sometimes sends up fast-growing sprouts below the graft union. Prune off these suckers as soon as they appear.

Companion Planting and Design

Witchhazels are most effective as specimen shrubs for the winter landscape. Locate them within view of a window or in shrub borders, mixed perennial beds, or woodland settings. Underplant with the earliest hardy spring bulbs, such as winter aconite, crocus, dwarf iris, or squill.

I Also Recommend

The light-yellow blossoms of hybrid witchhazel (*Hamamelis* × *intermedia* 'Arnold Promise') are pleasantly fragrant. This hardy survivor displays a mixture of yellow, red, and orange autumn foliage.

Fragrant, spiderlike blooms with twisting, ribbonlike petals that gleam in the winter sun make witchhazel the earliest flowering shrub in the landscape. Bright sunny days when temperatures remain below freezing tempt the sweet-scented yellow or orange-red flowers to unfurl with a spectacular show that lasts for weeks; the bewitching floral skirts retract in the cold and expand with milder temperatures. Common witchhazel (Hamamelis virginiana) is the hardiest, but vernal witchhazel is most widely available and grows successfully in most of our region. Hybrids of Hamamelis × intermedia are becoming more available; they are hardy to zone 5, with differences in flower size and color, time and profusion of bloom, fragrance, leaf retention, fall color, and plant habit. Count on witchhazel to brighten the late winter landscape.

Bloom Period and Seasonal Color
February through March blooms in yellow or orange-red

Mature Height × Spread
8 to 12 ft. × 10 to 12 ft.

Zones
To zone 4 (with protection)

Vines *for the Rockies*

Vines are opportunistic plants that extend their growth vertically using neighboring trees, shrubs, walls, or manmade supports to reach up towards the light. They provide vertical cover, shade, privacy, and landscape accent in a variety of colorful forms. Many vines have handsome foliage, beautiful flowers, and edible fruits, and their clinging, twining, or upright growth habits make a nice visual contrast with the other plants around them.

Considering Vines

Vines offer many choices. Some may be annual (living for just one growing season), while others are perennial and will last a lifetime. Some are herbaceous with soft stems, and some are woody. Some are tender and may die back each winter, while some are rather aggressive and long-lived. Some vines are fast growing, and some are more restrained. Annual vines are a good way to start—you can experiment by adding certain colors and textures to the landscape without making a long-term commitment. Many are easy to grow from seed in the spring, such as morning glories, sweet peas, and moonflowers. At the end of the season, many of these annuals produce seed that will self-seed and germinate the following spring, if conditions are right. Annual vines produce the largest leaves and bear more flowers when planted in full sun.

Perennial vines reward you with flowers, interesting foliage, and often, ornamental stems and bark for winter interest. Once established, vines do not like to be disturbed, so select your perennial vines thoughtfully and consider the best location for them to grow and prosper.

Let's Do the Twist

Vines vary in the way they climb. Clematis vines use tendrils or leaf-like appendages that grow out from the stems and wrap themselves around some kind of support. Some vines, including Boston ivy, Virginia creeper, and trumpet vine, have non-coiling, clinging tendrils with a different mechanism—an *adherent pad*. Like a super-strength adhesive, their stems are bonded to a rough surface or support structure. Other vines, such as English ivy and climbing hydrangea, have aerial rootlets called *holdfasts* that cement themselves to walls, trees, or other objects in their path as the vines grow. Most vines climb by twining themselves around a structure. In the wild, they use a tree for climbing; in your landscape, it could be a post, a pillar, a downspout, or a dead tree. The

Clematis
'Nelly Moser'

English Ivy 'California Gold'

vine will start to twine when it touches an object, producing growth faster on one side of the vine than the other. This causes the vine to twist as it grows, so it continues to bend round and round the object. Just as people are right- or left-handed, so are twining vines. They twist around the support either clockwise (to the right) or counterclockwise (to the left). This growth habit is easy to see when you observe a honeysuckle, which grows clockwise, and bittersweet, which grows counterclockwise. It helps to know this so when a vine starts to grow, you won't inadvertently twist it in the wrong direction. Instead, let nature take its course.

How to Grow a Happy Vine

If you want vines to establish more rapidly, heavy clay or sandy soils should be amended with organic matter. You may add 1/3 volume of compost or well-rotted manure to the soil removed from the planting hole. These organic amendments will improve soil structure and drainage. Dig the planting hole as deep as the rootball and two to three times as wide. Drive a stake into the planting hole before setting the vine in the hole. This will prevent damage to the developing roots later. Loosen the rootball, and gently untangle the longest roots so they can be spread into the hole. Position the vine in the hole so that the crown will be planted at the same level it was in the container. Fill in the planting hole with the prepared backfill soil, gently firm the soil around the plant, and water in thoroughly to eliminate any air pockets. Tie the stems loosely to the stake using soft twine or plastic-coated wire.

Most vines need an object to climb or twine on, and matching the vine to the support is one of the secrets for success. A twining vine will not grow up a brick wall, and you can't expect an ivy to climb a wire. Vines can be trained on arbors, trellises, pergolas, gazebos, fence posts, lattices, and trees. Clematis are often at their best when climbing through trees and shrubs. Some vines can be left to grow as a ground cover to hold the soil, and they are attractive when cascading over stones and embankments. Vines can dress up chain-link fences, and annual vines can be easily trained and grown on twine or string.

An Important Rule

The vines covered in this chapter represent some of my favorites and include some of the best tried-and-true vines for the Rockies; but they are by no means an exhaustive list. Most are hardy throughout our area; it is helpful, however, to provide some protection to newly planted vines by applying a winter mulch in late November or early December. Evergreen boughs, shredded cedar mulch, or coarse compost at the base of the vines will help to protect the roots and crown from heaving. A *Rule of Green Thumb:* Be sure to water vines periodically in the absence of rain or snow. During a dry fall and winter, water monthly — as long as the soil remains unfrozen and will accept moisture, and when temperatures are above freezing.

American Bittersweet
Celastrus scandens

A remarkable vine, American bittersweet is prized for its colorful fruit that clings to the stems throughout the fall and winter. Cuttings of the decorative yellow-orange berries are wonderful in dried flower arrangements. It grows relatively fast and will cover a trellis, arbor, or fence if given vertical support. The foliage provides a thick screen in summer and then turns lime-green to yellow in the fall. Clusters of creamy-white flowers appear in June. The female plants produce yellow and orange berries that burst open in autumn to reveal bright orange-red seeds. This is when the vine is the showiest. Be sure to plant both male and female plants if you want the yellow and orange berries in fall.

Bloom Period and Seasonal Color
Late spring with greenish white flowers; followed by yellow-orange berries in the fall

Mature Height × Spread
20 to 25 ft. × as permitted

Zones
To zone 4

When, Where, and How to Plant
Plant container-grown vines from spring through fall. Before planting bare-root vines, soak their roots in a bucket of warm water for a few hours. Clip off any damaged or broken roots to live, healthy tissue. Bittersweet prefers full sun, but will grow in partial shade. The more sun it receives, the more the vine produces colorful fruit for drying. It is adapted to most soil types and tolerates poor soil conditions. If the soil is too rich, this vine may threaten to cover everything in sight. Bittersweet climbs by twining and needs a strong support. Dig the planting hole twice as wide as the rootball. If your soil is a heavy clay or extremely sandy, add an organic amendment to improve drainage and to help retain moisture, respectively. If the roots in the container have become rootbound, gently pull them apart and loosen the longest roots so they can be spread into the hole. Add backfill soil, and water thoroughly.

Growing Tips
Water new transplants regularly during the growing season. Water thoroughly and deeply for the first season, but only as the soil starts to dry out. Spread compost mulch over the root zone. Fertilizer is generally not needed, but a complete 5-10-5 product can be applied in spring.

Care
Once established, bittersweet requires little care other than pruning in spring to increase flowering and fruiting. Should the vine grow out of bounds by means of underground roots, you can "root prune": Use a sharp shovel to cut unwanted plants out by the roots. Bittersweet is generally not bothered by any pests or diseases.

Companion Planting and Design
Train on fences or lattice panels for a screen. Pick a bouquet of berries for dried arrangements or wreaths, or display them in a bottleneck gourd for an elegant autumn display.

I Also Recommend
My favorite and always dependable is American bittersweet, though Loesener bittersweet (*Celastrus loeseneri*) and Oriental bittersweet (*Celastrus orbiculatus*) are adapted to some parts of our region.

Clematis

Clematis spp. and hybrids

When, Where, and How to Plant

Spring is the best time to plant. Clematis vines usually require two seasons to get established and start blooming. Choose a site that receives full sun to partial shade. An east- or northeast-facing site is ideal, but vines thrive in full sun if air circulation is good and if moisture is evenly provided. Before planting, loosen the soil deeply so there is good soil aeration and drainage. Clematis does remarkably well in alkaline soils. Consult page 241 for more details on soil preparation and planting techniques.

Growing Tips

Water new plants regularly. Clematis prefers soil kept evenly moist, but not waterlogged. Apply a slow-release granular 5-10-5 fertilizer in the spring. Grow clematis with its "head in the sun and its feet in the shade" to protect the roots from summer heat. Maintain a deep layer of mulch at the base of the vine or grow a ground cover to shade the crown.

Care

Clematis are hardy and need occasional pruning to maintain shape, height, and flowering. Pruning methods vary. Spring-blooming types that bloom on the previous year's growth should be pruned after flowering (no later than mid-July) to allow new growth to ripen. Remove dead wood or winter-killed tips. Deadheading can often stimulate new blooms later in the summer and early fall. Summer-flowering and early-fall-blooming varieties do best if cut back in early spring. Prune stems back to a pair of plump buds, and thin out weak and dead wood. Late-flowering cultivars and species produce flowers on the current season's growth, so prune in early spring, removing the previous season's stems down to a pair of plump, healthy buds 6 to 12 in. above the ground.

Companion Planting and Design

Train clematis on wooden lattice panels, arbors, posts, mailboxes, or fences. For an informal look, let clematis spill over rocks or twine through trees and shrubs.

My Personal Favorite

Clematis heracleifolia or tube clematis has wonderful hyacinth-blue flowers from July through September.

Clematis produces an abundance of exquisite blooms on vigorous, fast-growing vines. The flowers are made up not of petals but of sepals, the outer parts of the blossom that surround and protect the bud before it opens. Clematis × jackmanii is one of the most popular with its rich purple blossoms, but a rainbow of colors is available. The nodding, small yellow flowers of C. tangutica resemble tiny lanterns that glow in summer's evening garden. Hybrid clematis produces the biggest flowers in an array of colors. Clematis montana rubens is at home climbing through shrubs. Sweet autumn clematis (C. terniflora) produces clusters of small, white flowers with a sweet fragrance mornings and evenings. Our native western virgin's bower (C. ligusticifolia) is a useful ground cover.

Bloom Period and Seasonal Color

Late spring, summer, or late summer, depending on variety; blooms in purple, pink, blue, white, red, or rose

Mature Height × Spread

10 to 20 ft. × as permitted

Zones

To zone 4

Climbing Honeysuckle
Lonicera spp.

The fragrant honeysuckle vine evokes memories of Grandma's garden and the sounds of busy bees working the flowers. Generally hardy and vigorous, honeysuckle vines thrive with a minimum of care. The vines can become invasive, and pruning is necessary to keep them in bounds. Tubular flowers of red, orange, coral, yellow, and white are borne in whorls or clusters and release a sweet fragrance. One of the hardiest is Brown's honeysuckle (Lonicera × brownii), with fragrant orange-red blooms from May into June—a sure attraction for hummingbirds. Goldflame honeysuckle (Lonicera × heckrotti) has handsome blue-green foliage. Its red buds open to blossoms with yellow corollas and pink outer petals. In late summer and early autumn, honeysuckle berries are a source of food for wild birds.

Bloom Period and Seasonal Color
Late spring to fall frost; blooms in red, pink, scarlet, orange, white, or yellow

Mature Height × Spread
15 to 20 ft. × as permitted

Zones
To zone 3

When, Where, and How to Plant
Plant spring through fall. Bare-root plants transplant easily in early spring. Choose a site with full sun to partial shade. The soil should be well drained and enriched with compost. Dig the planting hole twice as wide as the root system and about 18 in. deep. If the soil in the planting area has not been prepared, follow the recommendations on page 241. Position the vine so that the crown is planted at the same level it was in the container. Add backfill soil, gently firm the soil around the plant, and water thoroughly.

Growing Tips
Water new transplants regularly to ensure healthy establishment—that is, water when the soil begins to dry out to a depth of 3 to 4 in. Once established, honeysuckle vines endure drought conditions. Keeping a layer of mulch underneath the plants helps conserve moisture and prevent weed invasion. Honeysuckle usually does not need fertilizer unless the soil quality is poor; if it is, apply a slow-release granular 5-10-5 fertilizer in the spring.

Care
To keep the plants growing vigorously and to promote prolific flowering, prune when the blooms fade. Prune back growth in the spring to maintain desired shape and to control growth. Thin out the oldest stems to ground level to encourage new growth from the crown. Aphids may invade some varieties; control them with homemade soap sprays or by hosing them off the plant.

Companion Planting and Design
Plant honeysuckles on fences, arbors, or trellises. Trumpet honeysuckle (*Lonicera sempervirens*), with its bright red tubular blooms, is sure to attract hummingbirds during the day and sphinx moths in the evening. Honeysuckle vines can also be grown as ground covers or allowed to sprawl over rocks and retaining walls.

My Personal Favorite
One of my favorites is Hall's honeysuckle (*Lonicera japonica* 'Halliana') with its light-green leaves and delightfully fragrant, creamy-white flowers that mature to yellow. It works well as a ground cover.

Climbing Hydrangea
Hydrangea anomala subsp. *petiolaris*

When, Where, and How to Plant
Plant bare-root plants in spring. Container-grown vines can be planted from spring to early summer. Climbing hydrangea prefers partial shade with a rich, moist, well-drained, slightly acidic soil. Dig the planting hole twice as wide as the rootball and only as deep. Amend the backfill soil with an equal proportion mix of compost and sphagnum peat moss, adding 50 percent by volume to the backfill to help create slightly more acidic soil conditions. To prevent damage to the developing roots later, drive a wooden stake into the hole. This stake can be removed once the vine has started to climb on its own. Gently untangle any crowded roots and spread them into the planting hole before adding the backfill soil. Plant the crown at the same level it was growing in the container. Add backfill, gently firming the soil around the plant, and water thoroughly. Finish by tying the stems loosely to the stake with soft twine or plastic-coated wire.

Growing Tips
Keep the soil evenly moist for the first few years until the vine is established. Once established, it tolerates drought well. Mulch with pine needles to maintain even moisture and to insulate the soil. Water the climbing hydrangea again when the soil begins to dry out 3 to 4 in. deep. Apply a slow-release granular fertilizer such as 10-10-10 as new growth begins in the spring.

Care
Prune regularly in the spring to keep the vine shapely and within bounds. Older, neglected hydrangea vines tend to lose vigor and produce few flowers. This vine is generally not bothered by pests or diseases.

Companion Planting and Design
Climbing hydrangea looks attractive against barren walls and fences, and this vine is very effective when sprawling over a retaining wall or large rocks. It does well growing up a large tree—without doing any harm.

My Personal Favorite
Look for the species, *Hydrangea anomala* subsp. *petiolaris*. You won't be disappointed.

When we think hydrangea, most think of the shrub, not a vine. But the climbing hydrangea is an excellent vine that should be more widely grown on north and northeast walls. It is a true clinging vine that cements itself to just about any structure by aerial rootlets called holdfasts. Climbing hydrangea can easily support itself and any of its lateral or side branches. As it matures, the vine requires a strong support for its weight—and to keep it somewhat tamed. Faintly scented, lacy, flat white flower clusters appear among the dark-green, serrated leaves in June and July. Peeling, reddish brown bark adds winter interest. Though this vine is somewhat slow to get started, it is worth the effort.

Bloom Period and Seasonal Color
Summer; blooms in white clusters

Mature Height × Spread
15 to 18 ft. × as permitted

Zones
To zone 4 (with protection)

Common Hop

Humulus lupulus

Common hop is a vine that can be both annual and perennial. It depends upon growing conditions and the area in which the vine is planted. The common or perennial hop is used to flavor beer and is fast becoming naturalized in our region. The handsome foliage on common hop vine twines upward on the support you designate. The variety 'Aureus' is the golden hop whose lovely foliage lightens up shady places. Hop vine grows quickly and can reach 25 ft. or more in a single season. It tolerates both low humidity and wind. The bright leaves, 6 to 8 in. wide, provide a nice, dense cover on a fence, lattice, arch, pillar, or other support. Female plants produce greenish yellow pinecone-like flowers.

Other Common Name
Hop vine

Bloom Period and Seasonal Color
Summer; yellowish green blooms that look like small pinecones

Mature Height × Spread
10 to 25 ft. × as permitted

Zones
To zone 3

When, Where, and How to Plant
Plant the common hop in spring. The Japanese hop (*Humulus japonicus*), an annual grown as a fast-growing vine, dies back to the ground in the fall. Plant the annual species outdoors in the spring after danger of frost has passed. If soil conditions are good, it will reseed and germinate the following spring. Easy to grow, hop vine thrives in a wide range of soils, as long as they are well drained. Plant them in full sun to partial shade. The common hop vine performs even in ordinary garden soil. Refer to page 241 for more information on soil preparation and planting techniques. Mound a rim of soil 3 to 4 in. high around the edge of the planting hole to hold water. When the soil begins to dry out, water again 4 to 6 in. deep.

Growing Tips
Keep new transplants watered regularly to ensure good establishment. Once established, it is well adapted to withstand drought conditions. Soak the soil deeply, but not frequently. Apply an organic mulch at the base of the vine to maintain moisture, keep the soil cool, and conserve water. Apply a slow-release 5-10-5 fertilizer in the spring.

Care
The common hop vine grows rather quickly and covers a support for the summer season. If the vine dies back due to severe winter desiccation, cut it back to the ground each spring and it will quickly grow back. If the stems survive, prune them back to live buds to clean out the dead wood and thin out the crowded stems.

Companion Planting and Design
Use hop vine to cover fences, unsightly walls, or rocks. It is effective when grown on older evergreens that have lost lower branches. The stems twine around the trunk and lower branches to lighten a shady area.

I Also Recommend
Besides the common hop vine, I like to plant *Humulus lupulus* 'Aureus'—golden hops. Its bright, golden-green foliage lightens shady spots.

English Ivy
Hedera helix

When, Where, and How to Plant

Plant in spring to allow for good root growth before hot weather. Ivy grows best in partial to full shade. Winter sun can bleach or scorch exposed leaves. Ivy prefers moist, organic-rich soils. Dig the planting hole twice as wide as the root system and about 18 in. deep. If the soil is not already prepared, mix 1 part compost, well-rotted manure, or sphagnum peat moss to 2 parts backfill soil. To avoid damaging the developing roots later, drive a wooden stake into the planting hole. Remove it once the vine starts to climb the support. Set transplants an inch below the soil surface to help in establishment and for added winter protection. Gently firm the soil around the plants, and water thoroughly. Tie the stems loosely to the stake with soft twine or plastic-coated wire.

Growing Tips

Water new transplants regularly during the growing season to ensure strong establishment. Mulch with shredded cedar or pine needles to maintain moisture and keep the soil cool. Once established, ivy is drought tolerant and requires only periodic watering during dry periods. Apply a slow-release granular 10-10-10 fertilizer in the spring.

Care

Prune as needed in early spring to restrict or train growth. Pinch back growing tips anytime to keep the vine compact. As it matures, it may bear clusters of small green flowers followed by tiny, black berries loved by birds. (But the seed can be toxic to humans.) If winter weather is extremely cold and harsh, the ivy may die back, but will regrow from the roots in spring. In hot summer weather, spider mites may attack the foliage. Turn the garden hose on the plant to reduce severe invasions.

Companion Planting and Design

Plant English ivy under trees as living ground cover to prevent trunk damage from lawn mowers and string trimmers. Use it to cover walls or sprawl over large boulders, or to prevent soil erosion in shady exposures.

My Personal Favorites

'Bulgaria', 'Hebron', and 'Thorndale' cultivars have good cold hardiness.

A very popular broadleaf evergreen vine for shady areas, English ivy clings tenaciously to most surfaces. This vine holds its leaves throughout the winter. And with special adaptations called holdfasts, *the ivy adheres tightly to walls, mortar, and support structures—so much so that it takes great strength to loosen their clinging grip. The shiny, leathery leaves have three to five lobes each, often with whitish veins, and will form a dense blanket on masonry walls. English ivy can be grown on trellises, rock walls, and other strong supports and can be used as a ground cover in shady areas. Use ivy to enhance the beauty of other plants in the shade garden, or allow it to sprawl along the ground to edge a pathway.*

Bloom Period and Seasonal Color
Evergreen; green (or variegated depending on species), leathery foliage

Mature Height × Spread
30 ft. × as permitted

Zones
To zone 4 (with protection)

Porcelain Vine
Ampelopsis brevipedunculata

A vigorous and attractive vine from Asia, porcelain vine rapidly covers a trellis or arbor. It moves upward by forked, twining tendrils and can grow 12 to 18 ft. a year. I enjoy looking at the variegated grapevine foliage draping my chain-link fence. Though the flowers are not porcelain vine's prominent feature, its colorful turquoise fruit draws the eye. One of the prettiest varieties with variegated foliage is Ampelopsis brevipedunculata 'Elegans'. The grapevine leaves are splashed a creamy-white and tinged pink, adding visual interest in the garden. Use porcelain vine effectively to cover unsightly walls, fences, or poles, or allow it to spill over large rocks. Keep in mind that porcelain vine is deciduous, so whatever it covers in summer will be bare in winter.

Other Common Name
Blueberry climber

Bloom Period and Seasonal Color
Summer through early fall; blooms are whitish green, followed by turquoise fruit

Mature Height × Spread
12 to 18 ft. × as permitted

Zones
To zone 4

When, Where, and How to Plant
Porcelain vine is easy to transplant from spring through early fall. For the most abundant and colorful fruit, plant this vine where it gets full sun or filtered shade. Be sure the soil is well drained, and provide a support for the vine to climb. If you plant near a tree or post, fasten chicken wire loosely around the support to help the vine's tendrils cling. Dig the hole outside the root spread of the tree, and use a wooden stake to lead the vine to the trunk. Dig the planting hole as deep as the rootball and three times as wide. If the soil in the planting area has not been prepared, mix 1 part compost to 2 parts backfill soil. Loosen the rootball and gently untangle the longest roots so that they can be spread into the hole. Add the backfill soil, gently firming it around the roots, and water thoroughly. If the vine is attached to a stake in the container, carefully untie it after planting and spread out the stems. Tie them loosely to the support.

Growing Tips
Water newly transplanted vines regularly throughout the first season. Mulch keeps the soil cool and helps it establish during the heat of summer. To maintain and conserve moisture, keep a 2-in. layer of organic mulch over the root zone year-round. Fertilize in early spring with a slow-release granular fertilizer, such as a 5-10-5 or 10-10-10.

Care
Somewhat slow to establish, porcelain vine is long lived and prolific. Prune as needed in the spring to control or direct vine growth. Pests and diseases don't bother this vine.

Companion Planting and Design
Use this vine on trellises or arbors, or let it wind its way around large trees. If you have a dead tree you don't want to remove, consider planting this vine at the base for landscape interest.

My Personal Favorite
My favorite is 'Elegans' with its handsome foliage, variegated with greenish white and a tinge of pink.

Silver Lace Vine
Polygonum aubertii

When, Where, and How to Plant

Plant container-grown plants in early spring. If you purchase bare-root plants, unpack the vine when it arrives, and clip the roots lightly to remove broken or damaged ends. Soak the roots in a bucket of water for an hour before planting. Plant silver lace vine in full sun to partial shade. Dig the planting hole twice as wide as the root system and about 18 in. deep. This vine is not particular about soil — as long as the soil is well drained. Refer to page 241 for information on preparing soil and planting techniques. Position the vine so that the crown is at the same level it was in the container. Add the backfill soil around the plant, gently firming it, and water in thoroughly.

Growing Tips

Water new vines regularly during the first growing season to ensure healthy and strong establishment. A true survivor, silver lace vine is drought tolerant once established. Water deeply when the soil begins to dry out to a depth of 3 to 4 in. Mulch with shredded cedar or pine needles to maintain moisture and to conserve water. Apply a slow-release granular 5-10-5 fertilizer in the spring as growth appears. Avoid overwatering and overfertilizing.

Care

This vine flowers on new wood and does best if pruned back hard (even to ground level) in early spring. It spreads by rhizomes and can sometimes become weedy. Dig out unwanted sections to keep it in bounds. Pests and diseases do not bother it.

Companion Planting and Design

Silver lace vine can be trained to grow on lattice panels, trellises, and chain-link fences. Or let it grow on a rocky slope as a ground cover. Ideal for hot, dry sites, this vine is a good water-thrifty landscape plant.

My Personal Favorite

The durable original species, *P. aubertii*, is the most readily available. It grows well even at elevations of 6,500 ft. or more.

Silver lace vine is prized not for its foliage, but for the masses of fleecy, greenish white blossoms that persist through the summer. It grows so vigorously that it will cover a fence or trellis in one growing season. It tolerates wind, drought, and city pollution. Old silver lace vines can be found growing in alleys and waste sites, testifying to its ability to survive a vast variety of soil conditions. Though it may die back to the ground if the winter is severe, the vine will recover in spring and produce many new vigorous shoots. This vine is a fast-growing deciduous vine that supports itself by twining. With the proper support from a trellis or arbor and careful pruning, silver lace vine is quite attractive.

Other Common Names
Fleece vine, mile-a-minute vine

Bloom Period and Seasonal Color
Late summer; sprays of white blooms

Mature Height × Spread
20 to 30 ft. × as permitted

Zones
To zone 3

Trumpet Vine
Campsis radicans

Trumpet vine's orange-scarlet trumpet-shaped blossoms highlight the summer landscape at a time when other vines have finished flowering. The colorful blossoms are magnets for hummingbirds and sphinx moths. If you've ever driven through western Colorado, then you've seen these bright-orange flowers on telephone poles. Quick-growing trumpet vine easily anchors itself to trellises, poles, fences, trees, and flat surfaces with aerial rootlets called holdfasts. Trumpet vine's pinnately compound leaves are glossy green, and they provide a nice background or screen. In late summer or early fall, this vine may produce spindle-shaped seed capsules that are 3 in. long and contain many winged seeds. If killed to the ground by a hard winter, trumpet vine readily sends up new shoots in the spring.

Other Common Name
Hummingbird vine

Bloom Period and Seasonal Color
Summer; blooms in orange or red

Mature Height × Spread
20 to 40 ft. × as permitted

Zones
To zone 4

When, Where, and How to Plant
Plant bare-root vines, root suckers, or container-grown vines in the spring. The sunniest locations suit trumpet vine, which continues flowering into fall. The soil must be well drained and can be amended with compost to improve soil porosity and drainage—especially if the soil is heavy clay or extremely sandy. Have the vine supports in place before planting. If you purchased a bare-root vine, soak the roots in a bucket of water for a few hours before planting. Add approximately 30 percent by volume of a quality compost to the backfill soil. Mix the compost uniformly with the soil. Dig the planting hole two to three times wider than the rootball or wide enough to accommodate the spread of bare roots. If the roots are crowded in the container, gently unwind the longest roots and spread them in the planting hole. Add backfill, gently firming it around the plant, and water thoroughly.

Growing Tips
Water new transplants regularly throughout the growing season. To maintain even moisture while the vine establishes itself, mulch with additional compost or shredded cedar shavings. Water when the soil begins to dry out 4 to 6 in. deep. Little or no fertilizer is needed. Overfertilizing stimulates too much leafy growth and too few flowers.

Care
Once established, trumpet vine is trouble free and hardy. Don't be afraid to prune—pruning is necessary to keep this vine in bounds. Flowers appear on new growth each year, so each spring, prune it back to the height you desire. Pests and diseases generally do not bother it.

Companion Planting and Design
Effective against a garden shed, fence, or wall, trumpet vine readily attaches itself by aerial roots that cling to walls or other supports.

My Personal Favorite
The most successful trumpet vine is the old-fashioned *Campsis radicans*. Most hybrid varieties are not fully winter hardy and often die back to ground level each winter without proper protection.

Virginia Creeper
Parthenocissus quinquefolia

When, Where, and How to Plant
Plant container-grown Virginia creeper spring through fall. In the spring, the vines transplant easily from rooted cuttings or plant divisions. Plant in full sun for vigorous growth and that spectacular scarlet transformation, but this vine tolerates partial shade. Set plants 2¹/₂ to 3 ft. apart near supports or walls on which they can grow. Dig the planting hole twice as wide as the root system and about 18 in. deep. If the soil has not been prepared, refer to the soil preparation recommendations on page 241. The plant should be placed in the hole so that the crown (where stem meets roots) is at the same level it was in the container. Add backfill soil around the roots, gently firming it around the plants, and water thoroughly.

Growing Tips
Water new vines regularly during the growing season—when the soil dries out to a depth of 3 to 4 in. Mulch with shredded cedar or pine needles to maintain moisture and to reduce weed invasions.

Care
Once established, Virginia creeper is an undisputed champion for fast vine growth. It requires periodic pruning and thinning to keep it in bounds. Prune back as needed in early spring and throughout the summer. Water this drought-tolerant plant thoroughly and deeply as needed throughout the growing season. This vine usually gets powdery mildew in late summer or early fall. Provide adequate air circulation to help prevent this disease. Turn to page 258 for a homemade mildew remedy.

Companion Planting and Design
Train Virginia creeper on trellises, lattice panels, or arbors, or let it cascade over large rocks. It can dress up a chain-link or wooden fence. I've seen it used effectively growing up older trees and mingling in shrubs without harming the supports.

I Also Recommend
Another favorite for shady walls is Boston ivy (*P. tricuspidata*). The glossy, dark-green grapelike foliage on this self-climber turns orange to red in the fall. The vine grows best on east- or north-facing exposures.

Virginia creeper puts on a striking display in autumn, when its dense foliage transforms, becoming a brilliant scarlet. This rapidly growing vine quickly produces a blanket of bright-green foliage that covers rough walls, trellises, arbors, fences, and other unsightly surfaces. Virginia creeper vine climbs by means of twisting tendrils tipped with adhesive discs. It produces dark bluish black berries that birds love to eat. Virginia creeper is especially effective in a naturalized setting where it can be allowed to grow around and to spill over large rocks. Similar to Virginia creeper, Engleman ivy (Parthenocissus quinquefolia var. engelmannii) has smaller leaves and denser growth. Its tendrils adhere tightly to masonry walls, so a firm pruning hand is necessary to keep these vines in bounds.

Other Common Name
Woodbine

Bloom Period and Seasonal Color
Grown for its foliage that turns scarlet in autumn

Mature Height × Spread
20 to 30 ft. × as permitted

Zones
To zone 3

Butterfly Gardening

The Rocky Mountain region is an excellent place for viewing and attracting butterflies. The West's differing habitats and climates allow for a good variety of butterfly species. Besides being beautiful to watch, butterflies play a part in the food chain, and to a small extent, they pollinate flowers.

Some Good Choices

To attract butterflies, you need plants on which their caterpillars can feed and flowers from which the adult butterflies can sip nectar. First, find a sunny location sheltered from strong winds; butterflies cannot feed well in windy conditions. Some of the best nectar-producing flowers planted in my garden—and ones sure to attract these winged beauties—include:

Butterfly bush (*Buddleia* spp.)
Aster (*Aster novae-angliae, Aster* 'September Ruby')
Butterfly weed (*Asclepias tuberosa*)
Coreopsis (*Coreopsis* spp.)
Joe-pye weed (*Eupatorium* spp.)

Liatris (*Liatris* spp.)
Black-eyed Susan (*Rudbeckia* spp.)
Purple coneflower (*Echinacea purpurea*)
Globe thistle (*Echinops exaltatus*)
Phlox (*Phlox* spp.)

Many of these flowers also attract hummingbirds and provide a food source for those acrobatic flying jewels as they migrate to warmer climates.

For an excellent butterfly garden, plant these flowers in large clusters sheltered by shrubs or a hedge, with the taller flowers in the back. Adding rocks and evergreens help to hold heat; the butterflies can perch on them to warm themselves.

In a separate area, plants that can feed the larva or caterpillar stage of butterflies will encourage egg laying and a larger number of butterflies. Many butterfly species are very specific about which species of plant the caterpillar will eat.

Larval food plants include: quaking aspen, cottonwoods, hackberry, white ash, clover, alfalfa, vetch, winter cress, willow, cabbage, and milkweed.

Some of the families of butterflies that you can attract to your landscape include: swallowtails, whites, sulphurs, coppers, hairstreaks, blues, snout butterfly, hackberry butterfly, longwings, angelwings, tortoiseshells (mourning cloak), painted ladies, red admiral, buckeye, fritillaries, crescents, admirals, satyrs, milkweed butterflies (monarch), and skippers.

Avoid the use of pesticides. Since butterflies are insects, pesticides kill them in the larval and adult stages. To control such pests as aphids in other areas of your landscape, use a homemade spray of soap-suds, garlic, chives, and hot sauce. Also see page 256 for homemade remedies.

Plants for Butterflies

A complete butterfly garden should contain plants that butterflies use during each stage of their life cycle—egg, larva (caterpillar), pupa (chrysalis), and adult (butterfly).

Unlike adult butterflies, young caterpillars are particular about their diet. Caterpillars prefer wild plants such as chokecherry, milkweed, hackberry, nettle, or Queen Anne's lace. When possible, let some of the native or wild plants flourish in a corner of your landscape. Some domestic plants, such as parsley, carrot, fennel, dill, and nasturtium, are also favorites for caterpillars. The idea is to have a balanced menu—host plants for caterpillars and nectar-producing plants for adult butterflies.

A mixture of annuals, perennials, and biennials provide a variety of combinations to attract a wide range of butterfly species to your garden. Choose old-fashioned or heirloom varieties since many of the newer hybrids have been bred for larger, showy flowers, but are not noted for better nectar production.

Perennials

Asclepias—Milkweed B
Alcea—Hollyhock B
Aster—single-flowered asters N
Achillea—Yarrow N
Coreopsis—Tickseed N
Dianthus—Sweet William, Dianthus N
Echinacea—Coneflower N
Eupatorium—Joe-pye weed N
Helenium—Sneezeweed N
Hemerocallis—Daylilies N
Linum—Flax H

Lupinus—Lupine H
Lychnis—Maltese cross, Campion N
Mentha—Mints N
Penstemon—Beardtongue N
Perovskia—Russian Sage N
Phlox—Perennial phlox N
Rudbeckia—Black-eyed Susan N
Scabiosa—Pincushion flower N
Sedum—Stonecrop N
Verbena—'Homestead Purple' verbena N

Annuals

Alyssum—Sweet alyssum B
Tropaeolum—Nasturtium B
Cosmos N
Dianthus—Annual pinks N
Lantana N
Pentas—Starflower N

Phlox—Annual phlox N
Salvia N
Tagetes—French marigold (single-flowered types) N
Tithonia—Mexican sunflower N
Verbena N
Zinnia N

Herbs

Allium—Chives N
Anethum—Dill H
Borago—Borage N
Foeniculum—Fennel H
Lavendula—Lavender N
Mentha—Mint N

Monarda—Bee balm N
Nepeta—Catmint N
Petroselinum—Parsley H
Salvia—Sage N
Thymus—Thyme N

Trees and Shrubs

Buddleia—Butterfly bush N
Caryopteris—Blue mist spirea N
Chrysothamnus—Rabbitbrush N
Cornus—Dogwood H
Crataegus—Hawthorn H

Fraxinus—Ash H
Prunus virginiana—Chokecherry H
Salix—Willow H
Syringa—Lilac N
Viburnum B

Key: N = Nectar Producing, H = Host plant for caterpillars, B = Both nectar and host plant

Nature's Little Helpers

Beneficial bugs keep your garden's insect population under control. Not everything that creeps, crawls, and flutters into your landscape and garden is an unwelcome pest or enemy. Many creatures that visit help to keep insect populations in check. Summer is a great time to observe, learn more about the life in your garden, and make friends with the many insects and other of Nature's little helpers. Get to know the friendly creatures before reaching for the bug killer. You soon learn to appreciate their contributions to a healthy yard and garden. Here are just a few to help you get started:

Parasitic Wasps There are thousands of parasitic wasp species from more than a dozen insect families. These tiny wasps are highly specific in their habits, attacking only one kind of insect. Some prey on aphids, others develop only on scale insects, while other wasps parasitize caterpillars.

Like the creature from the movie *Alien*, female parasitic wasps insert eggs into the body of these insect hosts. The eggs hatch within the host, and the developing wasp grubs usually kill the host insect within seven to ten days. Several generations of wasps are produced during one growing season.

Lady Beetles Better known as *ladybugs*, lady beetles are among the most widely recognized beneficial insects. Visit some of your local garden outlets; you'll find convergent lady beetles for sale in packets of five hundred or more. These are the classic reddish orange beetles with bright black spots. Voracious eaters, lady beetles consume large quantities of soft-bodied insects, including aphids, small caterpillars, and scales.

Some gardeners bring insect samples to nurseries and clinics to identify them and discover they have mistakenly killed the "ugly creatures" after finding them resting on the foliage and stems of evergreens. Upon closer examination, they learn that the creatures they've killed are the larval stages of the lady beetles.

At the immature or larval stage, the lady beetle looks nothing like the adult. Only $1/4$ to $1/2$ inch long, the black and orange larvae resemble miniature orange and black Gila monsters. But you want these tiny larvae around because they eat hundreds of aphids a day.

So don't reach for the bug killer until you've identified the creature in your garden. Pesticides kill lots more than you think and upset the natural balance in your garden.

Tip: If you purchase lady beetles, open the container and sprinkle a little water over them. Then close the container back up and keep them in the refrigerator until you're ready to release them. The best time to turn them loose is late evening, preferably after a rainstorm. Release them where there is a food source, preferably aphids, but pollen and nectar from flowers work temporarily.

Spiders Misrepresented by nursery rhymes and folklore, spiders have become feared and often hated in the home and garden. But most spiders should be welcomed to the yard and garden. Their webs trap hundreds of unsuspecting insect pests that would otherwise destroy plants.

Summer is a great time to watch for spiders finding new home sites. If you look at the right time of day-early morning when the sun is bright or early evening—you may spot the fine webs floating in the air.

After hatching, the tiny spiderlings climb onto a high perch (fence posts, tree branches, etc.) and spin fine threads of silk. When the summer breeze catches the threads, the tiny spiders are carried great distances to a new home. If they don't like where they land, they can take up residence elsewhere by simply repeating the process.

Dragonflies You don't need a pond in your backyard to attract dragonflies. These fascinating creatures of the insect world can be found in most gardens zigzagging over flowers and shrubs.

Dragonflies are fun to observe as they hover over garden plants like miniature helicopters, often moving rapidly in all directions—even backwards. They have the ability to capture insects on the wing, using their strong front legs as a scoop; then stuffing helpless victims into their mouths without even stopping. Once the task is completed, dragonflies land on the tip of a plant and rest, motionless, for long periods.

Dragonflies don't sting or bite, as many of us have been led to believe. But from an insect's perspective, the dragonfly is a monster with the skill to capture and devour an unsuspecting visitor.

Lacewings One of the most delicate-looking insect predators found in the garden is the lacewing. Their iridescent green wings shimmering in the sunlight, lacewings feed on aphids, thrips, small caterpillars, and spider mites. Both larvae and adults feed on insect pests.

Lacewings occur naturally throughout the Rocky Mountain region, but you can also buy them in the egg stage. Scatter about a thousand lacewing eggs around each 500 square feet of garden area.

How to Entice Friendly Critters to Your Garden

- Lay off the use of pesticides at the sign of a bug in your garden. Many pesticides kill beneficial insects, as well as the pests.
- Provide a source of water in the garden—a small birdbath, a shallow pond, or a small dish filled with gravel and water.
- Have a spot for shelter from wind and rain. A row of tall perennials, such as sunflowers, shrubbery, or ornamental grasses, provides a buffer zone for insect predators to hide and later come out to hunt down the "bad guys."
- Grow plants that are a source of nectar and pollen for beneficial insects. These plants attract the insects to the garden and give them something to eat while they wait for the insect prey to arrive or hatch from eggs. Some of the common herbs, such as dill, fennel, lemon balm, and spearmint, are favorite plants of beneficial insects. They also favor many wildflowers, daisies, cosmos, clovers, and other legumes.

Coping with Browsing Deer

Though charming to watch, deer and elk can cause considerable damage to our landscapes. There are various ways to discourage deer, but one solution is to grow plants that wildlife find unpalatable. The problem is that deer in different areas seem to adapt to different tastes. Plants not bothered in the spring may be consumed in the fall. Keep in mind that consistently watering and fertilizing landscape plants tends to make most species more palatable to deer. Despite these frustrations, the following is a **partial listing** of trees and shrubs browsed by deer, either "rarely," "sometimes," or "often." Avoid species rated "often."

Trees and Shrubs	Plant Species	Browsing Frequency
Alder	*Alnus tenuifolia*	sometimes
Apache plume	*Fallugia paradoxa*	sometimes-rarely
Apples (most)	*Malus* spp.	often
Aspen	*Populus tremuloides*	often
Bearberry	*Arctostaphylos uva-ursa*	sometimes
Buffaloberry	*Shepherdia canadensis*	sometimes
Ceanothus, Fendler	*Ceanothus fendleri*	sometimes
Chokecherry	*Prunus virginiana*	often
Coralberry	*Symphoricarpos chenaultii*	sometimes-rarely
Creeper, Virginia	*Parthenocissus quinquefolia*	rarely
Currant, golden	*Ribes aureum*	sometimes-rarely
Currant, wax	*Ribes cereum*	sometimes-rarely
Fir, Douglas	*Pseudotsuga menziesii*	rarely
Goldenrod	*Solidago* spp.	sometimes-rarely
Grapes	*Vitis* spp.	often
Hackberry	*Celtis reticulata*	sometimes-rarely
Hawthorn	*Crataegus succulenta*	rarely
Hazelnut, beaked	*Corylus cornuta*	rarely
Holly-grape, Oregon	*Mahonia repens*	sometimes-rarely
Honeysuckle, bush	*Lonicera involucrata*	sometimes-rarely
Ivy, English	*Hedera helix*	sometimes-rarely
Jamesia, cliff	*Jamesia americana*	sometimes
Juniper, common	*Juniperus communis*	rarely
Juniper, Rocky Mountain	*Juniperus scopulorum*	often
Lead plant	*Amorpha fruticosa*	rarely
Licorice, wild	*Glycyrrhiza obtusata*	sometimes
Maple, box elder	*Acer negundo*	rarely
Maple, mountain	*Acer glabrum*	sometimes
Mountain mahogany, evergreen	*Cerocarpus ledifolius*	sometimes-rarely
Mountain mahogany, true	*Cerocarpus montanus*	often
Ninebark	*Physocarpus monogynus*	sometimes
Pine, limber	*Pinus flexilis*	rarely
Pine, lodgepole	*Pinus contorta*	sometimes
Pine, mugo	*Pinus mugo mugo*	often
Pine, pinyon	*Pinus edulis*	rarely
Pine, ponderosa	*Pinus ponderosa*	sometimes
Plum, wild	*Prunus americana*	sometimes-rarely
Potentilla/cinquefoil	*Potentilla* spp.	rarely
Rabbitbrush	*Crysothammus nauseosus*	sometimes
Raspberry, Boulder	*Rubus deliciosus*	sometimes
Raspberry, wild red	*Rubus idaeus*	sometimes-often
Roses (most)	*Rosa* spp.	often
Skunk brush	*Rhus trilobata*	rarely
Snowberry, western	*Symphoricarpos occidentalis*	rarely
Spirea, blue mist	*Caryopteris incana*	rarely
Spruce, blue	*Picea pungens*	rarely
Spruce, Engelmann	*Picea engelmannii*	rarely

Old-Time Remedies for Pest and Disease Problems

With more than a million different species, insects are very adaptable, making them the most successful life forms on Earth. If you doubt that, think about the results of a century of human attempts to subdue insects with pesticides. Like many old techniques and remedies nearly forgotten with the advances in modern technology, the use of soaps, oils, and baking soda has made a comeback with gardeners looking for safe and effective ways to control pests and diseases.

I have used the following remedies passed down from my grandmother, aunts, and uncle, who at the time did not have the luxury of synthetic pesticides or fungicides. Yet their gardens and home orchard thrived and produced abundantly with relatively few pest problems.

Grandma's Garlic Bug Spray

Garlic has long been known as the herb of health; it can also be used in a homemade bug spray. It's an all-around ingredient that acts as both bug repellent and, reportedly, an antibiotic that helps to cure plant diseases.

Insects this spray controls include cabbage worms, earwigs, leafhoppers, aphids, whiteflies, mites, slugs, and mosquitoes. Larger caterpillars take longer to be affected, but give it a try. The following procedures tell you how to make a homemade garlic concentrate and how to mix the spray solution to keep insects off your garden plants.

Ingredients:
1 dozen garlic cloves	Dishwashing soap
Olive oil	1 pint water

Preparation:
- Soak a dozen finely minced garlic cloves in olive oil for twenty-four hours; then thoroughly strain the oil through cheesecloth.
- Mix 2 teaspoons of the oil into a pint of water.
- Add a few drops of dishwashing soap, such as Ivory or Joy; stir, and strain again.
- Store in a cool location and use as needed.
- Use 2 tablespoons of the garlic concentrate in a pint of water. Apply to insect-infested plants with a hand-held spray bottle or a small pressurized tank sprayer. The best time to spray is in the cool of the day, preferably very early morning or evening.

Molasses to the Rescue

For a natural fungicide to prevent diseases in her garden, Grandma used molasses and vinegar. If you've had trouble with fungus diseases in the past, start spraying susceptible plants before disease symptoms appear and then continue to spray at weekly intervals to prevent the problem. You can even add baking soda to give it an extra punch.

Ingredients:
1 tablespoon blackstrap molasses	1 gallon water
1 tablespoon apple cider vinegar	

Preparation:
- Mix ingredients together thoroughly. Place the mixture in a tank sprayer or spray bottle. Spray during the cool part of the day. You don't have to soak the foliage; just lightly spray the leaves. That's all that's needed.
- Clean your sprayer with soap and water thoroughly after use.
- *Tip:* To give an extra boost to this disease control, add 2 tablespoons baking soda to this recipe.

Weed Buster

The natural way to get rid of weeds in your garden is the "cowboy way"—pulling by hand or digging. If you're getting tired of this method, you can thwart them with a shot of vinegar spray. Grandma used this to kill weeds in the driveway and cracks in the sidewalk. It has a short residual in the soil, too, and can keep weeds from coming back up for several months.

Ingredients:
Vinegar (10% acidity)
Dishwashing soap, such as Ivory or Joy

Preparation:
- Fill a spray bottle with the undiluted vinegar or mix 3 parts vinegar to 1 part dishwashing soap. Spot-spray weeds, dousing the weed's foliage and the crown (the area at the base of the weed).
- *Tip:* Cut the bottom out of a plastic milk jug, and use the jug as a shield to keep spray off desirable plants. Place the milk jug over the weed and spray through the top opening of the bottle.
- *Note:* If you use a metal tank sprayer, be sure to rinse the sprayer with water because vinegar is corrosive.

Apple Worm Trap

Ingredients:

Water	1 cup sugar
1 cup apple cider vinegar	1 banana peel

Preparation:
- Combine the ingredients in a 1-gallon plastic milk jug, and fill the jug almost full with water. Place the cap on the jug and shake this brew vigorously to blend thoroughly. Hang the gallon jug of this homemade remedy in the middle of each apple or pear tree. Be sure to remove the cap after you've secured the jug to a branch. Soon this trap will be packed with codling moths, the mothers of those dreaded apple worms.

Deer and Rabbit Repellent

Ingredients:

6 egg yolks	1 teaspoon liquid lemon-scented dishwashing soap
2 to 3 tablespoons hot pepper sauce	1 gallon warm water

Preparation:
- Puree the egg yolks in your kitchen blender. Add the hot pepper sauce, and pour the mixture into the warm water. Add the dishwashing soap. Thoroughly mix the ingredients. Spray this homemade remedy on the bark of trees and shrubs, and around the bases of flowers and vegetables that are frequently visited by deer and rabbits.
- The aroma stops most deer, rabbits, and other browsing wildlife in their tracks. Reapply after a heavy rain or as often as needed.

Slug-Slaying Ammonia-Water Solution

Become a slug slayer with a squirt bottle filled with a 10 percent solution of household cleaning ammonia and water. Take a good flashlight out in the garden at night to search out the slimy slugs. One quick squirt with this homemade remedy causes death quickly while at the same time adding a bit of fertilizer—ammonia is a nitrogen compound that can be used by plants.

Homemade Slug Trap

They hide during the day but start their march at dusk in preparation for sneak attacks at night. They munch on the new and succulent leaves of flowers and vegetables, and they'll even raid our lawns. The enemy? **Slugs.** With their voracious appetites, slugs can quickly demolish plants.

You've most likely heard that beer attracts slugs, and it does. They crawl to containers filled with beer, glide down into the brew, and drown. But I'm not fond of sharing my beer with slugs. Here's a homemade remedy that works better than beer and reduces the incidence of intoxicated birds, dogs, and cats!

Ingredients:
1 cup water
1 teaspoon raw sugar
1/4 teaspoon yeast

Preparation:
- Warm the water in the microwave for one to two minutes. Add the sugar and stir until dissolved. Add the yeast, and mix thoroughly.
- Put this liquid slug bait in shallow containers, such as empty tuna cans or yogurt cups cut in half. Bury the containers in the ground to their rims. The slugs will crawl in and drown. Repeat as often as necessary.

Powdery Mildew Remedy

Powdery mildew infects a wide variety of plants, including roses, lilacs, honeysuckles, crabapples, woodbine, phlox, dahlias, bee balm, and zinnia. This fungus disease coats the leaves with a grayish white powdery substance that looks ugly, but seldom kills the plant. If you're growing plants that are susceptible to this fungus, here's an effective homemade remedy to keep the disease at bay.

Ingredients:
1 gallon water
2 tablespoons baking soda
1 tablespoon Murphy's oil soap or lemon-scented dishwashing soap

Preparation:
- Mix all ingredients together well. Place in a tank sprayer or spray bottle and start spraying when you spot the first signs of the disease. Apply to both sides of the leaves. You can spray every 7 to 10 days as a preventative treatment before any sign of the disease appears; reapply after a heavy rain.
- *Tip:* Remove badly infected leaves and dispose of them. Prune or thin plants to increase air circulation around the foliage. Keep your plants growing healthy with good cultural techniques as stressed plants are more susceptible to infection.

A Hot Tip to Repel Squirrels

The proliferation of squirrels has caused considerable concern for the health of our shade trees. Squirrels are known to damage bark and kill entire branches by their gnawing on the bark and often girdling the branches.

Hot pepper sauces, red pepper, and black pepper have been used for years as animal deterrents. Grandma sprinkled it on the ground around plants that were bothered by rabbits, mice, gophers, voles, chipmunks, raccoons, skunks, and deer.

Often called the "king of all peppers," the blistering hot habanero pepper is twenty times hotter than jalapeno and adds a new twist to squirrel busting. Handle it very carefully, and use sparingly. Habanero sauce mixed with water, plus a biodegradable soap to help with adhesion to the bark, can prove an effective repellent.

Ingredients:

1 tablespoon habanero sauce

1 tablespoon Murphy's oil soap

1 gallon warm or tepid water

Preparation:

- Carefully add the habanero sauce into the gallon of water. Then add the soap, and stir for two minutes to thoroughly blend the mixture. Add this homemade remedy to a pressure tank sprayer, and apply to the tree or shrub branches that are under attack. This spray may need to be repeated every two to three weeks or after a heavy rain.

Homemade Flower Preservative

When you buy a bouquet of flowers, the florist usually includes a packet of floral preservative. It contains the required ingredients to make the flowers last longer—a source of sugar to provide food to the rootless flowers, citric acid to lower the pH of the water, and a disinfectant to inhibit microorganisms that otherwise clog up the stems or the "plumbing system" of the flower.

Make your own flower preservative with this tried-and-true homemade solution. You probably have most of these ingredients at home already.

Ingredients:

1 tablespoon light corn syrup

$1/2$ teaspoon liquid bleach

2 tablespoons lemon or lime juice

1 quart warm water

Preparation:

- Combine the ingredients in the water, and mix thoroughly. Before placing the flowers in the vase of water, strip the lower leaves off the flower stems that would otherwise be underwater. It is well known that excessive foliage in the water increases bacteria and contaminates the water, shortening the shelf life of cut flowers.

Vegetable Tonic Plus Insect and Fungus Control

The summer vegetable garden can be vulnerable to attacks from various insect pests and diseases. The tomato is the target of aphids, psyllids, and white flies during summer. Here is Grandma's old-fashioned, homemade remedy that can help both prevent and reduce an outbreak of troublesome insects. The baking soda is proven to prevent leaf diseases such as powdery mildew.

Ingredients:

1 gallon warm or tepid water

1 tablespoon baking soda

1 tablespoon lemon-scented dishwashing liquid

1 tablespoon soluble plant food, such as 10-15-10

1 tablespoon epsom salt

1 tablespoon vegetable oil

$1/4$ cup rubbing alcohol

Preparation:

- Mix the ingredients in the gallon of water until all are thoroughly dissolved. Put this homemade remedy in a $1^{1}/2$- or 2-gallon tank sprayer, and close the lid tightly. Once you pressurize the tank, you're ready to spray the tomato plants with this tonic and pest control. Apply during the cool times of the day, early morning or late evening. Repeat every seven to ten days depending on weather conditions; repeat more often after a heavy rainfall.
- My grandmother used this tonic to rid plants of plant lice (aphids), white flies, and other pesky critters. It also reduced the incidence of powdery mildew on cucumbers, squash, and pumpkins.

Tired and Aching Roses? Try Some Epsom Salt!

Did you know that rose bushes like epsom salt? Epsom salt can be used as a supplemental fertilizer on your rose bushes. American Rose Society members at Portland, Oregon, found such use meant higher growth rate, increased basal breaks, stronger stems, and improved color and foliage.

Epsom salt is suggested for use on magnesium-deficient soils. Apply at the rate of **1 tablespoon** per rose bush each month throughout the growing season.

Never-Fail Christmas Tree Preservative

You can keep a fresh-cut Christmas tree green and the needles supple by using this homemade preservative solution. It is economical, and most ingredients can be found in your kitchen and laundry room. Always be sure to use a tree stand that holds a couple quarts or more of water. Before the tree is brought indoors, saw a few inches from the base (butt end) to open up the water-drinking tubes that often become clogged with resin. This allows the tree trunk to "drink" all the water and preservative it needs to maintain freshness and that evergreen scent.

Ingredients:
1 gallon hot water
1 cup light corn syrup
1 to 2 tablespoons liquid bleach

Preparation:
- Mix the ingredients, being careful not to spill the bleach on your clothing. Allow the mixture to cool to tepid, and then pour it into the tree stand bowl. Check the tree stand daily, and add more preservative as needed so that it always covers the butt end. Stir the solution each time before adding it to the tree stand bowl.
- *Caution:* Store unused preservative in a plastic gallon container that is labeled as tree preservative. Keep it out of the reach of small children and pets.

Homemade Horticultural Oil

It's easy to make your own horticultural oil from some familiar household products. Use it to suffocate eggs and immature and adult insect pests that attack trees, shrubs, roses, and flowers.

Ingredients:
1 tablespoon liquid dishwashing detergent or soap
    (Joy, Ivory, Palmolive—The soap is needed
    to emulsify the oil in water.)
1 cup corn, peanut, safflower, soybean, or sunflower oil
1 cup water

Preparation:
- Blend the soap and oil into a solution, then add 1 to $2^{1}/_{2}$ teaspoons of the solution to the water. (Use no more than a cup of water.) Pour into a plastic pump-handled spray bottle. Shake the bottle in between sprays to keep the mixture agitated; spray the undersides and topsides of infested leaves and the bark of trees and shrubs. It is very effective against oyster shell scale on aspen and lilac.

Ant Control Around the Home and Garden

Have ants in your pants—pantry? Ant mounds in the yard and garden? Don't fret. Here's a very effective way to rid your home and garden of nuisance ants.

Mix up a homemade bait that takes advantage of ants' feeding habits. Since ants share food with other members of the colony and eventually the queen, the concept is to use the appropriate food source baited with a slow-acting poison.

The following recipe can be modified to control sugar and grease ants. First, identify what food source the ants prefer, sweets or protein. Here's what you'll need: several pint canning jars with screw-top lids, cotton balls, sugar or tuna, boric acid or Borax®.

Sugar (sweet-loving) Ants
1 to 2 teaspoons boric acid or Borax®
1 cup sugar

Grease (protein-loving) Ants
1 to 2 teaspoons boric acid or Borax®
1 cup tuna packed in oil

Preparation:
- Use a nail to punch several holes in the lids of the jars. Then place the appropriate bait into the jars and add some cotton balls to soak it up. Screw the lids on tightly. To entice the ants to the bait, smear a bit of it on the outsides of the jars.
- *Caution:* Set the bait jars in an area out of the reach of children, pets, and wildlife. The ants soon find the bait and take some back to the nest.
- *Note:* Don't use too much boric acid—you want the ants to live long enough to take the bait back to the colony to kill other ants and, ultimately, the queen.

Glossary

aeration: A term to describe methods of introducing air movement into compacted or tight soils.

alkaline soil: Soil having the properties of a high pH above the neutral rating of 7.0.

amendment: Material added to soil that helps improve drainage, moisture-holding capacity, or nutrient-holding capabilities.

annual: A plant that starts from seed, flowers, and produces seed to complete its life cycle in one growing season.

backfill soil: Soil removed from the planting hole that is returned to the hole during the process of planting.

balled and burlapped: A method of wrapping the rootball of a large tree or shrub with burlap, rope, twine, and wire basket so that the plant can be brought to the nursery or transported to the planting site.

bare-root plant: A plant harvested without soil around the roots. This is done in the early spring or fall.

biennial: A plant that has a two-year life cycle. The first year it grows from seed and produces foliage. During the second year, it resumes foliage growth, blooms, develops seeds, and dies.

bleeders: A term used to describe trees that drip sap from a pruning cut or wound; especially trees such as maple, birch, cottonwood, aspen, and walnut.

bloom: 1. The flower of a plant. 2. The bluish gray coating on evergreen needles, fruit, or foliage that can be wiped off or removed by certain pesticide sprays.

bract: A modified leaf at the base of a flower or flower clusters.

broadleaf weed: A weed having flattened, broad leaves, as distinguished from thin, grasslike foliage.

bulb: A horticultural term for an underground leaf bud with fleshy scales; the tulip and onion are true bulbs. Often used to include corms, tubers, and thickened rhizomes.

calcareous soil: A soil that is alkaline because of the high amounts of calcium carbonate.

canopy: The height and width of a tree's branch area.

chlorosis: A condition when plants develop a yellowing of otherwise normal green foliage.

compaction: The compression of soil particles, collapsing air spaces in between.

compost: A mixture of decomposing and decomposed organic waste materials that have been layered in a pile, turned periodically to hasten decomposition, and used to condition garden soil. It provides a source of humus and slow-release nutrients.

corm: A solid, bulblike underground stem, such as crocus and gladiolus.

crown: 1. The highest portion of a tree. 2. The point on a herbaceous plant where stem and root meet.

cultivar: A variety or strain of a plant that has originated and persisted under cultivation. Cultivars are given a specific name, usually distinguished by single quotation marks, as is *Acer rubrum* 'Autumn Blaze'.

cyme: A more or less flat-topped flower.

deadheading: To remove dead or spent flower heads from flowering plants. Regular deadheading prevents seed formation, tidies the garden, and encourages prolonged blooming in many plants.

deciduous: A term used to describe plants that shed their leaves during the fall.

division: A method of propagation that involves cutting apart or separating root and crown clumps of perennials to create several new plants from the mother plant.

dormant: The resting period in a plant's life cycle when no growth occurs.

drip line: The imaginary line at ground level where water dripping from the outermost branches of a tree or shrub will fall.

establishment: Refers to a plant's acclimation after transplanting. Often refers to the time before a plant reaches its drought-resistance potential. A typical establishment period takes a full growing season, but some plants take several years.

establishment watering: Providing supplemental water during the stages of transplanting and establishing a plant before it can grow on its own with less frequent irrigation or natural precipitation.

fireblight: A bacterial disease that infects the tips of the branches and progresses toward the trunk; infects some varieties of crabapples, apples, pears, and mountain ashes. Symptoms appear as if the foliage has been scorched.

frog-eye sprinkler: One of the oldest and best sprinklers that delivers water with coarse droplets and in a low arc so there is little waste from evaporation. Also known as the twin-eye sprinkler.

frost cracks: The splits, fissures, or hairline cracks in the bark of a tree's trunk or branches caused from winter desiccation and temperature fluctuations.

gall: A swollen growth caused by insects or fungus that can occur on the stems, branches, and foliage. Most are generally harmless and may be pruned out.

germinate: The term used to describe a seed sprouting.

graft union: The point on the stem of a woody plant where a stem from another desirable ornamental plant is grafted or inserted into the roots of a hardier plant. Hybrid tea roses are commonly grafted.

growing season: The period between the last frost in spring and the first frost of autumn; the time when plants can grow without danger of frost.

ground cover: A plant that grows by spreading or trailing to cover or carpet an expanse of soil. Although most ground covers are low growing, including lawn grasses and woolly thyme, taller plants of spreading habit, such as ornamental grasses and cotoneaster, can also be used for this purpose.

hardening off: A process by which transplants started indoors are gradually acclimatized to outdoor conditions before they are permanently transplanted to the outdoor garden.

hardpan: A layer of hard soil or ground that impedes the downward movement of water.

hardy: The ability of a plant to grow in a specific area and survive low temperatures without protection.

heaving: The lifting or shifting of the plant crown caused by the repeated freezing and thawing of the soil.

heeling in: A technique of temporarily planting in a protected spot until the plants can be transplanted. The roots are protected from drying by covering with loose soil or a loose organic mulch.

hellstrip: A term used to describe the area between the street and sidewalk that is traditionally planted with grass and trees.

herbaceous: A plant whose aboveground parts are not hardy that will die back to the ground each winter.

holdfast: A rootlike structure by which a plant clings to a wall or other structures.

humus: The well-decomposed, fertile, and stable part of organic matter in the soil.

inorganic mulch: Inert material used to cover the ground, including gravel, cobblestone, plastic, and synthetic fabrics.

island bed: A free-standing garden bed that can be viewed and maintained from all sides.

layering: A method of starting plants by bending and securing a stem to the soil; roots and shoots then form along this stem to produce a new plant. Once the roots are established, the shoot is cut from the parent plant and transplanted.

lean soil: Soil lacking in organic matter and nutrients. Some plants, such as blue grama grass, saltbush, and mountain mahogany, do best in lean rather than rich soils.

limbing up: A type of pruning in which the lower limbs are removed from a tree. Often referred to as "skirting," specifically, for evergreen trees.

loam: Medium-textured soil that contains a balanced mix of sand, silt, clay, and organic matter; also known as the "ideal soil."

microclimate: The environmental conditions of a localized area that differ from the overall climate of the area, such as near a building, between large boulders, under a tree, or at the top of a hill.

mulch: Any of the various organic and inorganic materials used to cover the soil to prevent moisture loss, discourage weed growth, maintain soil temperature, and reduce soil cultivation. Verb: To spread mulch around the root zone of plants or over the soil.

mycorrhizae: Special fungi that live in and around plant roots and perform in symbiosis with plants to help extract water and nutrients from the soil.

native plants: Species indigenous to the region or of local origin. They have adapted to specific environments and geographic regions and are best equipped to tolerate the regional climate and local weather conditions.

naturalize: A technique of establishing plants in the landscape so that they adapt, grow, and spread unaided as though they were native, such as naturalizing daffodils.

pinching back: Removing the growing tips of plants using the thumb and forefinger. This stimulates plants to grow bushier and more compact.

perennial: A plant that continues to live from year to year. A short-lived perennial refers to a plant that may live three to five years; a long-lived perennial is likely to live indefinitely.

pH: The measure of the soil's acidity or alkalinity on a scale with a value of 7.0 representing neutral; the lower numbers indicate increasing acidity and the higher numbers increasing alkalinity.

plant stress: A disruption in normal plant growth generally caused from poor physiological or environmental conditions or insect, disease, or wildlife invasion.

pole peelings: An organic mulch made when branches, stems, and other woody byproducts are run through a grinder or wood chipper. The thin wood slivers that result will knit together so as not to blow away.

rhizome: A thickened underground stem or root that produces shoots above and roots below. Examples include bearded iris and bluegrass.

saline soil: A soil that contains a high level of soluble salts and can be injurious for plant growth.

slow-release fertilizer: Natural or synthetic materials that require microbial, chemical, or physical breakdown to become available to plants.

root zone: The area in which the plant's roots are growing and expanding.

scarification: Breaking the seed coat, such as by filing, to hasten seed germination.

side dress: To work fertilizer into the soil around the root zone of a plant. Also, to spread mulch around the bases of plants.

soil drainage: The rate at which water can move through the soil profile.

stolon: A horizontal stem that grows along the ground or just below the surface and roots along its nodes or tip, giving rise to new plants; an example is the strawberry.

sucker: A soft, fast-growing shoot that originates from the base of a tree trunk, on limbs, or from roots.

translocation: The movement of water, minerals, and nutrients within a plant.

tuber: A short, thickened underground organ, usually, but not always, a stem. Tubers bear buds, or eyes, from which new shoots and roots develop. Dahlia is an example.

waterlogged: A soil so saturated with water that it has poor aeration and is not conducive to healthy root growth.

watering in: The technique of watering plants after planting to ensure soil and root contact for the plant's establishment.

whorl: The arrangement of several leaves, flowers, or other organs around a common growth point or node.

xeriscape: A term used to describe a dry or desertlike (xeric) view or scene (scape); coined in 1981 by the Associated Landscape Contractors of Colorado to promote water conservation through water-efficient landscaping.

zone: An area used to describe a plant's hardiness restricted by a range of annual average minimum temperatures.

Bibliography

Bailey, Liberty Hyde. *Hortus Third*. Macmillan Publishing Company, 1976.
Bryan, John E. *John E. Bryan on Bulbs*. Macmillan Publishing, 1994.
Clausen, Ruth Rogers, and Nicolas H. Ekstrom. *Perennials for American Gardens*. Random House, 1989.
Crandall, Barbara and Chuck. *Flowering, Fruiting & Foliage Vines*. Sterling Publishing Company, 1995.
Darr, Shelia, and Helga and William Olkowski. *Common-Sense Pest Control*. The Tauton Press, Inc., 1991.
Dirr, Michael A. *Manual of Woody Landscape Plants*. Stipes Publishing Company, 1998.
DiSaabato-Aust, Tracy. *The Well-Tended Perennial Garden*. Timber, Press, 1998.
Evison, Raymond J. *Making the Most of Clematis*. Burall Floraprint Ltd., 1991.
Fairchild, D. H., and J.E. Klett. *Woody Landscape Plants for the High Plains*. Colorado State University, 1993.
Greenlee, John. *The Encyclopedia of Ornamental Grasses*. Michael Friedman Publishing Group, 1992.
Griffiths, Mark. *Index of Garden Plants: The New Royal Horticulture Society Dictionary*. Timber Press, 1994.
Harper, Pamela. *Designing with Perennials*. Macmillan Publishing Company, 1991.
Jimerson, Douglas A. *Successful Rose Gardening*. Meredith Books, 1993.
Kelly, George W. *Trees for the Rocky Mountains*. Rocky Mountain Horticultural Publishing Company, 1976.
Kelly, George W. *Rocky Mountain Horticulture*. Pruett Publishing Company, 1957.
Meyer, Mary Hockenberry. *Ornamental Grasses*. Charles Scribner's Sons, 1975.
Pesman, M. Walter. *Meet the Natives*. Pruett Publishing, 1988.
Phillips, Roger and Martyn. *Perennials*, Volumes 1 and 2. Random House, 1991.
Shigo, Alex L. *A New Tree Biology*. Shigo and Trees, Associates, 1986.
Still, Steven. *Manual of Herbaceous Ornamental Plants*. Stipes Publishing Company, 1994.
Strauch Jr., J.G., and J.E. Klett. *Flowering Herbaceous Perennials for the High Plains*. Colorado State University, 1989.
Turgeonn, A.J. *Turfgrass Management*. Prentice Hall, Inc., 1991.
Wyman, Donald. *Ground Cover Plants*. Macmillan Company, 1976.
Wyman, Donald. *Shrubs and Vines for American Gardens*. The Macmillan Company, 1969.

Photography Credits

Thomas Eltzroth: pages 14, 22, 24, 26, 27, 29, 30, 31, 32, 33, 35, 36, 37, 40, 41, 42, 43, 45, 47, 48, 50, 56, 58, 59, 60, 64, 67, 68, 69, 76, 80, 86, 87, 92, 94, 95, 101, 102, 106, 108, 112, 113, 117, 119, 121, 123, 124, 125, 128, 131, 134, 135, 136, 137, 138, 139, 147, 148, 149, 151, 156, 158, 160, 162, 164, 165, 167, 168, 169, 171, 172, 173, 175, 179, 180, 181, 183, 184, 185, 187, 188, 191, 192, 193, 194, 195, 196, 197, 198, 202, 203, 208, 209, 212, 216, 218, 223, 225, 235, 237, 240, 243, 246, 247, 248, 249, 251

Jerry Pavia: pages 10, 25, 28, 39, 44, 49, 55, 61, 63, 70, 75, 81, 91, 93, 98, 99, 107, 109, 111, 114, 120, 142, 145, 146, 150, 153, 159, 174, 182, 199, 206, 207, 210, 211, 238, 239, 241, 244, 250

Liz Ball and Rick Ray: pages 16, 20, 34, 52, 72, 79, 82, 89, 90, 97, 100, 110, 115, 116, 122, 141, 152, 154, 157, 163, 170, 177, 214, 220, 229, 230, 232, 236, 245

Charles Mann: page 8, 17, 38, 66, 85, 88, 103, 155, 200, 205, 215, 222, 226, 227, 228, 231, 233, 234

David Winger: pages 11, 12, 13, 84, 96, 118, 178, 204, 221, 242

John Pohly: pages 65, 71, 74, 224

Ralph Snodsmith: page 46, 201, 217

(c) Mark Turner: page 51, 54, 57

John Cretti: pages 161, 166

Mike Dirr: pages 104, 213

Pam Harper: pages 176, 219

Dave MacKenzie: pages 140, 144

Judy Mielke: pages 73, 126

Felder Rushing: pages 21, 23

William Adams: page 143

Karen Bussolini: page 15

Ohio State University: page 105

Andre Viette: page 53

Plant Index

Featured plant selections and articles are indicated in **boldface**.

Abies concolor, 68
Abies lasiocarpa, 68
Acer campestre, 90
Acer ginnala, 84
Acer platanoides, 94
aconite, winter, 59, 239
Aesculus glabra, 96
Aesculus hippocastanum, 96
African marigold, 32
Agastache barberi, 166
Agastache cana, 166
Agastache foeniculum, 166
Agastache rupestris, 166
Agastache spp., 166
ageratum, 32
Agropyron, 126
Agropyron desertorum, 126
Agropyron riparium, 126
ajuga, 108, 152
Ajuga reptans, 71, 108
alba rose, 198
allium, 55
 drumstick, 55
Allium aflatunense, 55
Allium cernuum, 55
Allium giganteum, 55
Allium hollandicum, 55
Allium sphaerocephalum, 55
Allium spp., 55
alpine
 aster, 149
 fir, 68
althea, shrub, 229
alum root, 157
alyssum, 195, 196
 sweet, 36
amelanchier, 100
Amelanchier alnifolia, 100
American
 arborvitae, 64
 bittersweet, 242
 linden, 92
 plum, 204
Amorpha canescens, 221
Amorpha fruticosa, 221
Ampelopsis
 brevipedunculata, 248
amur
 honeysuckle, 219
 maple, 84
Andropogon gerardii, 141
anemone, 181
 Japanese, 140, 145,
  167, 208
Anemone blanda, 59
Anemone × hybrida, 167
Anemone pulsatilla, 167
anglojap yew, 75
anise, 166

annual
 delphinium, 30
 sunflower, 38
Antennaria, 118
Antennaria dioica, 118
Antennaria parvifolia, 118
*Antennaria
 plantaginifolia*, 118
Antennaria rosea, 118
antique rose, 198
Antirrhinum majus, 37
Apache plume, 205
Aquilegia caerulea and
 hybrids, 178
arborvitae, 64
 American, 64
arctic willow, 215
Arctostaphylos uva-ursi, 115
artemisia, 36, 148, 176
Artemisia absinthium, 148
Artemisia frigida, 173
Artemisia spp. and
 hybrids, 148
Asclepias tuberosa, 154
ash
 green, 88
 white, 105
Asiatic lily, 53
aspen, 85, 98, 100, 237
 quaking, 98
**aster, 140, 142, 144, 145,
 149, 172, 177, 179,
 198, 208**
 alpine, 149
 blue, 156
Aster alpinus, 149
Aster frikartii, 162, 163, 180
Aster novae-angliae, 149
Aster spp. and hybrids, 149
Astilbe, 116, 120
Aubrieta, 112
Aubrieta deltoidea, 112
Aurinia saxatilis, 110
Austrian pine, 65
autumn crocus, 54
autumn-flowering crocus, 46
avena, blue, 137
bamboo, 143
baptisia, 153
Baptisia australis, 153
Baptisia australis var.
 minor, 153
Baptisia lactea, 153
barberry, 206
 Japanese, 206
basil, 22
basket of gold, 110
bean tree, Indian, 103
bearberry, 115

beard tongue, 173
bearded iris, 44, 182
beauty bush, 207
beauty-of-the-night, 27
begonia, wax, 195
Berberis spp., 206
Berberis thunbergii var.
 atropurpurea, 206
bergenia, 155
Bergenia cordifolia, 114
betony, big, 169
Betula nigra, 99
big
 betony, 169
 bluestem, 141
birch
 European white, 99
 paper, 99
 river, 99
birdcherry, 93
bittersweet
 American, 242
 Loesener, 242
 Oriental, 242
black-eyed Susan, 139, 156,
 162, 177, 180
blanket flower, 150
blazing star, 145, 151
bleeding heart, 152, 155
 fringed, 152
bloodroot, 155
blue
 aster, 156
 avena, 137
 false indigo, 153
 fescue, 136, 161
 flax, 175
 fountain willow, 215
 grama, 125, 126,
  127, 129
 mist spirea, 208
 oat grass, 137
 spruce, 67, 99
 stem willow, 215
 velvet honeysuckle, 219
bluebeard, 208
blueberry climber, 248
bluegrass, 125, 129
 Kentucky, 125, 131
blueleaf honeysuckle, 219
bluestem
 big, 141
 little, 141
bluestem willow, 215
borage, 22
Boston ivy, 251
botanical tulip, 123
bourbon rose, 198
Bouteloua gracilis, 126

Brassica oleracea, 26
bridal wreath spirea, 236
bristlecone pine, 66
brome, smooth, 127
Bromus inermis, 127
broom
 common, 231
 prostrate, 231
 scotch, 231
Brown's honeysuckle, 244
Buchloe dactyloides, 126
buckeye
 fetid, 96
 Ohio, 96
buckthorn
 common, 218
 glossy, 218
 sea, 232
 Smith's, 218
Buddleia, 210
Buddleia alternifolia, 210
Buddleia davidii, 210
buffalo currant, 213
buffaloberry, 234
 russet, 234
 silver, 234
buffalograss, 125, 126,
 127, 129
bugleweed, 108
 carpet, 108
bunchgrass, 127
bur oak, 95
burning bush, 54, 209
bush
 beauty, 207
 burning, 209
 butterfly, 210
 fountain butterfly, 210
bush cinquefoil, 226
Busy lizzie, 29
butterfly bush, 183, 210
 fountain, 210
butterfly weed, 154
Butterfly Gardening, 252
cabbage, ornamental, 26
*Calamagrostis ×
 acutiflora*, 138
calendula, 22, 26
Calendula officinalis, 22
callery pear, 97
Campsis radicans, 250
Canada red chokecherry, 93
candytuft, 37
canna, 45
 hybrid, 45
Canna × generalis, 45
Canna glauca, 45
Caragana arborescens, 233
cardinal climber, 33

carnation, 32
carpet bugleweed, 108
Caryopteris ×
  clandonensis, 208
Caryopteris incana, 208
catalpa
  hardy, 103
  northern, 103
  western, 103
Catalpa speciosa, 103
catmint, 159, 169
cedar
  eastern red, 74
  white, 64
Celastrus loeseneri, 242
Celastrus orbiculatus, 242
Celastrus scandens, 242
Celtis occidentalis, 104
centifolia rose, 198
Cerastium, 119
Cerastium biebersteinii, 119
Cerastium
  tomentosum, 119
Cerastium tomentosum var.
  columnae, 119
Cercocarpus ledifolius, 224
Cercocarpus montanus, 224
Chasmanthium
  latifolium, 143
chenault coralberry, 235
chewings fescue, 125
chiming bells, 155
china rose, 198
Chinese magnolia, 230
Chionodoxa, 51
Chionodoxa luciliae, 51
chives, 55
chokecherry, Canada red, 93
Christmas rose, 170
chrysanthemum, 32, 140,
  142, 167, 198
  florist's, 163
  garden, 163
  hardy, 163
Chrysanthemum ×
  grandiflorum, 163
cinquefoil
  bush, 226
  shrubby, 226
classic zinnia, 39
clematis, 243
  sweet autumn, 243
  tube, 243
Clematis heracleifolia, 243
Clematis × *jackmanii*, 243
Clematis ligusticifolia, 243
Clematis montana
  rubens, 243
Clematis spp. and
  hybrids, 243
Clematis tangutica, 243
Clematis terniflora, 243
cleome, 23
Cleome hassleriana, 23
climber

blueberry, 248
cardinal, 33
climbing
  honeysuckle, 244
  hydrangea, 245
  rose, 192
coffee tree, Kentucky, 91
colchicum, 54
  showy, 54
Colchicum autumnale, 54
Colchicum speciosum, 54
Colchicum spp. and
  hybrids, 54
Colorado
  redcedar, 74
  spruce, 67
columbine, 157, 178
common
  broom, 231
  buckthorn, 218
  crocus, 46
  garden zinnia, 39
  hackberry, 104
  honeylocust, 101
  hop, 246
  larch, 71
  mockorange, 223
  ninebark, 211
  witchhazel, 239
  wormwood, 148
concolor fir, 68
coneflower, 37, 149, 151,
  156, 177, 208
  cutleaf, 156
  purple, 145, 179
  yellow, 145
Consolida ambigua, 30
Convallaria majalis, 116
Convallaria majalis var.
  rosea, 116
Coping with Browsing
  Deer, 255
coral bells, 157, 178
coralberry
  chenault, 235
  red, 235
coreopsis, 158, 159, 163,
  172, 182, 183, 185
Coreopsis grandiflora, 158
Coreopsis rosea, 158
Coreopsis spp., 158
Coreopsis verticillata, 158
Cornus alba, 227
Cornus coloradensis, 227
Cornus sericea, 227
cosmos, 24, 32, 37
Cosmos bipinnatus, 24
cotoneaster, 212
  cranberry, 212
  hedge, 212
  rock, 212
Cotoneaster apiculatus, 212
Cotoneaster dammeri, 212
Cotoneaster
  horizontalis, 212

Cotoneaster lucidus, 212
Cotoneaster spp., 212
cottage
  pink, 184
  rose, 197
cottonwood, 85
  Plains, 85
coyote willow, 215
crabapple, 86
  flowering, 86
cranberry cotoneaster, 212
cranesbill, 164, 178
Crataegus ambigua, 89
Crataegus laevigata, 89
Crataegus spp., 89
creeper, Virginia, 251
creeping
  juniper, 66, 69, 73, 74
  mahonia, 109, 225
  mountain juniper, 69
  Oregon grape holly, 109
  phlox, 110
  thyme, 123, 169
  veronica, 111
crested wheatgrass, 126, 127
crocus, 46, 49, 239
  autumn, 54
  autumn-flowering, 46
  common, 46
  saffron, 46
  snow, 46
  Tomasini's, 46
Crocus chrysanthus, 46
Crocus kotschyanus, 46
Crocus sativus, 46
Crocus speciosus, 46
Crocus spp. and hybrids, 46
Crocus tommasinianus, 46
curlleaf mahogany, 224
currant, 213
  golden, 213
  hardy alpine, 213
  wax, 213
  buffalo, 213
cushion mum, 163
cutleaf coneflower, 156
Cytisus decumbens, 231
Cytisus hirsutus, 231
Cytisus purgans, 231
Cytisus scoparius, 231
daffodil, 35, 47, 51, 52, 54,
  56, 59, 111, 164
dahlia, 48
Dahlia spp. and hybrids, 48
damask rose, 198
daphne, 214
  rose, 214
Daphne × *burkwoodii*, 214
Daphne cneorum, 214
Daphne spp., 214
daylily, 108, 114, 159, 176,
  179, 181, 208
dead nettle, 120
Deer, Coping with
  Browsing, 255

Delosperma cooperi, 113
Delosperma nubigenum, 113
Delosperma spp., 113
delphinium
  annual, 30
  perennial, 30
devil-in-a-bush, 31
dianthus, 26, 176, 184,
  185, 195
Dianthus barbatus, 184
Dianthus deltoides, 184
Dianthus plumarius, 184
Dicentra eximia, 152
Dicentra spectabilis, 152
dogwood
  red-osier, 227
  redtwig, 99, 227
  yellow twig, 67, 227
double bubble mint, 166
Douglas fir, 70
dropseed, prairie, 144, 156
drumstick allium, 55
dusty miller, 25, 34, 36, 54
Dutchman's breeches, 152
dwarf
  arctic willow, 215
  bulbous iris, 49
  iris, 49, 123, 239
  ninebark, 211
eastern red cedar, 74
Echinacea, 177
Echinacea purpurea, 177
Elymus lanceolatus, 126
Engleman ivy, 251
English
  ivy, 247
  rose, 197
Erianthus, 140
euonymous, 209
  winged, 209
Euonymus alatus, 54, 209
Euonymus europaeus, 209
Euonymus fortunei, 71
Eupatorium maculatum, 168
Euonymus nanus var.
  turkestanicus, 209
Eupatorium purpureum, 168
European
  larch, 71
  spindle tree, 209
  white birch, 99
evening primrose, 160
everyman's gentian, 161
Fallugia paradoxa, 205
false
  indigo, 153
    blue, 153
  rockcress, 112
feather reed grass, 138
fennel flower, 31
fern, 29, 53, 114, 116, 152
fescue
  blue, 136, 161
  chewings, 125
  fine, 125

hard, 125
red, 125
sheep, 125, 136
turf-type, 125, 129, 131
Festuca arundinacea, 125
Festuca glauca, 136
Festuca ovina, 136
Festuca spp., 125
fetid buckeye, 96
field maple, 90
fine fescue, 125
fir, 68
    alpine, 68
    concolor, 68
    Douglas, 70
    white, 68, 99
firethorn, 216
    scarlet, 216
flag, 44
flax, blue 175
fleece vine, 249
floribunda rose, 193,
    194, 197
florist's chrysanthemum, 163
flowering
    crabapple, 86
    kale, 26
    onion, 55
forget-me-not, 152
forsythia, 67, **217**
Forsythia × intermedia, 217
fountain
    butterfly bush, 210
    grass, 139
        purple, 139
four o'clock, 27
    perennial, 27
foxtail pine, 66
Fraxinus americana, 105
Fraxinus pennsylvanica, 88
French marigold, 32
fringed bleeding heart, 152
Gaillardia, 150
Gaillardia × grandiflora, 150
Galanthus, 57
Galanthus nivalis, 57
Galium odoratum, 71, 122
gallica rose, 198
garden
    chrysanthemum, 163
    lily, 53
    tulip, 58
garland flower, 214
garlic, 55
gayfeather, 151
gentian, 161
    everyman's, 161
Gentiana parryi, 161
Gentiana septemfida, 161
Gentiana spp., 161
geranium, 25, **28**
    hardy, 152, 153, 157,
        164, 176, 182, 185
    ivy, 28
    scented, 28

zonal, 28
Geranium sanguineum var.
    striatum, 164
Geranium spp., 164
German iris, 44
ginnala maple, 84
glad, 50
gladiolus, 50
Gladiolus byzantinus, 50
Gladiolus × hortulanus, 50
Gleditsia triacanthos var.
    inermis, 101
globe willow, 102
glory-of-the-snow, 51
Glossary, 262
glossy buckthorn, 218
golden
    currant, 213
    hop, 246
goldenrain tree, 87
goldenrod, 140, 142, 144,
    149, **162**
goldflame honeysuckle, 244
goldmoss stonecrop, 121
grama, blue, 125, 126,
    127, 129
grandiflora rose, 194
grape
    holly, Oregon, 220, 225
    hyacinth, 52, 57
grass
    blue oat, 137
    feather reed, 138
    fountain, 139
    hardy pampas, 140
    Japanese silver, 142
    maiden, 142
    miscanthus, 142
    pampas, 140
    purple fountain, 139
    ravenna, 140
green ash, 88
ground cover
    juniper, 49
    rose, 197
Gymnocladus dioica, 91
hackberry, 104
    common, 104
    western, 104
Hall's honeysuckle, 244
Hamamelis ×
    intermedia, 239
Hamamelis vernalis, 239
Hamamelis virginiana, 239
hard fescue, 125
hardy
    alpine currant, 213
    catalpa, 103
    chrysanthemum, 163
    geranium, 152, 153, 157,
        164, 176, 182, 185
    iceplant, 113
    mum, 163
    pampas grass, 140
hawthorn, 89

Russian, 89
heart-leafed bergenia, 114
Hedera helix, 247
hedge
    cotoneaster, 212
    maple, 90
Helen's flower, 183
helenium, 142
Helenium autumnale, 183
Helianthus annuus, 38
Helictotrichon
    sempervirens, 137
hellebore, 170
Helleborus niger, 170
Helleborus orientalis, 51, 170
Hemerocallis, 159
Hemerocallis hybrids, 159
heritage rose, 198
heuchera, 157
Heuchera micrantha var.
    diversifolia, 157
Heuchera spp. and
    hybrids, 157
Hibiscus syriacus, 229
Hick's yew, 75
Hippophae rhamnoides, 232
holly, 109
    Oregon grape, 109,
        220, 225
Holodiscus dumosus, 228
honeylocust, 101
    common, 101
    thornless, 101
honeysuckle, 219
    amur, 219
    blue velvet, 219
    blueleaf, 219
    Brown's, 244
    climbing, 244
    goldflame, 244
    Hall's, 244
    shrub, 219
    trumpet, 219, 244
    twinberry, 219
hop
    common, 246
    golden, 246
hop vine, 246
horsechestnut, 96
hosta, 29, 108, 116,
    152, 155, **165**
Hosta sieboldiana, 165
Hosta spp. and hybrids, 165
hummingbird
    vine, 250
    mint, 166
Humulus japonicus, 246
Humulus lupulus, 246
hyacinth, 59
hybrid
    anemone, 153, 167
    canna, 45
    perpetual rose, 198
    tea rose, 193, 194, **195,**
        197, 198

witchhazel, 239
hydrangea, 220
    climbing, 245
    oakleaf, 220
    pee gee, 220
Hydrangea anomala subsp.
    petiolaris, 245
Hydrangea arborescens, 220
Hydrangea paniculata, 220
Hydrangea quercifolia, 220
Hydrangea spp., 220
hyssop, 166
iceplant, 166
    hardy, 113
Ilex, 109
impatiens, 29
Impatiens balsamina, 29
Impatiens walleriana, 29
Indian
    bean tree, 103
    cigar, 103
indigo, false, 153
indigobush, 221
Ipomoea × multifida, 33
Ipomoea purpurea, 33
iris, 141
    bearded, 44, 182
    dwarf, 49, 123, 239
    bulbous, 49
    German, 44
    reticulated, 49
    snow, 49
Iris germanica and hybrids, 44
Iris reticulata, 49
Iris reticulata danfordiae, 49
Iris sibirica, 182
ivy, 247
    Boston, 251
    Engleman, 251
    English, 247
ivy geranium, 28
Jacob's ladder, 114
Japanese
    anemone, 140, 145,
        167, 208
    barberry, 206
    magolia, 230
    silver grass, 142
joe-pye weed, 149, **168**
Johnny-jump-up, 35
jonquil, 47
juniper, 74
    creeping, 66, 69, 73, 74
    mountain, 69
    ground cover, 49
    Rocky Mountain, 74
Juniperus chinensis, 74
Juniperus communis var.
    montana, 69
Juniperus horizontalis, 66,
    69, 73
Juniperus scopulorum, 74
Juniperus virginiana, 74
kale
    flowering, 26

ornamental, 26
Kentucky
  bluegrass, 125, 131
  coffee tree, 91
king's crown roseroot, 121
kinnikinick, 115
Koelreuteria paniculata, 87
Kolkwitzia amabilis, 207
Koreanspice viburnum, 238
lady's mantle, 164, 178, 185
lamb's ears, 36, 54, 160, **169,** 176
Lamium, 120
Lamium maculatum, 120
landscape rose, 197
larch, 71
  common, 71
  European, 71
Larix decidua, 71
larkspur, 22, **30**
leadplant, 221
leadwort, 221
leek, 55
Lenten rose, 51, **170**
Leucanthemum × superbum, 181
Leucojum vernum, 57
Lewis mockorange, 223
liatris, 208
Liatris aspera, 151
Liatris spicata, 151
lilac, 222
  summer, 210
Lilium candidum, 53
Lilium spp. and hybrids, 53
lily, 53
  Asiatic, 53
  garden, 53
  madonna, 53
  Oriental, 53
  trumpet, 53
lily-of-the-valley, 116
limber pine, 72
linden, 92
  American, 92
  littleleaf, 92
Linum lewisii, 175
Linum perenne, 175
little bluestem, 141
littleleaf
  linden, 92
  mockorange, 223
Loesener bittersweet, 242
Lolium perenne, 125
lombardy poplar, 85
Lonicera × brownii, 244
Lonicera × heckrotti, 244
Lonicera involucrata, 219
Lonicera japonica, 244
Lonicera korolkowii, 219
Lonicera maackii, 219
Lonicera sempervirens, 244
Lonicera spp., 219, 244
Lonicera syringantha, 219
Lonicera tatarica, 219

love-in-a-mist, 22, **31**
lungwort, 29
lupine, 171
Lupinus argenteus, 171
Lupinus spp. and hybrids, 171
madonna lily, 53
magnolia, 230
  Chinese, 230
  Japanese, 230
  saucer, 230
Magnolia × soulangiana, 230
mahogany
  curlleaf, 224
  mountain, 224
mahonia, creeping, 225
Mahonia, 109
Mahonia aquifolium, 225
Mahonia repens, 109, 225
maiden grass, 142
Malus spp., 86
maple, 90
  amur, 84
  field, 90
  ginnala, 84
  hedge, 90
  Norway, 94
  sugar, 94
mapleleaf viburnum, 238
marigold, 32, 37
  African, 32
  French, 32
  pot, 22
  signet, 32
mayday tree, 93
meadow saffron, 54
Mertensia ciliata, 155
Mertensia virginica, 155
Mexican evening primrose, 160
mile-a-minute vine, 249
milkweed, 154
miniature rose, 29, **196**
mini-flora rose, 196
mini rose, 196
mint, double bubble, 166
Mirabilis jalapa, 27
Mirabilis multiflora, 27
miscanthus grass, 142
Miscanthus sinensis, 142, 166
mockorange, 223
  common, 223
  Lewis, 223
  littleleaf, 223
modern shrub rose, 197
morning glory, 33
moss rose, 34, 198
mother-of-thyme, 123
mountain
  bluebell, 155
  mahogany, 224
  ninebark, 211
  spray, 228
mum, 162, 163
  cushion, 163

hardy, 163
Muscari armeniacum, 52
Muscari azureum, 52
Muscari botryoides, 52
Muscari comosum, 52
Muscari latifolium, 52
Muscari macrocarpum, 52
narcissus, 47, 56
Narcissus poeticus, 47
Narcissus spp. and hybrids, 47
narrowleaf zinnia, 39
nasturtium, 22
New England aster, 149
nigella, 31
Nigella damascena, 31
Nigella hispanica, 31
ninebark
  common, 211
  dwarf, 211
  mountain, 211
noisette rose, 198
northern
  catalpa, 103
  sea oats, 143
Norway maple, 94
oak, 95
  bur, 95
  Rocky Mountain, 95
  swamp white, 95
oakleaf hydrangea, 220
oat grass, blue, 137
oats
  northern sea, 143
  wild, 143
Oenothera brachycarpa, 111, 160
Oenothera macrocarpa, 160
Oenothera speciosa, 160
Ohio buckeye, 96
old garden rose, 197, **198**
Old-Time Remedies for Pest and Disease Problems, 256
onion, 55
  flowering, 55
  ornamental, 55, 137
orchid beard tongue, 173
Oregon grape, 225
  holly, 220
Oriental
  bittersweet, 242
  lily, 53
  poppy, 172
ornamental
  cabbage, 26
  kale, 26
  onion, 55, 137
  pear, 97
Ozark sundrop, 160
Paeonia lactiflora and hybrids, 174
pampas grass, 140
  hardy, 140
Panicum virgatum, 145

pansy, 26, **35,** 52, 58, 195, 196
Papaver orientale, 172
paper birch, 99
Parry gentian, 161
Parthenocissus quinquefolia var. *engelmannii,* 251
Parthenocissus tricuspidata, 251
P*ascopyrum smithii,* 126
pasqueflower, 123, 167
pea shrub
  Siberian, 233
  weeping Siberian, 233
pea tree, Siberian, 233
pear
  callery, 97
  ornamental, 97
peashrub, 233
pee gee hydrangea, 220
Pelargonium × hortorum, 28
Pelargonium peltatum, 28
pennisetum, 139
Pennisetum alopecuroides, 139
Pennisetum setaceum, 139
penstemon, 173
Penstemon barbatus, 173
Penstemon pinifolius, 173
Penstemon secundiflorus, 173
Penstemon spp. and hybrids, 173
Penstemon strictus, 173
peony, 44, 153, **174,** 182
perennial
  delphinium, 30
  flax, 175
  four o'clock, 27
  ryegrass, 125, 131
  sage, 183
  salvia, 176
periwinkle, 117
Perovskia atriplicifolia, 179, 205
Pest and Disease Problems, Old-Time Remedies for, 256
petunia, 34, **36,** 195
Petunia × hybrida, 36
Philadelphus, 223
Philadelphus coronarius, 223
Philadelphus lewisii, 223
Philadelphus microphyllus, 223
Philadelphus spp., 223
phlox, 181
Phlox subulata, 110
Physocarpus monogynus, 211
Physocarpus opulifolius, 211
Picea pungens, 67
pincushion flower, 158
pine, 65, 71
  Austrian, 65
  bristlecone, 66
  foxtail, 66

limber, 72
pinyon, 73
ponderosa, 65
white, 65
pineleaf penstemon, 173
pink, 37
    cottage, 184
pink coreopsis, 158
Pinus aristata, 66
Pinus cembroides edulis, 73
Pinus flexilis, 72
Pinus nigra, 65
Pinus ponderosa, 65
pinyon pine, 73
pitcher sage, 172, 176
Plains cottonwood, 85
plantain lily, 165
plum
    American, 204
    wild, 204
plume, Apache, 205
Poa pratensis, 125
polyantha rose, 193
Polygonum aubertii, 249
ponderosa pine, 65
poplar
    lombardy, 85
    silver, 85
poppy, 141, 172, 182
Populus, 85
Populus alba, 85
Populus deltoides spp.
    monilifera, 85
Populus spp., 85
Populus tremula, 98
Populus tremuloides, 85, 98
porcelain vine, 248
Portland rose, 198
portulaca, 34
Portulaca grandiflora, 34
pot marigold, 22
potentilla, 208, 226
Potentilla fruticosa, 226
prairie
    dropseed, 144, 156
    flax, 175
    false indigo, 153
pride of India, 87
primrose, evening, 160
prostrate broom, 231
Prunus, 93, 204
Prunus americana, 204
Prunus besseyi, 204
Prunus padus, 93
Prunus virginiana, 93
Pseudotsuga menziesii, 70
Pseudotsuga menziesii var.
    glauca, 70
pulmonaria, 29
purple
    coneflower, 145, **177**,
        179, 180
    echinacea, 177
    fountain grass, 139
    iceplant, 113

pussytoes, 118
Pyracantha coccinea, 216
Pyrus calleryana, 97
quaking aspen, 98
quaky, 98
Quercus bicolor, 95
Quercus gambelii, 95
Quercus macrocarpa, 95
Quercus spp., 95
rabbit berry, 234
rambling rose, 192
ravenna grass, 140
red
    cedar, eastern, 74
    coralberry, 235
    fescue, 125
redcedar, Colorado, 74
red-osier dogwood, 227
redtwig dogwood, 99, 227
renaissance rose, 197
reticulated iris, 49
Rhamnus cathartica, 218
Rhamnus frangula, 218
Rhamnus smithii, 218
rhododendron, 220
Rhus glabra, 209
Rhus spp., 237
Rhus trilobata, 73, 237
Rhus typhina, 237
Ribes alpinum, 213
Ribes aureum, 213
Ribes cereum, 213
Ribes odoratum, 213
Ribes spp., 213
river birch, 99
rock
    cotoneaster, 212
    spirea, 228
rockspray, 228
Rocky Mountain
    columbine, 164, 178
    juniper, 74
    oak, 95
    penstemon, 173
    yellow stemless
        sundrop, 160
Rosa, 192, 193, 194, 195,
    196, 197
Rosa glauca, 199
Rosa hugonis, 199
Rosa spinosissima, 199
Rosa spp., 198, 199
rose, 31, 196
    alba, 198
    antique, 198
    bourbon, 198
    centifolia, 198
    china, 198
    Christmas, 170
    climbinig, 192
    cottage, 197
    damask, 198
    English, 197
    floribunda, 193, 194, 197
    gallica, 198

grandiflora, 194
ground cover, 197
heritage, 198
hybrid
    perpetual, 198
    tea, 193, 194, 195,
        197, 198
    landscape, 197
    Lenten, 51
    miniature, 29, 196
    mini-flora, 196
    modern shrub, 197
    moss, 34, 198
    noisette, 198
    old garden, 197, 198
    Portland, 198
    rambling, 192
    renaissance, 197
    shrub, 197
    species, 199
    tea, 195, 198
    wild, 199
rose daphne, 214
rose-of-Sharon, 229
rough blazing star, 151
rudbeckia, 142, 144, 151,
    156, 179
Rudbeckia fulgida var.
    sullivantii, 156
Rudbeckia hirta, 156
Rudbeckia laciniata, 156
Rudbeckia spp., 156
russet buffaloberry, 234
Russian
    hawthorn, 89
    sage, 137, 145, 151, 159,
        160, 166, 168, 169,
        179, 205
    ryegrass, perennial, 125, 131
Saccharum ravennae, 140
saffron crocus, 46
saffron, meadow, 54
sage, 173
    Russian, 137, 145, 151,
        159, 160, 166, 168,
        169, 179, 205
Salix exigua, 215
Salix irrorata, 215
Salix matsudana, 102
Salix purpurea, 215
Salix spp., 102
salvia, 148, 158, 169
Salvia azurea var.
    grandiflora, 176
Salvia jurisicii, 176
Salvia nemerosa, 176
Salvia sylvestris, 176
Salvia × *superba*, 176
sandcherry, western, 204
santolina, 54
saucer magnolia, 230
scarlet
    firethorn, 216
    bugler, 173
scented geranium, 28

Schizachyrium scoparium, 141
Scilla, 51
Scilla siberica, 56
scotch broom, 231
sea buckthorn, 232
sedum, 121, 139, 149, 166,
    177, 179, 180
    'Autumn Joy', 180
Sedum, 156, 163, 208
Sedum acre, 121
Sedum lanceolatum, 121
Sedum rosea var.
    integrifolium, 121
Sedum spp., 121
Sedum telephium ssp.
    maximum, 180
Sempervivum, 118
Senecio cineraria, 25
serviceberry, 100
shallot, 55
Shasta daisy, 181
sheep's fescue, 125, 136
Shepherdia argentea, 234
Shepherdia canadensis, 234
showy
    colchicum, 54
    stonecrop, 180
shrub
    althea, 229
    honeysuckle, 219
    rose, 197
shrubby cinquefoil, 226
Siberian
    bugloss, 120
    iris, 114, 153, 182
    pea shrub, 233
    pea tree, 233
    squill, 51, 56
signet marigold, 32
silver
    buffaloberry, 234
    grass, Japanese, 142
    lace vine, 249
    poplar, 85
silverberry, 234
silvery lupine, 171
Smith's buckthorn, 218
smokebush, 137
smooth brome, 127
snapdragon, 26, 37
snaps, 37
sneezeweed, 183
snow
    crocus, 46
    iris, 49
snowberry, 235
snowdrop, 49, 56, **57**, 59
snowflake, 57
snow-in-cerastium, 119
Solidago sphacelata, 162
Solidago spp. and
    hybrids, 162
species rose, 199
spider flower, 23
spiked speedwell, 185

spindle tree, European, 209
Spiraea, 208
Spiraea × bumalda, 236
Spiraea nipponica maxim var.
  tosaensis, 236
Spiraea spp. and hybrids, 236
Spiraea × vanhouttei, 236
spirea, 236
  blue mist, 208
  bridal wreath, 236
  rock, 228
Sporobolus heterolepis, 144
spotted dead nettle, 120
spray, mountain, 228
spruce, 67, 71
  blue, 67, 99
  Colorado, 67
squill, 57, 59, 239
  Siberian, 51, 56
Stachys byzantina, 169
Stachys macrantha, 169
staghorn sumac, 237
stonecrop, 121
streambank wheatgrass, 126
sugar maple, 94
sumac, 73, 209, **237**
  staghorn, 237
  three-leaf, 237
summer lilac, 210
sundrop, 111, 160
sunflower, 38
  annual, 38
swamp white oak, 95
sweet
  alyssum, 36
  autumn clematis, 243
  William, 184
  woodruff, 122, 152
switchgrass, 145
Symphoricarpos albus, 235
Symphoricarpos
  orbiculatus, 235
Symphoricarpos ×
  chenaultii, 235
Syringa spp., 222
Syringa vulgaris, 222
Tagetes erecta, 32
Tagetes patula, 32

Tagetes spp., 32
Tagetes tenuifolia, 32
tallhedge, 218
Taxus × media, 75
tea rose, 195, 198
thickspike wheatgrass, 126
thornless honeylocust, 101
thread-leaf coreopsis, 158
three-leaf sumac, 237
Thuja occidentalis, 64
thyme, 123
  creeping, 169
  woolly, 49, 123
Thymus praecox ssp.
  arcticus, 123
Thymus
  pseudolanuginosus, 123
tickseed, 158
Tilia americana, 92
Tilia cordata, 92
Tilia spp., 92
Tomasini's crocus, 46
touch-me-not, 29
trumpet
  honeysuckle, 219, 244
  lily, 53
  vine, 250
tube clematis, 243
tulip, 35, 47, 51, 52, 53, 54,
  58, 59, 137, 139
  botanical, 111, 123
  garden, 58
Tulipa greigii, 58
Tulipa spp., 58
turf-type fescue, 125,
  129, 131
Turkish veronica, 111
twinberry honeysuckle, 219
upside-down sage, 176
varnish tree, 87
verbena, 154, 183
veronica, 111, **185**
Veronica incana, 185
Veronica liwanensis, 111
Veronica pectinata, 111
Veronica prostrata, 111
Veronica repens, 111
Veronica species, 111

Veronica spicata, 185
viburnum, 220, **238**
  Koreanspice, 238
  mapleleaf, 238
Viburnum acerifolium, 238
Viburnum × burkwoodii, 238
Viburnum carlesii, 238
Viburnum lantana, 238
Viburnum opulus, 238
Viburnum ×
  rhytidophylloides, 238
Viburnum spp., 238
vinca, 117
Vinca minor, 117
vine
  fleece, 249
  hop, 246
  hummingbird, 250
  mile-a-minute, 249
  porcelain, 248
  silver lace, 249
  trumpet, 250
viola, 35, 58
Viola tricolor, 35
Viola × wittrockiana, 35
Violet sage, 176
Virginia
  bluebell, 155
  creeper, 251
wax
  begonia, 195
  currant, 213
weeping
  Siberian pea shrub, 233
  willow, 102
western
  catalpa, 103
  hackberry, 104
  sandcherry, 204
  virgin's bower, 243
  wheatgrass, 126, 127
wheatgrass, 126, 127
  crested, 126, 127
  streambank, 126
  thickspike, 126
  western, 126, 127
white
  ash, 105

cedar, 64
fir, 68, 99
pine, 65
sage, 148
wild
  geranium, 161
  oats, 143
  plum, 204
  rose, 199
willow, 102
  arctic, 215
  blue fountain, 215
  bluestem, 215
  coyote, 215
  dwarf arctic, 215
  globe, 102
  weeping, 102
windflower, 59
winged euonymous, 209
winter aconite, 59, 239
witchhazel, 67, **239**
  common, 239
  hybrid, 239
woodbine, 251
woodland fern, 155
woolly
  thyme, 49, **123**
  veronica, 185
wormwood, 148
  common, 148
yarrow, 148, 169, 172,
  181, 183
yellow
  coneflower, 145
  iceplant, 113
yellowtwig
  dogwood, 67, 227
yew, 75
  anglojap, 75
  Hick's, 75
zinnia, 32, 37, **39**
  classic, 39
  common garden, 39
  narrowleaf, 39
Zinnia angustifolia, 39
Zinnia elegans, 39
Zinnia spp., 39
zonal geranium, 28

Meet John Cretti

John Cretti is a respected and highly regarded horticulturist and gardening expert. Cretti's motto is, "To grow plants successfully, you have to *think* like a plant."

His multimedia approach to reach gardeners includes television, radio, and print. He is the long-time host of the popular "Winter Gardener" show, shown nationally on HGTV.

Along with his wife, Jeri, Cretti hosts "John and Jeri's Garden Talk" on KHOW-AM 630 radio, a live call-in program. Cretti also hosts "Gardening with an ALTITUDE" on KOA-AM 850 radio. Both are broadcast across the Rocky Mountain region.

Cretti also shares his gardening wisdom in numerous articles for local and national publications. He has been the Rocky Mountain and High Plains editor for *Flower & Garden Magazine*, and an editor for *Horticulture Magazine* and *Colorado Homes and Lifestyles*. Cretti writes a biweekly column featuring the Rocky Mountain region for Nationalgardening.com. In addition to authoring the *Rocky Mountain Gardener's Guide*, Cretti is the author of the *Colorado Gardener's Guide*, also for Cool Springs Press.

Cretti has received numerous awards and honors, including several from the Garden Writer's Association (GWA) for his radio and television programs. In addition, Cretti has been recognized an impressive six times as a recipient of the Quill and Trowel Award from GWA, as well as the Award of Excellence.

Cretti, his wife and partner, Jeri, and their children—Jason, Justin, Jonathan, and Jinny—reside in Bennett, Colorado, where they stay very busy and enjoy Life in the Rockies.